"In addition to exploring the critical issues of the Reformation, *Here We Stand* demonstrates how those issues are even more important today than they were hundreds of years ago. More than a study of history, *Here We Stand* looks backward in order to look forward to the return of Jesus and the Reformation finally finished."

—John Bradshaw, speaker and director, It Is Written

"The Protestant Reformation is one of the most pivotal events in the history of Christianity. Its catalyst and central figure, Martin Luther, is chronicled in this work and juxtaposed alongside the courageous gallantry of Adventism. This book is a must read for all church-history enthusiasts as the contributors adeptly offer keen insights on the interdependent relationship of Martin Luther, the Reformation, and Seventh-day Adventism."

—Carlton P. Byrd, speaker and director, Breath of Life

"This work on Luther is a tremendous contribution to the understanding of Adventism as a natural inheritor of the Protestant Reformation. This volume is full to the brim with insightful research on the connection of Luther and the Seventh-day Adventist Church. It should be in the library of anyone who desires to understand and proclaim the three angels' messages with power."

—Chris Holland, speaker/director, It Is Written Canada

"This a major work that firmly links Adventists to Luther and the Reformation. The editors have brought together a wide-ranging series of essays by stellar contributors. There is nothing comparable to this book in Adventist literature. I commend it highly."

—William G. Johnsson, former editor, *Adventist Review* and *Adventist World*

"I would highly recommend this book for all readers who want to deepen their understanding of the doctrines of the Seventh-day Adventist Church through the lens of key doctrines of Martin Luther and the early Reformation. In this book, Adventist scholars share unique perspectives that have not been gathered in one volume before. The result is a faith-affirming volume that is a must read!"

—Andrea Luxton, president, Andrews University

"This is the story of a courageous and fearless man who stood in the face of the then known world's power. May history continue to be repeated with individuals so convicted to stand on the promises of God. This is an essential read."

—Ivan L. Williams, ministerial director, North American Division of Seventh-day Adventists

CONTRIBUTORS

Sergio Becerra, Reinder Bruinsma, Heidi Campbell, Michael W. Campbell, Lisa Clark Diller, Abner P. Dizon, Denis Fortin, Daniel Heinz, Darius Jankiewicz, Denis Kaiser, Joel Klimkewicz, George R. Knight, Martin J. Lohrmann, Douglas Morgan, Jiří Moskala, Richard W. Müller, Trevor O'Reggio, John C. Peckham, Dennis Pettibone, Nikolaus Satelmajer, Dan Shultz, Michael Sokupa, Alberto R. Timm, Sigve K. Tonstad, Remwil R. Tornalejo, Timothy J. Wengert, Woodrow W. Whidden II, and Daniel Wildemann.

HERE WE STAND

Luther, the Reformation, and Seventh-day Adventism

EDITED BY

MICHAEL W.
CAMPBELL

AND

NIKOLAUS
SATELMAJER

WITH A FOREWORD BY

GEORGE R. KNIGHT

Pacific Press®
Publishing Association
Nampa, Idaho | Oshawa, Ontario, Canada
www.pacificpress.com

TABLE OF CONTENTS

Why Luther Matters

Five hundred years ago the world experienced one of its great turning points. On October 31, 1517, an unknown Augustinian monk in an obscure university posted ninety-five propositions to a church door in Wittenberg, Germany. His ideas challenged Roman Catholic doctrine and practice. The action itself was not remarkable. To the contrary, it was a common academic practice of the time for scholars to publicly post their positions as an invitation to debate. That was all Luther expected to happen. But Luther's Ninety-Five Theses soon jumped the fence separating the academic world from that of personal Christian piety and politics, and they ignited a revolution—a Reformation. They transformed not only the Western world but eventually affected the entire planet through worldwide mission.

Luther risked almost certain death for his challenge to the medieval establishment. But he was a man under conviction and moved forward in spite of the religious and civil powers arrayed against him. Yet, as strange as it may seem, some who carry the name *Lutheran* five centuries later no longer seem to appreciate the significance of Luther's ideals or beliefs that led not only to his attack on papal authority but also to his separation from the Roman Church. In the spirit of ecumenism, many in the church Luther founded (in harmony with several other denominations that grew out of the sixteenth-century Reformation) are tending back toward Rome.

That reality forces upon us the question of whether Luther and his teachings are still important. Is there anything in Luther that matters in the second decade of the twenty-first century?

The short answer is an emphatic Yes! Luther and his message matter today because he was propelled by those teachings that form the very heart of biblical Christianity. First among those teachings is the issue of religious authority. Heiko Oberman put his finger on the importance of that topic when he wrote, "What is new in Luther is the notion of absolute obedience to the Scriptures against any authorities; be they popes or councils."[1] From a Seventh-day Adventist perspective, *The Great Controversy* highlights that understanding repeatedly and carries it from Luther right through to the end of earthly history. "In our time," we read, "there is a wide departure from their [the Scriptures'] doctrines and precepts, and there is need of a return to the great Protestant principle—the Bible, and the Bible only, as the rule of faith and duty. . . . The same unswerving adherence to the word of God manifested at that crisis of the Reformation is the only hope of reform today."[2] That is essential truth for our day. Adventist history has witnessed episodes when the denomination has sought to solve its theological issues through ecclesiastical legislation guided by what Ellen G. White referred to as "kingly power."[3] One only has to think of the denomination's 1888 experience.[4]

A second teaching at the heart of why Luther still matters is Luther's understanding of justification, or righteousness by faith. His teaching of salvation by grace alone through faith alone has stood at the center of Christian history from Paul's time up to the present. Throughout its history, Christianity has had "evangelists" who add something that humans must do to be justified. And here we, creative Adventists, have not been a whit behind those who would propose "a different gospel," which in effect is "no gospel at all" (Galatians 1:6, 7, RSV). Luther speaks to all such gospel innovators in Adventism; a denomination that has the "eternal gospel" as the foundation of its message (Revelation 14:6, RSV).

A third sample of Luther's relevance for our day is his teaching on the priesthood of all believers. Luther uplifted the fact that every individual can come before the throne of grace without the aid of an earthly priest or other human intercessor. His understanding and emphasis on the priesthood of all believers continues to form the basis of personal spirituality. And it is especially dear to Adventists, with our emphasis on the book of Hebrews and the heavenly ministry of Jesus as our High Priest.

Does Luther matter in our day? Of course, he does! And we Adventists need to study and understand his life and message. A good place to begin is the chapters on Luther in *The Great Controversy*.[5] Beyond those pages are the many excellent one-volume biographies of the great Reformer. And, of course, there are the insightful and focused chapters of the present book.

As Adventist believers who follow in the heritage of Luther the Reformer, we can be thankful that Michael W. Campbell and Nikolaus Satelmajer have had the vision to develop, with the help of a cadre of scholars, a five hundredth anniversary reminder. The book shows the significance of Luther but, more particularly, highlights the intersection of Luther's thought with the ideas and themes that have not only made Seventh-day Adventists Protestants but Protestants with a very distinctive biblical flavor. A survey of the volume's table of contents indicates many themes in Luther's works that have informed the Adventist faith.

There is nothing like this book in Adventist literature. Perhaps the closest is W. L. Emmerson's *The Reformation and the Advent Movement* (1983) and some of the historical work of LeRoy Froom. But neither come anywhere near the scope and depth of the essays in this collection, which focus on more than two dozen areas where Luther and Adventism share common interests. As a denomination, we are indebted to the editors and authors for an insightful treatment of topics important for our day.

George R. Knight
Professor Emeritus of Church History
Andrews University

---

1. Heiko A. Oberman, *Luther: Man Between God and the Devil*, trans. Eileen Walliser-Schwarzbart (New York: Image Books, 1992), 204.

2. Ellen G. White, *The Great Controversy* (Mountain View, CA: Pacific Press® Pub. Assn., 1939), 204, 205.

3. A. Leroy Moore, "Kingly Power," in *The Ellen G. White Encyclopedia*, ed. Jerry Moon and Denis Fortin (Hagerstown, MD: Review and Herald® Pub. Assn., 2013), Kindle edition, loc. 32128.

4. The 1888 General Conference Session of Seventh-day Adventists, held in Minneapolis, Minnesota, is one of the most controversial and significant episodes in denominational history. For an overview, see George R. Knight, "General Conference Session of 1888," in *The Ellen G. White Encyclopedia*, 835–839.

5. White, *The Great Controversy*, 120–210.

INTRODUCTION

Although separated in time by centuries, Seventh-day Adventists see themselves as heirs of the Protestant Reformation started by Martin Luther five hundred years ago. Where does one begin with Martin Luther, described by biographer Paul Althaus as an "ocean" and whom Timothy George calls a "volcano of a personality"?[1] This volume explores the various facets and contours of Luther and compares them with Seventh-day Adventism.

Seventh-day Adventists, beginning as a revivalist reform movement that arose during the final pangs of the Second Great Awakening, saw themselves as restorationists. They viewed themselves as returning to the authority of Scripture and, based on biblical prophecy, proclaimed the literal return of Jesus Christ. In this way, Adventism is much closer to Luther, who also expected Christ's return. In this sense, early Adventists saw themselves as reliving and returning to the purity and simplicity of the early Christians. Even Ellen G. White connected and strongly featured the early Christian church and later Martin Luther as key highlights in the spiritual struggle between Christ and Satan. She devoted more space in her book *The Great Controversy* to his life than any other historical figure after the first Christians.[2]

Luther waged war during his time on scholastic theology. He revealed a deep-seated skepticism concerning the value of philosophy for the theological enterprise. Historian Timothy George observes, "Luther did not become a reformer because he attacked indulgences. He attacked indulgences because the Word had already taken deep root in his heart."[3] Thus, his phrase *fides ex auditu* (faith out of hearing) represents one of the best summaries of his Reformation discovery.

The basis of the Ninety-Five Theses was an appeal to Scripture. It was Luther's appeal to *sola scriptura* (scripture alone) that caused his view of justification by faith to fall "like a bombshell on the theological landscape of medieval Catholicism."[4] He went on to argue that all creeds, sayings of the early church fathers, and even conciliar decisions must be judged by the sure word of Scripture.

This book is a journey both across time as well as space. Today Seventh-day Adventists have some twenty million church members across a large portion of the globe. After more than 150 years of proclaiming Christ's soon return, and now 500 years after Luther protested against indulgences, the editors of this volume hope that the essays in this book will lead toward a better understanding of both Luther and Adventism. In some instances, the volume reveals strong areas of alignment and affinity, and upon other points, it showcases areas of critique to the extent that Adventists continue to base our authority upon the Word of God.

We express our deep appreciation to the diverse group of contributors. While they focused on the theme of the book, each one gives their own perspective on the topic. Some have revisited themes that have been discussed previously, while others are exploring new areas. Several of the writers had the privilege of making presentations in May 2016 at Friedensau Adventist University, Germany. We believe our readers will also enjoy the book from that symposium: Rolf J. Pöhler, ed., *Perceptions of the Protestant Reformation in Seventh-day Adventism* (Friedensau, Germany: Friedensau Adventist University, 2017).

We are grateful to Sheryl Beck and Ruth I. Satelmajer for their imput and editing. They focused on important details, and their imput makes the book more valuable. We express appreciation to the administration of the Adventist International Institute of Advanced Studies, that provided time and support for Michael W. Campbell to participate in this project. A special thanks to Dale E. Galusha, president, Jerry D. Thomas, vice president for product development, and Douglas Church, vice president for sales and marketing, of Pacific Press, who have enthusiastically supported the project. We thank them for their encouragement and support.

Michael W. Campbell and Nikolaus Satelmajer

1. Paul Althaus, *The Theology of Martin Luther*, trans. Robert C. Schultz (Philadelphia, PA: Fortress, 1966), vi; Timothy George, *Theology of the Reformers*, rev. ed. (Nashville, TN: B & H Academic, 2013), 182.

2. Ellen G. White, *The Great Controversy* (Mountain View, CA: Pacific Press® Pub. Assn., 1950).

3. George, *Theology of the Reformers*, 55, 56.

4. Ibid., 72.

HISTORICAL
FOUNDATIONS

CHAPTER 1

What Happened? An Overview of the Beginnings of Luther's Reformation

Timothy J. Wengert

What happened in October 1517 began fifteen years earlier in the city of Erfurt.[1] Two people, whose theologies—unbeknownst to them—were set on a collision course, crossed paths. One was a nineteen-year-old student at the university: Martin Ludher (as he was then spelling his name), who that year (1502) would receive his bachelor of arts degree in preparation to continue on for his master's (1505). In that same year, Raimund Peraudi,[2] the papal legate originally from France, also visited Erfurt to help organize and preach the jubilee indulgences of 1500.

One of the preachers under Peraudi's administration was Johann von Paltz, an Augustinian friar from the same Erfurt cloister where, in a surprising change of vocational direction, Martin Luther entered in 1505.[3] For the 1476 indulgence, Pope Sixtus IV, builder of the Sistine Chapel that

> For the 1476 indulgence, Pope Sixtus IV, builder of the Sistine Chapel that bears his name, decreed for the first time that letters of indulgence purchased by the faithful could apply not only to the living but also to the dead souls in purgatory.

bears his name, decreed for the first time that letters of indulgence purchased by the faithful could apply not only to the living but also to the dead souls in purgatory. When Luther questioned the theological basis for that very practice in 1517, he was directly contradicting both Peraudi and von Paltz.

Luther as preacher of indulgences

Luther and Peraudi were intertwined a second time. In January 1503, Peraudi took a side trip to Wittenberg, the capital of the Electorate of Saxony, where Frederick, the proud elector, had just started a university the previous fall. On January 17, 1503, Peraudi not only dedicated the Castle Church and its All Saints' Foundation—the backbone of the new university—but he decreed, on behalf of Pope Julius II, the nephew of Sixtus, that anyone worshiping in that church on the anniversary of its dedication would receive an indulgence of two hundred days. Each year, unless he was detained by business elsewhere, Elector Frederick would attend, surrounded by the graves of his predecessors, his massive collection of relics, and the courtiers and the learned teachers of his university.

Fast-forward fourteen years to January 1517, when the Saxon court decided to ask their up-and-coming Augustinian professor of theology, Martin Luther, to deliver the sermon. Depending on which of the two sources for that sermon one chooses, either on the eve of the celebration or on the day itself, Luther climbed into the unfamiliar pulpit of the Castle Church (his call as professor included regular preaching at the city church, St. Mary's) and delivered a sermon on the appointed text for such anniversaries—the story of Zacchaeus.[4] Not only did Luther question the motives of people who give money to found churches without changing their hearts, but he also talked, for the first time in such a public place, about indulgences.

Indulgences were a medieval way of lessening the burden of punishment for sin that the flesh of believers undergoes either in this life or in purgatory—a place of purgation intended to purify the soul for its vision of God in heaven ("Blessed are the pure in heart: for they shall see God" and no one else [Matthew 5:8]). The church, through the keys given to Peter and his successors by Christ in Matthew 16, could open the kingdom of heaven by forgiving guilt and reducing that punishment. Baptism, a stronger sacrament, removed all guilt and punishment for original sin and any sins committed before baptism. Becoming a monk or a nun could serve as a kind of second baptism by removing all guilt and punishment. But for everyday sinners, the church offered the sacrament of Penance, which consisted of sorrow for sin (contrition), confession (privately to a priest), and "satisfaction." In Penance, guilt was removed, but the punishment, or discipline, of the flesh was only reduced from an eternal one (mortal sins earned a person a one-way ticket to hell) to temporal disciplines of the flesh. A person, now moved from a state of sin to a state of grace, could satisfy (hence the name of the third part), usually through fasting, almsgiving, and prayer (as in the Sermon on the Mount). But the church could be indulgent and reduce this penalty either partially (e.g., by attending Mass on the anniversary of a church's dedication) or fully. Full, or plenary, indulgences, as they were called, had not been around for more than four hundred years and were the sole prerogative of the pope. The most regular were the so-called jubilee indulgences, such as the one Peraudi preached in 1502 and which Pope Leo X had expressly issued in 1516 to raise funds to construct anew the Basilica of Saint Peter in Rome—the results of which still dominate the Vatican's skyline.

In January 1517, this new plenary indulgence was about to be preached in towns adjacent to electoral Saxony. Elector Frederick banned the sale in his territory for fear of a drain of gold and to avoid undermining his own burgeoning collection of relics. While not offering a plenary indulgence, his relics did offer well over one hundred thousand years of indulgence to those lucky enough to view them when on display, either on November 1 or May 1. And Luther, in his sermon preached for the much smaller anniversary indulgence of two hundred days, made some comments. He wondered aloud how one could preach this (or any other) indulgence on the one hand and still lead people to true sorrow for their sin on the other. He does not seem to know a way out of this dilemma: "You see, therefore, how dangerous a thing the preaching of indulgences is, which teaches a mutilated grace, namely, to flee satisfaction and punishment. . . . For how easily can true contrition and so lax and bountiful an indulgence be preached at one and the same time, when true contrition desires a rigid exaction [of punishment] and such an indulgence relaxes it too much?"[5]

According to Luther's later recollection, the elector was incensed with such an attack on his religious foundation and its indulgences. Without a doubt, that anger forced Luther to do his homework; therefore, throughout the coming months, he poured over church law, the latest New Testament commentary (annotations on the Greek text just published the previous year by Erasmus of Rotterdam), and even the defense of indulgences penned by the Augustinian preacher Johann von Paltz.[6] At the same time, the preaching of Johann Tetzel, the latest indulgence salesman, and the booklet defining this preaching, which was published by the archbishop of Mainz and in whose territories Tetzel was preaching, had come to Luther's attention. As a result, Luther became even more worried that something was wrong with the preaching and teaching surrounding this indulgence. His examination of church law convinced him that originally indulgences did not apply to God's discipline and penalties for sin at all but only to ecclesiastical penalties for flagrant sins that were hurtful to the community—penalties that, of course, a priest, a bishop, or a pope could relax for the sake of the sinner. His reading of the Bible convinced him of what he had already come to cherish; namely, that the entire life of the Christian is to be one of penitence.

The Ninety-Five Theses: Attacking bad preaching

To demonstrate the uncertainty surrounding the church's teaching of indulgences, Luther (since 1512 a *doctor ecclesiae*—that is, a teacher of the church) informed his superiors of his misgivings and, as was the right of every professor at a medieval university, wrote some theses for debate on the subject. Following the statutes of the University of Wittenberg, he then posted these theses on the doors of the town's churches—doors that functioned rather as university bulletin boards for official announcements.[7] On October 31, 1517, he also wrote a letter to the archbishop of Mainz, Albrecht, expressing his dismay at what the people thought the preachers were saying (e.g., "As soon as money clinks in the chest and the cash bell rings, a soul flies out of purgatory and sings";[8] even raping the virgin Mary could be covered by this indulgence; the papal coat of arms displayed during the preaching was more powerful than Christ's cross) and enclosing a copy of these theses—ninety-five in number, as everyone knows.[9]

What do the Ninety-Five Theses tell us about Luther's Reformation? First, his motivation, as he recounted the next year in his open letter to Pope Leo,[10] was in the very opening words of his Ninety-Five Theses: "Out of love and zeal for the truth."[11] And what about the proof text for indulgences, Matthew 4:17, which in the Latin text reads, "Do penance"? Thesis 1—based upon the comments on this very text by Erasmus of Rotterdam—hinted at Luther's growing knowledge of Greek, where the Greek text read *metanoeite* (change one's mind) and not, as in the Latin version, *poenitentiam agite* (do penance): "Our Lord and Master Jesus Christ, in saying 'Do penance . . . ,' wanted the entire life of the faithful to be one of penitence."[12] Luther states the very concern expressed in the January sermon. But, after such an opening, Luther then continued with what he thought was the solution to the problem, based upon his reading of the history of indulgences: "The pope neither desires nor is able to remit any penalties except those imposed by his own authority or that of the canons."[13] Suddenly, the entire system of purchasing a way around God's discipline and penalty of the flesh has been lifted from indulgences, and they have been returned to their original purpose of ecclesiastical discipline and mercy. Then Luther argues, quoting Saint Bonaventure, that the only power the pope has over souls in purgatory is *per modum suffragii*; that is, by the mode of praying for those souls. Then there is thesis 39: "It is extremely difficult, even for the most learned theologians, to lift up before the people the liberality of indulgences and the truth about contrition at one and the same time."[14] Here Luther reflects his own difficulty, already revealed in his sermon of January 1517.

> Underneath the letter to Albrecht and the Ninety-Five Theses themselves runs another theme: bad preaching.

Underneath the letter to Albrecht and the Ninety-Five Theses themselves runs another theme: bad preaching. Once Luther thinks he has proven that indulgences have only a limited, ecclesiastical purpose (theses 5–20), he starts after the preachers, contrasting their wild claims not only with his own uncertainty but also with how good works ought to be preached: in care for the poor. "Christians are to be taught that anyone who sees a destitute person and, while passing such a one by, gives money for indulgences does not buy [gracious] indulgence of the pope but God's wrath."[15] After warning bishops and others about their responsibility and listing the commoners' objections to indulgences, Luther concludes with a rhetorical flourish: "Christians must be encouraged diligently to follow Christ, their head, through penalties, death, and hell, and in this way they may be confident of 'entering heaven through many tribulations' rather than through the [false] security of peace."[16] But the actual heart of the theses comes in a corollary discussion of the nature of the treasures of the church. The standard teaching of indulgences had insisted that God had graciously set up a treasure containing the merits of Christ, Mary, and the saints that could then be applied through indulgences to those who purchased the letters. Instead, Luther insisted, "The true treasure of the church is the most holy gospel of the glory and grace of God."[17]

The "unexpected" Reformation

What happened next surprised everyone, not least of all Martin Luther (who had Hellenized his name, as many humanist scholars of the time did, to match the Greek *Eleutherius*, which means "the free one"). Archbishop Albrecht, suspecting heresy and also worrying about a drop in revenue that would affect his ability to repay a loan for having purchased the right to hold multiple sees, sent the theses to his own theology faculty in Mainz for their opinion and also to Rome. In early 1518, a friend from Nuremberg sent Luther a German translation of the theses, which Luther nixed, preparing instead a German-language essay (of only twenty points): "A Sermon on Indulgences and Grace."[18] This, and not so much the Ninety-Five Theses, turned Luther into a household name and the first living best-selling author the world had ever seen (the sermon was reprinted more than twenty times within two years). The result was, to use Heiko Oberman's apt phrase, the "unexpected Reformation."[19] Many in the early sixteenth century were looking for reform of the feudal system, economic system, and the structure and practices of the church. No one expected a frontal assault on the church's theology, especially on a cornerstone of the medieval penitential system, to which all Western Christians adhered.

When the story of the Reformation's beginnings is told in this way, certain myths disappear. We no longer hear of a guilt-ridden monk eager to rid his soul of a psychological illness. The pictures of an angry Luther nailing a piece of paper to a door (we do not know whether or when he posted them for sure—and he would have more likely used wax or paste) slips back into the nineteenth century, where it was invented. Although there were immediate political and ecclesial consequences, Luther's own motives also had nothing to do with such things. Instead, Luther was concerned with one thing and one thing only: bad preaching and teaching and what it did to the common Christians subject to it. This unexpected Reformation led to the formation of Evangelical, Reformed, and even Anabaptist churches and to the reform of the Roman Catholic Church at the Council of Trent.

The heart of Martin Luther's witness to the gospel

As became clear in the years that followed, Luther's proposal to improve Christian proclamation of the gospel embraced several things that still remain central to the Lutheran witness to the gospel. All have to do with the human creature's standing before God; all were in place in Luther's theology by 1518.

"*We are justified by grace through faith on account of Christ.*"[20] This famous line from the Augsburg Confession, the Lutheran confession of faith presented to the Emperor Charles V on June 25, 1530, in Augsburg, echoes Luther's initial insight into the gospel: "We are justified"; that is, made or declared righteous before God. Already in 1515, as Luther was lecturing on Romans at the University of Wittenberg, he began to realize the fatal flaw in the theologians of his day. (In one German outburst in his Latin-language lecture, he calls them "pig theologians.")[21] One's standing before God cannot depend upon works in any way. Not only are works insufficient over and against sin, but the very claim that they contribute something to a relation with God reflects the worst human sin of all: pride and self-love. Luther's phrase "by grace" reflects a shift in Luther's thinking that occurred rather late in the process, around 1520. Early on, following the medieval scholastic consensus, Luther defined grace (*gratia*) as a force or power of love infused into the human soul to make it acceptable to God by providing it the proper disposition. In the *Annotations on the New Testament* of 1516, however, Erasmus of Rotterdam noted that the Greek word *charis* designated something quite different—namely, the *favor Dei*, God's favor or mercy. At first, Luther was skeptical and tried to combine both definitions. By 1521 at the latest, probably influenced by Philip Melanchthon, his colleague and expert in Greek, Luther changed his mind and thereafter, with every chance he got, would define grace as God's mercy. "Through faith" signaled a complete rejection of works in the relation with God. This shift from the medieval claims

> One's standing before God cannot depend upon works in any way. Not only are works insufficient over and against sin, but the very claim that they contribute something to a relation with God reflects the worst human sin of all: pride and self-love.

to merit grace is sometimes lost on many Christians, who imagine faith is a work or decision that the Christian offers to God in return for grace—a view far closer to Luther's late-medieval teachers and later opponents. Faith for the Reformers is not a work but rather a relation of trust and assurance brought to life by the Holy Spirit through the hearing of God's gracious promise in Christ. Finally, "on account of Christ" reflects perhaps the most important aspect of Luther's theology, often summarized by him as "Christ alone" (not, of course, to the exclusion of the Trinity but rather as a way of focusing upon the incarnation of Christ and His salvific death and resurrection). Thus, we have the three most important *solas* (alones) of Luther's thought: grace alone, faith alone, and Christ alone.

"*To obtain such faith God instituted the office of preaching, giving the gospel and the sacraments.*"[22] This excerpt from the next article of the Augsburg Confession insists that God works through means to effect human salvation. Luther insists that God works through "means of grace"—that is, baptism, the Lord's Supper, and the proclamation of God's Word. He traces this to the Incarnation itself, where the Word becomes flesh (John 1:1–14). God comes to His people in the physical means of words, water, and bread and wine. Indeed, by insisting with Augustine that the sacraments were "visible words," Luther actually developed another *sola*; namely *solo verbo* (by the Word alone). Sometimes mistakenly rendered as *sola scriptura* by later Protestants—Luther used that term less than a dozen times—Luther insisted that the proclaimed aural word and celebrated visible word were the means God used to awaken faith and justify the sinner. But, for Luther, because human beings are sinners, God's Word must work on us in two ways: first, doing a work alien to God's nature (an *opus alienum*) before doing God's proper work (*opus proprium*). Because of sin, God's Word first acts to condemn, terrify, and put to death the "old Adam" in us; what Luther calls "the Law." Only then does God work to forgive, console, and make alive; what Luther calls "the Gospel." This twofold action is reflected in baptism (understood as a drowning and rising that joins the sinner to Christ's death and resurrection). It also redefines Penance by reducing the threefold division of medieval theology to two parts: sorrow for sin (contrition) and forgiveness, so that sometimes Luther will even call it the sacrament of Absolution.

A theologian of the cross is one who speaks of the crucified and hidden God.[23] The third leg of Luther's theology, taken from Luther's defense of the Ninety-Five Theses, is usually called the "theology of the cross"—not a theology about the cross (explaining a theory of atonement) but rather the revelation of God in the last place one would reasonably look.[24] Luther is forever being surprised, turned upside down, by the God who would choose Moses over Pharaoh, the children of Israel over the Egyptians, a young woman from Nazareth rather than a daughter of Caiaphas, and fishermen rather than scribes and Pharisees. But the chief surprise is finding God in a manger, standing dripping wet in the

Jordan, surrounded by all the wrong people (tax collectors, sinners, women, and children), and hanging on a cross between two criminals. The very justification of sinners reflects this same paradoxical revelation, as does the alien and proper work of God (Law and Gospel) and the work of God through ordinary means: the words of a preacher, the waters of baptism, and the bread and wine providing Christ's real presence to sinners of all kinds.

There are, of course, other aspects of Luther's theology as well. Especially his distinction between God's rule in this world through a "civil use" of the law and God's rule in the church through the "theological use" of the law (described above) and the gospel. This is often designated as the "doctrine" of the two kingdoms but better understood as the distinction between God's two hands, where the left hand rules this world and the right ushers in the world to come. But the Reformation started with a single professor's effort to raise a theological question about the nature of indulgences and the state of preaching in his world.[25]

1. For this reconstruction, see Martin Brecht, *Martin Luther: His Road to Reformation, 1483–1521*, trans. James L. Schaaf (Philadelphia: Fortress, 1985), 23–50; Scott Hendrix, *Martin Luther: Visionary Reformer* (New Haven, CT: Yale University Press, 2015), 27–33; and Timothy J. Wengert, ed., *Martin Luther's 95 Theses With Introduction, Commentary, and Study Guide* (Minneapolis, MN: Fortress, 2015), xxi–xxxi.

2. He is also known as Cardinal Raymund von Gurk, and the spelling of his name varied.

3. See Berndt Hamm, *Ablass und Reformation: Erstaunliche Kohärenzen* (Tübingen: Mohr Siebeck, 2016), 121–175.

4. For the most recent study of this sermon, see Timothy J. Wengert, "Martin Luther's Preaching an Indulgence in January 1517," *Lutheran Quarterly* 29 (2015): 62–75. For a more traditional view of this sermon, see David Bagchi, "Luther's *Ninety-Five Theses* and the Contemporary Criticism of Indulgences," in *Promissory Notes on the Treasury of Merits: Indulgences in Late Medieval Europe*, ed. R. N. Swanson (Leiden: Brill, 2006), 331–355.

5. Martin Luther, *D. Martin Luthers Werke: Kritische Gesamtausgabe*, vol. 1 (Weimar: Hermann Böhlau, 1883), 94–99, quoted in Wengert, "Martin Luther's Preaching an Indulgence in January 1517," 69, 70.

6. Johannes von Paltz, *Supplementum Coelifodinae* (1504), ed. Berndt Hamm et al. (Berlin: De Gruyter, 1983).

7. The question of whether the theses were posted is a matter of scholarly debate. For the most recent discussion of the issue, see Volker Leppin and Timothy J. Wengert, "Sources for and Against the Posting of the *Ninety-Five Theses*," *Lutheran Quarterly* 29 (2015): 373–398. For the

most recent translation into English, see Wengert, *Martin Luther's 95 Theses*, 1–26.

8. This jingle has been attributed to Johann Tetzel.

9. For the letter, see Wengert, *Martin Luther's 95 Theses*, 27–36.

10. Luther, *D. Martin Luthers Werke*, 1:527–529.

11. Martin Luther, *Luther's Works*, vol. 31, *Career of the Reformer 1*, ed. Jaroslav Pelikan (St. Louis, MO: Concordia; Philadelphia: Fortress, 1968), 25.

12. Wengert, *Martin Luther's 95 Theses*, 13.

13. Luther, *Luther's Works*, 31:25–33.

14. Timothy J. Wengert, "[The 95 Theses or] Disputations for Clarifying the Power of Indulgences, 1517," in *The Annotated Luther*, vol. 1, *The Roots of Reform*, ed. Timothy J. Wengert (Minneapolis, MN: Fortress, 2015), 39.

15. Ibid., 40.

16. Ibid., 46.

17. Ibid., 42.

18. For this sermon, see Wengert, *Martin Luther's 95 Theses*, 37–48.

19. Heiko A. Oberman, *Luther: Man Between God and the Devil*, trans. Eileen Walliser-Schwarzbart (New Haven, CT: Yale University Press, 1989), 113–206.

20. Art. 4 of "The Augsburg Confession," in *The Book of Concord*, ed. Robert Kolb and Timothy J. Wengert, trans. Eric Gritsch (Minneapolis, MN: Fortress, 2000), 38–41.

21. See Martin Luther, *Luther's Works*, vol. 25, *Lectures on the Romans*, ed. Jaroslav Pelikan (St. Louis, MO: Concordia, 1972), 261. See also Berndt Hamm, *The Early Luther: Stages in a Reformation Reorientation*, trans. Martin Lohrmann (Grand Rapids, MI: Eerdmans, 2014), 59–84.

22. Art. 5 of "The Augsburg Confession," 40, 41. For one of the best overviews of Luther's thought, see Gerhard Forde, *Where God Meets Man: Luther's Down-to-Earth Approach to the Gospel* (Minneapolis, MN: Augsburg, 1972).

23. See Dennis Bielfeldt, "Heidelberg Disputation, 1518," in *The Annotated Luther*, vol. 1, *The Roots of Reform*, ed. Timothy J. Wengert (Minneapolis, MN: Fortress, 2015), 67–120.

24. For the classic treatment of this aspect of Luther's teaching, see Walther von Loewenich, *Luther's Theology of the Cross*, trans. Herbert J. A. Bouman (Minneapolis, MN: Augsburg, 1976). For its use in Luther's *Explanations of the Disputes Concerning the Power of Indulgences*, see Timothy J. Wengert, " 'Peace, Peace . . . Cross, Cross': Reflections on How Martin Luther Relates the Theology of the Cross to Suffering," *Theology Today* 59 (2002): 190–205.

25. For a helpful overview of Luther's teaching, see Robert Kolb and Charles P. Arand, *The Genius of Luther's Theology: A Wittenberg Way of Thinking for the Contemporary Church* (Grand Rapids, MI: Baker, 2008).

CHAPTER 2

Sola Scriptura:
A Comparison of Luther
and the Adventist Understanding

Remwil R. Tornalejo

S *ola scriptura* was one of the principles of the Reformation.[1] Although not unique to Martin Luther, it is a concept popularized by him.[2] One of the earliest references to it occurs during a debate with Johann Eck at Leipzig in 1519. Luther declared, "No Christian believer can be forced [to believe an article of faith] beyond Holy Scripture."[3] The same idea is embodied in his defense at Worms on April 18, 1521: "Unless I am convinced by the testimony of the Scriptures or by clear reason (for I do not trust either in the pope or in councils alone, since it is well known that they have often erred and contradicted themselves), I am bound by the Scriptures I have quoted and my conscience is captive to the Word of God. I cannot and I will not retract anything, since it is neither safe nor right to go against conscience. I cannot do otherwise, here I stand, may God help me, Amen."[4]

Seventh-day Adventists affirm the *sola scriptura* principle. They are known as "the people of the Book" and place a high regard upon Scripture. But what Luther meant by *sola scriptura* is a contested subject among church historians and theologians.[5] This chapter explores and compares the meaning of the *sola scriptura* principle by Luther and as understood by Seventh-day Adventists.

Luther and *sola scriptura*

Several recent studies maintain that it is a misconception, or at least an over-simplification, to argue that Scripture was the sole authority for the Reformers and that tradition had no role.[6] For example, Irena Backus states, "It is by now a well-known fact that the reformers did not reject the tradition of the Early Church, which in their eyes was to be sharply distinguished from the corruptions of mediaeval ecclesiastical structures."[7] These developments necessitate a more careful look at what the term *sola scriptura* meant for Luther. To understand this phrase, it is necessary to place the issue in its historical context.

> During Luther's time, the issue was not the authority of Scripture itself but rather to what extent this authority has vis-à-vis the Roman Catholic Church and its leaders.

Sola scriptura principle in historical context

During Luther's time, the issue was not the authority of Scripture itself but rather to what extent this authority has vis-à-vis the Roman Catholic Church and its leaders. Catholic leaders taught "the unwritten tradition could be just as authoritative as Scripture." At times, it could even be superior since it was the church's creation.[8] Luther, as priest, adhered to this belief during his early life. Even after posting his Ninety-Five Theses, he maintained a high regard for the writings of the church fathers and papal decrees. He declared, "First, I testify that I desire to say or maintain absolutely nothing except, first of all, what is in the Holy Scriptures and can be maintained from them; and then what is in and from the writings of the church fathers and is accepted by the Roman church and preserved both in the canons and papal decrees."[9]

In addition, another common understanding maintained that the pope or a church council represented the ultimate authority to determine the meaning of the Bible.[10]

Luther's view of the church fathers and their teachings

Luther did not altogether discard tradition. He fought against the Radical Reformers who wanted to eliminate all church traditions.[11] He warned, "One needs a more cautious, discreet spirit, which attacks the accretion which threatens the temple without destroying the temple of God itself."[12] And to those who accused him of rejecting all the teachings of the church fathers, he answered,

"I do not reject them. But everyone, indeed, knows that at times they have erred, as men will; therefore, I am ready to trust them only when they give me evidence for their opinions from Scripture, which has never erred."[13]

Luther, after several disputations with papal representatives, rejected the common understanding that "the teaching of the Scripture and the teaching of the Roman Catholic Church were necessarily identical."[14] He wrote, "What else do I contend for but to bring everyone to understand the difference between the divine Scripture and human teaching or custom."[15] The Holy Scriptures are "more reliable than any other writings" and by which one can judge all other writings, for it is the only "true lord and master of all writings and doctrine on earth."[16] He advised that "the Sacred Scriptures must be sharply distinguished from those that have been invented by men in the Church, it matters not how eminent they be for saintliness and scholarship."[17]

Luther argued for the primacy of the Scriptures over the writings of the church fathers, but at the same time he upheld their value. In 1539, he wrote, "We Gentiles must not value the writings of our fathers as highly as the Holy Scripture, but as worth a little less."[18] He added, "The teachings of the Fathers are useful only to lead us to the Scriptures, as they were led, and then we must hold to the Scriptures alone."[19] Furthermore, he explained, "The writings of all the holy fathers should be read only for a time, in order that through them we may be led to the Holy Scriptures. . . . The dear fathers wished, by their writings, to lead us to the Scriptures, but we so use them as to be led away from the Scriptures, though the Scriptures alone are our vineyard in which we ought all to work and toil."[20]

Luther and religious authority

Luther did not despise church authority without qualification. His strong objection was against the pope's claim that the church has authority above the Word of God and therefore must be its arbiter.[21] For him, Scripture is its own interpreter, and therefore it must be interpreted by comparing Scripture with Scripture.[22] He protested against the Catholic teaching that Scripture is insufficient "apart from the treasury of popes and councils."[23] Contrary to the popular belief of his time, he disagreed that the church is above Scripture. Instead, he believed that the Word of God bore and nourished the church. Thus, he claimed that "the Word of God is incomparably superior to the Church, and in this Word the Church, being a creature, has nothing to decree, ordain, or make, but only to be decreed, ordained, and made."[24]

Arthur Wood attests that Luther quoted profusely from the church fathers, but he subjected their authority to Scripture and refused to accept them whenever they appeared to contradict the Word of God.[25] According to Luther, "All the holy fathers, when they speak apart from the Scriptures, are as fallible as anyone else."[26] He added, "I will not listen to the Church or the fathers or the apostles unless they bring and teach the pure Word of God."[27] In his *Sermons on the Gospel of John*, he referred to apostle Paul's message to the Galatians (Galatians 1:8) when he emphasized that any person (regardless of his or her status or rank) and even angels would be suspect if they preached contrary to the Word of God.[28] Professed prophets who work wonders and miracles also must be judged "in the light of God's Word."[29]

Summary of Luther and *sola scriptura*

The idea of *sola scriptura* for Luther does not mean that Scripture is the *sole* religious authority. It is evident that the above statements were not intended to mean that Luther despised all the teachings of the church fathers. Although he made it clear that Scripture must be above creeds and papal decrees, his acceptance of church authority and the creeds depended upon their biblical authority.[30]

> Although he made it clear that Scripture must be above creeds and papal decrees, his acceptance of church authority and the creeds depended upon their biblical authority.

James R. Payton Jr. aptly summarizes Luther's understanding of *sola scriptura* by stating that, for Luther, "Scripture was the *only unquestioned* religious authority. It did not mean that Scripture was the *only* religious authority—as has often been assumed or misunderstood in subsequent Protestantism."[31]

For Luther, *sola scriptura* meant that the Word of God is the ultimate standard and norm, the proper touchstone, and the final authority for faith and practice. All other authorities must be judged and evaluated in light of Scripture. Moreover, for him, the Word of God is self-sufficient. It is its own interpreter and should never be beholden to any other authority for authentication.[32]

Seventh-day Adventist understanding of *sola scriptura*

Seventh-day Adventists adhere to the *sola scriptura* principle.[33] The first fundamental belief of the Seventh-day Adventist Church states, "The Holy Scriptures, Old and New Testaments, are the written Word of God, given by divine inspiration. The inspired authors spoke and wrote as they were moved by the Holy Spirit. In this Word, God has committed to humanity the knowledge necessary for salvation. The Holy Scriptures are the supreme, authoritative, and the infallible revelation of His will. They are the standard of character, the test of experience, the definitive revealer of doctrines, and the trustworthy record of God's acts in history."[34] Yet Adventist thinkers have differed in their understanding of *sola scriptura*.[35] In order to grasp the Adventist understanding of the *sola scriptura* principle, I will examine the writings of Ellen G. White in order to establish an Adventist baseline view. It is important to note that when she referenced the idea of *sola scriptura* she connected the idea to the Reformation understanding on this topic. She wrote, "In our time there is a wide departure from their doctrines and precepts, and there is need of a return to the great Protestant principle—the Bible, and the Bible only, as the rule of faith and duty."[36]

Ellen G. White and *sola scriptura*

Ellen White consistently affirmed the *sola scriptura* principle. For her, "the Bible, and the Bible alone, is our rule of faith."[37] In another place, she wrote, "The Bible is its own expositor. One passage will prove to be a key that will unlock other passages, and in this way light will be shed upon the hidden meaning of the word. By comparing different texts treating on the same subject, viewing their bearing on every side, the true meaning of the Scriptures will be made evident."[38]

Contrary to her detractors' assertions, Ellen White never claimed that her writings should ever be considered as equal to Scripture. She is emphatic on this point: "God's Word is the unerring standard. The Testimonies [her writings] are not to take the place of the Word. . . . Let all prove their positions from the Scriptures and substantiate every point they claim as truth from the revealed Word of God."[39] In comparison to the Bible, she claimed that her writings were a "lesser light" to lead people to the "greater light."[40] She penned that "if the *Testimonies* speak not according to the word of God, reject them."[41] She also wrote, "Our position and faith is in the Bible. And never do we want any soul to bring in the Testimonies ahead of the Bible"[42] and that the Testimonies would not be necessary if God's people diligently study the Scriptures.[43] She explained, "The written testimonies are not to give new light, but to impress vividly upon the heart the truths of inspiration already revealed."[44]

Ellen G. White and the use of other sources

Ellen White's adherence to the *sola scriptura* principle does not mean that she never considered other sources. She cautioned, "Many think that they must consult commentaries on the Scriptures in order to understand the meaning of the word of God, and we would not take the position that commentaries should not be studied; but it will take much discernment to discover the truth of God under the mass of the words of men."[45] She consistently maintained that Scripture is the ultimate gauge of faith and practice. Furthermore, she affirmed "the Bible, and the Bible only, as the standard of all doctrines and the basis of all reforms"[46] and all other teachings and practices must pass the test of the Scriptures.[47]

Summary of Ellen G. White's understanding of *sola scriptura*

Ellen White understood *sola scriptura* to mean that the Bible and the Bible alone is the foundation of Christian faith and practice. Yet, this does not mean she disregarded other religious material. She claimed that her writings did not have the same function as Scripture but instead were intended to lead people back to the Word of God. Even though she maintained the principle that Scripture interprets itself, she allowed for the fact that other biblical tools and resources can be helpful as an aid to study the Bible. She emphasized that Scripture must always be given priority over other sources of authority in order to determine the meaning of the text.

Conclusion

Luther and Seventh-day Adventists share two main commonalities about the principle of *sola scriptura*. First, both decisively affirm that the Bible is the only infallible and final touchstone of faith and practice. It means that all doctrine must pass the test of Scripture in order to be considered valid. The Bible is the only source of religious knowledge. Second, both agree that Scripture is its own interpreter. It is not dependent upon external authorities or science to authenticate its claim. A difficult Scriptural passage must be understood in the light of the witness of Scripture as a whole. Finally, in application of the *sola scripture* principle, any teaching or doctrine that does not pass the test of the Scripture must be rejected.

---

1. *Sola scriptura* is generally accepted to mean that the Bible alone is the authority in matters of faith and practice. The other two principles that complete the three *solas* are *sola gratia* (grace alone) and *sola fide* (faith alone).

2. See Arthur Skevington Wood, *Captive to the Word: Martin Luther, Doctor of Sacred Scripture* (London: Paternoster, 1969), 31–40. Wood labors to explain that Luther is indebted in many ways to his predecessors, especially Augustine of Hippo and William of Occam, and to later Occamist theologians regarding his view of the Scriptures. Nevertheless, *sola scriptura* as a theological formula is a by-product of the Reformation rather than its presupposition. See Bernhard Lohse, *Martin Luther: An Introduction to His Life and Work* (Edinburgh: T & T Clark, 1986), 153; cf. Bernhard Lohse, *Martin Luther's Theology: Its Historical and Systematic Development*, trans. and ed. Roy A. Harrisville (Minneapolis, MN: Fortress, 2011), 22, 23. The phrase *sola scriptura* per se is not found in the works of Luther. Nevertheless, the idea that Scripture stands supreme in authority over the church and other religious authorities is central in his more developed theology.

3. Lohse, *Martin Luther's Theology*, 123.

4. Martin Luther, *Luther's Works*, vol. 32, *Career of the Reformer 2*, ed. George W. Forell (Philadelphia, PA: Fortress, 1958), 113.

5. For a discussion on the meaning of *sola scriptura*, see James R. Payton Jr., *Getting the*

Reformation Wrong: Correcting Some Misunderstandings (Downers Grove, IL: IVP Academic, 2010), 132–159; John C. Peckham, "*Sola Scriptura: Reductio ad Absurdum?*" *Trinity Journal*, n.s., 35, no. 2 (Fall 2014): 195–223; Aleksandar S. Santrac, "The *Sola Scriptura* Principle in the Current Debate," *Journal of the Adventist Theological Society* 24, no. 1 (2013): 107–126; Kwabena Donkor, "Contemporary Responses to *Sola Scriptura*: Implications for Adventist Theology," *Reflections: The BRI Newsletter* 41 (January 2013): 5–8.

6. Payton, *Getting the Reformation Wrong*, 133.

7. Irena Backus, "The Disputation of Baden, 1526, and Berne, 1528: Neutralizing the Early Church," special issue, *Studies in Reformed Theology and History* 1, no. 1 (Winter 1993): 81, accessed December 18, 2016, http://scdc.library.ptsem.edu/mets/mets .aspx?src=SRTH199311&div=11&img=3.

8. Roger E. Olson, *The Story of Christian Theology: Twenty Centuries of Tradition and Reform* (Downers Grove, IL: IVP Academic, 1999), 385.

9. Martin Luther, *Luther's Works*, vol. 31, *Career of the Reformer 1*, ed. Harold J. Grimm (Philadelphia, PA: Fortress, 1957), 83.

10. Wood, *Captive to the Word*, 120.

11. The Radical Reformers or Anabaptists were more consistent in applying the *sola scriptura* principle. See Alister E. McGrath, *Reformation Thought: An Introduction*, 3rd ed. (Malden, MA: Blackwell, 1999), 155.

12. Martin Luther, *Martin Luther's Basic Theological Writings*, ed. Timothy F. Lull and William R. Russell (Minneapolis, MN: Fortress, 1989), 346.

13. Luther, *Luther's Works,* 32:11.

14. Wood, *Captive to the Word*, 120; cf. Lohse, *Martin Luther's Theology*, 188. According to Ernst Zeeden, "Luther was not breaking new ground when he turned to the Bible, but only when he cut the Bible off from the pope and Church, or subordinated them." Ernst W. Zeeden, *The Legacy of Luther: Martin Luther and the Reformation* (Westminster, MD: Newman Press, 1954), quoted in Wood, *Captive to the Word*, 119.

15. Martin Luther, "Answer to the Superchristian, Superspiritual, and Superlearned Book of Goat Emser," quoted in Hugh T. Kerr, ed., *A Compend of Luther's Theology* (Philadelphia, PA: Westminster Press, 1974), 15.

16. Luther, *Luther's Works,* 32:11.

17. Martin Luther, "The Babylonian Captivity of the Church," quoted in Kerr, *A Compend of Luther's Theology*, 12.

18. Martin Luther, *On the Councils and the Church, 1539*, in *Selected Writings of Martin Luther, 1529–1546*, ed. Theodore G. Tappert (Minneapolis, MN: Fortress, 2007), 243.

19. Luther, "Answer to the Superchristian," 14.

20. Martin Luther, "An Open Letter to the Christian Nobility," quoted in Kerr, *A Compend of Luther's Theology*, 13.

21. Martin Luther, *Luther's Works*, ed. Jaroslav Pelikan, vol. 26, *Lectures on Galatians, Chapters 1–4* (St. Louis, MO: Concordia, 1963), 51.

22. Martin Luther, *Luther's Works*, ed. Jaroslav Pelikan, vol. 9, *Lectures on Deuteronomy* (St. Louis, MO: Concordia, 1960), 21.

23. Michael S. Horton, "Scripture Alone: Luther's Doctrine of Scripture," in *The Legacy of Luther*, ed. R. C. Sproul and Stephen J. Nichols (Orlando, FL: Reformation Trust, 2016), 121.

24. Martin Luther, *Luther's Works*, vol. 36, *Word and Sacrament 2*, ed. Abdel R. Wentz (Philadelphia, PA: Fortress, 1959), 107.

25. See Wood, *Captive to the Word*, 125.

26. Martin Luther, quoted in the introduction to Luther's 1521 *Avoiding the Doctrine of Men*, in Tappert, *Selected Writings of Martin Luther, 1529–1546*, 204.

27. Luther, *Luther's Works*, 26:67.

28. See Martin Luther, *Luther's Works*, vol. 23, *Sermons on the Gospel of St. John, Chapters 6–8*, ed. Hilton C. Oswald (St. Louis, MO: Concordia, 1959), 191, 192.

29. Martin Luther, *Luther's Works*, ed. Jaroslav Pelikan, vol. 24, *Sermons on the Gospel of St. John, Chapters 14–16* (St. Louis, MO: Concordia, 1961), 75; cf. Luther, *Luther's Works*, 26:383.

30. See Martin Luther, *Luther's Works*, vol. 41, *Church and Ministry 3*, ed. Eric W. Gritsch (Philadelphia, PA: Fortress, 1966), 123. Alberto R. Timm observes that for the Magisterial Reformers, such as Luther and Calvin, *sola scriptura* does not mean the rejection of other sources of religious knowledge. Alberto R. Timm, "*Sola Scriptura* and Ellen G. White: Historical Reflections," in *The Gift of Prophecy in Scripture and History*, ed. Alberto R. Timm and Dwain N. Esmond (Silver Spring, MD: Review and Herald® Pub. Assn., 2015), 288.

31. Payton, *Getting the Reformation Wrong*, 142 (italics in the original). Frank M. Hasel reaches a similar conclusion. He writes, "When Luther maintained the principle of *sola scriptura*, he was not suggesting that the tradition of the church was without value. Rather, he was arguing a case of relative clarity and weight. In other words, if a conflict arises in the interpretation of faith, then the Scripture carries the authority that transcends and judges any of the church's traditions." Frank M. Hasel, "Presuppositions in the Interpretation of Scripture," in *Understanding Scripture: An Adventist Approach*, vol. 1, ed. George W. Reid (Silver Spring, MD: Biblical Research Institute, 2005), 37.

32. Although Luther asserted the *sola scriptura* principle, it is evident that he did not agree with the principle of *tota scriptura*—the idea that all Scriptures are equally inspired. He calls the book of James the "epistle of straw" for the reason that it seemingly contradicts the idea of righteousness by faith alone. Luther wrote, " 'Away with James.' 'His authority is not great enough to cause me to abandon the doctrine of faith and to deviate from the authority of the other apostles and the entire Scripture.' " Martin Luther, quoted in Paul Althaus, *The Theology of Martin Luther*, trans. Robert C. Shultz (Philadelphia: PA, Fortress, 1966), 81. On the other hand, Adventists assert *tota scriptura* in consideration that "all Scriptures" are equally inspired and are profitable to the believer.

33. See Hasel, "Presuppositions in the Interpretation of Scripture," 36.

34. See 2015 edition of the Seventh-day Adventist 28 fundamental beliefs. Accessed August 10, 2017, http://szu.adventist.org/wp-content/uploads/2016/04/28_Beliefs.pdf.

35. E.g., see Tim Crosby, "Why I Don't Believe in *Sola Scriptura*," Viewpoint, *Ministry*, October 1987, 11–15; Woodrow W. Whidden II, "*Sola Scriptura*, Inerrantist Fundamentalism, and the Wesleyan Quadrilateral: Is 'No Creed but the Bible' a Workable Solution?" *Andrews University Seminary Studies* 35, no. 2 (Autumn 1997): 211–226.

36. Ellen G. White, *The Great Controversy* (Mountain View, CA: Pacific Press® Pub. Assn., 1950), 204.

37. Ellen G. White, *Counsels on Sabbath School Work* (Washington, DC: Review and Herald® Pub. Assn., 1938), 84; cf. Ellen G. White, *Selected Messages*, vol. 2 (Washington, DC: Review and Herald® Pub. Assn., 1958), 85.

38. Ellen G. White, *Fundamentals of Christian Education* (Nashville, TN: Southern Pub. Assn., 1923), 187. In line with E. G. White, Hasel comments that to take *sola scriptura* as a hermeneutical principle does not mean to "exclude the help of other sources in the task of interpretation, such as biblical lexicons, dictionaries, concordances, and other books and commentaries. However, in the proper interpretation of the Bible, the text of Scripture has priority over all other aspects, sciences, and secondary helps. Other viewpoints have to be carefully evaluated from the standpoint of Scripture as a whole." Hasel, "Presuppositions in the Interpretation of Scripture," 36.

39. Ellen G. White, *Evangelism* (Washington, DC: Review and Herald® Pub. Assn., 1946), 256.

40. Ellen G. White, *Colporteur Ministry* (Mountain View, CA: Pacific Press® Pub. Assn., 1953), 125.

41. Ellen G. White, *Testimonies for the Church* (Mountain View, CA: Pacific Press® Pub. Assn., 1948), 5:691.

42. White, *Evangelism*, 256.

43. White, *Testimonies for the Church*, 2:605, 606. White claimed that her Testimonies are to point people to the Scriptures that they have neglected. White, *Evangelism*, 257.

44. White, *Testimonies for the Church*, 2:605.

45. White, *Fundamentals of Christian Education*, 187.

46. White, *The Great Controversy*, 595.

47. According to Ellen G. White, "The opinions of learned men, the deductions of science, the creed or decisions of ecclesiastical councils, as numerous and discordant as are the churches which they represent, the voice of the majority—not one nor all of these should be regarded as evidence for or against any point of religious faith. Before accepting any doctrine or precept, we should demand a plain 'Thus saith the Lord' in its support." White, *The Great Controversy*, 595; cf. White, *Testimonies for the Church*, 5:575.

CHAPTER 3

Priesthood of Believers
in Luther and Adventism

Michael Sokupa

M artin Luther's understanding of the priesthood of all believers is widely recognized by most Reformation scholars. Timothy George contends, "Luther's greatest contribution to Protestant ecclesiology was his doctrine of the priesthood of all believers."[1] Oswald Bayer notes that Luther's address *To the Christian Nobility* was "a document that had great effect, in the public realm as well, which one might call the Magna Carta for Luther's understanding of the *priesthood of all believers*."[2] At the same time, this was not Luther's original contribution, even though he certainly placed great emphasis on it and even though his understanding came at a critical moment in the history of the Christian church. During the early church, Tertullian presented baptism as the ordination to priesthood. He understood that in baptism believers "are thoroughly anointed with a blessed unction."[3] Many centuries later Luther expressed the same thought when he wrote, "We are all priests, as many of us as are Christians."[4] Thus, according to Robert Muthiah, the Reformation was a turning point in terms of this understanding of the priesthood of all believers.[5] Such a shift in thinking, as part of the Reformation, is largely attributed to Martin Luther. This chapter examines both Luther and Adventist reflections about this vital doctrine. The emphasis is on how Luther's understanding resonates or varies from Seventh-day Adventists.

Luther and the priesthood of believers

Martin Luther discussed the topic of the priesthood of believers throughout his literary works. As a consequence, there are many ways scholars have viewed this topic. Hank Voss proposes a chronological treatment. He suggests "a Roman Catholic period (1505–17); a period of strong emphasis (1518–23); a transitional period (1524–25); and a period of weaker emphasis (1526–46)."[6] In the first stage, the Roman Catholic Church's understanding of the priesthood influenced Luther. During the second phase of development, his literary output was at its peak. He produced eleven of the fifteen works on the topic during this period; and it is in these works that most of his thoughts on this subject are found. Luther's focus during the transitional period is on Christian freedom; his polemic against Karlstadt was the intellectual driving force behind the German Peasants' War.[7] According to Voss, the last twenty years of Luther's life show a decline in his emphasis upon the priesthood of all believers as a result of fallout from the Peasants' War, along with the growing influence of Anabaptist teaching.[8] The doctrine, however, remained central in Luther's ecclesiology. Three centuries after Luther, Adventism emerged during the 1830s as a lay-driven, transdenominational, Scripture-focused movement. As the movement grew, it drew from both the Radical and Magisterial Reformations; from the Radical Reformation, it gained a heritage that sought to conform everything to Scripture.

The essence of Luther's teaching

Luther's ideas on the priesthood of believers were formulated within the socio-political and religious context of his time. At that point, the major division within society concerned the difference between laity and clergy.[9] According to Voss, "Luther's ecclesial world was divided into three estates: clerics, monastics, and laics."[10] On July 2, 1505, Luther became a monk, and two years later a priest in the Roman Catholic Church.[11] Another important division that impacted society at that time was between the spiritual and secular. Based on biblical grounds, Luther rejected these divisions. His rejection of these divisions may be observed in a number of his literary works. Voss highlights two such works that provide the clearest evidence: "*On Monastic Vows* (1521) and his vigorous 1521 debate with Jerome Esmer (d. 1527) over 'priesthood' in 1 Pet 2:5–9."[12] In these works, Luther argued against the spiritual-secular divide; the lay-clergy division is also rejected. Luther believed that the priesthood of all Christians flows from the priesthood of Christ.[13] He argued that "as Christ's brothers, Christians receive a share in his priestly office, namely, through baptism, regeneration, and the anointing with the Holy Spirit."[14] It is, however, important to note that Luther's position on the division between laity and clergy "did not rule out church office."[15] Therefore, he did not reject the ministry as a special calling and function. The public character of the ministerial office is the main difference that sets it apart from the priesthood of all believers.

The function of the priesthood

"In the treatise *On Appointing Ministers of the Church* he [Luther] lists seven priestly functions: teaching or preaching, baptism, consecration or the administration of the Lord's Supper, binding and loosing sins, intercession, sacrifice, and the judging of doctrines."[16] A number of scholars discuss these functions with reference to both ministers and laity. Brian Gerrish observes that Luther "assigns to the royal priesthood all the functions that, in other places, are assigned to the church's official ministry."[17] Uche Anizor interprets Luther to be saying "all Christians are permitted to perform those same functions."[18] For Gerrish, Luther simply demonstrates that the function belongs to the whole priesthood and every member.[19]

> In the treatise *On Appointing Ministers of the Church* he [Luther] lists seven priestly functions: teaching or preaching, baptism, consecration or the administration of the Lord's Supper, binding and loosing sins, intercession, sacrifice, and the judging of doctrines."

Luther's biblical foundation for the priesthood of all believers

Old Testament. Among the prominent texts used by scholars about the priesthood of all believers is Exodus 19:5, 6. Luther, however, does not engage this passage in his major arguments. Instead, he opts for the New Testament passage based upon the Septuagint. But he notes some echoes and allusions to the priesthood of believers across the Old Testament. For example, he applies ecclesiological language to Cain and Adam when he states, "But the words which Cain adds—'I shall be hidden from your face'—deal with an ecclesiastical punishment and with true excommunication. Since Adam was in possession of the priesthood and of royal rule, and Cain is excommunicated by Adam because of his sin, he is at the same time deprived of the glory of the priesthood and of royal rule."[20] He summarizes the loss Cain sustained this way: "He [Cain] is compelled to leave not only the common home, dear parents, and the protection of parents but also his hereditary birthright, the prerogative of rule and priesthood, and the fellowship of the church."[21] Luther's understanding about the origin of the priesthood and his treatment of the subject in the Old

Testament seems to be individualistic rather than corporate. He concludes, "Therefore the true priesthood was in existence from the very beginning of the world, first covertly but later on promised more clearly to Abraham."[22] Luther recognizes the Levites had a special priesthood. They were "appointed by God as priests; but they were mortal, and therefore they gave a blessing that was only temporal. For as the priest, so the blessing. They could not do away with sin and death; nor could they purify hearts."[23] The approach that Luther uses to draw attention to the echoes of the priesthood in the Old Testament presents some challenges. There is no mention of a priesthood in the texts that he picks in Genesis. This may be viewed as eisegesis; however, Luther also uses a typological method to relate this to the church. While this may be appreciated, it raises more questions as to whether typology was indeed intended in those passages. The best way is to make a judgment based upon the tools available to him at that time.

New Testament. In his argument against Jerome Emser,[24] Luther draws upon biblical evidence in the New Testament.[25] In Luther's own words, Scripture is the primary foundation of his argument on the priesthood of believers. He states,

> "For it stands in Scripture. . . .
> "But you are a chosen race, a royal priesthood. . . ."
> Tell me, can anyone be so crude as not to understand to whom St. Peter speaks here? Or do the passages from the fathers have to step forward here and provide the interpretation? He [Peter] names the people and the congregation very clearly; and he calls them all together a royal priesthood.[26]

This appeal represents Luther's approach throughout his writings in support of his argument for the priesthood of believers. This passage also is part of the debate Luther had with Emser, who represented the Roman Catholic Church. Emser wrote a treatise against Luther's position, and Luther responded. "He may interpret 'priests' as he pleases, but all Christians are nevertheless such priests through this passage. If all of us should preach, then the tonsure-bearers [what he chose to call the Roman Catholic priests] must keep silent, since they have a different, special priesthood above all Christians."[27] In the course of the debate, Luther used several New Testament passages, including 1 Peter 2:9 and Revelation 5:9, 10; 20:6. He concludes, "Thereby the Holy Spirit teaches us that the ointments, consecrations, tonsures, chasubles, albs, chalices, masses, sermons, etc., do not make priests or give power. Rather, priesthood and power have to be there first, brought from baptism and common to all Christians through the faith which builds them upon Christ the true high priest."[28] Luther always buttressed his argument, including this one with Esmer, with evidence based upon Scripture.

Luther, Adventism, and the priesthood of believers

In this chapter, I have summarized the essence of Luther's views on the priesthood of believers into two areas: biblical and ecclesiological. These two areas form the basis for engaging Luther's doctrine from an Adventist perspective. While separated by centuries, a comparison of key points is helpful to understand the connection that Adventism has with Martin Luther. This can be seen especially in a recent dialogue between Lutherans and Seventh-day Adventists.

From 1994 to 1998, the Lutheran World Federation engaged in a series of meetings with Seventh-day Adventist leaders, which resulted in a joint theological consultation. Lutheran and Adventist representatives shared their theological perspectives. Out of the ten points, the fifth point reads: "Stressing the priesthood of all baptized believers to indicate the equality of all Christians before God and the apostolic obligation of the whole Christian community."[29] The consultation meetings held on November 1–5, 1994, revealed that both Adventists and Lutherans understood the church as a community of believers. There was also a strong appreciation for the work of Martin Luther among Adventist theologians.[30]

The priesthood of believers is a scriptural teaching that lies at the heart of Seventh-day Adventist beliefs. Adventist theologians and historians have highlighted the importance of this concept. According to Norskov Olsen, "The Lutheran Reformation grew out of Luther's own religious experience in which he found justification by 'faith alone' and 'grace alone' through 'Christ alone' and 'the Bible alone.' "[31] Among other things, the emphasis here is on *sola scriptura* as reflected in Luther's teaching of the priesthood of believers. Olsen summarizes

> The priesthood of believers is a scriptural teaching that lies at the heart of Seventh-day Adventist beliefs.

Luther's ecclesiology: "From this experience stems his ecclesiology: negatively as a reaction against sacerdotalism and positively in the doctrine of the priesthood of all believers."[32] Reflecting on Luther's teaching in general, Philip Schaff mentions three principles of Luther's Reformation: "The supremacy of the *Scriptures* over tradition, the supremacy of *faith* over works, and the supremacy of the Christian *people* over an exclusive priesthood."[33]

Demonstrating how Scripture plays a foundational role for his teaching on the priesthood of believers, Luther boldly states, "Therefore, when we grant the Word to anyone we cannot deny anything to him pertaining to the exercise of his priesthood."[34] Luther's ideas on the priesthood of believers "signaled a revolution in the concept of the church. In place of a hierarchical and stratified ecclesiastical structure, Luther proposed a model based on the equality of all members under the head, Christ. He replaced the rule of the oligarchical few and the rule of the democratic many, with the rule of the eternal Son of God who was active in all true members."[35] Such reflections demonstrate that teaching of the priesthood of believers played a central role for both Luther and his spiritual descendants and remains an important part of the Seventh-day Adventist Church. Adventists view a strong consistency between *sola scriptura* and the priesthood of all believers.

Conclusion

This chapter hopefully stimulates further discussion on the connections between Luther and Adventism on the subject of the priesthood of believers. We need to reflect upon Luther's understanding and the continued legacy of this concept. Luther must be understood on his own terms. He believed that every doctrine should be based upon Scripture. Such an approach must begin with Scripture as its foundation. The application of the doctrine should also find relevance and application for the church today. Luther balanced these two principles in his approach as he addressed relevant issues of his time.

1. Timothy George, *Theology of the Reformers*, rev. ed. (Nashville, TN: B & H Academic, 2013), 96.

2. Oswald Bayer, *Martin Luther's Theology: A Contemporary Interpretation*, trans. Thomas H. Trapp (Grand Rapids, MI: Eerdmans, 2008), 274 (italics in the original).

3. Alexander Roberts and James Donaldson, eds., "On Baptism," in *Tertullian*, vol. 3 of *Ante-Nicene Fathers* (Grand Rapids, MI: Eerdmans, 1956), chap. 7, 672.

4. Martin Luther, *Luther's Works*, vol. 36, *Word and Sacrament 2*, ed. Abdel R. Wentz (Philadelphia, PA: Fortress, 1959), 113; Martin Luther, *Luther's Works*, vol. 44, *The Christian in Society 1*, ed. James Atkinson (Philadelphia, PA: Fortress, 1966), 127.

5. Robert Muthiah, *The Priesthood of All Believers in the Twenty-First Century* (Eugene, OR: Pickwick Publications, 2009), 6.

6. Hank Voss, *The Priesthood of All Believers and the* Missio Dei: *A Canonical, Catholic, and Contextual Perspective* (Eugene, OR: Pickwick Publications, 2016), 132.

7. Brett Muhlhan, *Being Shaped by Freedom: An Examination of Luther's Development of Christian Liberty, 1520–1525* (Eugene, OR: Pickwick Publications, 2012), viii.

8. Voss, *The Priesthood of All Believers*, 133.

9. Ibid., 131.

10. Ibid., 130.

11. Ibid.

12. Ibid., 131.

13. Paul Althaus, *The Theology of Martin Luther*, trans. Robert C. Schultz (Philadelphia, PA: Fortress, 1970), 314.

14. Ibid.

15. Muthiah, *The Priesthood of All Believers in the Twenty-First Century*, 19.

16. Brian Gerrish, *The Old Protestantism and the New* (New York: T & T Clark, 2004), 97.

17. Ibid.

18. Uche Anizor, "Martin Luther, the Priesthood of Believers, and the Theological Interpretation of Scripture," in *Aspects of Reforming: Theology and Practice in Sixteenth Century Europe*, ed. Michael Parsons (Milton Keynes, UK: Paternoster, 2013), 6.

19. Gerrish, *The Old Protestantism and the New*, 98.

20. Martin Luther, *Luther's Works*, vol. 1, *Lectures on Genesis, Chapter 1–5*, ed. Jaroslav Pelikan (Philadelphia, PA: Fortress, 1955), 299.

21. Ibid., 1:308.

22. Martin Luther, *Luther's Works*, vol. 4, *Lectures on Genesis, Chapters 21–25*, ed. Jaroslav Pelikan (Philadelphia, PA: Fortress, 1964), 177.

23. Ibid.

24. Some background information about Emser, Luther's opponent, is helpful: "Jerome Emser (1477-1527), the 'goat of Leipzig'—Luther's designation because Emser's coat of arms, a shield and helmet adorned with a goat, was displayed on the title page of his writings—had pursued a variegated career before engaging Luther in a bitter literary feud. After studying law and theology at the universities of Tübingen and Basel, he became secretary to Cardinal Raymund von Gurk, papal legate in the matter of indulgencies until 1505." Martin Luther, *Luther's Works*, vol. 39, *Church and Ministry 1*, ed. Jaroslav Pelikan (Philadelphia, PA: Fortress Press, 1970), 107.

25. Michael Sokupa, "Martin Luther on the Priesthood of All Believers" (master's thesis, University of Stellenbosch, 2004).

26. Luther, *Luther's Works*, 39:236.

27. Ibid.

28. Ibid., 39:236, 237.

29. General Conference of Seventh-day Adventists and Lutheran World Federation, *Lutherans and Adventists in Conversation* (Silver Spring, MD: General Conference of Seventh-day Adventists, 2000), 75.

30. Ibid., 6.

31. V. Norskov Olsen, *Myth and Truth: Church, Priesthood, and Ordination* (Riverside, CA: Loma Linda University Press, 1990), 105.

32. Ibid.

33. Philip Schaff, *History of the Christian Church*, vol. 6 (New York: Charles Scribner's Sons, 1916), 16 (italics in the original), quoted in Rex Edwards, "Priesthood of Believers," Biblical Research Institute, 12, accessed July 11, 2017, https://www.adventistbiblicalresearch.org/sites/default/files/pdf/Edwards-Priesthood_of_believers.pdf.

34. Martin Luther, *Luther's Works*, vol. 40, *Church and Ministry 2*, ed. Conrad Bergendoff (Philadelphia, PA: Fortress, 1958), 21, quoted in Edwards, "Priesthood of Believers," 13.

35. Edwards, "Priesthood of Believers," 17, 18.

CHAPTER 4

Predestination and Justification by Faith: Was Luther a Calvinist?

Darius Jankiewicz and Joel Klimkewicz

The Protestant Reformation Martin Luther initiated in October 1517 not only altered the theological landscape of Christianity but also forever changed the Western world. Even though he is not considered a systematician of Reformation thought—a title later attributed to John Calvin—Luther's contribution to Christian theology cannot be overestimated. His call for a return to the teaching of Scripture in all areas of Christian life and theology reverberated throughout Europe and still echoes today. His Ninety-Five Theses provided a starting point for a new theology of justification, where believers were to be reckoned righteous by God rather than made righteous, as taught by medieval Catholicism. Most important, this entire miraculous process of transforming an enemy of God into a believer was accomplished solely by faith rather than through meritorious action. Unsurprisingly, such radical teachings shook the late medieval Christian establishment to its core and changed the matrix of Christianity forever. Luther, argues Alister

> The Protestant Reformation Martin Luther initiated in October 1517 not only altered the theological landscape of Christianity but also forever changed the Western world.

McGrath, "must be regarded as a transitional figure, standing at the junction of two rival understandings of the nature of justification."[1]

In some ways, all Protestant denominations trace their roots to Luther's insurgency against medieval soteriological conventions and consider him a theological forefather. The same applies to the Seventh-day Adventist Church, which is a denomination that considers itself firmly rooted in the Protestant Reformation. For Adventists, writes Johann Heinz, the Reformation "is not simply a historic turning point but an act of God on behalf of the Christian world for a renewal of the center of the gospel and for the adjustment of faith and life according to the Word of God and not according to human tradition. This event can be summed up in the person and work of Martin Luther, for 'he *is the Reformation.'* "[2] Bert B. Beach further concludes that "Adventists see themselves in many ways as 'children' of Luther, the great Reformer."[3] Many decades earlier Ellen G. White speaks of Luther as "God's chosen instrument" and as a man raised by God "to do a special work."[4] Luther's particular theological contribution, she believes, lies in highlighting again the doctrine of justification by faith. "The great doctrine of justification by faith, so clearly taught by Luther," White writes, "had been almost wholly lost sight of," being replaced by the "principle of trusting to good works for salvation."[5]

As breathtaking as it was, however, Luther's doctrine of justification by faith has proven challenging to interpret. It has been the subject of scrutiny by generations of theologians; many arriving at different conclusions regarding his understanding of the doctrine of justification by faith. This is likely because Luther was not a systematic theologian and tended to react to various theological controversies somewhat imprecisely and often with erratic language.[6] Thus, it is not an easy task to pigeonhole Luther's views.

Many Protestant theologians and lay members, Adventists and others, agree with Luther on the definition of justification: "The doctrine of Justification is this, that we are pronounced righteous and are saved solely by faith in Christ, and without work."[7] This belief is also expressed in the classic Reformation slogan that refers to salvation as *sola gratia et fides*; that is, by grace and faith alone. It is a common assumption that this definition of justification means that God offers His righteousness to all humanity and it is the role of those who believe to grasp God's offer by faith and respond affirmatively. Clearly, such a view precludes the view of salvation accomplished by God's eternal decree or election, as taught by John Calvin. While Luther certainly used the term *predestination* in his writings, it is a popular belief that his understanding of predestination was not the same as that of Calvin.[8] More often than not, Luther's view of predestination is perceived as based on God's foreknowledge of the free action of those who would believe, rather than on His eternal, immutable decision.[9]

Luther did not hold such a view. The view of justification presented above is more akin to the synergistic views of Philip Melanchthon and is echoed, to some extent, in the Formula of Concord (1577), rather than the views of Luther himself.[10] While Luther's *sola gratia et fides* doctrine is clearly present in the articles of the Formula of Concord, it is also evident that, under the influence of Melanchthon's synergism, the authors of the document deviated from the classical Lutheran understanding of justification by faith. Clearly, this was facilitated by the authors' decision to depart ever so slightly from Luther's understanding of predestination. During later centuries, this departure aided a large-scale Lutheran abandonment of Luther's monergism in favor of a synergistic understanding of salvation, while at the same time creating clear discontinuity between the teachings of Luther and modern Lutheran churches. We now turn to Luther's understanding of predestination and the implications for his doctrine of justification by faith. To further elucidate Luther's teachings on predestination, we begin with a brief clarification of the term *predestination*.

Degrees of predestination

Luther used the word *predestination*; but after John Calvin, theologians began to speak of degrees of predestination—that is, double predestination, single predestination, and predestination based on God's foreknowledge of future human free action.[11] The term *double predestination* generally refers to God's sovereign election for both salvation and condemnation (reprobation).[12] The rise of this understanding of predestination has traditionally been associated with John Calvin.[13] His emphasis was not so much on the fact that there are two groups of people in existence—one elected for heaven and one for reprobation—but rather on the belief that humans cannot make a choice regarding their ultimate destiny. The stress is on the proposition that our salvation and damnation depend *solely* on God's grace rather than on any human action.[14] In other words, humans possess no ability to influence their destiny. Salvation is *all* by God's grace and His volitional election. It is this ideology that forms the backbone of the well-known Reformation slogan *soli Deo gloria* (glory to God alone).[15]

On the other hand, the term *single predestination* is distinguished from *double predestination* and indicates that God only determines the saved but allows for the natural consequence of sin to determine the lost. It is, in Ted Campbell's words, a "milder" view of predestination because "God does not really choose persons for damnation; rather, damnation was chosen for all human beings by Adam and Eve."[16] This understanding of predestination seeks to absolve God of the culpability involved in the decisions of sinners.[17]

It is often argued that the authors of the Formula of Concord adopted a single rather than double predestination theory.[18] A single predestination view, however, is fraught with complications. First, it quickly becomes evident, once a person moves away from the strict monergism of double predestination, that the lines between monergism and synergism become blurred. This was precisely the problem faced by the authors of the Formula of Concord.[19] Attempting to steer a middle course between Luther's monergism and the view that salvation involves human choice, they made it impossible for future theologians to clearly understand their intentions.[20] Second, the single-predestination view does not absolve God of evil; it still makes Him, albeit passively, responsible for the demise of reprobates. Finally, a single-predestination view may lead to a universalist soteriology, in which God saves all indiscriminately, thereby making a mockery of God's justice.[21] In an attempt to soften the hard edges of strict determinism, some are willing to conclude that Luther taught single, rather than double, predestination.[22]

The final view of predestination is the traditional synergistic interpretation; that is, predestination as God's foreknowledge of future human choices, also referred to as conditional predestination or conditional election. This view is adopted by most nonmonergistic Christians, including Seventh-day Adventists.[23] The view among many Protestants is that this was Luther's understanding of predestination.

While the debate about degrees of predestination belongs in the post-Reformation era, the concept of deterministic predestination has been debated throughout Christian history, finding its roots in the anti-Pelagian writings by Augustine of Hippo.[24] Alister McGrath argues that Luther's view on predestination is the fruit of a well-concluded Augustinianism. In an attempt to counter the human-centered synergism of the medieval church, Luther took Augustine's view to the extreme, resulting in a firm determinism. As McGrath states, "Luther explicitly teaches a doctrine of double predestination, whereas Augustine was reluctant to acknowledge such a doctrine, no matter how logically appropriate it might appear."[25] Luther's views on predestination are correlated with his understanding of human free will and are encapsulated in *The Bondage of the Will*, written against Erasmus, in 1525. It is in this work where one finds a systematic and scathing rebuke of libertarian free will.

God's deterministic foreknowledge and assurance of salvation

Luther's acceptance of double predestination goes hand in hand with his views on God's foreknowledge. In *The Bondage of the Will*, he stressed that "God foreknows nothing contingently"—that is, nothing that God foreknows is subject to change. All that God foreknows, therefore, must come to fruition, because the basis of such foreknowledge lies in His "immutable, eternal, and infallible will." Such a view of God's foreknowledge and His will led Luther to conclude that "free choice is completely prostrated and shattered, so that those who want free choice asserted must either deny or explain away this thunderbolt, or get rid of it by some other means."[26] He further wrote,

From this it follows irrefutably that everything we do, everything that happens, even if it seems to us to happen mutably and contingently, happens in fact nonetheless necessarily and immutably, if you have regard to the will of God. For the will of God is effectual and cannot be hindered, since it is the power of the divine nature itself; moreover it is wise, so that it cannot be deceived. Now, if his will is not hindered, there is nothing to prevent the work itself from being done, in the place, time, manner, and measure that he himself both foresees and wills.[27]

Thus, in Luther's view, the will of God is not dependent on future human action. Furthermore, it is the declarative property of God's will that is external to humans and, based on the ontology of God, that determines our status as saved or lost. God does not just will; He *is will*.[28] Accordingly, Luther advocated for the strongest form of determinism; that is, all things happen necessarily by divine decree.[29] Such determinism is concomitant with the irresistible grace of God to save and the unbridled power of God to condemn. With unmitigated directness, he continued, "I admit that the question is difficult, and indeed impossible, if you wish to maintain at the same time both God's foreknowledge and man's freedom."[30] For Luther, belief in human free will amounts to "a refusal to accept God's action on our behalf as the sole hope for salvation."[31]

Luther also believed that natural revelation confirmed his views. He argued that humans intuitively understood that the foreknowledge of God was determinative when they uttered such statements as, "God's will be done," or "God willing, we will do it." He wrote, "From this we can see that the knowledge of God's predestination and foreknowledge remained with the common people no less than the awareness of his existence itself. But those who wished to appear wise went so far astray in their reasonings that their hearts were darkened and they became fools . . . , and denied or explained away the things that the poets and common people, and even their own conscience, regarded as entirely familiar, certain, and true."[32]

For Luther, evidence of God's determinism in natural revelation was important, for it provided further support for what was already known about God's foreknowledge from the Scriptures. This foreknowledge was not contingent on humans and was only revealed to those who were saved, for whom Christian assurance was found through trusting that God had saved them. Luther passionately believed that assurance of salvation came from the revelation that God keeps His promises to the elect; therefore, faith was about the faithfulness of God to save those whom He had chosen. Luther wrote the following:

"But God's firm foundation stands, bearing this seal: 'The Lord knows those who are his' " (II Tim. 2:19). . . .

Therefore, Christian faith is entirely extinguished, the promises of God and the whole gospel are completely destroyed, if we teach and believe that it is not for us to know the necessary foreknowledge of God and the necessity of the things that are to come to pass. For this is the one supreme consolation of Christians in all adversities, to know that God does not lie, but does all things immutably, and that his will can neither be resisted nor changed nor hindered.[33]

From this passage, it is clear that the foundation of a believer's assurance was God's necessary and irresistible will. At the same time, Luther never addressed the subject of what happens to reprobates and why. The question of why God saves some and condemns others if He has the ability to save all does not appear to be addressed. Instead, Luther appeals to the distinction between "God preached" and "God hidden." God's love, mercy, forgiveness, and justification—truths that are revealed to humans through Scripture—belong to the sphere of "God preached"; however, the reason why some are saved and some damned belongs to the category of "God hidden." Thus, Luther wrote, "To the extent, therefore, that God hides himself and wills to be unknown to us, it is no business of ours. For here the saying truly applies, 'Things above us are no business of ours.' "[34]

This is perhaps why, in his later years, Luther refused to engage in conversation on predestination, essentially forbidding any debate on this topic.[35] As a result, some commentators conclude that Luther rejected deterministic predestinarianism; however, as Harry Buis notes, "Luther is not condemning predestination, he is simply pointing out one abuse of the doctrine against which we must guard ourselves."[36]

Double predestination in Luther

By the time Luther published *The Bondage of the Will* in 1525, he had embraced a strict view of God's sovereignty, also referred to in theological literature as God's "meticulous providence."[37] There seems to be little doubt that, while he did not use the term *double predestination*—a phrase that postdates the Magisterial Reformation—Luther was comfortable with its premise: human salvation and damnation are based on God's foreordination rather than contingent foreknowledge. Luther clearly spoke of strictly unmovable foreknowledge in the fate of both the saved and the lost. While Luther might, at times, have implied that humans had a degree of what could be termed as *compatibilist free will* in relation to God's foreknowledge,[38] he never taught that God bows His will to human will.[39]

If predestination goes together with deterministic foreordination, speaking of degrees of predestination, whether single or double, is irrelevant and can only be used as an attempt to mitigate or disassociate Luther from the Reformed theology of Calvin. As stated above, there is then only a short step from speaking of single predestination to the synergistic understanding of predestination. Such a softening of purely deterministic predestination would surely be unacceptable to Luther. He strongly objected to Erasmus's view on human free will:

> In these and similar bits of juggling with words, her [Erasmus's Diatribe] only aim is to gain time by distracting our attention for a while from the main issue ["the First Cause does everything"] to something else. She credits us with being as stupid and senseless or as little concerned about the subject as she is herself. . . . Just as little children in fear or at play will put their hands over their eyes and then imagine that nobody sees them because they see nobody, so in all sorts of ways Diatribe . . . pretends that she does not see the real truth of the matter.[40]

Luther's beliefs about God's foreknowledge (the First Cause) comingled with his belief in the ultimate sovereignty of God, which inevitably resulted in a Calvinistic understanding of predestination. Buis writes: "Martin Luther held as strong a doctrine of predestination as did John Calvin."[41] Similarly, Jairzinho Lopes Pereira concludes, "Although it may not seem so to the unprepared reader, [double] predestination lay at the core of Luther's understanding of the salvation process."[42]

Thus, as Luther was a strict determinist, distinguishing between single and double predestination in his thinking was irrelevant, as the latter was his only choice. But the question remains: how did Luther's determinism affect his doctrine of justification? Before we turn to justification, however, we must first unpack Luther's concept of *alien righteousness*.

Alien righteousness

The adjective "alien" in the construct *alien righteousness* points to the fact that such righteousness stands apart from any human derivation. This righteousness is foreign and external to the sinner; it never belongs to the sinner, even when the sinner becomes a believer. Luther's earliest views on righteousness and justification were influenced by nominalist soteriology (via moderna) that formed the backbone of his theological education.[43] The most important feature of *via moderna soteriology* was a pactum between God and humanity, where humans were encouraged to do their best according to their internal abilities (inherent righteousness).[44] Luther was uncomfortable with the nominalist focus on inherent righteousness, as he felt he could never measure up to God's righteousness with his own internal righteousness, and thus, he felt condemned by God. At some point before 1517, Luther broke with *via moderna* soteriology, concluding that humanity had nothing to offer as far as salvation was concerned and that the only righteousness that counted in salvation was God's.[45] This is often referred to as "Luther's theological breakthrough."[46]

This concept of alien righteousness, or Christ's righteousness, is grounded in Scripture, particularly in Pauline writings. For Luther, any hint of "human" or inherent righteousness implies a return to some form of postbiblical Pelagianism. At the same time, in his quest against medieval synergistic *pactum* theology, Luther embraced the Augustinian version of divine determinism. It is the marriage of these two conceptions—alien righteousness and Augustinian determinism—that transformed the biblical notion of Christ's (alien) righteousness into a mutant form of Christianity, which was an amalgam of biblical faith and Greek philosophy. This amalgam is the a priori lens through which all of Luther's writings on salvation must be read. The implications for the doctrine of justification by faith are troubling.

Justification by faith

Left unpolluted, the doctrine of justification teaches that humans who avail themselves of God's offer of salvation are pronounced righteous and saved solely by faith in Christ. Biblically speaking, this righteousness is always Christ's, and never inherently human. When determinism is added to the mix, however, all this changes because the process of salvation no longer has a human element. Thus, for Luther, justification of the sinner did not involve human faith or faithfulness. Rather, it was God's declaration that justified the sinner, *not on account of his or her faith* but *solely* through the efficacy of God's eternal decree. Such an understanding of justification by faith was so essential to Luther that he declared:

> Nothing in this article can be given up or compromised. . . .
> On this article rests all that we teach and practice against the pope, the devil, and the world.[47]

In Luther's deterministic soteriology, God was active and humans passive. This was also why Luther often referred to God's righteousness as "passive."[48] Faith, or *trust*, as Luther would often refer to it, was the believer's discovery that he or she was reckoned as righteous through the eternal decree of God and nothing more. Faith was not instrumental in salvation; it was passive.[49] For Luther, the phrase "justification by faith" was synonymous with determined salvation based on God's declarative will and did not include the human action of accepting God's offer by faith. Accepting God's offer of righteousness involves human choice, and that was not acceptable to Luther. He was devastatingly clear on this point when he wrote the following:

[The apostle Paul wrote,] "We hold that a man is justified by faith apart from works of law" (Rom. 3:28), and as he [Paul] has said above: "No human being will be justified in his sight by works of the law" (Rom. 3:20). From all of which it is very clearly evident that all the devoted endeavors of free choice are worth absolutely nothing. For if the righteousness of God exists apart from law and the works of law, must it not much more exist apart from free choice? Especially as the highest aspiration of free choice is to practice moral righteousness, or the works of the law, with the help afforded by the law to its own blindness and ignorance.[50]

It is evident that the Reformation slogan *sola fide* has different meanings for different believers. For the majority of Protestants, the slogan means receiving God's offer of salvation through the means of faith, based on a free human choice. Not so for Luther, for whom *sola fide* was basically reduced to the "aha" moment when the elect believer recognized what had been already accomplished. For Luther, introducing any human element into the process of salvation, including faith based on a free human choice, implies a return to medieval Catholicism.

Conclusion

While Protestants, including Seventh-day Adventists, look to Luther as a forefather, his views on predestination are not widely known or accepted. As a result, it is a popular misconception that Luther was either not deterministic[51] or he embraced a mild version of deterministic predestination (single predestination). This misimpression is perhaps due to the fact that many Protestant scholars and historians appear to filter Luther's soteriology through the lens of the Formula of Concord. This document was strongly influenced by Philip Melanchthon and later Lutherans.[52] In contrast to Luther, Melanchthon eventually rejected the divine determinism taught by his mentor and embraced an understanding of synergism[53] that allowed for participation of human will in the salvation process.[54] Ultimately, seventeenth-century (and later) Lutheranism deviated from Luther and warmed up to Melanchthon's synergistic, albeit still thoroughly Protestant, understanding of salvation.[55]

Within Adventism, the popular misconception that Luther taught a Pauline version of justification by faith most likely resulted from the high praise the Reformer received from Ellen White, especially in *The Great Controversy*. To be sure, the Protestant Reformation initiated by Luther in 1517 was a major turn away from medieval Catholicism and toward a scriptural understanding of justification by faith. This is probably why Ellen White lavished such praise on Luther. And rightly so! Luther's embrace of divine determinism, however, significantly hampered his complete return toward a scriptural understanding of justification by faith. In his desire to move away from the high anthropology and merit-based view of salvation, which was advocated by the Catholicism of his day, Luther embraced the view that advocated God's extreme sovereignty to the complete exclusion of human free will. As a result, "faith," in the "justification by faith" phrase, became a passive acceptance of the election that was accomplished without human input. Luther's journey toward a Pauline understanding of justification by faith was stopped a few centuries short when he lingered too long in conversation with Augustine. It was left to others, including Philip Melanchthon and Jacobus Arminius,[56] to offer a correction to Luther's deterministic understanding of salvation. An Adventist understanding of salvation finds its roots in their theology.

While Luther ceased to speak of deterministic predestination in his later years, even forbidding speculation on the topic, he never departed from Augustinian determinism. Such a departure certainly undermined his understanding of justification by faith, destroying what he treasured the most: complete assurance of salvation through election. Although he never used the term *double predestination*, Luther unquestioningly believed, both in his early and later years, that God's will determines the salvation and reprobation of humanity. In fact, as late as 1537, he insisted that of all the books he had ever written only two deserved preservation: *The Bondage of the Will* and the *Catechism*.[57]

We return to the original question posed in the title of this chapter: Was Luther a Calvinist? Being chronologically sensitive, we should rather ask, was Calvin a Lutheran, in a classical sense? The answer to both questions is an unequivocal Yes. Both of these great thinkers of the Reformation embraced a deterministic understanding of salvation. While their emphases and ways of expressing themselves differed to a significant degree, they both drank deeply from the Augustinian theological well.

1. Alister E. McGrath, *Iustitia Dei: A History of the Christian Doctrine of Justification*, 3rd ed. (Cambridge: Cambridge University Press, 2005), 213.

2. Johann Heinz, "Luther, Martin," in *The Ellen G. White Encyclopedia*, ed. Jerry Moon and Denis Fortin (Hagerstown, MD: Review and Herald® Pub. Assn., 2013), 954 (italics in the original).

3. Bert B. Beach, *Ambassador for Liberty: Building Bridges of Faith, Friendship, and Freedom* (Hagerstown, MD: Review and Herald® Pub. Assn., 2012), 122.

4. Ellen G. White, *Testimonies for the Church* (Mountain View, CA: Pacific Press® Pub. Assn., 1948), 1:372.

5. Ellen G. White, *The Great Controversy* (Mountain View, CA: Pacific Press® Pub. Assn.,

1950), 253; cf. Ellen G. White, *Early Writings* (Washington, DC: Review and Herald® Pub. Assn., 1945), 222, 223.

6. Roger E. Olson, *The Story of Christian Theology: Twenty Centuries of Tradition and Reform* (Downers Grove, IL: IVP Academic, 1999), 379; cf. Hans J. Hillerbrand, "The Legacy of Martin Luther," in *The Cambridge Companion to Martin Luther*, ed. Donald K. McKim (Cambridge: Cambridge University Press, 2003), 230.

7. Martin Luther, *Luther's Works*, vol. 26, *Lectures on Galatians, 1535, Chapters 1–4*, ed. Walter A. Hansen (St. Louis, MO: Concordia, 1963), 223.

8. The centuries-long debate on Luther's determinism is well encapsulated in Harry J. McSorley's *Luther: Right or Wrong? An Ecumenical-Theological Study of Luther's Major Work, The Bondage of the Will* (New York: Newman Press, 1969), 256–260. Victor A. Shepherd states, "For Luther, predestination is simply the efficacy of the crucified and risen Lord Jesus Christ surging over us in the power of the Spirit in such a way as to fulfill his promise and thereby eclipse our unbelief." Victor A. Shepherd, *Interpreting Martin Luther: An Introduction to His Life and Thought* (Toronto: BPS Books, 2008), 115.

9. In the sixteenth century, Lutheran orthodoxy embraced the view that predestination was based on God's foreknowledge. Thus, it is possible that Luther has, at times, been interpreted through the lens of later Lutheran theological developments. See Gerrit C. Berkouwer, *Divine Election*, Studies in Dogmatics (Grand Rapids, MI: Eerdmans, 1960), 40–42; cf. Hans J. Hillebrand, ed., *The Encyclopedia of Protestantism*, vol. 3 (New York: Routledge, 2014), 1858; and Erwin Fahlbusch et al., eds., *The Encyclopedia of Christianity*, vol. 4 (Grand Rapids, MI: Eerdmans, 2005), 342. This view concurs with the Adventist understanding of predestination. See F. Nichol, ed., *The Seventh-day Adventist Bible Commentary*, vol. 6 (Washington, DC: Review and Herald® Pub. Assn., 1957), 575.

10. The Formula of Concord represents an authoritative confession of the post-Luther Lutheran Church. Completed in 1577, it was later included in *The Book of Concord* (1580). "The Formula of Concord," in *The Creeds of Christendom*, vol. 3, ed. Philip Schaff (Grand Rapids, MI: Baker Book House, 1985), 168, 171.

11. It is beyond the scope of this work to develop a systematic theology for the doctrine of predestination. A brief clarification of what is meant by these terms is, however, necessary.

12. Oswald Bayer, *Martin Luther's Theology: A Contemporary Interpretation*, trans. Thomas H. Trapp (Grand Rapids, MI: Eerdmans, 2007), 209.

13. John Calvin, *Institutes of the Christian Religion*, ed. John T. McNeill (Philadelphia, PA: Westminster Press, 1960), bk. 2, chap. 21, 920.

14. Ibid., 921; cf. Herman J. Selderhuis, *John Calvin: A Pilgrim's Life* (Downers Grove, IL: IVP Academic, 2009), 190.

15. It must be emphasized that Protestants who do not subscribe to a monergistic view of salvation can also adopt the slogan *soli Deo gloria*. Those who follow Melanchthon's view of salvation, as well as that of Jacobus Arminius, can readily acknowledge that it is God who is solely responsible for human salvation through the agency of prevenient grace. While Melanchthon never wrote of prevenient grace, the concept is clearly present in his writings.

16. Ted A. Campbell, *Christian Confessions: A Historical Introduction* (Louisville, KY: Westminster John Knox Press, 1996), 155.

17. Martin Luther, "The Bondage of the Will," in *Luther and Erasmus: Free Will and Salvation*, ed. E. Gordon Rupp and Philip S. Watson (Philadelphia, PA: Westminster Press, 1969), 234.

18. Campbell, *Christian Confessions*, 157; cf. Ralph W. Quere, "The Community of Faith as a Confessional Norm: Universalism and Evangelism," in *The Difficult but Indispensable Church*, ed. Norma Cook Everist (Minneapolis, MN: Fortress Press, 2002), 86.

19. E.g., how can one reconcile statements such as, "Christ calls all sinners to him, and promises to give them rest. And he earnestly wishes that all men may come to him" and that "the cause of the damnation of the ungodly is that they either do not hear the Word of God at all, but contumaciously contemn it, stop their ears, and harder their hearts" with "[there is no] cause in us, on account of which cause God has chosen us to eternal life"? "The Formula of Concord," 167, 168, 172.

20. The original intent of the Formula of Concord was to unite the warring Lutheran factions. The hopes of its authors, however, were largely unfulfilled. While the Formula of Concord's teachings had some unitive effect, it also led to more divisions. For an excellent overview of the Lutheran struggles prior to the Formula of Concord, see Robert Kolb, *Bound Choice, Election, and Wittenberg Theological Method* (Grand Rapids, MI: Eerdmans, 2005), 103–134. For a discussion of the mixed reception of the Formula of Concord, see Paul Douglas Lockhart, *Frederik II and the Protestant Cause: Denmark's Role in the Wars of Religion, 1559–1596* (Leiden: Brill, 2004), 164; cf. Euan Cameron, "One Reformation or Many? Protestant Identities in the Later Reformation in Germany," in *Tolerance and Intolerance in the European Reformation*, ed. Ole Peter Grell and Bob Scribner (Cambridge: Cambridge University Press, 1996), 108, 109.

21. Duane H. Larson, "Universality of the Church," in *The A to Z of Lutheranism*, ed. Günther Gassmann, Duane H. Larson, and Mark W. Oldenburg (London: Scarecrow Press, 2007), 338.

22. See, e.g., John Dillenberger and Claude Welch, who insist that Luther only spoke of single predestination: *Protestant Christianity* (New York: Charles Scribner's Sons, 1954), 34; cf. Jonathan Hill, *The History of Christian Thought* (Downers Grove, IL: InterVarsity Press, 2003), 202; Campbell, *Christian Confessions*, 155.

23. See Nichol, *The Seventh-day Adventist Bible Commentary*, 6:575. For an excellent overview of this understanding of predestination, see Roger E. Olson, *Arminian Theology: Myths and Realities* (Downers Grove, IL: InterVarsity Press, 2006), 179–199.

24. Thus, Jairzinho Lopes Pereira concludes, "Augustine's notion of grace and the way it works points to an undeniably deterministic account of salvation. The fact is that, according to Augustine, humans do not even decide whether they want or not to be in God's path. By the time they will make such a decision (which is necessarily a predetermined decision), a previous decision has already been made in God's eternal decree of predestination. If that divine decision is for condemnation there is nothing that a human can do in order [to] change the course of things. That human being will necessarily desire to go astray from God and then meet condemnation." Jairzinho Lopes Pereira, *Augustine of Hippo and Martin Luther on Original Sin and Justification of the Sinner* (Göttingen: Vandenhoeck and Ruprecht, 2013), 262.

25. McGrath, *Iustitia Dei*, 230.

26. Luther, "The Bondage of the Will," 118.

27. Ibid., 119.

28. Luther's ontology of God follows a voluntarist system of thought, according to which the will of God has primacy over all else. Voluntarism teaches that whatever God commands is necessarily good. In this view, God may be identified with His will. Peter Harrison, "Philosophy and the Crisis of Religion," in *The Cambridge Companion to Renaissance Philosophy*, ed. James Hankins (Cambridge: Cambridge University Press, 2007), 245; cf. J. B. Schneewind, *Essays on the History of Moral Philosophy* (Oxford: Oxford University Press, 2010), 203.

29. Harrison, "Philosophy and the Crisis of Religion," 242, 243.

30. Martin Luther, *Luther's Works*, vol. 33, *Career of the Reformer 2*, ed. Helmut T. Lehman (Philadelphia, PA: Fortress, 1955), 188.

31. Olson, *The Story of Christian Theology*, 383.

32. Luther, "The Bondage of the Will," 121, 122.

33. Ibid., 122.

34. Ibid., 200, 201; cf. John Peckham, "An Investigation of Luther's View of the Bondage of the Will With Implications for Soteriology and Theodicy," *Journal of the Adventist Theological Society* 18, no. 2 (Autumn 2007): 294, 295.

35. Martin Luther, *Luther's Table Talk; or, Some Choice Fragments From the Familiar Discourse of That Godly, Learned Man* (London: Longman, 1832), 270, 271.

36. Harry Buis, *Historic Protestantism and Predestination* (Eugene, OR: Wipf and Stock, 2007), 57.

37. Kenneth J. Stewart, *Ten Myths About Calvinism: Recovering the Breadth of the Reformed Tradition* (Downers Grove, IL: IVP Academic, 2011), 54.

38. Ronald H. Nash, *The Concept of God* (Grand Rapids, MI: Zondervan, 1983), 54.

39. *Compatibilism* is the belief that freedom of human will is compatible with divine determinism. In simple terms, it is an attempt to absolve God as the creator of sin and evil in the world. While some determinists, such as Huldrych Zwingli, did not shy away from naming God as the creator of sin and evil, both Luther and Calvin were decidedly uneasy with the idea. Instead, it is the human "free" will that is blamed for evil. Thus, Luther refers to the human free will as "the beast of burden." He thus wrote, "The human will is placed between the two [God and Satan] like a beast of burden. If God rides it, it wills and goes where God wills. . . . If Satan rides it, it wills and goes where Satan wills; nor can it choose to run to either of the two riders or to seek him out, but the riders themselves contend for the possession and control of it." Luther, "The Bondage of the Will," 140. At the same time, it must be stated that Luther had a difficult time maneuvering around the problem of God as the source of evil, as illustrated by the following passage: "Let no one suppose, therefore, when God is said to harden or to work evil in us (for to harden is to make evil), that he does so by creating evil in us from scratch. You must not imagine him like an evil-minded innkeeper, full of wickedness himself, who pours or blends poisons into an innocent vessel, which itself does nothing but receive or suffer the malignity of the blender. . . . God works in us good things and bad, and that we are subject by sheer passive necessity to God's working; for they do not sufficiently consider how unrestingly active God is in all his creatures, allowing none of them to take a holiday. But anyone who wishes to have any understanding of such matters should think as follows. God works evil in us, i.e., by means of us, not through any fault of his . . . he carries us along by his own activity in accordance with his omnipotence, good as he is

himself he cannot help but do evil with an evil instrument, though he makes good use of this evil in accordance with his wisdom for his own glory and our salvation." Ibid., 234. As Gregory Boyd rightly points out, in wanting to absolve God as the creator of evil, Luther places the blame for sin and evil on the human will; but, with other Augustinians, he sees the will as even performing evil for a greater good as part of God's foreordination. Gregory A. Boyd, *God at War: The Bible and Spiritual Conflict* (Downers Grove, IL: InterVarsity Press, 1997), 47, 48.

40. Luther, "The Bondage of the Will," 240.

41. Buis, *Historic Protestantism and Predestination*, 2.

42. Pereira, *Augustine of Hippo and Martin Luther*, 453. For a further study of Luther's position, the reader is directed to Brian G. Mattson, "Double or Nothing: Martin Luther's Doctrine of Predestination," Contra Mundum, accessed July 12, 2017, http://www.contra-mundum.org/essays /mattson/Luther-predestination.pdf.

43. Heiko A. Oberman, *Luther: Man Between God and the Devil*, trans. Eileen Walliser-Schwarzbart (New Haven, CT: Yale University Press, 1989), 120–122. *Nominalism* was a medieval school of thought that emphasized free will and humanity's internal moral capabilities. Pereira, *Augustine of Hippo and Martin Luther*, 295.

44. Alister E. McGrath, *Historical Theology* (Oxford: Blackwell Publishing, 1998), 151; cf. McGrath, *Iustitia Dei*, 198–201.

45. Alister E. McGrath, *Luther's Theology of the Cross* (Oxford: Basil Blackwell, 1985), 133; cf. Pereira, *Augustine of Hippo and Martin Luther*, 280. In 1545, Luther himself admitted this move was precipitated by his rediscovery of Augustine. Martin Luther, "Autobiographical Fragment," in *Martin Luther*, ed. E. G. Rupp and Benjamin Drewery (New York: St. Martin's Press, 1970), 6.

46. Pereira, *Augustine of Hippo and Martin Luther*, 322; McGrath, *Iustitia Dei*, 224; cf. Michael G. Baylor, *Action and Person: Conscience in the Late Scholasticism and the Young Luther* (Leiden: Brill, 1977), 125.

47. Martin Luther, "The Smalcald Articles," in *The Book of Concord: The Confessions of the Evangelical Lutheran Church*, ed. Theodore G. Tappert (Philadelphia, PA: Fortress Press, 1959), pt. 2, art. 1, 292. Reading this article may give the reader the impression that Luther believed in an active human role in justification; however, it must once again be emphasized that only "to the untrained eye" does deterministic predestination not "assume a crucial role in young Luther's soteriology." Pereira, *Augustine of Hippo and Martin Luther*, 362.

48. Luther, *Luther's Works*, 26:4–7. Even as late as 1545, Luther still strongly held to his views on "passive righteousness." Luther, "Autobiographical Fragment," 6. Keeping in mind that throughout his lifetime Luther held to an *a priori* presupposition of divine determinism allows us to truly comprehend his teachings on justification by faith. Without this knowledge, passages such as those found in *Luther's Works*, vol. 26, cited above, sound very much like a textbook soteriology.

49. Martin Luther, *Commentary on Psalm 51*, in *Luther's Works*, vol. 12, *Selections Psalms 1*, ed. Jaroslav Pelikan (Philadelphia, PA: Fortress, 1955), 368; cf. Mark C. Mattes, *The Role of Justification in Contemporary Theology* (Grand Rapids, MI: Eerdmans, 2004), 69.

50. Luther, "The Bondage of the Will," 307.

51. In recent years, a particular group known as the "Finnish school" avoided the topic of

Luther's determinism altogether by offering an alternative interpretation that makes Luther more palatable to ecumenically minded groups. As a result of ecumenical discussions between Finnish Lutherans and Russian Orthodox churches "from 1970 to 1995, significant soteriological statements were adopted in Kiev (1977), Turku (1980), and Järvenpää (1992). The best known and most influential of these have been the theses on 'Salvation as Justification and Deification,' drafted in Kiev in 1977." The most controversial aspect of these conversations regarding Luther's theology on justification and free will are found in this statement: "Grace never does violence to a man's personal will, but exerts its influence through it and with it. Every one has the opportunity to refuse consent to God's will or, by the help of the Holy Spirit, to consent to it." Risto Saarinen, "Salvation in the Lutheran-Orthodox Dialogue," in *Union With Christ: The New Finnish Interpretation of Luther*, ed. Carl E. Braaten and Robert W. Jensen (Grand Rapids, MI: Eerdmans, 1998), 167–169.

52. Harry Buis is certainly correct when he states that the Formula of Concord is a contradictory document that, on the one hand, appeared to oppose Melanchthon's synergism, but on the other hand, "it denied irresistible grace and affirmed the universality of the offer of the Gospel." As a result, Buis argues, "The position of the Formula of Concord amounted to conditional predestination which became the accepted Lutheran doctrine in the seventeenth century." Buis, *Historic Protestantism and Predestination*, 82.

53. In contrast to Catholic synergism, evangelical synergism rejects the possibility of inherent righteousness. In this view, salvation is still *soli Deo gloria* and thus not dependent on human merit.

54. Buis, *Historic Protestantism and Predestination*, 2, 3, 81, 82. To be sure, the Formula of Concord clearly rejects a synergism that suggests that humans have the ability to turn themselves to God and thus appears to advocate a single-predestination view. At the same time, however, the Formula appears to leave room for Melanchthon's view that "through and in the working of grace . . . one can be capable of one's own consent of the will." Such a position would be unacceptable to Luther. Peter Neuner, "Synergism," in *The Encyclopedia of Christianity*, ed. Erwin Fahlbusch et al., vol. 5 (Grand Rapids, MI: Eerdmans, 2008), 272; cf. Buis, *Historic Protestantism and Predestination*, 82.

55. Joel R. Beeke, *The Quest for Full Assurance* (Carlise: Banner of Truth Trust, 1999), 25, 26.

56. It must be noted that while Jacobus Arminius was reacting to the extremes of Calvinism rather than that of Luther, Calvin himself was strongly influenced by Luther and Augustine. In one way or another, all Protestant theological roads lead to Luther.

57. In a letter to Wolfgang Capito regarding the publishing of his complete works, Luther says, "I would rather see them devoured. For I acknowledge none of them to be really a book of mine, except for perhaps the one *On the Bound Will*, and the *Catechism*." Martin Luther, "Letter to Wolfgang Capito, Wittenberg, July 9, 1537," in *Luther's Works*, vol. 50, *Letters 3*, ed. Gottfried G. Krodel (Philadelphia, PA: Fortress, 1975), 172, 173; cf. J. I. Packer and O. R. Johnson, "Historical and Theological Introduction," in *The Bondage of the Will*, trans. J. I. Packer and O. R. Johnston (Grand Rapids, MI: Fleming H. Revell, 1957), 40.

CHAPTER 5

Understanding *Sola Scriptura*: A Working Approach for the Church

John C. Peckham

A great deal of debate and confusion exists about what *sola scriptura* means. *Sola scriptura* is often translated as "Scripture alone" or "by Scripture alone," and its historical meaning is a matter of considerable dispute. This chapter, however, does not deal primarily with the history of the phrase but attempts a constructive approach to what this principle should mean for the church today.

There are two primary dangers in approaching *sola scriptura*: isolationism and creedalism (or some other form of communitarianism). By *isolationism*, I mean the tendency of some to think their theological understanding is the product of "me and my Bible" alone.[1] Such an approach favors a private interpretation of Scripture that lends itself to idiosyncrasies and divisiveness. Furthermore, the one who practices it often mistakenly confuses one's private interpretation with the meaning of the Bible, unwittingly shifting authority from Scripture to oneself.

Creedalism, on the other hand, makes creeds or confessional statements the normative standard for the interpretation of Scripture. Although many creed-alists *formally* uphold the supremacy of Scripture, creedalism results in shifting *functional* authority from Scripture to whatever confessions, creeds, or state-ments the community adopts. Creedalism is one kind of communitarianism among many that is rapidly growing among Protestants.[2] By *communitarianism*, I mean any approach that proposes a normative standard beyond Scripture that is determined by the community, whether it is a community-determined rule of faith or the community itself.

Beyond these, an additional danger exists of attempting to avoid one of these "ditches" by overcorrecting and ending up in the other "ditch." We can be so wary of isolationism that we fall into the practice of creedalism, or vice versa. This chapter reminds us to be aware of these dangers; but at the same time, it also suggests a working approach to *sola scriptura* that might help us steer a course between either extreme—both in terms of our individual reading of Scripture and our reading of Scripture together as a church.

The danger of isolationism

In reality, no person reads Scripture in a way that is entirely free from the influence of factors outside the Bible. Each person reads Scripture from his or her own perspective. There is no neutral standpoint from which we can approach Scripture. Each of us brings a framework of previous understandings to our interpretation of the Bible, whether we intend to or not. Whereas the influences of known presuppositions can be *mitigated* and corrected, one cannot arrive at an interpretation that is free from all presuppositions.

> In reality, no person reads Scripture in a way that is entirely free from the influence of factors outside the Bible. Each person reads Scripture from his or her own perspective.

For one thing, we automatically bring to our reading some previous understanding of the meaning of the very words we read. Further, whereas I am no advocate of any normative tradition or creed, *tradition* simply refers to that which has been passed down; and we are all deeply affected by traditions, from inside and outside the church. Some are good, while others are not so good; but we cannot escape the fact that we are always affected by tradition in some way. Indeed, Scripture itself has been passed down to us (cf. 1 Corinthians 11:2; 2 Thessalonians 2:15; 3:6). Yet, Scripture also strongly cautions against the "tradition of men" (Colossians 2:8)[3] and any tradition that invalidates "the word of God" (Mark 7:13; cf. Matthew 15:2–6; Galatians 1:14–16).

If we think that we are not influenced by presuppositions or traditions, then an even greater tendency exists to read presuppositions into Scripture, often called *eisegesis*. The very expectation that we can read Scripture in isolation from other factors makes us more susceptible to the danger of unintentionally allowing such factors to *determine* our reading. The attempt to read Scripture in isolation, with the goal of keeping our reading from being infected by things outside of Scripture, often has the opposite effect.

Such an approach often leads to a simplistic and superficial reading of Scripture that fails to dig deeply into God's Word and thus we miss many of its treasures. Although the gospel message of Scripture is so simple that even a child can understand, Peter taught that "some things" in Scripture are "hard to understand, which the untaught and unstable distort" to "their own destruction" (2 Peter 3:16). A superficial approach to the Bible ignores this inspired counsel and breeds overconfidence. This leads some to extreme forms of individualism and separatism. As Woodrow W. Whidden II argues, the result "has all too often been highly individualistic persons with a very autocratic sense of their exclusivist strangle hold on truth."[4]

In this and other ways, the attempt to read Scripture entirely by oneself is detrimental to the individual and the church. Such an endeavor requires a rejection of what could be learned from others who have studied the text deeply, and it often harbors an anti-intellectual bias that serves neither the reader nor the church.

The danger of communitarianism

No one should develop his or her theology in isolation from the Christian community (cf. Hebrews 10:23–25). Fellowship and study within the church are essential, and much can be learned from resources, such as good commentaries, and from dialogue with competent interpreters (cf. Acts 8:30–35). Yet, communitarianism goes beyond the healthy role of the community by elevating the community or its resources to a level that inevitably competes with Scripture, subjecting infallible Scripture to fallible human opinions, intentionally or not.

Various forms of communitarianism are rapidly growing among Protestants. As Peter Leithart puts it, "Evangelicalism is awash in the 3Rs: retrieval, renewal, and *ressourcement*."[5] "Retrieval" (or ressourcement) calls Christians to "retrieve" the classical Christian tradition as the norm or rule of faith. This movement is rooted in the developments leading up to, and influential on the ecumenical trajectory of, the Second Vatican Council of the Roman Catholic Church (1962–1965).[6]

Today there are a number of fast-growing Protestant communitarian movements. Each emphasizes (to some extent) the community's normative role in deciding theological truth. Whereas most of these continue to claim that Scripture holds primacy, and some even advocate the phrase *sola scriptura*, many add that something outside Scripture must provide the rule or key to interpreting Scripture. This means, however, that biblical interpretation is controlled by a standard external to Scripture, thus undercutting Scripture's *functional* authority.

Some of these approaches strongly advocate retrieval of the first few centuries of Christian tradition, whether emphasizing primarily the ecumenical creeds (and/or the creeds or confessions of their denominations) or the broader tradition of the patristic age of at least the first five centuries. These approaches go by labels such as *paleo-orthodoxy, consensual orthodoxy, ancient-future Christianity,* and others.[7]

On the other hand, some approaches view the contemporary community as the authoritative standard. For instance, some postconservatives[8] emphasize that the Spirit guides and even "inspires" the contemporary community, which should engage with Scripture and tradition but should also expect to be led by the Spirit in surprising new directions.[9] At the popular level, Brian McLaren and others have taken one stream of such thought to form movements such as the emerging church.[10]

In both paleo-orthodox and postconservative kinds of approaches, the community—past or present—becomes the normative rule in a way that tends to displace Scripture as the rule of faith and practice. If biblical interpretation is determined by a standard outside of Scripture, then Scripture's authority is *functionally* superseded by that external standard. Whatever one concludes regarding just how Luther himself understood *sola scriptura,* the *consistent* adoption of the normativity of the community or community-determined standards would have excluded the Protestant Reformation from taking place and likewise would have rendered impossible the origination of Seventh-day Adventism.

A canonical approach to *sola scriptura*

What sola scriptura *should mean.* How, then, might we approach *sola scriptura* and avoid the pitfalls of isolationism and communitarianism? If none of us can read Scripture in a way that is entirely free from the influence of extrabiblical factors, can *sola scriptura* be practiced at all?

While no approach by itself will guard against all pitfalls, I propose here what I call a canonical approach to *sola scriptura,* which takes Scripture to be the unique rule (*canon*), or standard, of faith and practice while recognizing that we never approach Scripture *alone.*[11] Specifically, canonical *sola scriptura* recognizes Scripture's unique (*sola*) authority in the following three ways:

1. Scripture is the uniquely infallible source of divine revelation that is collectively available;
2. Scripture alone provides a sufficient and fully trustworthy basis of theology; and
3. Scripture is the uniquely authoritative and final norm of theological interpretation.[12]

As such, canonical *sola scriptura* rejects the supposition of any normative authority other than Scripture (except God Himself), including any norm that is to govern biblical interpretation, whether a creed, group of people, or an individual. If Scripture is to rule, its interpretation cannot be ruled by anything else, including one's private interpretation. This is why interpreters individually and collectively should return to Scripture to continually test interpretations against the standard of the canon (rule) itself.

In this regard, four integral corollaries of canonical *sola scriptura* indicate further how *sola scriptura* should function. First, *tota scriptura* holds that *all* of Scripture serves as the infallible source, sufficient basis, and final norm of theological interpretation (2 Timothy 3:16). Thus, we should not emphasize parts of Scripture while neglecting or downplaying others. The whole canon of Scripture must be allowed to function as the rule of our faith and practice.

> I f Scripture is to rule, its interpretation cannot be ruled by anything else, including one's private interpretation.

This undergirds the second corollary—the analogy of Scripture (*analogia scriptura*). This approaches Scripture as a unified and internally coherent corpus, so that each text is understood in light of the entire canon (Isaiah 8:20; Luke 24:27, 44, 45). As such, Scripture should be allowed to provide its own model of interpretation. This closely relates to the often-misunderstood saying, "Scripture interprets itself." This does not mean that Scripture requires no interpretation. Every reading of Scripture (or anything else) is already an interpretation, and it is obvious that Scripture *can* be variously interpreted in that so many people and denominations arrive at differing interpretations. Jesus Himself pointed out that Scripture can be interpreted in various ways when He asked, "What is written in the Law? How does it read to you?" (Luke 10:26). While Scripture *can* be variously interpreted, not all interpretations are valid. The interpreter should always seek the wider teaching of Scripture to help understand any part of it, and every interpretation of Scripture should be continually subjected back to the rule of Scripture itself.

This brings us to the third corollary: Spiritual things are spiritually discerned (1 Corinthians 2:11–14). This teaches that the Holy Spirit must be continually sought for guidance and illumination. The biblical canon is the *rule* because it was given by the Divine *Ruler*, and as such, one should seek and submit to the guidance of the One who inspired Scripture.

In the final corollary, the primacy of Scripture recognizes that, although Scripture is the uniquely infallible source of revelation, it is not the only source of revelation (e.g., Romans 1:18–23; 1 Corinthians 14:29), as discussed below.

What sola scriptura *should not mean.* In addition to what canonical *sola scriptura* means, it is important to clarify what it does not mean. Canonical *sola scriptura* does *not* mean that (1) Scripture is the only source of knowledge; (2) Scripture excludes reason, requires no interpretation, or one's private interpretation is the correct understanding of Scripture; (3) communities and tradition(s), past and present, should be ignored; or (4) all doctrine requires a *direct* biblical statement(s).

First, Scripture is not the only source of knowledge in general, or of revelation in particular. Scripture itself teaches that there is a *partial* revelation of God in nature, often called general revelation (Psalm 19:1–4; Romans 1:18–23).[13] Scripture also teaches that there is genuine prophecy outside of Scripture (Acts 2:17; 1 Corinthians 14:29).[14] However, Scripture is the uniquely infallible source of revelation collectively available today and is thus the prime revelation by which any other supposed source or factor should be judged.

Second, we cannot even read Scripture—let alone properly interpret it—without using our faculty of reason. Scripture advocates the careful use of reason (e.g., Isaiah 1:18; Acts 17:2; 18:4), but it is crucial to recognize that we have cognitive shortcomings and are subject to presuppositions, idiosyncrasies, and blind spots. This brings us to the third point: we can and should learn from communities and traditions, past and present, without treating them as normative. Many errors could be avoided by seriously engaging historical theology. Further, reading within and across communities might allow the wonderful diversity of readers to help individual readers to see beyond their own narrow perspectives.

Finally, whereas a direct biblical statement for each doctrine or practice is not required, theological doctrine should be derived from Scripture directly or by sound induction or deduction that corresponds to Scripture as a whole. Since Scripture is selective in what it addresses, ecclesial policy and practice enjoy a wider range of acceptable derivation than does theological doctrine. But just for this reason, ecclesial policy and practice should not be confused with or elevated to the level of theological doctrine, and even church doctrines must be correctable by Scripture.[15] *Scripture should test all faith and practice*, but Scripture itself should never be subjected to any external standard, even the church itself.

The goal of *sola scriptura* as process rather than destination

Despite the best of intentions, however, it is not possible to ever arrive at a pure *sola scriptura* understanding. Recognition of this fact should, in turn, drive us to even more careful attention to Scripture itself. We should never think that we have finally fully understood everything therein. Whereas Scripture is infallible, human interpretation of it is not.

This *sola scriptura* approach thus proposes that all extrabiblical factors, including one's known presuppositions, insofar as possible, should be intentionally judged by the unique rule (*canon*) of Scripture. At the same time, it is crucial to recognize that every interpreter and interpretive community is influenced, for good or for ill, by various factors.

This recognition should motivate us to subject ever more presuppositions and factors to Scripture at every opportunity. This requires honest self-criticism and humility, setting aside the faulty notion that Scripture is something to be mastered or that one's interpretation is a final destination. We should recognize, instead, that coming to know the Living God better through Scripture is a never-ending process. There is always more to be mined from the inexhaustible riches of Scripture.

Sadly, some church members might get the impression that the important points of Scripture already have been extracted for them. One by-product of this is that some read Scripture without

> We should recognize, instead, that coming to know the Living God better through Scripture is a never-ending process.

expecting their views to be reformed by it. Mistakenly thinking they have exhausted the important matters of Scripture might lead them to become bored with reading the Bible, sometimes leading to neglect and at other times motivating an unhealthy desire for sensationalistic theories. Either outcome detracts from the sanctification of the mind that might be progressively enjoyed by continually subjecting our understanding to Scripture and allowing it to speak anew each day and renew our minds, "taking every thought captive to the obedience of Christ" (2 Corinthians 10:5).

Conclusion

Canonical *sola scriptura* takes Scripture to be the unique rule (*canon*) of faith and practice while recognizing that we never approach Scripture *alone*. As such, individual and collective interpreters should continually submit to all of Scripture (*tota scriptura*). This might allow it, under the guidance of the Holy Spirit, to function as the uniquely infallible, sufficient basis and final norm of theological interpretation. This aims at avoiding both the adoption of an external standard (communitarianism) and the elevation of private interpretation (isolationism).

---

1. This corresponds roughly to what Alister E. McGrath labeled "tradition 0." Alister E. McGrath, *Reformation Thought: An Introduction*, 3rd ed. (Malden, MA: Blackwell, 2001), 154.

2. Some use Heiko A. Oberman's label of "tradition 1" to refer to this kind of view wherein Scripture has prime authority but should be interpreted according to tradition. See Heiko A. Oberman, *The Dawn of the Reformation* (Edinburgh: T & T Clark, 1986), 280–296. However, "tradition 1" is used by some to refer to approaches that are not communitarian but treat tradition as purely ancillary. Tradition 1 is thus too broad a label for our purposes.

3. Unless otherwise noted, all Scripture quotations in this chapter are from the New American Standard Bible.

4. Woodrow W. Whidden II, "*Sola Scriptura*, Inerrantist Fundamentalism, and the Wesleyan

64 | HERE WE STAND

Quadrilateral: Is 'No Creed but the Bible' a Workable Solution?" *Andrews University Seminary Studies* 35, no. 2 (Autumn 1997): 226.

5. Peter J. Leithart, "The Word and the Rule of Faith," *First Things*, January 30, 2015, http://www.firstthings.com/web-exclusives/2015/01/the-word-and-the-rule-of-faith (italics in the original).

6. See Gabriel Flynn and Paul D. Murray, eds., *Ressourcement: A Movement for Renewal in Twentieth-Century Catholic Theology* (Oxford: Oxford University Press, 2012). Vatican II included numerous Protestant luminaries invited as delegated observers, including George Lindbeck, who heavily influenced the communitarian trajectory of Protestantism via his postliberal approach.

7. See, e.g., Thomas C. Oden, *The Rebirth of Orthodoxy* (San Francisco, CA: HarperSanFrancisco, 2003).

8. There is a diversity of opinion among those who take this and other labels, however. The reader is thus cautioned not to use such labels to pigeonhole individuals or groups.

9. See Stanley J. Grenz, *Renewing the Center: Evangelical Theology in a Post-Theological Era*, 2nd ed. (Grand Rapids, MI: Baker, 2006).

10. See Brian D. McLaren, *A Generous Orthodoxy* (Grand Rapids, MI: Zondervan, 2006).

11. See the fuller explanation in John C. Peckham, *Canonical Theology: The Biblical Canon, Sola Scriptura, and Theological Method* (Grand Rapids, MI: Eerdmans, 2016), 140–165.

12. Although the phrase *sola scriptura* does not appear in Scripture, these three tenets are derived from Scripture, which consistently proclaims the divinely commissioned authority of Scripture as rule (2 Timothy 3:16; 2 Peter 1:20, 21; cf. Isaiah 8:20; 1 Thessalonians 2:13) over and against all other factors (Acts 5:29; cf. Jeremiah 17:9; Matthew 15:3, 6). See the discussion in Peckham, *Canonical Theology*, 145–148.

13. Nature, properly understood, does not contradict Scripture (Psalm 19:1–6); yet post-Fall nature includes much that does not reveal God (Genesis 3:17, 18; Romans 8:20).

14. Notice that Ellen White consistently pointed back to the Bible, advocating a robust conception of *sola scriptura* and maintaining that doctrine should be derived from, and understood by, Scripture itself. See Merlin D. Burt's excellent essay, "Ellen G. White and Sola Scriptura," Biblical Research Institute, accessed July 13, 2017, https://adventistbiblicalresearch.org/sites/default/files/pdf/Burt%2C%20Ellen%20White%20%26%20Sola%20Scriptura.pdf.

15. See the preamble of the Seventh-day Adventist Fundamental Beliefs, which affirms that Adventists "accept the Bible as their only creed" and allow for "revision" based on "a fuller understanding of Bible truth." "28 Fundamental Beliefs," Seventh-day Adventist Church, accessed July 13, 2017, https://www.adventist.org/fileadmin/adventist.org/files/articles/official-statements/28Beliefs-Web.pdf.

CHAPTER 6

Lutherans and Adventists in Nineteenth-Century America

Martin J. Lohrmann

Often separated by language, ethnicity, and theological heritage, Lutherans and Seventh-day Adventists in the United States during the nineteenth century did not regularly interact with each other. For different reasons, however, they both existed at the edges of the more dominant strains of American Protestantism. For American Lutherans, this marginal status derived from their origins in Lutheran Germany and Scandinavia rather than from the Reformed or Anglican roots of so many other American Protestants.[1] While early Seventh-day Adventists shared traits of the Second Great Awakening with other American Protestants, they differed on their views of Christ's coming, Sabbath observance, and care for the body.[2]

While early Seventh-day Adventists shared traits of the Second Great Awakening with other American Protestants, they differed on their views of Christ's coming, Sabbath observance, and care for the body.

The study of how Lutherans and Adventists viewed each other in the nineteenth century raises new possibilities for understanding how Christians have balanced issues of faith and culture over time. The high esteem Ellen G. White held for the Reformers Martin Luther and Philip Melanchthon, for instance, reveals the Adventist sense of connection with the past and a desire to continue effective reform for both church and daily life. Similarly, the fact that nineteenth-century Lutherans discussed such topics as millennialism and Sabbath observance shows that they were not only interested in preserving certain Old World beliefs but were engaged in the theological and social questions of their time. Shared concerns for rootedness in Scripture and tradition and a willingness to address contemporary religious issues can serve as foundations for ongoing dialogue and partnership between Adventists and Lutherans.

Lutheran Reformers and early Adventists

The German church reformer Martin Luther (1483–1546) had a good reputation among early Adventists. William Miller cited Luther and the Lutheran Augsburg Confession (1530) approvingly in articles on Christ's second coming and the resurrection of the dead. He also sympathized with Luther's rejection of fanatical believers during the Reformation.[3] In their respective careers, both Luther and Miller needed to distance themselves from more radical colleagues and from accusations that they harbored unorthodox views.

For her part, Ellen White devoted several chapters of her work *The Great Controversy* to Luther and the Lutheran Reformation, writing that "through him God accomplished a great work for the reformation of the church and the enlightenment of the world."[4] In *Testimonies for the Church*, White described Luther as an example of faithful courage and perseverance in the face of opposition; positive traits for Christians of any era.[5]

White also valued the contributions of Luther's coworker Philip Melanchthon (1497–1560): "When Luther so much needed the sympathy and counsel of a true friend, God's providence sent Melanchthon to Wittenberg. Young in years, modest and diffident in his manners, Melanchthon's sound judgment, extensive knowledge, and winning eloquence, combined with the purity and uprightness of his character, won universal admiration and esteem."[6] Because Melanchthon has often been negatively identified with controversies that took place among Lutherans after Luther's death, such lofty praise of Melanchthon in White's work is a notable and welcome contribution to historical views of this important Reformer.

Employing the common, if frequently overstated, view that Luther and Melanchthon possessed nearly opposite personality traits, White highlighted the complementary nature of their work together for the sake of the gospel.[7] Glimpsing the benefits that came from this partnership, White wrote, "Melanchthon's farseeing caution often averted trouble which would have come upon the cause had the work been left alone to Luther; and ofttimes the work would not have been pushed forward had it been left to Melanchthon alone. I was shown the wisdom of God in choosing these two men to carry on the work of reformation."[8] By recognizing Luther and Melanchthon as effective coworkers, White identified an element of collegiality in the Lutheran Reformation that is often overlooked.

These positive Adventist references to Luther and Melanchthon continued into the twentieth century. A 1957 summary of Adventist teachings, for instance, approvingly cited Luther on the sleep of the soul.[9] The same collection of teachings also favorably referred to the Augsburg Confession's view that the primacy of Sunday as a day of worship was a human institution and not a divine transference of the Old Testament command.[10] Although Lutherans have come to different conclusions than Adventists about the significance of this particular human institution for faith and practice, the consistently positive use of Lutheran sources in Adventist writings is striking nonetheless.

> These positive Adventist references to Luther and Melanchthon continued into the twentieth century. A 1957 summary of Adventist teachings, for instance, approvingly cited Luther on the sleep of the soul.

Ellen White and Johann Albrecht Bengel

Another connection between Lutherans and early Adventists appears in the works of the German Lutheran biblical scholar Johann Albrecht Bengel (1687–1752). Known for his groundbreaking work in text criticism, Bengel's study of the New Testament included careful readings of the book of Revelation. A century before William Miller, Bengel found cause to suggest the year 1836 as the beginning of the biblical prophecy of the millennium.[11] For this reason, Ellen White identified Bengel as a proto-Adventist. She wrote,

It was while preparing a sermon from Revelation 21 for advent Sunday that the light of Christ's second coming broke in upon Bengel's mind. . . . From that time he devoted himself to the study of the prophecies, especially those of the Apocalypse, and soon arrived at the belief that they pointed to the coming of Christ as near. The date which he fixed upon [1836] as the time of the second advent was within a very few years of that afterward held by Miller.

Bengel's writings have been spread throughout Christendom. His views of prophecy were quite generally received in his own state of Württemberg, and to some extent in other parts of Germany. The movement continued after his death, and the advent message was heard in Germany at the same time that it was attracting attention in other lands.[12]

For Bengel, knowledge of the end times was a "summons to further efforts, not fatalistic resignation."[13] This view about the spirituality of Christ's second coming and its significance for believers in leading lives of faith and service resonates well with that of White and the Seventh-day Adventists.

Sabbath observance and nineteenth-century American Lutherans

As members of a different branch of the Protestant Reformation, Lutherans in the United States generally experienced the Second Great Awakening of the early nineteenth century as observers rather than participants. Nevertheless, religious and social themes of the eras, including revival worship, millennial expectations, and Sabbath observance, greatly influenced Lutheran church life. While Lutherans usually addressed these topics by going back to earlier sources within their own tradition, their engagement with these themes shows that they took these issues seriously and were actively negotiating the same religious context as early Seventh-day Adventists.

Prominent themes of early Adventism, such as Sabbath observance and the coming reign of Christ (chiliasm or millennialism), appeared in many Lutheran debates of the nineteenth century. These doctrinal questions crossed several branches of Lutheranism. Sabbath observance and millennial expectation were as likely to be discussed by new immigrant communities (often in the American Midwest) as by more established church bodies in the eastern United States.

The American context is evident because Sabbath observance had not typically been a controversial issue for Lutherans. Concerning the commandment to remember the Sabbath day, for instance, Martin Luther wrote in his *Large Catechism*, "According to its outward meaning, this commandment does not concern us Christians. It is an entirely external matter, like the other regulations of the Old Testament associated with particular customs, person, times, and places, from all of which we are now set free through Christ."[14] Luther believed that every day should include time for worship and hearing God's Word; but because Sunday had been especially set aside for corporate worship as a customary practice of the church, "it should not be changed."[15] The Augsburg Confession—written primarily by Melanchthon—provides a similarly pragmatic view of Sunday worship in its article 28: "The Christian church instituted Sunday because it became necessary to set apart a specific day so that the people might know when to assemble."[16]

In the context of nineteenth-century American religion, however, Lutherans needed to revisit their views. Influenced by Puritanism, questions of Sabbath observance had grown prominent among North American Protestants. In light of this contextual reality, one major Lutheran leader of the period, Samuel S. Schmucker (1799–1873), suggested revising the Augsburg Confession for the sake of cooperation with other American Protestants. In Schmucker's view, the Augsburg Confession's "denial of the divine obligation of the Christian Sabbath" was one of the points that Lutherans should emend in order to come into closer accord with more dominant Reformed views.[17]

Schmucker's proposed recension of the Augsburg Confession provides a clear example of Lutherans engaging the theological questions of the wider culture. In the intra-Lutheran debates that followed, it might appear as if American Lutherans were talking only to each other and not to other communities; however, the prevalence of questions such as Sabbath observance in the surrounding Protestant culture shows that Lutherans were active participants in the broader religious issues of the day.

In contrast with Schmucker's position, most other American Lutherans of the period affirmed the traditional Lutheran view that the commandment to observe the Sabbath had been abrogated and was not in itself a binding command on Christians. In 1869, Henry E. Jacobs, who went on to teach at the Lutheran seminary in Philadelphia for more than fifty years, wrote two extended essays on the topic in the *Evangelical Quarterly Review*.[18] He identified the theological and moral issue at stake not as one primarily of Sabbath observance but of honoring God's Word: "Sabbatarianism in its origin in the Protestant Church, resembles many other attempts at Reformation, which have been made by striking at the branches, instead of at the root of error. The desecration of the Lord's Day, should not have been regarded the sin, against which the Church was to array herself. The contempt of God's Word, was the crime which should have been charged against those, who thus despised the ordinances of God's house, and the preaching of the Gospel."[19] With views like these, many American Lutherans tried to balance gospel freedom with the importance of nurturing communities through strong regular worship. Following Luther's *Large Catechism*, these Lutherans invoked passages such as Romans 14:5, 6: "Some judge one day to be better than another, while others judge all days to be alike. Let all be fully convinced in their own minds. Those who observe the day, observe it in honor of the Lord. Also those who eat, eat in honor of the Lord, since they give thanks to God; while those who abstain, abstain in honor of the Lord and give thanks to God" (NRSV). The goal of this position was not to deny the importance of weekly worship as such but rather to make sure that divine worship served personal faith, gospel preaching, and congregational experiences that would enrich lives and communities.

Even with these convictions, American Lutherans noted that their Protestant counterparts varied widely among themselves on the meaning of Sabbath observance. Jacobs, for instance, differentiated between a strict Sabbatarianism, Puritanic Sabbatarianism, and a mild Sabbatarianism, which held a good deal in common with the Lutheran view.[20] Though Jacobs showed a clear desire to maintain the traditional Lutheran understandings of the Sabbath, he also expressed openness to other perspectives based upon shared concern for biblical worship and gospel faith.

The differences on this issue among German Lutherans in the Midwest manifested themselves in a sharp controversy between the Evangelical Lutheran Synod of Iowa and the Lutheran Church—Missouri Synod. The Missouri Synod believed that having the precise doctrine about the Sabbath was an essential matter for saving faith, while the Iowa Synod was open to a number of interpretations on how Christians might observe the Sabbath and honor God's Word through worship.[21] Rather than fight about exact views of the Sabbath, the Iowa Synod considered it an "open question," to be treated with a generosity of spirit.

Millennialism among nineteenth-century American Lutherans

Willing to tolerate—or even expect—some differences among its members, the Iowa Synod also welcomed pastors who preached more strongly about Christ's second coming than was typical for Lutherans. Although this position drew criticism from the Missouri Synod, the leaders of the Iowa Synod defended their openness to preaching about Christ's second coming on the basis of biblical passages such as Revelation 20 and the historical creeds of the church.[22] (The New Testament and creeds of the church clearly say that Christians can expect Christ's return.) They also cited article 17 of the Augsburg Confession, which affirms Christ's return for judgment and denies that this return necessitates a temporal Messianic kingdom.[23] This reveals a cautious Lutheran approach to millennial views, as found in the work of Bengel mentioned above.

Some Lutherans brought this nuanced perspective to their views of Seventh-day Adventism. In an 1896 essay in the *Lutheran Quarterly*, on the topic "Millennialism," John F. Pollock wrote, "Some of these [denominational] bodies hold more of orthodox truth than others. The Adventists, as represented by Millennium Dawn, are in the main orthodox concerning the subjects of theology, anthropology and soteriology. In regard to pneumatology they are somewhat Montanistic, and in eschatology, they teach the annihilation of the wicked."[24] Here Pastor Pollock represented Seventh-day Adventism in a relatively positive manner. From the Lutheran perspective, Pollock's use of "Montanism" is negative, as it refers to a heretical sect of the third century. Nevertheless, he accurately described Adventism's openness to the continuing revelation of the Holy Spirit, an abiding gift of prophecy, which remains a positive claim of Seventh-day Adventists when it occurs in harmony with God's Word.[25]

> Nevertheless, he accurately described Adventism's openness to the continuing revelation of the Holy Spirit, an abiding gift of prophecy, which remains a positive claim of Seventh-day Adventists when it occurs in harmony with God's Word.

A similar Lutheran view of Adventism continued into the twentieth century.

In a book titled *Your Neighbor's Faith: A Lutheran Looks at Other Churches*, William Poovey wrote this about Seventh-day Adventists: "While most Christians are not as concerned as they should be about the future, Seventh-Day Adventists find great strength in this direction. Stirred by the prospect of the immediate return of Christ, the church is zealous in its missionary activity and has spread into many foreign countries. While we do not share their interpretations of prophecy, we can learn something about zealous work from these people."[26] Poovey provides an example of honesty in naming differences between church bodies, while respecting and lifting up the good that another tradition offers.

Conclusion

The five hundredth anniversary of the Reformation provides a good occasion for various branches of Protestantism to get better acquainted with each other. This is true for groups, such as Lutherans and Seventh-day Adventists, that developed in different contexts, yet still share many theological convictions and social commitments.

Lutherans and Adventists, for instance, share a clear affinity when it comes to trusting that Christ's spiritual kingdom reshapes, redefines, and reinvigorates life in this world. Furthermore, both traditions have high views of the gospel message as preached by Martin Luther and his colleagues during the Reformation, believing that the Holy Spirit continues to work for freedom and life through Christian faith in the hearts of believers. Lutherans and Adventists also share a strong dedication to social ministry, as represented by organizations such as Lutheran Services in America and Adventist Community Services, respectively.

Though quite distinct in their historical origins, the care with which Lutherans and Adventists in the nineteenth century addressed common religious concerns suggests positive directions for work together in the twenty-first century.

1. Mark A. Noll, *A History of Christianity in the United States and Canada* (Grand Rapids, MI: Eerdmans, 1992), 216.

2. Noll, *A History of Christianity*, 192; and Edwin S. Gaustad and Leigh Schmidt, *The Religious History of America: The Heart of the American Story From Colonial Times to Today* (New York: HarperCollins, 2002), 154.

3. Sylvester Bliss, *Memoirs of William Miller, Generally Known as a Lecturer on the Prophecies, and the Second Coming of Christ* (Boston: Joshua V. Himes, 1853), 200, 201, 233, 239.

4. Ellen G. White, *The Great Controversy* (Mountain View, CA: Pacific Press® Pub. Assn., 1950), 120.

5. Ellen G. White, *Testimonies for the Church* (Mountain View, CA: Pacific Press® Pub. Assn., 1948), 1:372–375.

6. White, *The Great Controversy*, 134.

7. Heinz Scheible, "Fifty Years of Melanchthon Research," *Lutheran Quarterly* 26, no. 2 (Summer 2012): 164–180.

8. Ellen G. White, *Early Writings of Ellen G. White* (Washington DC: Review and Herald® Pub. Assn., 1945), 224.

9. *Seventh-day Adventists Answer Questions on Doctrine* (Washington, DC: Review and Herald® Pub. Assn., 1957), 570–573.

10. Ibid., 171, 172.

11. John C. Weborg, "Bengel, J(ohann) A(lbrecht)," in *Dictionary of Major Biblical Interpreters*, ed. Donald K. McKim (Downers Grove, IL: IVP Academic, 2007), 184–188. See also John Sandys-Wunsch, *What Have They Done to the Bible? A History of Modern Biblical Interpretation* (Collegeville, MN: Liturgical, 2005), 268–270.

12. White, *The Great Controversy*, 363, 364.

13. Sandys-Wunsch, *What Have They Done to the Bible?* 270.

14. Robert Kolb and Timothy J. Wengert, eds., *The Book of Concord: The Confessions of the Evangelical Lutheran Church* (Minneapolis, MN: Fortress, 2000), 397.82.

15. Kolb and Wengert, *The Book of Concord*, 398.85.

16. Ibid., 100.57–60.

17. Richard C. Wolf, *Documents of Lutheran Unity in America* (Philadelphia, PA: Fortress, 1966), 102.

18. Henry E. Jacobs, "The Lutheran Doctrine of the Sabbath, and the Lord's Day," *Evangelical Quarterly Review* 20 (1869): 125–152; Henry E. Jacobs, "The Sabbath Question, in Its Historical Relations, and Bearings Upon the Faith and Life of the Church," *Evangelical Quarterly Review* 20 (1869): 524–555. The author thanks his research assistant Katelin Bingner for her assistance in locating these and other articles from the period.

19. Jacobs, "The Sabbath Question," 540.

20. Ibid., 525–527.

21. Martin J. Lohrmann, " 'A Monument to American Intolerance': The Iowa Synod's 'Open Questions' in Their American Context," in *Wilhelm Löhe: Erbe und Vision*, ed. Dietrich Blaufuß (Gütersloh: Gütersloher Verlagshaus, 2009), 304.

22. Ibid., 302, 303.

23. Kolb and Wengert, *The Book of Concord*, 50.1–5.

24. John F. Pollock, "Millennialism," *Lutheran Quarterly* 26, no. 1 (January 1896): 19.

25. *Seventh-day Adventists Answer Questions on Doctrine*, 94–96.

26. William A. Poovey, *Your Neighbor's Faith: A Lutheran Looks at Other Churches* (Minneapolis, MN: Augsburg, 1961), 87.

CHAPTER 7

Ellen White's Portrait
of Martin Luther

Denis Kaiser

E llen G. White (1827–1915) viewed Martin Luther as *the* Protestant Reformer par excellence and *the* historical example for those living at the time of the end.* She held this view despite the fact that the most obvious roots for Seventh-day Adventist theology come from the Wesleyan-Methodist and Restorationist traditions. White mentions Luther more than four times as often as Philip Melanchthon, Huldrych Zwingli, John Calvin, John Knox, and John Wesley combined. Ellen White certainly saw something very special in this German Reformer.[1]

On the surface, it might seem that Ellen White did not have much in common with Luther. Not only did three hundred years and a large ocean

---

* This chapter is based on Denis Kaiser, "God Is Our Refuge and Strength: Martin Luther in the Perception of Ellen G. White" (paper, Perceptions of the Protestant Reformation in Seventh-day Adventism Symposium, Institute of Adventist Studies, Friedensau Adventist University, Germany, May 9–12, 2016).

separate them, they also came from very different cultural, educational, philosophical, and theological backgrounds.[2] Despite such obvious differences, they shared a number of common experiences that, in one sense, might have created a spiritual kinship between them.

Both Martin Luther and Ellen White were at the forefront of religious reform and revival movements in their own nations and beyond. They were expelled from the churches of their early years for circulating their religious convictions. Both highlighted the ultimate authority of Scripture for faith and practice, the importance of Scripture as its own interpreter, the close relationship between the Old and the New Testament, and the central role of Jesus Christ. They strongly believed in the merits of Christ's atoning sacrifice as the provision for the justification of the sinner by faith; yet for both Luther and White, a conspicuous eschatological outlook accompanied salvation. Their theological framework has influenced their fellow believers and is still held in high regard by their respective denominational traditions to the point that it continues to impact the broader surrounding culture.

Ellen White's chronological sketch of Luther's life is characterized by an interlacing of the motifs of the central role and authority of Scripture, justification by faith in Christ, God's providential working in Luther's experience, and Luther's gradual separation from Roman Catholicism. This chapter describes her appropriation of each of these motifs.

The authority of the Bible

Ellen White, throughout her description of the life of Martin Luther, emphasized the growing importance that the Bible played in his experience. She highlighted that upon finding a Latin Bible in the University of Erfurt's library, he felt deeply moved as he could read "the words of life" for the first time for himself. Angels came close to Luther and illumed his understanding as he sighed, "O that God would give me such a book for myself." As a result, he became deeply convicted of his own sinfulness. Luther greatly delighted to study the Bible that was "chained to the convent wall." The growing conviction of his own sin caused him to seek forgiveness by earning it through his own works. Johann von Staupitz, Luther's confessor, eventually explained the Bible to him and pointed him to Jesus.[3]

Later, in Wittenberg, he was able to study the Bible in its original languages and soon began to lecture on biblical books. Ellen White stressed that Luther nevertheless still felt unworthy to preach the Word of God and needed Staupitz's encouragement. After earning his doctoral degree in 1512, he became a professor at the university, so that he could "devote himself, as never before, to the Scriptures that he loved." It was at this point that White saw him making the crucial resolution to study Scripture carefully, receive only such doctrines that rested upon its authority, and faithfully teach others in it. That resolution points already to the later "vital principle of the Reformation."[4] Theologians have termed it the *formal principle* (the authoritative source) of the Reformation. Luther was sure that a person's intellect and research were insufficient to obtain a proper understanding of the Bible. What a person needs is to pray with an open heart for God, the Author of Scripture, to provide a better understanding of it. Ellen White emphasized that he perceived Scripture as the only rule of faith and practice;[5] this is a motif that appears throughout her own writings and the publications of other early Seventh-day Adventists and contemporary American Protestant writers.

After the inception of the Protestant Reformation, Luther even "urged" his detractors to "show him his errors from the Scriptures."[6] Writing about his stay at Wartburg Castle from May 1521 to March 1522, White stated that Luther was "filling his lamp from the storehouse of truth."[7] Indeed, it was there that he "performed a most important service for his countrymen by translating the New Testament into the German tongue." (Published six months after his return from Wartburg Castle, it became known as the September Testament.) From this "rocky Patmos," Luther issued a host of tracts that proclaimed the gospel and rebuked the errors of his time.[8] Yet, instead of turning only against Roman Catholicism and rationalism, he also opposed the spiritualizing fanaticism of the Zwickau prophets and Thomas Müntzer, who stressed the significance of spiritual communications, thus diminishing the authority of the Written Word.[9] Neither Luther nor White saw any value

> Ellen White perceived Martin Luther as the prime advocate of "true Christianity" because of the role and authority he placed upon Scripture.

in the Catholic rite of the Mass; yet she sided with Luther in his rejection of its violent abolishment because she believed that the power of the Word of God was more effective than the use of force in turning people away from both apostate worship and fanatical excitement.[10] Ellen White perceived Martin Luther as the prime advocate of "true Christianity" because of the role and authority he placed upon Scripture.[11]

Justification by faith in Christ

The second motif running through Ellen White's narrative on Luther is "the great truth of justification by faith . . . a mighty beacon to guide repentant sinners into the way of life."[12] Denis Fortin, a historical theologian, notes that Ellen White credits Martin Luther with "the greatest role in restoring the second distinctive doctrine of Protestantism: salvation through faith in Christ."[13] In addition, Hans Heinz states that by discovering that teaching "Luther established the *material principle* [the central doctrine] of the Reformation."[14]

As mentioned before, Ellen White pointed out that Martin Luther was searching for forgiveness and peace through discipline and spiritual exercises when his confessor, Staupitz, eventually asked him to "look away from himself" and the "infinite punishment for the violation of God's law, and look to Jesus, his sin-pardoning Saviour."[15] She first mentioned Staupitz's statement in an article in late May 1883.[16] Interestingly, at the General Conference session of the Seventh-day Adventists less than six months later, she repeatedly emphasized the need to refrain from focusing on one's own lack of perfection and to look firmly to Christ for one's personal salvation. As her sermons were published, she impressed on her readers the thought to look away from self and focus on the Cross—"Look and live."[17]

Luther's new insight had a positive impact on his life, yet it did not necessarily transform his view of salvation. Thus, Ellen White described Luther in the winter of 1510–1511, together with other pilgrims, as "devoutly" climbing the Scala Sancta in Rome when "suddenly a voice like thunder seemed to say to him: 'The just shall live by faith.' [Romans 1:17]." She wrote that Luther left the scene in horror and "that text never lost its power upon his soul." He realized "more clearly than ever before the fallacy of trusting to human works for salvation, and the necessity of constant faith in the merits of Christ."[18] Commenting on the nature and impact of his teachings on those listening to him from 1512 to 1517, White wrote, "The glad tidings of a Saviour's love, the assurance of pardon and peace through His atoning blood, rejoiced their hearts and inspired within them an immortal hope."[19]

Since 1904, Reformation scholars have emphasized Luther's Reformational breakthrough, the *Turmerlebnis* (tower experience), an event that Ellen White never mentioned.[20] Nevertheless, scholars disagree on the time of that event. Some place it about three years before the beginning of the Reformation, while others suppose that it did not happen until 1518. More recently scholars assert that Luther's Reformational insight may have been a process rather than a single event, suggesting that earlier scholars may have failed to do justice to his complex development between 1510 and 1520. This reasoning is in harmony with Ellen White's view of his experience. Luther himself may not have ascribed too much significance to the *Turmerlebnis* because he mentioned it only once in his writings (and even this lone reference was about thirty years later).[21]

Talking about Luther's response to those who had purchased indulgences from Johann Tetzel (1465–1519), she wrote, "Nothing but repentance toward God and faith in Christ can save the sinner. The grace of Christ cannot be purchased; it is a free gift. He [Luther] counseled the people not to buy indulgences, but to look in faith to a crucified Redeemer. He related his own painful experience in vainly seeking by humiliation and penance to secure salvation, and assured his hearers that it was by looking away from himself and believing in Christ that he found peace and joy."[22]

On his way to the Diet of Worms in 1521, Luther preached a sermon at Erfurt in which he made a similar remark, "We are saved by His [Christ's] work, and not by our own," and that "since God has saved us" through Him, we are to live as redeemed people and show unselfish love to the needy. Ellen White perceived his sermon as "the bread of life . . . broken to those starving souls." As Luther tried to present Christ as "the sinner's Redeemer," "he hid behind the Man of Calvary," and he "lost sight of self" and the peril of his situation.[23]

Divine providence in Luther's experience

Ellen White was convinced that God was deeply interested in Martin Luther's destiny and God's providence was actively operating in specific events and circumstances in his life. She believed that God placed people in Luther's life who became instrumental to his personal development and the cause of reform. According to her, "God raised up" Staupitz as "a friend and helper" for Luther.[24] She similarly perceived God's providence at work when Melanchthon came to Wittenberg, because he and Luther complemented each other and strengthened the Reformation.[25]

Even some enemies of the Reformation spoke and acted in ways that Ellen White could explain only by divine providence. Thus, she equated Emperor Charles V's call for Luther to present his views at the Diet of Worms in 1521 with God's call.[26] Similarly, the appearance of Jerome Aleander (1480–1542), "the ablest of . . . [Rome's] orators," at the diet was calculated by God to bring both positions to a direct encounter.[27] She further believed that God must have worked on the heart of Duke George of Saxony (1471–1539), who was "a determined enemy" of the Reformation, when he offered one of the most eloquent critiques of the papal tyranny.[28]

White described several experiences as God's means to educate Luther and further his efforts. Thus, the despondency Luther experienced at Worms was permitted by "an all-wise Providence." He was "to realize his peril, that he might not trust to his own strength and rush presumptuously into danger." Like Jacob, he was to wrestle with God and fasten his faith "in his utter helplessness . . . upon Christ, the mighty Deliverer."[29] Luther being asked to present his speech not only in German but also in Latin was another circumstance that Ellen White perceived as God's providence, because it allowed many of the attendees to understand the force of Luther's argument who had not felt it the first time.[30] Luther's planned abduction on his return from the diet was, in White's view, a divine "way of escape." Besides preserving his life, God had more significant goals in mind. To prepare Luther for walking again "upon the dizzy heights to which he had been so suddenly exalted," God saved him "from the pride and self-confidence that are so often caused by success" by shutting him out from public and human praise and therefore preventing the endeavors of the Reformation from being thwarted.[31]

Luther's separation from Rome

As Luther grew in his understanding of the Bible and its gospel message, he grew increasingly apart from the church of his childhood. Ellen White's first chapter on Luther in *The Great Controversy* is aptly titled "Luther's Separation From Rome," thus encapsulating the theme of an extended process of dissociation from the Roman Catholic system. The following chapters on the Reformation in Germany illustrate the widening gap between Luther and his former church. White stated that Luther found joy in studying the Bible as well as relief in Staupitz's advice; yet for years, he was "still a true son of the papal church" and "had no thought that he would ever be anything else."[32] His visit to Rome in 1510–1511 made him aware more than ever before that one was to rely on the merits of Christ rather than one's own works for salvation. White wrote, "His eyes had been opened, and were never again to be closed, to the delusions of the papacy. When he turned his face from Rome he had turned away also in heart, and from that time the separation grew wider, until he severed all connection with the papal church."[33]

After Luther completed his doctoral degree in October 1512, Ellen White saw him resolve "that Christians should receive no other doctrines than those which rest on the authority of the Sacred Scriptures"; this was a principle that "struck at the very foundation of papal supremacy."[34] That resolution did not make him a Protestant, however, for she pointed out that even when he learned of Tetzel's "blasphemous assumptions" in 1517, he was "still a papist of the straitest sort."[35] And even after his return from the Diet of Augsburg in October 1518, White saw him as "a supporter of the Roman Church," who had "no thought that he would ever separate from her communion."[36] Luther's final and outward separation came as a result of a terrible inner struggle, manifested in the burning of the papal bull in December 1520.[37]

The events during and surrounding the Diet of Worms in the spring of 1521 (about two months) compose about one-third of Ellen White's sketch on Luther. She may have given such prominence to that event because it brought face-to-face the conflict between Rome and Luther—between darkness and light. The character and foundation of each side were revealed more directly than ever before. She perceived Luther's appearance before Emperor Charles V, the papal party, and the German nobility as a showdown between the two sides. It signaled the success of the Reformation: a condemned heretic was not only granted safe conduct but was even permitted to present his teachings before the assembly, thus disregarding the authority of the pope who had just condemned him.[38]

Despite the stark contrast that Ellen White saw between Catholicism and Protestantism, she nevertheless perceived a paradox in the lives of Luther and others. Although he moved away from Rome by placing his faith on the authority of Scripture and salvation by the merits of Christ, he was still a strict supporter of the papal system. She saw each person being swayed by two great principles—divine, self-sacrificing, other-oriented love versus selfish, self-oriented love. That struggle entered "into every phase of human experience" and influenced people to make choices in one or the other direction.[39] Instead of judging people based on their "occasional good deeds and occasional misdeeds," she stressed the significance of "the tendency of the habitual words and acts."[40] Luther's example illustrates the paradox that some people may be led by God's Spirit and progress in their understanding despite their loyalty to a particular religious system.

Conclusion

Interestingly, the above motifs do not just characterize Ellen White's Luther narrative but harmonize with her writings in general. Throughout her writings, she stressed the authority of Scripture, salvation by faith in Christ, and the great-controversy theme between good and evil. Luther was the epitome of revival and reform. In fact, she thought that Luther's courage in preaching "present truth" in the face of opposition seemed to be an example for those called by God to promote the "present truth" in the end time. White remarked that as "there was a present truth in the days of Luther,—a truth at that time of special importance; there is [similarly] a present truth for the church today." The term *present truth* was and still is highly significant for Seventh-day Adventists, yet many readers may be surprised to learn that Ellen White used that term only two times in *The Great Controversy* and both times in connection with Luther.[41] Ellen White's Luther narrative was an illustration of the tension between the two contending principles that are present in the life of each person. They are, therefore, an example for those preparing themselves for coming events. The experience of clinging to Jesus and His Word in the midst of the universal, global, and personal conflict is not just an experience reserved for Martin Luther or Ellen White but an experience in which each person is invited to participate.

> Throughout her writings, she stressed the authority of Scripture, salvation by faith in Christ, and the great-controversy theme between good and evil.

---

1. Ellen G. White described Luther's experience in Ellen G. White, *Spiritual Gifts: The Great Controversy Between Christ and His Angels, and Satan and His Angels*, vol. 1 (Battle Creek, MI: James White, 1858), 120–122; Ellen G. White, *Testimony for the Church, No. 9* (Battle Creek, MI: Steam Press of the Seventh-day Adventist Pub. Assn., 1863), 16–20; a series of twenty *Signs of the Times* articles, May 31–November 1, 1883; Ellen G. White, *The Spirit of Prophecy: The*

Great Controversy Between Christ and Satan From the Destruction of Jerusalem to the End of the Controversy, vol. 4 (Battle Creek, MI: Steam Press of the Seventh-day Adventist Pub. Assn., 1884), 94–169; and Ellen G. White, *The Great Controversy Between Christ and Satan During the Christian Dispensation*, rev. and enl. ed. (Oakland, CA: Pacific Press® Pub. Assn., 1888), 120–170, 185–210.

2. George R. Knight, *A Search for Identity: The Development of Seventh-day Adventist Beliefs*, Adventist Heritage Series (Hagerstown, MD: Review and Herald® Pub. Assn., 2000), 32; Woodrow W. Whidden II, *The Judgment and Assurance: The Dynamics of Personal Salvation*, Library of Adventist Theology, vol. 4 (Hagerstown, MD: Review and Herald® Pub. Assn., 2012), 13; Denis Fortin, "The Theology of Ellen G. White," in *The Ellen G. White Encyclopedia*, ed. Denis Fortin and Jerry Moon (Hagerstown, MD: Review and Herald® Pub. Assn., 2013), 248–255.

3. White, *The Great Controversy*, 122, 123.

4. Ibid., 125, 126.

5. Ibid., 132; cf. 186.

6. Ibid., 138. See also 156, 157, 159, 160, 166–168.

7. Ibid., 168.

8. Ibid., 169. See also 193, 194.

9. Ibid., 186–193.

10. Ibid., 189.

11. Ibid., 193.

12. Ellen G. White, *The Acts of the Apostles* (Mountain View, CA: Pacific Press® Pub. Assn., 1911), 373.

13. Fortin, "The Theology of Ellen G. White," 246.

14. Johann Heinz, "Luther, Martin," in *The Ellen G. White Encyclopedia*, ed. Denis Fortin and Jerry Moon (Hagerstown, MD: Review and Herald® Pub. Assn., 2013), 954 (emphasis added).

15. White, *The Great Controversy*, 123.

16. Ellen G. White, "Martin Luther—His Character and Early Life," *Signs of the Times*, May 31, 1883, 242.

17. See Ellen G. White, "The Christian's Refuge," *Review and Herald*, April 15, 1884, 241; Ellen G. White, "Effectual Prayer," *Review and Herald*, April 22, 1884, 257; Ellen G. White, "Christ's Followers the Light of the World," *Review and Herald*, May 13, 1884, 306; Ellen G. White, "Our Mighty Helper," *Review and Herald*, July 1, 1884, 417.

18. White, *The Great Controversy*, 125.

19. Ibid., 126.

20. Heinz, "Luther, Martin," 955.

21. Martin H. Jung, *Reformation und Konfessionelles Zeitalter, (1517–1658)*, Basiswissen Theologie und Religionswissenschaften, vol. 3628 (Göttingen: Vandenhoeck and Ruprecht, 2012), 27, 28; Christian Danz, *Einführung in die Theologie Martin Luthers*, Einführung Theologie (Darmstadt: Wissenschaftliche Buchgesellschaft, 2013), 24–29.

22. White, *The Great Controversy* , 129.

23. Ibid., 152.

24. Ibid., 123.

25. Ibid., 134, 135.

26. Ibid., 146.

27. Ibid., 147.

28. Ibid., 150. See also ibid., 149.

29. Ibid., 156.

30. Ibid., 159.

31. Ibid., 168, 169.

32. Ibid., 124.

33. Ibid., 125.

34. Ibid., 126.

35. Ibid., 128.

36. Ibid., 139.

37. Ibid., 142.

38. Ibid., 145–170, esp. 146.

39. Ellen G. White, *Education* (Oakland, CA: Pacific Press® Pub. Assn., 1903), 190.

40. Ellen G. White, *Steps to Christ* (Battle Creek, MI: Review and Herald® Pub. Assn., 1896), 58.

41. White, *The Great Controversy*, 143.

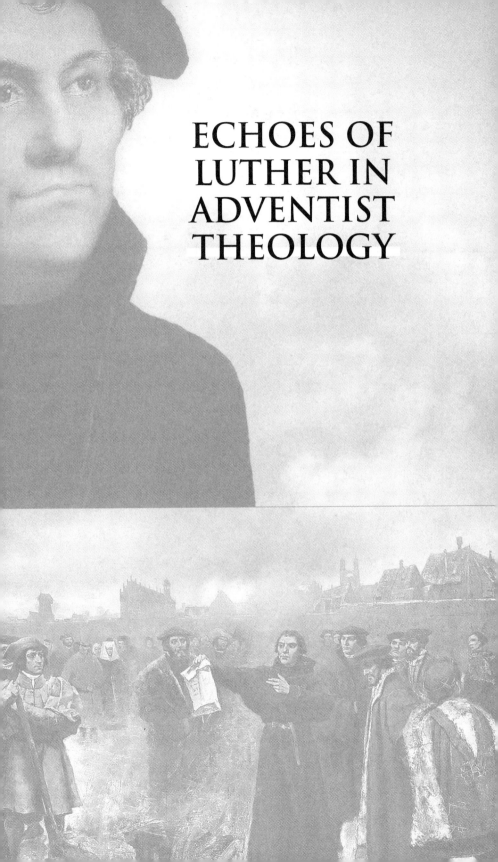

ECHOES OF LUTHER IN ADVENTIST THEOLOGY

CHAPTER 8

The Priesthood of Christ in Luther and Adventism

Alberto R. Timm

G od's salvation plan was foreshadowed in the Old Testament and realized in the New Testament (Hebrews 8:1–5). The plan gravitates around Christ's atoning sacrifice on the cross and His priestly ministry in heaven. Jesus stressed the centrality of the cross by His statement, "And I, when I am lifted up from the earth, will draw all people to myself" (John 12:32, NRSV). Paul affirmed that "God was in Christ reconciling the world to Himself" (2 Corinthians 5:19).[1]

After His sacrifice on the cross, Christ became the High Priest of the heavenly sanctuary, where He intercedes "in the presence of God on our behalf" (Hebrews 9:24, NRSV). Hebrews 4:14–16 assures us that we have a High Priest, who sympathizes with our weaknesses and invites us to come boldly to the throne of grace.

Martin Luther's emphasis was on Christ's atoning sacrifice for the forgiveness of sins, which is also known as the theology of the cross (*theologia crucis*). But Seventh-day Adventists have focused on Christ's priestly ministry in the heavenly sanctuary. These two approaches raise some questions: Did Luther's emphasis on the Cross undermine Christ's heavenly priesthood? Does the Adventists' stress on priesthood overshadow the meaning of the Cross? Are these approaches mutually exclusive, or can they be harmonized?

MARTIN LUTHER

Martin Luther challenged the medieval Roman Catholic philosophical theology.[2] This process involved a substantial rupture with Aristotelian theological reasoning[3] and a hermeneutical pilgrimage from the medieval allegorical method to the grammatical-historical method of biblical interpretation.[4] By September 1517, Luther recognized that "virtually the entire *Ethics* of Aristotle is the worst enemy of grace" and that "the whole Aristotle is to theology as darkness is to light."[5] But this does not mean that he eliminated all philosophical-dichotomist traces from his thinking.

> Luther viewed the cross as a historical event with deep spiritual meaning.

Luther viewed the Cross as a historical event with deep spiritual meaning. Yet his notion of heavenly realms continued to be portrayed mainly in dichotomist terms, with a strong emphasis upon a theocentric heaven with almost nothing else added to it.[6] Even so, Luther made a significant contribution to a better understanding of Christ's sacrifice and heavenly priesthood.

Old Testament types

Luther saw Christ as a true high priest to whom the Mosaic tabernacle, the Levitical priesthood, and the priesthood of Melchizedek all converged and in whom all were fulfilled. As "shadows or pictures of the Christ who was to come, and of His sacrifice,"[7] they were considered by Luther to be of great significance for the understanding of Christ's priesthood.

In his reflections upon Hebrews 9:1–5 from 1517, Luther interpreted the Mosaic tabernacle and its furniture from a Christ-centered perspective.[8] Although the Mosaic tabernacle itself was typologically related to the priesthood of Christ, it was in the service of the tabernacle that Christ's priesthood was more foreshadowed. Luther explained that the reason the Levitical priests were called priests was "to show by means of such dramatic symbols and shadows that the true Priest, the promised Christ, would come, reconcile all men by His sacrifice, and preach and publish this fact in all the world through the Gospel."[9] That priesthood, with Aaron as its high priest, was instituted by God (Exodus 28:1), had the "books of Moses" as its laws, and "irrational animals and physical things" as its sacrifices.[10] After distinguishing between the moral law and the ceremonial law, Luther recognized that everything contained in the latter was "promised and prefigured with reference to Christ and in Christ."[11]

Foundational for the Levitical priesthood was the concept of transference of sin. Luther argued that the expressions "the iniquity of the sanctuary" and "the iniquity of your priesthood" (Numbers 18:1) were used "not because the sanctuary or the priesthood have committed them, but because it is the nature and the duty of the priesthood to be the bearer and the carrier of sins."[12] By carrying the sins of the people, the Levitical priests typified Christ as the One who would vicariously bear "our griefs" and carry "our sorrows" (Isaiah 53:4).

Luther noted that the typological relationship between the Levitical priesthood and Christ's priesthood was inadequate for two reasons. First, God chose the tribe of Levi, particularly the house of Aaron, for the priesthood (Numbers 8:5–26). "Since Christ was to be born of the tribe of Judah, He could not logically be a priest."[13] Second, "God clearly wanted the two offices, king and priest, separately maintained. This is something which secular insight has also discerned as necessary."[14] Christ would unite in Himself both priestly and kingly offices (Zechariah 6:13) in a new "spiritual" and "not temporal" dimension.[15]

Therefore, Melchizedek, a king and a priest of the time of Abraham (Genesis 14:17–20; cf. Psalm 110:4; Hebrews 6:19–7:28), was a more appropriate type of our Priest Christ than Aaron.[16] In the expression "You are a priest forever according to the order of Melchizedek" (Psalm 110:4, NRSV), Luther saw an element that transcends the human level of existence, pointing toward the eternity of Christ.[17]

The nature of Christ

Johannes Zachhuber argues, "Luther's theology is strongly Christocentric, but Christology is rarely the central focus of his writings." This means that his Christology must be "reconstructed from . . . various strands in his thought."[18] Some of his most significant insights about Christ as a High Priest are found in his remarks on Psalm 110:4 (1535), in which Christ is portrayed as the everlasting King and Priest according to the order of Melchizedek. For the Reformer, "this is an extraordinary statement. It is marvelous."[19]

While dealing with the divine and human natures of Christ, Luther was able to distinguish "between the *duality* of natures and the *singularity* of the person."[20] In his book *The Babylonian Captivity of the Church* (1520), he argued that "in order for the divine nature to dwell in him bodily, it is not necessary for the human nature to be transubstantiated and the divine nature contained under the accidents of the human nature. Both natures are simply there in their entirety."[21] In the book *The Freedom of a Christian*, he added in clear terms, "Christ is God and man in one person."[22] He stated elsewhere that Christ is "a man who is supernaturally one person with God, and apart from this man there is no God."[23]

This mysterious union also accounted for the fact that Christ remained uncorrupted and incorruptible by sin (John 8:46; Hebrews 4:15; 1 Peter 1:19). In his "Disputation on the Divinity and Humanity of Christ" (1540), Luther argued, "Every man is corrupted by original sin, with the exception of Christ. Every man who is not a divine Person [*personaliter Deus*], as is Christ, has concupiscence, but the man Christ has none, because he is a divine Person, and in conception the flesh and blood of Mary were entirely purged, so that nothing of sin remained."[24] Because Christ is "a lamb without blemish and without spot"

(1 Peter 1:19), He was able to offer Himself as "the Lamb of God who takes away the sin of the world" (John 1:29).

Christ's atoning sacrifice

According to Luther, the events of the cross were not merely preparatory in allowing Christ to become a true High Priest but the beginning of His priestly office. The Reformer stated that Jesus "has been a Priest since the day He became the Christ and began to sacrifice His body."[25] Luther referred to the cross as "the altar on which He [Christ], consumed by the fire of the boundless love which burned in His heart, presented the living and holy sacrifice of His body and blood to the Father with fervent intercession, loud cries, and hot, anxious tears (Heb. 5:7)."[26] Ulrich Asendorf concluded that "at the cross Christ comes to his right priestly office."[27]

> According to Luther, the events of the cross were not merely preparatory in allowing Christ to become a true High Priest but the beginning of His priestly office.

Christ's sacrifice on the cross was a real sacrifice, consisting of the shedding of His blood "for the remission of sins," through which Christ Himself became "the end of sins and the beginning of righteousness, as Gabriel said in Dan. 9:24, 'to put an end to sin and to bring in everlasting righteousness.' "[28] While "the blood of Abel cries out for wrath and vengeance, . . . the blood of Christ cries out for forgiveness and mercy."[29]

While recognizing that God, as the Source of life, cannot suffer and die, Luther suggested that Christ's divine nature was so blended with His human nature that it also suffered and died. Luther argues,

> If it cannot be said that God died for us, but only a man, we are lost; but if God's death and a dead God lie in the balance, his side goes down and ours goes up like a light and empty scale. Yet he can also readily go up again, or leap out of the scale! But he could not sit on the scale unless he had become a man like us, so that it could be called God's dying, God's martyrdom, God's blood, and God's death. For God in his own nature cannot die; but now that God and man are united in one person, it is called God's death when the man dies who is one substance or one person with God.[30]

In his "The Misuse of the Mass" (1521), Luther criticized Roman Catholic priests for teaching that at the Eucharist they were repeating Christ's sacrifice, whereas Hebrews 9:26 states that the sacrifice was "once for all" (NRSV). He affirmed that "Christ has sacrificed himself once [Heb. 7:27; 9:25-26]; henceforth he will not be sacrificed by anyone else." Since His "sacrifice is a living sacrifice," it is powerful and effective forever, and there is no need for any other atoning sacrifice.[31]

Christ's heavenly priesthood

Luther was indebted to the Greek dichotomist perspective of the earthly and heavenly realities. Consequently, he could not conceive of the existence of a real and concrete sanctuary or temple in a spiritual heaven. In 1525, he stated, "In the new order, the tabernacle or house is spiritual; for it is heaven, or the presence of God."[32] He saw Christ Himself as that sanctuary. But if this is the case, how do we understand passages that affirm that Christ, after His ascension, "entered once for all into the holy places" (Hebrews 9:12, ESV) and became "a minister in the holy places" (Hebrews 8:2, ESV)?

> We must recognize that Luther did not limit the priesthood of Christ to His atoning sacrifice on the cross, as some are inclined to do. Luther regarded Christ's priestly ministry in heaven as absolutely crucial for our salvation.

We must recognize that Luther did not limit the priesthood of Christ to His atoning sacrifice on the cross, as some are inclined to do. Luther regarded Christ's priestly ministry in heaven as absolutely crucial for our salvation. He confessed that "nothing in Scripture is more comforting than what is said about the priestly office of our dear Christ."[33]

As a High Priest, Christ represents God's people "before God and speaks in their interests."[34] But even more, He is also "the true King of Righteousness, who rules us through His priestly office. Through Him we are redeemed from sin and the power of the devil and come to eternal righteousness."[35] In reality, Christ "intercede[s] for us that such weakness and sin may not be reckoned to our account." In doing so, Christ does not only "pray for us" but also applies the merits of His sacrifice to us. He "continues to present His sacrifice to the Father, to plead for us without ceasing, until the end of the world."[36] According to the Reformer, after "Christ, by his own sacrifice and blood, has taken away the true sin," "He has gone in once for all through the curtain to God to make atonement for us [Heb. 9:12]."[37] In this statement, Luther suggests that Christ's priestly work in heaven is still an atoning work on our behalf.

For Luther, Christ's heavenly priesthood had an incredibly meaningful existential dimension. We are encouraged to do the following:

> Do not despair after sin, but lift your eyes on high to where Christ intercedes for us. He is our Advocate. He intercedes for us and says: "Father, I have suffered for this person; I am looking after him." This prayer cannot be in vain. In Heb. 4:14 we read: "We have a great High Priest." But even though we have had Christ as our High Priest, Advocate, Mediator, Reconciler, and Comforter, yet we have fled for refuge to the saints and have

regarded Christ as Judge. Accordingly, this text should be written with golden letters and should be painted in the heart. Therefore you should get understanding and say: "Christ, I know Thee alone as the Advocate, the Comforter, and the Mediator; and I do not doubt that Thou art such a Person for me but cling firmly to this with my heart and believe." Christ is born for us, suffers, ascends into heaven for our sakes, sits at the right hand of the Father, and intercedes for us.[38]

By contrast, Luther regretted that Catholic priests taught "the people absolutely nothing concerning this priestly office of Christ."[39] He saw the Catholic priesthood as an abomination intended to cast away the truth about Christ's priesthood. He stated that "into this holy, glorious, happy, gracious priesthood [of Christ] the devil's swine, the pope, has fallen snout and all; not only defiling it, but completely destroying and suppressing it, and setting up another priesthood, one of his own, stirred together out of all the heathen priesthoods like a stew of abominations."[40]

Luther declared, "Every promise of God includes Christ; for if it is separated from this Mediator, God is not dealing with us at all."[41]

We have highlighted the basic concepts of Luther's understanding of Christ's priesthood as comprising the atoning sacrifice of the cross and also a mediatory work in heaven. Keeping these concepts in mind, we turn to the Adventist understanding of the theme, with special attention to Ellen G. White's contributions.

SEVENTH-DAY ADVENTISM

While there are many similarities between Luther's and Seventh-day Adventism's understanding of Christ's priesthood, some basic differences exist. The Roman Catholic and Protestant worldviews were largely shaped by the Greek concept of the immortality of the soul or spirit that survives the death of the body.[42] This view became the basis of their anthropologies and distinctions between the present *tangible* world and the heavenly *spiritual* reality.

By contrast, Seventh-day Adventists have a more Hebrew, wholistic perspective of reality.[43] According to H. Wheeler Robinson, in Hebrew psychology there is no trichotomy, dividing "human personality into body, soul, and spirit" and "not even a dichotomy in any strict sense." "The Hebrew idea of personality is an animated body, and not an incarnated soul."[44]

For Roman Catholics and many Protestants, the idea of a real sanctuary in heaven sounds too *literalistic*. At the same time, Adventists find this notion in harmony with the Bible. While Luther provided insightful glimpses into the ongoing conflict between Christ and Satan,[45] Adventist theology is shaped by the great cosmic-historical controversy between good and evil.

Old Testament types

Luther viewed the Mosaic tabernacle, Levitical priesthood, and priesthood of Melchizedek as pointing to Christ's atoning sacrifice and His heavenly priesthood. But at times he tended to overemphasize the distinction between the Old and the New Testaments, between the law and the gospel.[46] Ellen White, for example, softened that distinction by speaking of the gospel of salvation by grace through faith as already available in the Old Testament (Genesis 15:6; Isaiah 55:1–3; Ephesians 2:8–10).[47]

White argued that "there is no such contrast as is often claimed to exist between the Old and the New Testament, the law of God and the gospel of Christ, the requirements of the Jewish and those of the Christian dispensation."[48] "The whole system of types and symbols was a compacted prophecy of the gospel, a presentation in which were bound up the promises of redemption."[49] "The Old Testament is the gospel in figures and symbols. The New Testament is the substance. One is as essential as the other."[50]

The most significant difference between Luther and an Adventist's view of Christ's priesthood concerns their understandings about the typological relationship between the earthly and the heavenly sanctuaries. Both hold to a Christ-centered interpretation of the former. Luther reduced the latter to the Person of Christ, enthroned on the right side of God the Father (John 2:21; Hebrews 10:19, 20). Adventists expand upon this notion[51] to encompass also Christ's priestly ministry *within* His heavenly sanctuary or temple (Hebrews 8:2; Revelation 11:19).[52]

Ellen White explains that God not only presented to Moses "a view of the heavenly sanctuary" itself but also gave him "the plan of that structure"—"a miniature representation of the heavenly temple"—as a model for the earthly sanctuary (Exodus 25:9, 40).[53] Richard M. Davidson argues, "In Exod. 25:9, 40, it appears probably that תינכת (and τύπος in vs. 40, LXX) refers to a *Nachbild* [copy] of an original *Urbild* (or perhaps the *Urbild* itself) that serves as a *Vorbild* [model]. It has in view the 'pattern' for the earthly sanctuary that is simultaneously a miniature of the heavenly sanctuary and ultimately encompasses a vision of the heavenly sanctuary itself."[54]

Ellen White, like Luther, defined the Old Testament sanctuary services as foreshadowing Christ's atoning sacrifice and His heavenly priestly ministry. She explains, "Christ was the foundation and life of the temple. Its services were typical of the sacrifice of the Son of God. The priesthood was established to represent the mediatorial character and work of Christ. The entire plan of sacrificial worship was a foreshadowing of the Saviour's death to redeem the world."[55] She also stated, "In the sacrificial offering on every altar was seen a Redeemer. With the cloud of incense arose from every contrite heart the prayer that God would accept their offerings as showing faith in the coming Saviour."[56]

While Luther spoke of the sanctuary services in more general terms,

Adventists draw a clearer distinction between the daily and the annual services. By 1843, William Miller suggested that as the spring feasts of Israel were fulfilled at Christ's first coming (Leviticus 23:4–22; cf. John 13:1; Acts 2:1–4), so the autumn ones pointed toward events related to His second coming (Leviticus 23:23–43).[57] In an article from 1846, "The Law of Moses," O. R. L. Crosier argued that the two chambers of the earthly tabernacle—the Holy Place and the Most Holy Place—reflected the two compartments of the heavenly sanctuary or temple (Hebrews 9:1–3) and that they foreshadowed two distinct phases of Christ's heavenly priesthood.[58]

The nature of Christ

Over the years, several discussions and tensions emerged within Seventh-day Adventism about the nature of Christ.[59] The important point for this chapter is to observe a few statements and expressions by Ellen White that represent her stand on this topic.

In agreement with Luther, Ellen White declared, "In Christ, divinity and humanity were combined. Divinity was not degraded to humanity; divinity held its place, but humanity by being united to divinity, withstood the fiercest test of temptation in the wilderness."[60] For her, Christ's claim of being "the resurrection and the life" (John 11:25) implied that "in Christ is life, original, unborrowed, underived."[61] In reality, "the Lord Jesus Christ, the divine Son of God, existed from eternity, a distinct person, yet one with the Father."[62]

White acknowledged, "Jesus accepted humanity when the race had been weakened by four thousand years of sin" and that He "took upon Him[self] the infirmities of degenerate humanity," "with the possibility of yielding to temptation."[63] But she also warned, "Be careful, exceedingly careful, as to how you dwell upon the human nature of Christ. . . . He could have sinned; He could have fallen, but not for one moment was there in Him an evil propensity."[64]

Christ's atoning sacrifice

Ellen White stated that Christ's "whole life was a preface to His death on the cross."[65] Like Luther, she also emphasized the value of Christ's atoning sacrifice for the salvation of the sinners. She explained that "Christ was treated as we deserve, that we might be treated as He deserves. He was condemned for our sins, in which He had no share, that we might be justified by His righteousness, in which we had no share. He suffered the death which was ours, that we might receive the life which was His. 'With His stripes we are healed.' "[66]

White saw the Cross as having a broader and far-enduring cosmic influence. She declared, "But the work of human redemption is not all that is accomplished by the cross. The love of God is manifested to the universe."[67] Indeed, "all the blessings of this life and of the life to come are delivered to us stamped with the cross of Calvary."[68]

She even recognized the Cross as the only means to prevent any future rebellion after sin and sinners are finally destroyed (Malachi 4:1). In her words,

> The death of Christ upon the cross made sure the destruction of him who has the power of death, who was the originator of sin. When Satan is destroyed, there will be none to tempt to [do] evil; the atonement will never need to be repeated; and there will be no danger of another rebellion in the universe of God. That which alone can effectually restrain from sin in this world of darkness, will prevent sin in heaven. The significance of the death of Christ will be seen by saints and angels. . . . The angels ascribe honor and glory to Christ, for even they are not secure except by looking to the sufferings of the Son of God. It is through the efficacy of the cross that the angels of heaven are guarded from apostasy. . . . The death of Christ on the cross of Calvary is our only hope in this world, and it will be our theme in the world to come.[69]

Luther recognized that only by becoming human could Christ die on the cross. But Ellen White stated this more explicitly, "When Christ was crucified, it was His human nature that died. Deity did not sink and die; that would have been impossible."[70] In a magazine article, after quoting John 11:25 ("I am the resurrection and the life"), she added, "He who had said, 'I lay down my life, that I might take it again' (John 10:17), came forth from the grave to life that was in Himself. Humanity died; divinity did not die. In His divinity, Christ possessed the power to break the bonds of death. He declares that He has life in Himself to quicken whom He will."[71]

The apostle Paul says that at the cross "God was in Christ reconciling the world to Himself," and now, through Christ's mediation in the heavenly sanctuary, we can be individually "reconciled to God" (2 Corinthians 5:19, 20). No wonder Ellen White acknowledged that "the intercession of Christ in man's behalf in the sanctuary above is as essential to the plan of salvation as was His death upon the cross."[72]

Christ's heavenly priesthood

Both Luther and early Adventists saw Christ's heavenly priesthood as crucial for salvation. Agreeing with the Reformer, Ellen White stated, "By the atoning sacrifice of Christ, and his work of mediation in our behalf, we may become reconciled to God."[73]

But Adventists differ from Luther in two major aspects. The first is with the *place* of Christ's mediatory work in heaven. While Luther's view of the heavenly sanctuary was focused on the biblical image of God's throne (Acts 7:55, 56; Hebrews 10:12; 12:2; 1 Peter 3:22; etc.), Adventists have expanded that view to include the many biblical allusions to a real sanctuary or temple in heaven

(Psalm 11:4; Hebrews 8:1, 2; 9:11, 12; Revelation 11:19; 14:17; 15:5; 16:17; etc.).[74]

The notion that the heavenly sanctuary or temple comprises two compartments—a Holy Place *and* a Most Holy Place—derived from (1) the concept that both the Mosaic tabernacle and the Jerusalem temple were built with two holy places that at the same time resembled (Exodus 25:8, 9, 40; 39:32–43; 1 Chronicles 28:10–19; Wisdom 9:8) and foreshadowed (Hebrews 9:1–9) the heavenly sanctuary; (2) the use of the plural "holy places" (from the original Greek *ta hágia*) in reference to the heavenly sanctuary (Hebrews 8:2; 9:8, 12; 10:19); and (3) those descriptions of God's heavenly temple in which allusions are made to such Holy Place furniture as the candlestick with seven lamps (Revelation 4:5; cf. Zechariah 4:2), the golden altar of incense (Revelation 8:3; 9:13), and the golden censer (Revelation 8:3) and to the ark of God's testament in the Most Holy Place (Revelation 11:19; cf. Psalm 99:1).[75]

The second area in which Adventists diverge from Luther is the actual *nature* of Christ's priesthood in heaven. While Luther limited it to a single mediatory work of atonement for the forgiveness of sin, Adventists describe it as a two-phase priesthood carried on in the two-apartment heavenly sanctuary or temple. The first phase corresponded to a mediatory work in the Holy Place (1 Timothy 2:5; Hebrews 4:14–16; 1 John 2:1, 2); this is very much in terms of what Luther described. But the second phase was seen as taking place in the Most Holy Place and added to the mediatory work the cleansing of that sanctuary (Daniel 8:14; Hebrews 9:23) by means of a pre-Advent investigative judgment (Daniel 7:9–14; Revelation 11:19; 14:6, 7).[76] The transition between the two phases was marked in 1844 by the end of the 2,300 symbolic evenings and mornings of Daniel 8:14.[77]

When describing the installment of that judgment, Daniel 7 mentions that "thrones were put in place" (verse 9), the movable throne of God had wheels like "a burning fire" (verse 9), and the "Son of Man" (Christ) went to the "Ancient of Days" (God the Father) (verse 13).[78] Daniel 7 explains that the judgment is at the same time against the "horn" that persecuted the saints and "in favor of the saints of the Most High" (verses 21, 22).

When Christ finishes His mediatory and judicial work in the heavenly sanctuary or temple, He will take His faithful children to heaven, where they will serve Him in His temple. As foreseen by the apostle John, "Therefore they are before the throne of God, and serve Him day and night in His temple. And He who sits on the throne will dwell among them" (Revelation 7:15).

In line with Luther, Adventists view the Roman Catholic papacy and its priestly system—including the sacrifice of the Mass and the claim that Catholic priests can forgive sins—as a counterfeit to Christ's sacrifice on the cross and His heavenly priesthood (Daniel 7:20–25; 8:9–13; Matthew 24:15; 2 Thessalonians 2:1–12).[79] Ellen White declared that the "compromise between paganism and Christianity resulted in the development" of a "gigantic system of false religion" that can be considered "a masterpiece of Satan's power."[80]

In part, the Catholic priesthood challenged Luther to start the Reformation of the sixteenth century. More than three centuries later, early Adventists felt the burden to continue that restoration process. As Luther restored the centrality of Christ's atoning sacrifice on the cross and, to some extent, His heavenly priesthood, so Adventists viewed themselves as restoring both dimensions.

CONCLUSION

One of the most meaningful themes of Scripture is the sanctuary and its services. This theme flows from the early patriarchal altars through the Mosaic tabernacle and the temple of Jerusalem. It reaches its climax at Christ's sacrifice on the cross and His priestly ministry in the heavenly sanctuary. The sanctuary is the abiding place of God (Exodus 25:8; Isaiah 6:1; Revelation 11:19), the depository of His law (Exodus 25:16; 31:18; Revelation 11:19), and the place where salvation is available to all (Hebrews 4:14–16; 1 John 2:1, 2).[81] Luther confessed, "Nothing in Scripture is more comforting than what is said about the priestly office of our dear Christ."[82] And Ellen White added, "The correct understanding of the ministration in the heavenly sanctuary is the foundation of our faith."[83]

According to Luther, Christ offered Himself as a single, self-sufficient, and unrepeatable atoning sacrifice for the sins of the whole world. At the right hand of God, Christ now "make[s] atonement for us [Heb. 9:12],"[84] and He "continues to present His sacrifice to the Father, to plead for us without ceasing, until the end of the world."[85] Luther claimed that the Catholic papacy and priesthood attempted to overthrow Christ's sacrifice on the cross and His heavenly priesthood.

Adventists resonate with Luther's view of the atoning nature of both Christ's sacrifice on the cross and His priesthood in heaven. Luther limited the heavenly priesthood exclusively to the biblical image of God's throne. Adventists see Christ's priesthood as taking place within a real heavenly sanctuary or temple, which is comprised of two compartments—a Holy Place and a Most Holy Place—or at least of two distinct phases. In 1844, at the end of the 2,300 symbolic evenings and mornings of Daniel 8:14, Christ began a special work of pre-Advent investigative judgment (Daniel 7:9–14; Revelation 11:19; 14:6, 7).

As I argue elsewhere, "The everlasting gospel flows through the sanctuary motif, integrating the plan of salvation into an unfolding whole."[86] We can better understand what Christ already did, what He is now doing, and what He will still do for our salvation. We can, by faith, accept His atoning sacrifice on the cross, behold His priesthood in the heavenly sanctuary or temple, and look for that glorious day when we will worship Him "in His temple" (Revelation 7:15).

1. Unless otherwise noted, all Scripture references in this chapter are from the New King James Version.

2. The section is largely based on my chapter "The Priesthood of Christ According to Martin Luther," in *Christ, Salvation, and the Eschaton: Essays in Honor of Hans K. LaRondelle*, ed. Daniel Heinz, Jiří Moskala, and Peter M. van Bemmelen (Berrien Springs, MI: Old Testament Department, Seventh-day Adventist Theological Seminary, Andrews University, 2009), 171–187.

3. For further study of Luther's early dependence on Aristotelianism and his later breaking away from it, see, e.g., Theodor Dieter, *Der junge Luther und Aristoteles: Eine historisch-systematische Untersuchung zum Verhältnis von Theologie und Philosophie* (Berlin: Walter de Gruyter, 2001); Robert Kolb, Irene Dingel, and Ľubomír Batka, eds., *The Oxford Handbook of Martin Luther's Theology* (Oxford: Oxford University Press, 2014), 91–114.

4. In 1520, Luther argued that Scriptures "are to be retained in their simplest meaning ever possible, and to be understood in their grammatical and literal sense unless the context plainly forbids." Martin Luther, *Luther's Works*, vol. 36, *Word and Sacrament 2*, ed. Abdel R. Wentz (Philadelphia, PA: Fortress, 1959), 30. See also Martin Luther, *Luther's Works*, vol. 1, *Lectures on Genesis, Chapter 1–5*, ed. Jaroslav Pelikan (Philadelphia, PA: Fortress, 1958), 232, 233.

5. Martin Luther, *Luther's Works*, vol. 31, *Career of the Reformer 1*, ed. Harold J. Grimm (Philadelphia, PA: Fortress, 1957), 12 (thesis 41 and 50 of Luther's "Disputation Against Scholastic Theology"). In a letter dated February 8, 1517, Luther wrote to Johannes Lang, "If Aristotle had not lived in the flesh I should not hesitate to call him a devil." Preserved Smith, *The Life and Letters of Martin Luther* (Boston, MA: Houghton Mifflin, 1911), 26.

6. Miriam van Scott, "Theocentric Heaven," in *Encyclopedia of Heaven* (New York: Thomas Dunne Books, 1999).

7. Martin Luther, *Luther's Works*, vol. 13, *Selected Psalms 2*, ed. Jaroslav Pelikan (St. Louis, MO: Concordia, 1956), 317.

8. See Martin Luther, *Luther's Works*, vol. 29, *Lectures on Titus, Philemon, and Hebrews*, ed. Hilton C. Oswald (St. Louis, MO: Concordia, 1968), 200–203.

9. Ibid., 13:317.

10. Ibid., 36:200, 219.

11. Ibid., 29:213. Luther refers to the "Ceremonial Law" also in Martin Luther, *Luther's Works*, vol. 4, *Lectures on Genesis, Chapters 21–25*, ed. Jaroslav Pelikan (St. Louis, MO: Concordia, 1964), 81; Martin Luther, *Luther's Works*, vol. 12, *Selected Psalms 1*, ed. Jaroslav Pelikan (St. Louis, MO: Concordia, 1955), 85, 398, 401, 402; Martin Luther, *Luther's Works*, vol. 26, *Lectures on Galatians, 1535, Chapters 1–4*, ed. Walter A. Hansen (St. Louis, MO: Concordia, 1963), 121–123, 130, 138, 156, 157, 180, 181, 202, 203, 330, 333, 446, 447; Martin Luther, *Luther's Works*, vol. 32, *Career of the Reformer 2*, ed. George W. Forell (St. Louis, MO: Concordia, 1958), 178; Martin Luther, *Luther's Works*, vol. 46, *The Christian in Society 3*, ed. Robert Schultz (St. Louis, MO: Concordia, 1967), 146; Martin Luther, *Luther's Works*, vol. 47, *The Christian in Society 4*, ed. Jaroslav Pelikan (St. Louis, MO: Concordia, 1971), 88n25.

12. Luther, *Luther's Works*, 29:168.

13. Ibid., 13:305.

14. Ibid.

15. Ibid., 13:306.

16. Martin Luther, *Luther's Works*, vol. 2, *Lectures on Genesis, Chapters 6–14*, ed. Jaroslav Pelikan (St. Louis, MO: Concordia, 1960), 381.

17. Ibid., 13:312, 313.

18. Johannes Zachhuber, "Jesus Christ in Martin Luther," Academia, 1, accessed July 17, 2017, https://www.academia.edu/29044077/Jesus_Christ_in_Martin_Luther. Cf. Jan D. Kingston Siggins, *Martin Luther's Doctrine of Christ* (New Haven, CT: Yale University Press, 1970); Marc Lienhard, *Luther: Witness to Jesus Christ*, trans. Edwin H. Robertson (Minneapolis, MN: Augsburg, 1982).

19. Luther, *Luther's Works*, 13:304.

20. Zachhuber, "Jesus Christ in Martin Luther," 15 (italics in the original).

21. Luther, *Luther's Works*, 36:35.

22. Ibid., 31:351.

23. Martin Luther, *Luther's Works*, vol. 37, *Word and Sacrament 3*, ed. Robert H. Fischer (Minneapolis, MN: Fortress, 1970), 218.

24. Martin Luther, "Disputation on the Divinity and Humanity of Christ," trans. Christopher B. Brown, Internet Christian Library, accessed July 17, 2017, http://www.iclnet.org/pub/resources/text/wittenberg/luther/luther-divinity.txt. Originally published as Martin Luther, "Die Disputation de divinitate et humanitate Christi," in *D. Martin Luthers Werke: Kritische Gesamtausgabe*, vol. 39, bk. 2 (Weimar: Hermann Böhlau, 1932), 107.

25. Luther, *Luther's Works*, 13:326.

26. Ibid., 13:319.

27. Ulrich Asendorf, *Die Theologie Martin Luthers nach seinen Predigten* (Göttingen: Vandenhoeck and Ruprecht, 1988), 103.

28. Luther, *Luther's Works*, 29:210, 212.

29. Ibid., 29:169.

30. Martin Luther, *Luther's Works*, vol. 41, *Church and Ministry 3*, ed. Eric W Gritsch (St. Louis, MO: Concordia, 1966), 103, 104.

31. Ibid., 36:147, 201.

32. Martin Luther, *Luther's Epistle Sermons: Epiphany, Easter and Pentecost*, trans. John Nicholas Lenker, vol. 2 (Minneapolis, MN: Luther Press), 164.

33. Luther, *Luther's Works*, 13:306.

34. Ibid., 13:308.

35. Ibid., 13:311.

36. Ibid., 13:320, 326.

37. Martin Luther, *Luther's Works*, vol. 35, *Word and Sacrament 1*, ed. E. Theodore Bachmann (St. Louis, MO: Concordia, 1960), 247.

38. Martin Luther, *Luther's Works*, vol. 30, *The Catholic Epistles*, ed. Jaroslav Pelika, (St. Louis, MO: Concordia, 1967), 236.

39. Ibid., 13:326.

40. Ibid., 36:201.

41. Martin Luther, *Luther's Works*, vol. 3, *Lectures on Genesis, Chapters 15–20*, ed. Jaroslav Pelikan (St. Louis, MO: Concordia, 1961), 26.

42. A classic exposition of this theory is found in Dante Alighieri's *The Divine Comedy*, trans. Henry W. Longfellow (New York: Barnes and Noble, 2008). This epic poem was written between 1308 and 1321.

43. A helpful analysis of how philosophical presuppositions can influence one's understanding of the biblical sanctuary is provided in Fernando L. Canale, "Philosophical Foundations and the Biblical Sanctuary," *Andrews University Seminary Studies* 36, no. 2 (Autumn 1998): 183–206.

44. H. Wheeler Robinson, "Hebrew Psychology," in *The People and the Book*, ed. Arthur S. Peake (Oxford: Clarendon, 1925), 362.

45. See Hans-Martin Barth, *Der Teufel und Jesus Christus in der Theologie Martin Luthers*, Forschungen zur Kirchen- und Dogmengeschichte 19 (Göttingen: Vandenhoeck and Ruprecht, 1967).

46. See Paul Althaus's analysis of Luther's distinction between the law and the gospel in *The Theology of Martin Luther*, trans. Robert C. Schultz (Philadelphia, PA: Fortress, 1966), 251–273; Gerhard Ebeling, *Luther: An Introduction to His Thought*, trans. R. A. Wilson (Minneapolis, MN: Fortress, 1972), 110–124; William M. Landeen, *Martin Luther's Religious Thought* (Mountain View, CA: Pacific Press® Pub. Assn., 1971), 174–190.

47. Ellen G. White, "Obedience Better Than Sacrifice," *Signs of the Times*, September 14, 1882, 409.

48. Ibid.

49. Ellen G. White, *The Acts of the Apostles* (Mountain View, CA: Pacific Press® Pub. Assn., 1911), 14.

50. Ellen G. White, *Selected Messages*, vol. 2 (Washington, DC: Review and Herald® Pub. Assn., 1958), 104.

51. For Adventist reflections on God's throne motif, see, e.g., Daegeuk Nam, *The "Throne of God" Motif in the Hebrew Bible*, Sahmyook University Doctoral Dissertation Series 1 (Seoul: Institute for Theological Research, Sahmyook University, 1994); Laszlo Gallusz, *The Throne Motif in the Book of Revelation*, Library of New Testament Studies (London: Bloomsbury, 2014).

52. Helpful Adventist assessments of the heavenly sanctuary or temple motif in the Bible are provided by Sanglae Kim, "The Heavenly Sanctuary/Temple in the Hebrew Bible" (PhD diss., University of Sheffield, 2002); Elias Brasil de Souza, *The Heavenly Sanctuary/Temple Motif in the Hebrew Bible: Function and Relationship to the Earthly Counterparts*, Adventist Theological Society Dissertation Series (Berrien Springs, MI: Adventist Theological Society Publications, 2005), published also as *Toward a Theology of the Heavenly Sanctuary in the Hebrew Bible* (Saarbrücken, Germany: VDM Verlag, 2008); Leonardo G. Nunes, "Function and Nature of the Heavenly Sanctuary/Temple in the New Testament: A Motif Study" (ThD diss., Andrews University, forthcoming).

53. Ellen G. White, *Patriarchs and Prophets* (Washington, DC: Review and Herald® Pub. Assn., 1958), 343.

54. Richard M. Davidson, *Typology in Scripture: A Study of Hermeneutical τύπος Structures*, Andrews University Seminary Doctoral Dissertation Series (Berrien Springs, MI: Andrews University Press, 1981), 388. See also ibid., 367–388; Richard M. Davidson, "Typology in the Book of Hebrews," in *Issues in the Book of Hebrews*, ed. Frank B. Holbrook, Daniel and Revelation

Committee Series (Silver Spring, MD: Biblical Research Institute, 1989), 121–186.

55. Ellen G. White, *The Desire of Ages* (Mountain View, CA: Pacific Press® Pub. Assn., 1940), 165.

56. Ellen G. White, "The Two Dispensations," *Review and Herald*, March 2, 1886, 129.

57. William Miller, "Letter From Wm. Miller," *Signs of the Times* [Millerite], May 17, 1843, 85, accessed July 18, 2017, https://adventistdigitallibrary.org/islandora/object/adl:367580/datastream/PDF/view.

58. O. R. L. Crosier, "The Law of Moses," *Day-Star* Extra, February 7, 1846, 37–44.

59. For an introduction to the Seventh-day Adventist Christological discussions, see Eric C. Webster, *Crosscurrents in Adventist Christology* (New York: Peter Lang, 1984).

60. Ellen G. White, "How to Meet a Controverted Point of Doctrine," *Review and Herald*, February 18, 1890, 97.

61. White, *The Desire of Ages*, 530. Ellen White borrowed the language of John Cumming who, in 1856, stated in his *Sabbath Evening Readings on the New Testament: St. John* (Boston, MA: John P. Jewett and Co., 1856), 5, that " 'in him [Christ] was life,'—that is, original, unborrowed, underived."

62. Ellen G. White, "The Word Made Flesh," *Signs of the Times*, April 26, 1899, 1, repr. in Ellen G. White, *Selected Messages*, vol. 1 (Washington, DC: Review and Herald® Pub. Assn., 1958), 247.

63. White, *The Desire of Ages*, 49, 117.

64. Ellen G. White to W. L. H. Baker, February 9, 1896, Lt. 8, 1895, Ellen G. White Writings, accessed July 18, 2017, https://m.egwwritings.org/en/book/6474.2000001#20.

65. Ellen G. White to W. W. Prescott, Granville, New South Wales, Australia, June 12, 1895, Lt. 67, 1895, Ellen G. White Writings, accessed July 18, 2017, https://m.egwwritings.org/en/book/5403.2000001#11.

66. White, *The Desire of Ages*, 25.

67. Ibid., 626.

68. Ellen G. White, *Christ's Object Lessons* (Washington, DC: Review and Herald® Pub. Assn., 1941), 362.

69. Ellen G. White, "What Was Secured by the Death of Christ," *Signs of the Times*, December 30, 1889, 786. See also Ellen G. White, *The Truth About Angels* (Boise, ID: Pacific Press® Pub. Assn., 1996), 296.

70. Ellen G. White to Ministers, Physicians, and Teachers, Middletown, Connecticut, September 3, 1904, Lt. 280, 1904, Ellen G. White Writings, accessed July 18, 2017, https://m.egwwritings.org/en/book/10626.2000001#16, repr. in Francis D. Nichol, ed., *The Seventh-day Adventist Bible Commentary*, vol. 5 (Washington, DC: Review and Herald® Pub. Assn., 1956), 1113.

71. White, *Selected Messages*, 1:301.

72. White, *The Great Controversy*, 489.

73. Ellen G. White, "The Cities of Refuge," *Signs of the Times*, January 20, 1881, 26.

74. E.g., O. R. L. Crosier, "The Law of Moses," 38, 40, 41; J. N. Andrews, *The Sanctuary and Twenty-Three Hundred Days* (Rochester, NY: James White, 1853), 52–54; [Uriah Smith],

"Synopsis of the Present Truth, No. 15," *Review and Herald*, February 18, 1858, 116, 117; Uriah Smith, *The Sanctuary and Twenty-Three Hundred Days of Daniel VIII, 14* (Battle Creek, MI: Steam Press of the Seventh-day Adventist Publishing Association, 1863), 36–51.

75. E.g., Crosier, "The Law of Moses," 38, 40, 41; Andrews, *The Sanctuary and Twenty-Three Hundred Days*, 52–54; [Smith], "Synopsis of the Present Truth, No. 15," 116, 117; Smith, *The Sanctuary and Twenty-Three Hundred Days of Daniel VIII, 14*, 36–51.

76. E.g., Crosier, "The Law of Moses," 42–44; Joseph Bates, *An Explanation of the Typical and Anti-typical Sanctuary, by the Scriptures, With a Chart* (New Bedford, MA: Benjamin Lindsey, 1850), 10; Smith, *The Sanctuary and Twenty-Three Hundred Days of Daniel VIII, 14*, 51–78.

For further study of the early Adventist understanding of the cleansing of the sanctuary and the investigative judgment, see Timm, *The Sanctuary and the Three Angels' Messages: Integrating Factors in the Development of Seventh-day Adventist Doctrines*, Adventist Theological Society Dissertation Series (Berrien Springs, MI: Andrews University Press, 1995), 70–78, 161–174.

For a more detailed Adventist exposition of the biblical bases for an investigative judgment, see William H. Shea, *Selected Studies on Prophetic Interpretation*, rev. ed., Daniel and Revelation Committee Series (Silver Spring, MD: Biblical Research Institute, 1992).

77. More in-depth historical-chronological studies of the 2,300 evenings and mornings of Daniel 8:14 are provided in Siegfried H. Horn and Lynn H. Wood, *The Chronology of Ezra 7*, 2nd and rev. ed. (Washington, DC: Review and Herald® Pub. Assn., 1970); Frank B. Holbrook, ed., *Symposium on Daniel*, Daniel and Revelation Committee Series (Washington, DC: Biblical Research Institute, 1986); Frank B. Holbrook, ed., *The Seventy Weeks, Leviticus, and the Nature of Prophecy*, Daniel and Revelation Committee Series (Washington, DC: Biblical Research Institute, 1986); Brempong Owusu-Antwi, *The Chronology of Daniel 9:24–27*, Adventist Theological Society Dissertation Series (Berrien Springs, MI: Adventist Theological Society, 1995); Juarez R. de Oliveira, *Chronological Studies Related to Daniel 8:14 and 9:24–27* (São Paulo, Brazil: Imprensa Universitária Adventista, 2004). See also Alberto R. Timm, "Miniature Symbolization and the Year-Day Principle of Prophetic Interpretation," *Andrews University Seminary Studies* 42, no. 1 (Spring 2004): 149–167.

78. See Ellen G. White, *Early Writings of Ellen G. White* (Washington, DC: Review and Herald® Pub. Assn., 1945), 55.

79. See *Seventh-day Adventists Believe*, 2nd ed. (Silver Spring, MD: Ministerial Association, General Conference of Seventh-day Adventists, 2005), 181–189.

80. White, *The Great Controversy*, 50.

81. Alberto R. Timm, "Recognizing Heavenly Realities: Ellen White's Insights Into the Heavenly Sanctuary," *Adventist World*, February 2013, 24.

82. Luther, *Luther's Works*, 13:306.

83. Ellen G. White to George C. Tenney, St. Helena, California, June 29, 1906, Lt. 208, 1906, Ellen G. White Writings, accessed July 18, 2017, https://m.egwwritings.org/en/book/8906.2000001#.

84. Luther, *Luther's Works*, 35:247.

85. Ibid., 13:320, 326.

86. Timm, "Recognizing Heavenly Realities," 25.

CHAPTER 9

The Decalogue
in Luther and Adventism

Jiří Moskala

The Decalogue forms the heart of God's revelation and biblical ethics. It is the Magna Carta of biblical teaching, and its summation is the norm of all norms. It forms the substance and foundation of divine standards for all humanity; its principles are eternal. The Pentateuchal account underlines that it was announced by God (Exodus 19:19; 20:1; Deuteronomy 5:4, 5, 24) and also was written by Him (Exodus 24:12; 31:18; Deuteronomy 5:22). It was twice given to Moses as a special gift (Exodus 32:19; 34:1; Deuteronomy 10:1, 2). In the book of Exodus, the Decalogue is called "the Testimony" (Hebrew *'edut*; Exodus 31:18); and in the book of Deuteronomy, it is named "the words of the covenant" (Hebrew *dibre habberit*; Exodus 34:28). Neither of the books uses the term *Ten Commandments* (Hebrew *mitswah*; however, see Exodus 20:6), but three references call it "the Ten Words" (Hebrew *'aseret haddebarim*, from *dabar* meaning "word," "sentence," "matter," "thing," "speech," "story," "promise," "utterance"; see Exodus 34:28; Deuteronomy 4:13; 10:4). In both Exodus and Deuteronomy, the Decalogue lies at the beginning of the law collections and their interpretation. There are seven main collections of legal material prescribed in the Pentateuch, and the first and principal one is the Decalogue.[1] The legal section of the book of Deuteronomy (Deuteronomy 12–26) is structured according to the Decalogue.[2] There are two versions of the Decalogue with very slight differences: the first one is recorded in Exodus 20:1–17, and the second one in Deuteronomy 5:6–21. The second form, presented orally by Moses to Israel just before entering the Promise Land (Deuteronomy 1:3, 4; 4:44–47), occurred forty years after the first one. These circumstances explain the slight variances that exist between these two versions of the Decalogue.[3] When Paul summarized the law as being love, he quotes from the Decalogue (Romans 8:34; 13:8–10; Galatians 6:5). Love is indeed the sum of God's law because He is the God of love (1 John 4:16).

This is not an exhaustive study on Luther and the Adventist understanding of God's law, because it is a very complex issue. It examines only Luther's crucial references to the law as representative of general ideas in his thinking and then analyzes the significance of these patterns for Adventist thought on the Decalogue.

The Decalogue in Martin Luther

A decade after Martin Luther posted the Ninety-Five Theses, "Erasmus asserted that 'the Lutherans seek two things only—wealth and wives (*censum et uxorem*)' and that to them the Gospel meant 'the right to live as they please.' "[4] This was a challenge because the Reformer was stressing God's grace and people could easily mistake this emphasis to mean that good works and obedience are not vital in a believer's behavior. Yet Luther perceived that the Decalogue does play an important place in the life of a Christian. He considered the Ten Commandments as "a complete guide for Christian living"[5] and that they "are to be used so that the people be exhorted to fear God."[6] For Luther, the primary function of God's law was to show how humans discover their deficiencies and sinfulness. In this way, the law then leads to Christ because the law cannot cleanse people or forgive their sins, otherwise Christ's life and death for us would be of no benefit and in vain. Luther declares that the law "merely drives the conscience to thirst and yearn for the promise of God and to look at Christ."[7]

> Thus the Law serves to indicate the will of God, and it leads us to a realization that we cannot keep it. It also acquaints us with the nature of man, with his capabilities, and with his limitations. The Law was given to us for the revelation of sin; but it does not have the power to save us from sin and rid us of it. It holds a mirror before us; we peer into it and perceive that we are devoid of righteousness and life. And this image impels us to cry: "Oh, come, Lord Jesus Christ, help us and give us grace to enable us to fulfill the Law's demands!"[8]

He states that "whoever knows well this art of distinguishing between Law and Gospel" places such a person "at the head" and he or she deserves to be called "a doctor of Holy Scripture."[9]

Luther wrote his clearest and most comprehensive commentary about the Ten Commandments in his 1529 catechism, particularly in the *Large Catechism* (half of the catechism deals with the Decalogue).[10] He wanted God's people to know how to live an authentic Christian life. He encouraged them to be occupied "with God's commandments and words and to speak, sing, or think about them."[11] He aptly declares, "Nothing is so powerfully effective against the devil, the world, the flesh, and all evil thoughts as to occupy one's self with God's word, to speak about it and meditate on it, in the way that Psalm 1[:2] calls those blessed who 'meditate on God's law day and night.' "[12] In the catechism's introduction, Luther declares, "Those who know the Ten Commandments perfectly know the entire Scriptures."[13] In the catechism's conclusion, he claims that the Decalogue is "a summary of divine teaching" and "the true fountain from which all good works must spring, the true channel through which all good works must flow,"[14] thus being the only reliable source of knowing God's will. The last sentence highlights a significant climax: "Therefore we should prize and value them [the Ten Commandments] above all other teachings as the greatest treasure God has given us."[15]

Luther also believed that before Sinai God's law was given in principles to people within their hearts: " 'Love your neighbor as yourself,' is of no concern to him [Cain]; and likewise the command (Matt. 7:12), 'What you do not want done to yourself, do not do to another.' This Law was not promulgated for the first time in the Decalog [*sic*] but it is written in the hearts of all men. Cain contends against it."[16]

In the *Small Catechism*, Luther underlines the fact that God "promises grace and every blessing to all who keep these Commandments. Therefore, we should also love and trust in Him and willingly do according to His Commandments."[17] Faith and trust in God, for Luther, are the bases for a right relationship with God. They furthermore lead to a correct faith, doctrines, and life. In the *Small Catechism*, Luther explains each commandment with the phrase that "we should fear and love God." For the first commandment, he expanded it with the statement that "we should fear, love, and trust in God above all things"[18] because this commandment is the foundation for the rest of the Decalogue. Luther understands all of God's commandments in the light of the first commandment: "Let each and everyone, then, see to it that you esteem this commandment above all things and not make light of it. Search and examine your own heart thoroughly, and you will discover whether or not it clings to God alone."[19] This commandment is "to illuminate and impart its splendor to all the others. In order that this may be constantly repeated and never forgotten, you must let these concluding words run through all the commandments, like the clasp or hoop of a wreath that binds the end to the beginning and holds everything together."[20] Luther maintains, "All divine promises are based" and "spring from faith in the First Commandment."[21] He states, "All promises have their origin in the First Commandment."[22]

When Luther explains the first commandment, he underlines that it declares war on all forms of idolatry.

> There is, moreover, another false worship. This is the greatest idolatry that we have practiced up until now, and it is still rampant in the world. All the religious orders are founded upon it. This kind of worship involves only the kind of conscience that seeks help, comfort, and salvation in its own works and presumes to wrest heaven from God. Such worship keeps track of the endowments, fasts, and celebrations of the Mass, etc. It relies on such things and boasts of them, unwilling to receive anything as a gift of God, but desiring to earn everything by itself or to merit everything by works of supererogation, just as if God were in our service or debt and we were God's liege lords. What is this but to have made God into an idol . . . and to have set ourselves up as God?[23]

For Luther, faith in God is the most important condition of the heart. This is why unbelief is sin: "Truly, therefore, this temptation [of Eve in the Garden of Eden] is the sum of all temptations; it brings with it the overthrow or the violation of the entire Decalog [sic]. Unbelief is the source of all sins; when Satan brought about this unbelief by driving out or corrupting the Word, the rest was easy for him."[24]

Luther explains the relationship between the first three commandments (directed toward God) and the second table with the other seven commandments (directed toward our neighbor) of the Decalogue.[25] Note their sequence:

> First, we are to trust, fear, and love God with our whole heart all our lives. Second, we should not misuse God's holy name to support lies or any evil purpose whatsoever, but use it for the praise of God and the benefit and salvation of our neighbor and ourselves. Third, on holy days or days of rest we should diligently devote ourselves to God's word so that all our conduct and life may be regulated by it. Now follow the other seven, which relate to our neighbor. Among these the first and greatest is: "You are to honor your father and mother."[26]

Luther states, "The sins against the First Table are far more serious than those against the Second Table."[27] He explains with an illustration: "The First Table must be given precedence over the Second Table. If parents prescribe or command something contrary to God, then the Fourth Commandment, which previously was valid and unalterable, is abrogated. For in the First Commandment it is stated that one must love and honor God above all things."[28] The principle is clear: "The simple and correct method is that . . . the Second is ordered to yield to the First, for God is the Creator, the Head, and the Lord of father and mother, the state, and the home. . . . For the First Table takes precedence, and when it has been obeyed, then also the Second Table has its place."[29]

Luther interprets the sixth commandment in a broader sense to demonstrate that his understanding of the commandments was not literalistic. He rightly points to the intention of this divine regulation: "But inasmuch as there is such a shameless mess and cesspool of all sorts of immorality and indecency among us, this commandment is also directed against every form of unchastity, no matter what it is called."[30] Luther then explains how purity of the heart, lips, and the entire body is crucial; and this purity can be accomplished only when one is truly devoted to God. This is also apparent in the way he treats the last two commandments against covetousness: "So these commandments are aimed directly against envy and miserable covetousness, so that God may remove the root and cause from which arise all injuries to our neighbors. Therefore God sets it in plain words. . . . God wants the heart to be pure, even though, as long as we live here, we cannot accomplish that. So this commandment remains, like all the rest, one that constantly accuses us and shows just how upright we really are in God's sight."[31] The law cannot save, but it can show us our real situation before God and lead us to Him so that He can purify, change, and sanctify us. Thus, the law guides the believer to Christ and, through His grace, to obedience.[32]

Luther denies that the Decalogue is a source of life or the way to salvation. The law cannot impart righteousness. It does not give life nor justify in spite of the fact that it "contains God's eternal commandments."[33] Luther proclaims, "Indeed, even the fulfilment of the Ten Commandments does not save us or make us holy, but only the grace of Christ accomplishes this."[34] "The entire Law, including the Law of the Decalog [sic], is also fatal without faith in Christ. . . . This does not mean that the Law is evil; it means that it cannot contribute anything to justification."[35] "For no matter how much the Law is taught or observed, it does not purify the heart itself."[36]

The Law does not inform man how to live eternally and how to be saved. There we are told what we must do, for the Ten Commandments preach about our works; but we cannot keep them. This message by itself does not lead us to the light. It does teach good works, but man cannot perform these if he has only the Law. Man needs another doctrine, namely, that of the Gospel, which declares: "I, Christ, am the Light." Without this you cannot be saved, for you are and remain in sin and are enveloped in darkness. The Law is detrimental rather than helpful.[37]

Luther emphasizes that there are no merits in obedience: "Thus the Law terrifies you and makes you thirsty, so that you finally ask with fear and trembling: 'What must I do to gain God's favor? I must obtain God's grace. But how? By keeping the Ten Commandments? By amassing good works and much merit? That is impossible.' "[38] For Luther, the law in Galatians represents the entire law. When he deals with Galatians 2:16, he states, "I have warned before, Paul is speaking here not about the Ceremonial Law alone but about the entire Law. For the Ceremonial Law was as much the divine Law as the moral laws were. Thus circumcision, the institution of the priesthood, the service of worship, and the rituals were commanded by God as much as the Decalog [sic] was."[39]

> For Luther, the law and gospel must go together and "should accompany one another."

For Luther, the law and gospel must go together and "should accompany one another."[40] This is documented in his two sermons on the eighteenth Sunday after Trinity Sunday, focusing on Matthew 22:34–46: "Therefore learn, who can learn, and learn well, so that we may know, first the ten commandments, what we owe God. For if we do not know this, then we know nothing and we will not inquire about Christ in the least."[41]

Christ has through his death secured for us the Holy Spirit; and he fulfills the law in us, and not we. For that Spirit, whom God sends into your heart for the sake of his Son, makes an entirely new man out of you, who does with joy and love from the heart everything the law requires, which before would have been impossible for you to do. . . . Then everything God commands is sweet, lovely and agreeable, and I do everything he desires of me; not in my own strength, but by the strength of him that is in me.[42]

"For no one is able to keep the law unless his nature is thoroughly renewed."[43] "The law is to be only an exercise to prove our love."[44] "You may indeed do the works outwardly, but God is not thus satisfied, when they are not done from the heart, out of love; and this is never done except man is born anew through the Holy Spirit."[45] He explains that the Decalogue "teaches what we are to become,"[46] and he adds, "For the Law is not abolished thus by grace."[47] Again he underlines, "It must come to the point that you keep the commandments."[48] "Christ does not only thus cover and protect us, but he will also nourish and feed us as the hen does her little chickens, that is, he gives us the Holy Spirit and strength, to begin to love God and to keep his commandments."[49]

For the redeemed in Christ, the attitude toward the law changes: it is not a source of life but a guide to do good deeds. Luther stresses, "Again and again the Ten Commandments are to be assiduously taught, for all good works are therein comprehended."[50] "To be sure, the Commandments must be kept. Of course, observe them! . . . 'Ah!' you say. 'Don't you preach faith?' Yes, but we also want to see good works performed; yet faith must come first. Then good works will follow."[51] Referring to a person who accepted Christ's righteousness and trusts in Him, Luther writes, "It is therefore impossible that sin should remain in him. This [Christ's] righteousness is primary; it is the basis, the cause, the source of all our own actual righteousness." He adds, "The second kind of righteousness [growth in holiness] is our proper righteousness, not because we alone work it, but because we work with that first and alien righteousness." He explains, "This [second] righteousness is the product of the righteousness of the first type, actually its fruit and consequence."[52] In *The Bondage of the Will*, Luther declares that the Decalogue demonstrates our moral inability. We can love, follow, and obey God only because of His grace and the supernatural work of the Holy Spirit who unites us to Christ.[53]

Luther explains that Christ and His grace liberated us from the condemnation of the law but not from the law itself along with obedience: "Christ frees us from the might of God's Law, from the accusation of the Law or the Decalog [*sic*], and from the obligations of ceremonies."[54] "The Ten Commandments, which deal with holy life and conduct toward God and man, cease too, in the sense that they cannot damn us believers in Christ. He became subject to the Law in order to redeem us who were under the Law (Gal. 4:5); yes, He became a curse for us to save us from the curse of the Law (Gal. 3:13). However, the Ten Commandments are still in force and do concern us Christians so far as obedience to them is concerned."[55]

The Decalogue in Adventism

The Seventh-day Adventist Church's position on the law of God is rooted in the Reformation tradition; whereby, all three uses of the law (civic, pedagogical, and didactic or normative) are included. They can furthermore be perceived as being in harmony with Luther's teaching, even though the emphasis is definitely more positive:

The great principles of God's law are embodied in the Ten Commandments and exemplified in the life of Christ. They express God's love, will, and purposes concerning human conduct and relationships and are binding upon all people in every age. These precepts are the basis of God's covenant with His people and the standard in God's judgment. Through the agency of the Holy Spirit they point out sin and awaken a sense of need for a Saviour. Salvation is all of grace and not of works, but its fruitage is obedience to the Commandments. This obedience develops Christian character and results in a sense of wellbeing. It is an evidence of our love for the Lord and our concern for our fellow human men. The obedience of faith demonstrates the power of Christ to transform lives and therefore strengthens Christian witness.[56]

Both Luther and Seventh-day Adventists emphasize that the function of the law is not to gain salvation through its observance but instead stress that the Decalogue reveals our sinfulness and leads us to Christ.[57] Even though these laws were already known in a nutshell before Sinai,[58] God Himself chose to present the Decalogue to His people and to humanity because these commandments reflect, in a systematic way, who He is, His character, and His values.

> Both Luther and Seventh-day Adventists emphasize that the function of the law is not to gain salvation through its observance but instead stress that the Decalogue reveals our sinfulness and leads us to Christ.

Adventists hold that believers should not keep the law of God in order to be saved but because they are saved. The law of God is not given to build a highway to heaven by our obedience or observance of the law. It is not a source of life but instead is a means to maintain life. The priority and primacy of God's grace is stressed in Adventist circles. Even though obedience and good works are not causes of salvation, they do express the fruit of salvation. They represent love and form an integral part of the redeemed individual's life (Galatians 5:6; Ephesians 2:10; 1 Peter 2:9–12). When saved by grace through faith, faith will not stay alone, but it will be accompanied by deeds of love.

In the Bible, the law of God is seen also in a very positive light (Matthew 5:16, 17; John 14:15; Galatians 3:31; 1 Corinthians 7:19). One may create poems on the law (such as the Psalm 119 masterpiece), sing about the law (Psalm 19), and meditate on it day and night (Psalm 1:2; Joshua 1:8) because it keeps one from evil and gives wisdom, understanding, health, prosperity, and peace (Deuteronomy 4:1–6; Proverbs 2; 3). God's law is a warrant of freedom (Genesis 2:16, 17; James 2:12). It is like a fence that creates a large free space for life and warns that, beyond a specific point, danger, problems, complications, and death await. There is no future for those who step outside the circle of freedom. The law is a mirror in which we can recognize how dirty we are and how much we need to be cleansed (James 1:23–25). (One should not misuse the mirror by looking at it in order to know who is the most beautiful.) Yet the law cannot purify (Romans 3:20). In this way, it leads us as a *paidagogos* to Christ (Galatians 3:24). Thus, the law is a signpost pointing to Jesus, who forgives our sins and changes our lives (2 Corinthians 5:17; 1 John 1:7–9). Louis Berkhof calls the law and the gospel "the two parts of the Word of God as a means of grace."[59] The law and the gospel must always go together, with priority being on the gospel.

Ellen G. White offers an insight into the function of the Decalogue: "The Ten Commandments . . . are ten promises."[60] She stresses that "the voice of God from heaven" speaks "to the soul in promise, 'This do, and you will not come under the dominion and control of Satan.' "[61]

This is why in Seventh-day Adventist thought the Decalogue is perceived as the promise of God.

This is why in Seventh-day Adventist thought the Decalogue is perceived as the promise of God. The Ten Commandments are a special gift from God to guide believers so they will know what He can do for and in them when they let Him. Ellen White declares,

> In the Ten Commandments God has laid down the laws of His kingdom. . . .
> The Lord has given His holy commandments to be a wall of protection around His created beings.[62]

God's law is not a whip to punish—even though if observed, it then restricts evil and directs to the right path—in the same way that reins direct a horse. The Decalogue first needs to be taken as a promise and then as a permanent commandment in order to become a reality in life. It is not merely a prohibition. Ellen White also proclaims, "The ten holy precepts spoken by Christ upon Sinai's mount were the revelation of the character of God."[63] She asserts that the Decalogue is "the greatest love that can be presented to man."[64]

In Hebrew grammar, an infinitive absolute has two meanings in legal material: a command or an emphatic promise.[65] The negative command is expressed in the Decalogue by the negation particle *lʾo* (not) plus the jussive, and the meaning of such a Hebrew expression refers to (1) a permanent prohibition, thus a commandment, or (2) a future situation, thus a promise.[66] The Hebrew meaning of the term *dabar* used in the Pentateuch to describe the Ten Commandments (*dabarim*) does not mean "commandment" but "words." This noun can have the meaning of "a promise," along with its verbal root.[67]

Like Luther, Ellen White unmasks different forms of idolatry, with false conceptions of God being the worst: "It is as easy to make an idol of cherished ideas or objects as to fashion gods of wood or stone. Thousands have a false conception of God and His attributes. They are as verily serving a false god as were the servants of Baal."[68] This is an explanation of the first two commandments.

Adventists understand the law in Galatians as the entire law, including the Decalogue, the same as Luther.[69] Ellen White states,

"The law was our schoolmaster [tutor] to bring us unto Christ, that we might be justified by faith." (Galatians 3:24.) In this scripture, the Holy Spirit through the apostle is speaking especially of the moral law. The law reveals sin to us, and causes us to feel our need of Christ, and to flee unto Him for pardon and peace. . . .

The law of Ten Commandments is not to be looked upon as much from the prohibitory side, as from the mercy side. Its prohibitions are the sure guarantee of happiness in obedience. . . . To the obedient it is a wall of protection. We behold in it the goodness of God, who by revealing to men the immutable principles of righteousness, seeks to shield them from the evils that result from transgression.[70]

Ellen White affirms, "There is not a negative in that law, although it may appear thus."[71] The law's seeming restrictions are only for our good in order to maintain happiness and life (Micah 6:8; John 10:10). The law for those who trust God and are saved by His grace through faith in Christ is a norm of conduct. White states, "God's law is not a new thing. . . . It is a code of principles expressing mercy, goodness, and love. It presents to fallen humanity the character of God, and states plainly the whole duty of man."[72]

The place of the law in the new covenant is amazing—it is planted in the heart. The law should be internalized and should not be seen as a burden but as a joy (Matthew 5:21–48). Those who keep the Decalogue properly need to follow its promises with right motives and obey out of gratitude and thankfulness for what God has done for them. Grace does not change the law, but our attitude toward it does change.

> Grace does not change the law, but our attitude toward it does change.

Paul is against legalism but not against the law of God (Romans 7:9–12). He was against the misuse of the law as well as against the transgression of God's law. Christ took upon Himself the curse, which was the punishment of the law (Galatians 3:13, 14). Because of Christ, we are not under the condemnation of the law and its demands for salvation but under God's grace (Romans 6:14, 15).

Jesus Christ is the *telos* of the law (1 Corinthians 10:4), meaning He is its goal and purpose and not the end in the sense of a termination or cessation of its validity. Robert Badenas concluded that the semantic impact of the word *telos* is primarily teleological, not temporal, and rightly claims, "Christ is the hermeneutical key which makes intelligible what was always the law's true meaning and purpose."[73] Thus, it would be incorrect to state that Christ invalidated, terminated, superseded, or abrogated the law. While the law does not lead only to Christ, Christ is its goal. He gives meaning to the law, so it makes sense that, for believers, the law has a normative function as it advocates the *tertius usus legis* (third use of the law).

Whatever God commands, He enables His followers to do. Ellen White states, "All His biddings are enablings."[74] From that perspective, the Ten Commandments are actually ten beatitudes. The theology of the book of Ezekiel makes this point very clear. Ezekiel explains this thought in the core of his theological summary in chapter 36, verses 26 and 27. We humans, by ourselves, are not able to change our hearts. This is solely the work of God. Only He can transplant our hearts. He removes our hearts of stone and replaces them with sensitive hearts of flesh. We are not able to obey God as Joshua reminded his audience: "You are not able to serve the Lord" (Joshua 24:19, ESV). We can only decide for Him. This is our role. While we do not have the power to fulfill our decision, God will make us strong when we give our weakness to Him. He will give us His Holy Spirit, who will move us to obey Him. Paul says, "When I am weak, then I am strong" (2 Corinthians 12:10, ESV).

Observe the divine *I* in Ezekiel 36:24–30: God gathers, cleanses, removes, gives, puts, and moves you to carefully keep His law. What He is doing, you will do. He identifies with you, and if you associate closely with Him, His doing will be your active doing. The unity between God and you will be dynamic, powerful, and lively. Good work is accomplished only by the power of the Holy Spirit! The emphasis in this passage is on God's doing. The literal translation of verse 27 reads, "I will give My Spirit in you, and I will do that you will walk in My statutes and keep My laws, and you will do." In summary, God says, "I will do that you will do! I will move and cause you to obey!" In other words, God charges people to obey; however, He will help them. He will give them His Spirit to accomplish His instructions, because only the Holy Spirit helps us to obey. God makes obedience happen! What God commands, He provides! What God requires of His people, He always helps them to do! Obedience is God's gift (not our performance or achievement), just as justification and salvation are His gifts too. This is the gospel par excellence!

As humans, we can only decide to do what is right. We need to make a decision to obey God, but we have no power to fulfill our decision or follow Him.[75] We need help in our fragility and weakness—help from outside of ourselves. The good news is that He provides willingness (which is a response to His call of love) and the power to obey (Philippians 2:13). Both justification and sanctification are gifts from God. All is given by God's grace and received through faith! His requirements are fulfilled only by the power of the Holy Spirit. The Holy Spirit moves us to a real and authentic obedience, not a forced or superficial obedience but genuine and springing from a grateful heart. When God's Word and His Spirit are accepted, genuine spiritual life occurs (Ezekiel 37:11–14).

Conclusion

There are strong similarities between Luther and the Adventist approaches to the Decalogue. Both agree about the use of the Ten Commandments. The Decalogue is given to maintain but not produce life, reveals to us the ideal, and how far we are from it. The law has no power to cleanse or save us, but it leads us to Jesus Christ who is our Savior. Perhaps the only dissimilarity is that Adventists do not underline the negative role of God's law as much as Luther does.[76] For both, the Decalogue still plays an important role in showing how to live when we are in Christ. These commandments represent God's model for godly lives, which we cannot live without the power of the Holy Spirit. We are enabled to live in harmony with God's precepts when we accept them, not as the way to heaven or simply as negative commands or demands, but as His guide. In this way, He reins in our life, and we can rejoice in our walk with the Lord. However, Adventists go further than Luther to stress that the Ten Commandments are not only a fence, a mirror, or a signpost but God's promise about what He wants to accomplish for and in us when we stay in a vibrant relationship with Him. By His power, these ten promises can become a permanent lifestyle for God's people.

1. The seven codes in the Pentateuch are (1) the Decalogue (Exodus 20:1–17); (2) the Covenant Code (Exodus 20:22–23:33); (3) the Ritual Code (Exodus 34:10–26); (4) the Sacrificial Code (Leviticus 1–7); (5) the Purity Code (Leviticus 11–15); (6) the Holiness Code (Leviticus 17–27); and (7) the Deuteronomic Code (Deuteronomy 12–26).

2. Stephen A. Kaufman, "The Structure of the Deuteronomic Law," *Maarav* 1, no. 2 (1979): 105–158; Walter C. Kaiser Jr., *Toward Old Testament Ethics* (Grand Rapids, MI: Zondervan, 1983), 127–137.

3. See Ekkehardt Mueller, "Why Is the Reason Given for Keeping in Deuteronomy 5 Different From That Given in Exodus 20," in *Interpreting Scripture: Bible Questions and Answers*, ed. Gerhard Pfandl, vol. 2 (Silver Spring, MD: Biblical Research Institute, 2010), 169–173.

4. Desiderius Erasmus to W. Pirkheimer, March 20, 1528, quoted in John Warwick Montgomery, *The Suicide of Christian Theology* (Minneapolis, MN: Bethany Fellowship, 1970), 423.

5. Martin Luther, *Luther's Works*, vol. 39, *Church and Ministry 1*, ed. Eric Gritsch and Helmut T. Lehman (Philadelphia, PA: Fortress Press, 1970), 37. (See note 16.)

6. Martin Luther, *Luther's Works*, vol. 40, *Church and Ministry 2*, ed. Conrad Bergendoff and Helmut T. Lehman (St. Louis, MO: Concordia, 1958), 308.

7. Martin Luther, *Luther's Works*, vol. 26, *Lectures on Galatians, 1535, Chapters 1–4*, ed. Jaroslav Pelikan and Walter A. Hansen (St. Louis, MO: Concordia, 1963), 364.

8. Martin Luther, *Luther's Works*, vol. 22, *Sermons on the Gospel of St. John, Chapters 1–4*, ed.

Jaroslav Pelikan (St. Louis, MO: Concordia, 1957), 143.

9. Martin Luther, *Dr. Martin Luthers Sämmtliche Schriften*, vol. 9 (St. Louis, MO: Concordia, n.d.), col. 802.

10. For a theology of the Ten Commandments in Luther, see Charles P. Arand, *That I May Be His Own: An Overview of Luther's Catechisms* (St. Louis: Concordia, 2000); Robert Kolb, *Teaching God's Children His Teaching: A Guide for the Study of Luther's Catechism* (St. Louis, MO: Concordia, 2012); Albrecht Peters, *Kommentar zu Luthers Katechismen*, vol. 1, *Die Zehn Gebote*, ed. Gottfried Seebass (Göttingen: Vandenhoeck and Ruprecht, 1990); Timothy J. Wengert, "Martin Luther and the Ten Commandments in the Large Catechism," *Currents in Theology and Mission* 31, no. 2 (April 2004): 104–114; Timothy J. Wengert, *Martin Luther's Catechisms: Forming the Faith* (Minneapolis, MN: Fortress Press, 2009).

11. Kirsi I. Stjerna, ed., *The Large Catechism of Dr. Martin Luther, 1529*, Annotated Luther Study ed. (Minneapolis, MN: Fortress Press, 2016), 292.

12. Ibid.

13. Ibid., 294.

14. Robert Kolb and Timothy J. Wengert, eds., *The Book of Concord: The Confessions of the Evangelical Lutheran Church*, trans. Charles Arand et al. (Minneapolis, MN: Augsburg Fortress Press, 2000), 428, para. 311.

15. Ibid., 431, para. 333.

16. Martin Luther, *Luther's Works*, vol. 1, *Lectures on Genesis, Chapters 1–5*, ed. Jaroslav Pelikan (St. Louis, MO: Concordia, 1958), 277, 278.

17. Martin Luther, *Luther's Small Catechism* (St. Louis, MO: Concordia, 1943), 8.

18. Ibid., 5.

19. Stjerna, *The Large Catechism of Dr. Martin Luther*, 304.

20. Kolb and Wengert, *The Book of Concord*, 430, para. 326.

21. Martin Luther, *Luther's Works*, vol. 17, *Lectures on Isaiah, Chapters 40–66*, ed. Hilton C. Oswald (St. Louis, MO: Concordia, 1972), 52.

22. Ibid., 17:143.

23. Stjerna, *The Large Catechism of Dr. Martin Luther*, 303.

24. Luther, *Luther's Works*, 1:147.

25. Luther follows the reading of the Vulgate and the medieval tradition in which the first two commandments are put together and the tenth commandment is split in two. In this way, he still maintains the same number of ten.

26. Stjerna, *The Large Catechism of Dr. Martin Luther*, 314.

27. Martin Luther, *Luther's Works*, vol. 23, *Sermons on the Gospel of St. John, Chapters 6–8*, ed. Jaroslav Pelikan and Daniel E. Poellot (St. Louis, MO: Concordia, 1959), 317.

28. Martin Luther, *Luther's Works*, vol. 5, *Lectures on Genesis, Chapters 26–30*, ed. Jaroslav Pelikan and Helmut T. Lehman (St. Louis, MO: Concordia, 1968), 115.

29. Martin Luther, *Luther's Works*, vol. 6, *Lectures on Genesis, Chapters 31–37*, ed. Jaroslav Pelikan and Hilton C. Oswald (St. Louis, MO: Concordia, 1970), 27.

30. Stjerna, *The Large Catechism of Dr. Martin Luther*, 331.

31. Ibid., 351.

32. On the debate about the "third use of the Law" (*tertius usus legis*) in the Lutheran tradition, see Bradley G. Green, *Covenant and Commandment: Works, Obedience and Faithfulness in the Christian Life* (Downers Grove, IL: InterVarsity Press, 2014), 60, 61; also *Concordia Theological Quarterly* 69, nos. 3–4 (July–October 2005) that deals with this question. The three uses of the moral law (*lex moralis*) are (1) the political or civic use; (2) the elenctical or pedagogical use; and (3) the didactic or normative use. See the Heidelberg Catechism, "Lord's Day" 2–4, 32–52.

33. Martin Luther, *Luther's Works*, vol. 27, *Lectures on Galatians, 1519, Chapters 1–6*, ed. Jaroslav Pelikan and Walter A. Hansen (St. Louis, MO: Concordia, 1964), 188.

34. Ibid., 40:329.

35. Ibid., 26:139.

36. Ibid., 27:188.

37. Ibid., 23:324.

38. Ibid., 23:270, 271.

39. Ibid., 26:138.

40. Martin Luther, *Sermons of Martin Luther*, ed. John Nicholas Lenker, trans. John Nicholas Lenker et al., vol. 5 (Grand Rapids, MI: Baker, 1983), 190.

41. Ibid., 192.

42. Ibid., 181, 182.

43. Ibid., 177.

44. Ibid.

45. Ibid., 180.

46. Ibid., 187.

47. Ibid., 189.

48. Ibid., 186.

49. Ibid., 192, 193. Luther states also, "Therefore another thing is necessary, Christ will say, for you to know, namely, that you know and possess the man called Christ, who helps us to the end that this doctrine of the Law may be established and perfected in you." Ibid., 193.

50. Luther, *Luther's Works*, 40:277.

51. Ibid., 22:425.

52. Martin Luther, "Two Kinds of Righteousness," in *Martin Luther: Selections From His Writings*, ed. John Dillenberger (New York: Doubleday, 1962), 88, 89.

53. Volker Leppin and Kirsi I. Stjerna, eds., *The Bondage of the Will, 1525*, Annotated Luther Study ed. (Minneapolis, MN: Fortress Press, 2016).

54. Martin Luther, *Luther's Works*, vol. 8, *Lectures on Genesis, Chapters 45–50*, ed. Jaroslav Pelikan and Walter A. Hansen (St. Louis, MO: Concordia, 1966), 284.

55. Ibid., 22:38, 39.

56. "The Law of God," in *Seventh-day Adventists Believe*, 2nd ed. (Silver Spring, MD: Ministerial Association, General Conference of Seventh-day Adventists, 2005), 263.

57. To understand the relationship between the gospel and the law from the Adventist perspective, see Ekkehardt Mueller, "The Law and the Gospel," Biblical Research Institute, 1–27, accessed July 20, 2017, https://adventistbiblicalresearch.org/sites/default/files/pdf/mueller,%20 Law%20%26%20the%20Gospel.pdf. See also the article by Mario Veloso, "The Law of God,"

in *Handbook of Seventh-day Adventist Theology*, ed. Raoul Dederen, Seventh-day Adventist Commentary Reference Series (Hagerstown, MD: Review and Herald® Pub. Assn., 2000), 457–492.

58. See Jo Ann Davidson, "The Decalogue Predates Mount Sinai: Indicators From the Book of Genesis," *Journal of the Adventist Theological Society* 19, nos. 1–2 (2008): 61–81.

59. Louis Berkhof, *Systematic Theology* (Grand Rapids, MI: Eerdmans, 1979), 612.

60. Ellen G. White, "Words of Comfort," MS 41, 1897, quoted in *The Seventh-day Adventist Bible Commentary*, ed. Francis D. Nichol, vol. 1 (Washington, DC: Review and Herald® Pub. Assn., 1953), 1105.

61. Ellen G. White to J. E. White, Brisbane, Queensland, Australia, October 30, 1898, Lt. 89, 1898, Ellen G. White Writings, accessed July 19, 2017, https://m.egwwritings.org/en/book/4959.2000001#20.

62. Ellen G. White, "Victory Over Temptation," MS 153, 1899, quoted in *The Seventh-day Adventist Bible Commentary*, ed. Francis D. Nichol, vol. 1 (Washington, DC: Review and Herald® Pub. Assn., 1953), 1105.

63. Ellen G. White to J. E. White, Lt. 89, 1898.

64. Ibid.

65. See E. Kautzsch, ed., *Gesenius' Hebrew Grammar*, trans. Arthur E. Cowley (Oxford: Clarendon, 1910), paras. 113bb and 113ee.

66. See Jacques B. Doukhan, *Hebrew for Theologians: A Textbook for the Study of Biblical Hebrew in Relation to Hebrew Thinking* (Lanham, MD: University Press of America, 1993), 41.

67. It depends on the English versions, but see, e.g., *dabar* (promise) as a noun (1 Kings 8:56; 2 Chronicles 1:9; Nehemiah 5:12, 13; Psalm 105:42) and *dabar* as a verb with the same meaning of promising (Deuteronomy 1:11; 6:3; 9:28; Joshua 9:21; 22:4; 23:5; etc.).

68. Ellen G. White, "The Privileges and Duties of the Followers of Christ," *Review and Herald*, December 3, 1908, 8.

69. See Denis Fortin, "Galatians, Law In," in *The Ellen G. White Encyclopedia*, ed. Denis Fortin and Jerry Moon (Hagerstown, MD: Review and Herald® Pub. Assn., 2013), 829–831. See also George R. Knight, *From 1888 to Apostasy: The Case of A. T. Jones* (Hagerstown, MD: Review and Herald® Pub. Assn., 1987), 23–27, 37–41; and Richard W. Schwarz, *Light Bearers to the Remnant* (Mountain View, CA: Pacific Press® Pub. Assn., 1979), 394, 395.

70. Ellen G. White to Uriah Smith, Cooranbong, New South Wales, Australia, June 6, 1896, Lt. 96, 1896, Ellen G. White Writings, accessed July 19, 2017, https://m.egwwritings.org/en/book/5508.2000001#0.

71. Ellen G. White to J. E. White, Lt. 89, 1898.

72. Ellen G. White, "As It Was in the Days of Noah," MS 88, 1897, quoted in *The Seventh-day Adventist Bible Commentary*, ed. Francis D. Nichol, vol. 1 (Washington, DC: Review and Herald® Pub. Assn., 1953), 1104, 1105.

73. Robert Badenas, *Christ the End of the Law: Romans 10.4 in Pauline Perspective*, Journal for the Study of the New Testament, Supplement Series 10 (Sheffield: University of Sheffield, 1985), 150.

74. Ellen G. White, *Christ's Object Lessons* (Battle Creek, MI: Review and Herald® Pub. Assn., 1900), 333.

75. E.g., Moses strongly admonished God's people: "Choose life" (Deuteronomy 30:19); Joshua encouraged Israel: "Choose for yourselves this day whom you will serve" (Joshua 24:15). Moses begged the people not to delay but to decide to follow God *today* (the word *hayyom* meaning "today" or "this day" is employed seventy-four times in the book of Deuteronomy).

76. Adventists disagree with one particular point in Luther's otherwise excellent interpretation of the Sabbath commandment: he states that Sabbath belongs to the ceremonial law and defends Sunday as the pragmatic day of keeping this commandment. See, e.g., his following quotations: "Thus it is not true that there is no ceremonial or judicial law in the Ten Commandments. Such laws are in the Decalogue, depend on it, and belong there. And to indicate this God himself has expressly introduced two ceremonial laws, namely, concerning images and the sabbath. We can show that these two parts are ceremonial laws which are also each in its way abrogated in the New Testament." Luther, *Luther's Works*, 40:93. Luther in his *Large Catechism* also expresses reservations regarding the Sabbath commandment in its application to Christians (see Stjerna, *The Large Catechism of Dr. Martin Luther*, 310–313). Seventh-day Adventists also divide the Decalogue differently: the first four commandments form the first table and describe the vertical relationship with God, and the last six, the second table, point to the horizontal relationship with other human beings.

CHAPTER 10

Luther, Seventh-day Adventists, and Righteousness by Faith

Woodrow W. Whidden II

The key question that this chapter seeks to answer is, what do Seventh-day Adventists owe Luther for their understanding of righteousness by faith or Christ and His righteousness? After a review of Luther's understanding of justification and sanctification (and how they relate to each other) and Melanchthon's, as he helped Luther to shape his soteriological views, we will then review the major passages in the history of Seventh-day Adventists regarding this theme. Finally, we will look at how these themes have been given expression by two key late twentieth- and early twenty-first-century Seventh-day Adventist thinkers—Ivan Blazen and Hans K. LaRondelle.

A summary of Luther's views on salvation by faith in Christ

I lay no claim to special expertise regarding the soteriology of Luther and his fellow sixteenth-century Reformers (both Protestant and Roman Catholic). From my study, however, I sense that contemporary British historical theologian Anthony "Tony" N. S. Lane has stated Luther's views succinctly and reliably in the following paragraphs:

Luther is known especially for his doctrine of justification by faith alone. But this doctrine does not figure in the ninety-five theses and it was not

117

the original cause of the reform. Furthermore, it was not until several years *after* the ninety-five theses that Luther reached a distinctively Protestant doctrine of justification. In the early years he still held to a basically Augustinian position. Augustine taught justification by faith, in the following sense. When the sinner recognizes his inability to keep God's law and his need of salvation he turns to God in faith. God then gives him his Holy Spirit, who heals his will and pours love into his heart. This is justification—being made righteous, being changed from a selfish into a loving person. Having been justified or changed, the believer can now proceed to keep God's law from the heart, motivated by love.

In the early years of the reform, Luther returned to this Augustinian teaching, but with a greater stress on the need for faith. He was especially against the mediaeval idea that the sacraments bestow salvation like medicine or like an injection, no more being required from the recipient than not placing an obstacle in the way. Thus Luther's stress lay on the need for a living, personal faith, against a mechanical view of the sacraments—not on the meaning of the word justification. But in due course, in the early 1520s, Luther came to see that for Paul, "justify" does not mean "make righteous," or "change into a good person," but [to] "reckon righteous," or "acquit." Justification [thus] concerns my status rather than my state, how God looks upon me rather than what he does in me, God accepting me rather than changing me. Thus Luther arrived at the Protestant distinction between justification (my standing before God) and sanctification (my growth in holiness).

But if we are justified or accepted by God on the basis of faith alone, without good works, surely the believer can "live it up" without worrying about the consequences? Luther was accused of teaching just this, but unfairly. While he *distinguished* justification and sanctification, he did not *separate* them. He did not imagine that one could exist without the other. When God accepts someone he also changes them. But if they always go together, what is so wonderful about distinguishing them? Simply this: Justification by faith alone (or, more accurately, *by* Christ alone, *through* faith alone) means that I can be confident of my acceptance by God, not because I am living a good life, but because Christ has died for me. The point is not whether justification can exist without sanctification (it cannot), but the *basis* of justification. If our acceptance by God is based on our good works, there can be no assurance—except for the morally smug like the Pharisee in Luke 18.9–14. But justification by faith alone means that we can have assurance before God—on the basis of the cross of Jesus Christ. This means that we can proceed to do good works not *in order to* win God's approval and acceptance but *because* God has already accepted us. Obedience to God is the free, loving response of his children, not the mercenary accumulation of merits by those striving for approval.[1]

While Seventh-day Adventism owes debts of influence to Luther and other sixteenth-century Magisterial Reformers on the issues of the four great Protestant *solas* (*sola fide, sola gratia, sola scriptura,* and *sola Christi*), it is primarily to Luther that Sabbatarian Adventism stands indebted for its interest in and pursuit of *sola fide*, especially as it has been described by Tony Lane. It is, however, to Melanchthon and his subsequent impact on Jacobus Arminius and John Wesley that we owe our strong emphasis on free grace—the latter being seen as standing in marked contrast to the Augustinian irresistible-grace emphases (that is, predestinarian impulses).[2]

But it took a number of decades before Seventh-day Adventism more self-consciously and intensively sought to clarify its relationship to the European Reformers (from the sixteenth to the eighteenth centuries). And the reasons for this renewed emphasis on a more Christocentric, grace-informed salvation perspective arose in reaction to early Adventism's emphasis (from the late 1840s up to the mid-1870s) on apocalyptic prophecy and the proper role and authority of the Ten Commandments. This was particularly so as they related to the doctrine of the pre-Advent investigative judgment and the particular role that the seventh-day Sabbath would play in last-day prophetic events.[3]

Much of this more polemical emphasis on and defense of the law of God, and its special role in prophetic fulfillments, came from formative Adventist pioneers, such as Joseph Bates, Uriah Smith, and James and Ellen White. But it was the Whites who especially sensed that something was amiss in this preoccupation with the law, the Sabbath, and the judgment (carried out according to works and based on the celestial record of these works of obedience to God's eternal law). However, at this very critical juncture, it must be pointed out that the Whites were not averse to any of these key teachings on law, prophecy, and the judgment. But they had begun to sense that Christ and His saving graces had fallen out of the truth-burdened focus of Adventist theology and gospel proclamation.

In the late 1870s and early 1880s, the Whites began to seek for and develop a more grace- and Christ-centered exposition of the prophecies, along with the other distinctive teachings of the Seventh-day Adventists, such as the state of the dead, hell, health reform, and so on. Ultimately, it was in this setting that the Whites began what can be characterized as their salvation revival.

There were two key moments in this revival, subsequent to the untimely death of James White in 1881. The first one was Ellen White's presentations at the 1883 General Conference Session of Seventh-day Adventists that greatly spotlighted the need for the Advent movement's revival and evangelistic presentations to be more Christ- and grace-focused. It was this 1883 conference that seemed to prepare the way for the stirring work of Ellen White, A. T. Jones, and E. J. Waggoner at, and subsequent to, the famed Minneapolis, Minnesota, 1888 General Conference Session. So what was the sum of the key components of the righteousness by faith message of Ellen White and her two younger allies, Jones and Waggoner?

The grace of Christ draws sinners to Himself through the conviction of sin and the truth that the Godhead loves us and wants to (1) forgive us of our sins (justification by faith alone) and (2) transform or cleanse our characters (habitual attitudes, words, and acts) through the sanctifying, perfecting power of the subjective (internal) workings of the Holy Spirit. The crucial point in this experience is to theologically and practically negotiate the appropriate linkages between converting, justifying, and sanctifying grace. It is on (or at) this crucially important juncture that most of the debates about righteousness by faith have been focused.

At this consequential intersection in Adventist thought and experience, three basic approaches unfolded. The first viewpoint was essentially justification by works of obedience to the law; this seemed to be the pit or ditch that Joseph Bates, Uriah Smith, and their partisans had fallen into. In opposition to that theme was the second perspective coming from the "Messengers of Minneapolis," A. T. Jones and E. J. Waggoner, who had received strong but not carte blanche support from Ellen White and her son W. C. "Willie" White. The Whites' approach (the third option), though it took a while to manifest itself, ultimately emerged from the more grace-centered approach of Jones and Waggoner. But it is crucial to note that while Jones and Waggoner were initially on the right track, they both eventually went off the rails into a species of perfectionism. Though claiming a great emphasis on grace, they went in a very subjective direction, especially Waggoner. And thus, in their basic principles, they arrived at a position that was not all that far from the Roman Catholic Council of Trent version of justification: the experience of sanctification by grace brings the believer to the point where, through the internal workings of the Spirit, the believer becomes so sanctified as to be declared just before God. But ultimately there emerged a third alternative, presented by Ellen White, that can essentially be called the effective/forensic version of salvation by grace.

> **B**ut ultimately there emerged a third alternative, presented by Ellen White, that can essentially be called the effective/forensic version of salvation by grace.

To get a fuller grasp of the situation, it is important to note that in the tradition of the later theology of Jones and Waggoner and their subjectively oriented concepts, there arose the so-called last generation theology of M. L. Andreasen. Evidently influenced by Waggoner's later, very subjective version of justification through perfecting sanctification and Jones's "post-Fall" Christology, Andreasen also seemed to pick up ideas from E. J. Waggoner that claimed God needs a final generation of saints on earth to vindicate Himself through their demonstration that perfect obedience to the law is possible. In other words, the perfect obedience of this remnant is absolutely essential if God is to win out against Lucifer's challenge that obedience to the law of God is impossible. Under the sway of this very alluring line of thought, there eventuated a widespread embrace of this subjective, perfectionistic vision, and it gained a notable predominance in Seventh-day Adventism for most of the first half of the twentieth century.

But in the 1950s, under the leadership of L. E. Froom, at the General Conference of Seventh-day Adventists, and British theologians, especially Edward "Ted" Heppenstall, a strong resurgence of emphasis on a more Protestant-informed soteriology was manifested, which would be associated with the effective or forensic view of theology. Raoul Dederen and Hans K. LaRondelle in the Theology Department of the Seventh-day Adventist Theological Seminary at Andrews University and Ivan Blazen in the seminary's New Testament Department, subsequently embraced this direction. It is in the wake of these developments that this more Reformationist-Evangelical strain of theology, tempered by Arminian-Wesleyan free-grace, sanctificationist themes, has arisen in Adventist academia as a reaction (corrective) to Jones's, Waggoner's, and Andreasen's perfectionist versions of soteriology.

At the same time that this more Protestant- or Evangelical-oriented direction was being promoted, there was also a strong resurgence of the later Jones- and Waggoner-inspired theology of Andreasen that was ably and forcefully set forth by such figures as Herbert Douglass, Kenneth H. Wood, C. Mervyn Maxwell, and ministers and laypersons who have styled themselves as "Historic Adventists." There were also others who sought to revive the later theology of Jones and Waggoner (the "1888 Message Study Committee," greatly energized by Robert J. Wieland and Donald K. Short).

So who has the truth on righteousness by faith?

The outcome of this long-running "debate" about the meaning of Christ and His righteousness is most ably represented in two key summary pieces published by Hans K. LaRondelle and Ivan Blazen. Their arguments are compelling because of the clarity and force of their biblical interpretations and theological expositions. Blazen's essay, titled "Salvation," was published in the *Handbook of Seventh-day Adventist Theology*;[4] and LaRondelle's presentation (titled "The Seventh-day Adventist View of the Relationship of Justification—Sanctification—the Final Judgment") was presented at the Seventh-day Adventist international dialogues with the Lutheran World Federation and published in *Lutherans and Adventists in Conversation: Report and Papers Presented, 1994–1998*.[5]

Once more we must remember that at the heart of all the Seventh-day Adventist discussions and debates about soteriology there still lurk the questions of (1) what we really mean by justification, sanctification, and perfection; (2) how these particular facets of soteriology properly interrelate with the actual experience of personal salvation; and (3) how they inform every aspect of the church's evangelistic proclamation. So what have Blazen and LaRondelle contributed to the clarification of these pressing righteousness-by-faith questions?

Blazen's soteriology: Justification, presumption, and true assurance of salvation

Blazen's carefully crafted interpretation of both justification and sanctification by faith suggests that justifying grace provides the only merit basis for justification and that sanctifying grace effectually redeems from cheap-grace presumption. It is grace that saves from the guilt, power (now), and ultimate presence (at the Second Coming) of sin. But Blazen's most appealing lines of insight deal with how he relates the forensic aspects of justification to the relational categories of salvation: "[The] forensic usage, with its covenantal context in the relationship between God and Israel, is the primary background for the NT teaching of justification by faith. However, this background . . . does not exhaust it. Court judgments and relationships are translated into the higher key of forgiving grace and a personal relationship between humans and God. The concept of God as judge is exceeded, though not superseded, by the concept of God as Father."[6] These legal or relational categories then translate into visions of adoption that speak of a profoundly assuring hope: Since "Christ died for us while we were morally weak, ungodly, sinners, and enemies toward God," we can conclude that "if God was willing to do the hardest thing—give His Son to die to justify" sinners, "how much more will the risen Christ be willing to save His new friends from the ultimate wrath of God. . . . Thus, believers can rejoice in their reconciliation ([Romans 5] verse 11), for it promises glorification to come."[7]

> Blazen's carefully crafted interpretation of both justification and sanctification by faith suggests that justifying grace provides the only merit basis for justification and that sanctifying grace effectually redeems from cheap-grace presumption.

But how does this theology address the Adventist's fear of cheap grace (attitudes of presuming on the merciful grace of God)? Blazen offers the following: "As the biblical texts on God's love and grace do not allow for the false view, 'Never quite saved at all, no matter what Christ has done,' so the judgment texts disallow the erroneous view, 'Once saved, always saved, no matter what I do.' Salvation is always a gift, but the gift does not remain when the Giver is rejected as the Lord of one's life."[8] He then neatly pulls the loose ends together: "The conclusion [therefore] that may be drawn is that if justification grants assurance, judgment guards it from the dangerous illusion that assurance is possible without a committed relationship to, and following of, Christ. Good works do not impart assurance, but the One who motivates such works does."[9]

LaRondelle and effective forensic justification

It is in the use of the term *effective forensic justification* that LaRondelle forges his views as to how justifying grace seamlessly relates to sanctifying or transforming grace in the setting of judgment and the believer's assurance of salvation.[10] LaRondelle's terminology articulates essentially the same dynamics as Blazen; that is, the term *forensic* references our objective or legal standing before God (being legally declared to be just). Whereas the term *effective* evocatively points to the inherent nature of the Christian's moral and spiritual character that results from the internal workings of the Spirit's transforming power in the believer's soul. It is a power that imparts real victory over the most tenaciously besetting, taunting character defects. The problem with retaining such defects, or faults, is that they can harden the believer into a presumptive insensitivity to the goodness of God. And such a hardening can subtly lead to a deadly erosion of the believer's appreciation for and dependence upon the reconciling goodness of God's grace—both its inseparable legal and experiential aspects: "The soteriologies of Ellen White [and the consensus of Seventh-day Adventism] and of the Reformers are governed by the principles of grace and faith in Christ," as they have recognized "that the grace of God in Christ is the sole meritorious ground for the believer's salvation, and that all human efforts are excluded from the basis of man's justification or forgiveness by God. . . . The good works of a sanctified life are the visible signs that demonstrate and vindicate the presence of genuine faith."[11] Quite possibly one of Adventism's most succinct expressions of this dynamic, inseparable interrelationship between forgiving and transforming grace comes from Ellen White's summation of Wesley's later experience of the gospel: "He continued his strict and self-denying life, not now as the *ground*, but the *result* of faith; not the *root*, but the *fruit* of holiness. The grace of God in Christ is the foundation of the Christian's hope, and that grace will be manifested in obedience."[12]

Conclusion

So what are the key debts that Seventh-day Adventists owe to Martin Luther regarding the meaning of righteousness by faith in Christ? Clearly, Luther's mature view on justification by faith alone (*sola fide*) in Christ's imputed righteousness is his key gift. Yet it was the more advanced views of Melanchthon on free grace and *sola fide*, united with Luther's other great themes of *sola scriptura* and *sola gratia*, as they were reset in the subsequent theologies of Jacobus Arminius and John Wesley, that became the key themes we owe to Luther at this moment of reflective commemoration on the five hundredth anniversary

To God "alone" be the glory for His unique gift of the gospel of righteousness by faith in Jesus Christ.

of Luther promulgating his Ninety-Five Theses on October 31, 1517. To God "alone" be the glory for His unique gift of the gospel of righteousness by faith in Jesus Christ.

1. Tony Lane, *A Concise History of Christian Thought*, rev. ed. (Grand Rapids, MI: Baker Academic, 2006), 159, 160 (italics in the original). For further background on Luther and his breakthrough on justification, see Alister E. McGrath, *Reformation Thought: An Introduction*, 4th ed. (Malden, MA: Wiley-Blackwell, 2012), 117–128.

2. For insights on Melanchthon's influence on Arminius and the Arminian tradition, see Timothy Arena, "The Soteriology of Philip Melanchthon and the Importance of Its Legacy for Seventh-day Adventists" (paper, Perceptions of the Protestant Reformation in Seventh-day Adventism Symposium, Institute of Adventist Studies, Friedensau Adventist University, Germany, May 9–12, 2016).

3. This historical analysis has been outlined by George Knight in his study titled *A Search for Identity: The Development of Seventh-day Adventist Beliefs* (Hagerstown, MD: Review and Herald® Pub. Assn., 2000); Woodrow W. Whidden II, *Ellen White on Salvation* (Hagerstown, MD: Review and Herald® Pub. Assn., 1995); and Woodrow W. Whidden II, *Ellen White on the Humanity of Christ* (Hagerstown, MD: Review and Herald® Pub. Assn., 1997). Thus, much of the historical development that follows is drawn from these studies.

4. Ivan Blazen, "Salvation," in *Handbook of Seventh-day Adventist Theology*, ed. Raoul Dederen, Seventh-day Adventist Commentary Reference Series (Hagerstown, MD: Review and Herald® Pub. Assn., 2000), 271–313.

5. Hans K. LaRondelle, "The Seventh-day Adventist View of the Relationship of Justification—Sanctification—the Final Judgment," in *Lutherans and Adventists in Conversation: Report and Papers Presented, 1994–1998* (Silver Spring, MD: General Conference of Seventh-day Adventists, 2000). See also Hans K. LaRondelle, "The Seventh-day Adventist View of the Relationship of Justification—Sanctification—the Final Judgment," in *E. J. Waggoner: From the Physician of Good News to Agent of Division*, by Woodrow W. Whidden II (Hagerstown, MD: Review and Herald® Pub. Assn., 2008), 384–397.

6. Blazen, "Salvation," 279.

7. Ibid., 289.

8. Ibid., 290.

9. Ibid., 291.

10. See LaRondelle, "The Seventh-day Adventist View of the Relationship of Justification," in Whidden, *E. J. Waggoner, 384–397*.

11. Ibid., 391.

12. Ellen G. White, *The Great Controversy* (Mountain View, CA: Pacific Press® Pub. Assn., 1950), 256; emphasis in the original.

CHAPTER 11

Martin Luther and the Lord's Supper for Seventh-day Adventism

Michael W. Campbell

A central aspect of medieval piety was the Mass. This is not surprising since the Eucharist[1] was instituted by Jesus Christ as a lasting ordinance of the Christian church. It was pregnant with meaning and purpose and was interpreted in many different ways through the centuries.

During the late medieval period, specifically at the Fourth Lateran Council (1215), the Roman Catholic Church articulated the concept of transubstantiation that effectively stated that the elements of the bread and wine literally changed into Christ's body and blood. The later bull, *Unam sanctam* (1302), written by Pope Boniface VIII, boldly asserted, "There is one holy, Catholic and apostolic church . . . and that outside this church there is no salvation or remission of sins."[2] During earlier periods, the mystical body of Christ (*corpus mysticum Christi*) was taken to mean the sacrament of the Eucharist, signifying the entire church. The conflation of meaning demonstrates that the Eucharist or Mass remained important during the time of Martin Luther. "The Church was not just likened to the body of Christ; it *was* the body of Christ." In this way, the Mass became "the central sacrament of the middle ages."[3]

> During the Reformation, the Mass became a symbol of a perverted church that needed to be abolished.

Martin Luther, and a host of Reformers in his wake, challenged this Latin claim. During the Reformation, the Mass became a symbol of a perverted church that needed to be abolished.[4] Tragically, fine theological distinctions about the Lord's Supper (as it became known in Protestant circles) led to further divisions within the Protestant Reformation. Although Protestants were far from united in terms of their theology of the Eucharist, it was generally agreed that it was the main Christian sacrament. Christ was present in substance, and all other sacraments had no meaning without it. It thus became a reenactment of Christ's sacrifice. Martin Luther and other Reformers "completely redefined Christian thinking on the sacrament and how the body of Christ should be understood in relation to the community of the faithful."[5] Of special note is how Luther described the Eucharist in a figurative and a symbolic sense. Later on he grew increasingly conservative in his stance, particularly as he became embroiled in debates with others. His view, described as *consubstantiation*, contends that the bread and wine do not become Christ's actual body and blood, but that it truly is present "in, with, and under" the elements. Finally, other Reformers viewed the Lord's Supper as the *spiritual presence* of Jesus Christ. The bread and wine cannot be empty symbols. They must be signs that Christ is actually present.[6]

This chapter reviews the development of the Lord's Supper, particularly as it relates to Seventh-day Adventists.[7] Amid the opposition of the Roman Catholic understanding of the Mass were a host of related issues, including the role of priests, the priesthood of all believers, and the need to allow everyone access to the rite's symbols (both the bread and the wine).[8] This chapter briefly reviews the development of Luther's understanding.

Martin Luther and the Lord's Supper

Luther wrote extensively on the Lord's Supper.[9] His "writings on the sacraments are vast" and "constitute one of his finest contributions to Christian theology."[10] Most scholars see a fourfold development in his views.[11] The earliest stage focuses on the Word as a source of assurance and forgiveness. The second stage, beginning in 1525, is when Luther connects the body and blood as a means of forgiveness. In a third stage (after 1526), Luther merged these two emphases. Finally, after the Marburg Colloquy of 1529, Luther argues for a more conservative position that focuses on the sacramental union itself.[12]

Obviously, Luther reflected the medieval tradition, but his radical reorientation through Scripture meant that his views quickly changed. The earliest evidence of this change appears in his 1518 pamphlet *Sermon on the Proper Preparation of the Heart for the Sacramental Reception on the Eucharist* that expressed pastoral concerns.[13] The next year he published another treatise: *The Blessed Sacrament of the Holy and True Body of Christ and the Brotherhoods*.[14] It differentiated between the Augustinian notion of an outward sign (*signum*) of the bread and wine that ultimately points to the community of believers (*communion*) and the importance of inward faith. This inward acting out of faith (*opus operantis*) is particularly distinctive for Luther at this early, formative stage in his understanding of the Lord's Supper.[15]

Luther further developed his views with the 1520 publication of *A Treatise on the New Testament, That Is, the Holy Mass*.[16] Here he described the Lord's Supper as a testament or will, given by Christ as a seal or sign expressed through bread and wine. "This shift in understanding begins to open the floodgates to Luther's critiques of multiple eucharistic practices," observes Gordon A. Jensen.[17] This critique centered on how people offer something to God, but the Lord's Supper is a gift or promise given by a testator to the heirs. It is not a " 'benefit received [by God] but a benefit conferred' by God to us."[18] Central to Luther's thinking is the notion of promise. This led him to criticize the practice of Masses for the dead (what amounted to mere works being used to reduce one's time in purgatory), priests who mumbled "the words of institution into the cup" (because it prevented those listening from being able to hear what was in the will), and Communion of one kind. He also disavowed the idea that the Mass was some kind of magic to ward off evil, as well as the commercialization of the sacrament (whether in private or for the dead).[19] Altogether such corrupt practices detracted from this foundational idea of God's gift. While faith was still necessary, he emphasized the life-giving Word in the sacrament that strengthens and creates faith.

Luther's boldest attack on the doctrine of transubstantiation is his treatise *The Babylonian Captivity of the Church* (1520).[20] While he did not outright reject transubstantiation, as he wished to protect the notion of a real presence, Luther felt the doctrine was simply wrong. At best, it was unhelpful; at worst, it was simply illogical. The real issue, for Luther, was forgiveness, and that could only happen if Christ was truly present in the Supper. *The Babylonian Captivity of the Church* is also notable because he "decried the practice of withholding the cup from the laity"—a direct violation of Christ's command in Matthew 26:27 ("Drink of it, all of you" [ESV]). At the heart of Luther's critique was his concern that the Mass had become merely another good work. Instead, the real focus should be "on the benefits God gives, not what humans offer." In doing so, Luther shifted the emphasis from the action of priests to God's saving activity.[21]

Luther's views about the Lord's Supper developed further after a series of perceived religious extremes, including the practice of the Lord's Supper that led him to come out of hiding at Wartburg Castle in late 1521. Once again this illustrates Luther's primary pastoral concern. While he initially argued that receiving the cup was possible for everyone, he did not feel that this view was mandatory. Two years later, in January 1523, Luther was, in fact, willing to offer the cup to all. The use of the altar then became reserved solely for the Lord's Supper (carrying over a strong proclivity among Protestants to decorate the table with a depiction of the Lord's Supper).[22]

Challenges to Luther's understanding of the Lord's Supper came from two directions: first, from within Wittenberg itself; and then later, from the Swiss Reformers. This becomes apparent in a sixteenth-century biography of the medieval theologian Wessel Gansfort (*Vita Wesseli Groningensis*). "In 1521 Hinne Rode, rector of the Brethren of the Common Life in Utrecht, arrived in Wittenberg with a manuscript treatise on the Lord's Supper. The purported author was Cornelius Henricxz Hoen (d. 1524), an affluent court lawyer from The Hague."[23] It is unclear whether he wrote the tract or not, but the tract was extremely influential both in Wittenberg and for Zwingli and others in Switzerland. His *Epistle on the Eucharist* was the first systematic defense of the symbolic interpretation of the sacrament to surface during the Reformation. He argued that the phrase "this is my body" should be interpreted in a symbolic or figurative manner. It was effectively a pledge of forgiveness, in the same way that a pledge represents a promise. According to the *Vita*, the manuscript fell into Luther's hands around 1521. He promptly read it, rejected it, and wrote against it.[24]

Others, such as Andreas Karlstadt, reacted differently. He followed Luther in rejecting the Roman Catholic notion of sacrifice and transubstantiation, but over time he moved toward Hoen's position in his *Epistle*. Thus, Karlstadt became the first to publish against Luther. Of note was his emphasis upon a typological interpretation (or "ardent remembrance") that stressed the subsequent words "given for you" rather than the real presence. The Eucharist for Karlstadt was not a re-creation of the New Testament supper but rather was something that could only be experienced in a symbolic or typological sense.[25] Similarly, Hoen's *Epistle*, which had been published anonymously in Worms and Strasbourg in 1525, influenced Huldrych Zwingli. It clearly reached him years earlier because he mentions both the work and its author by name.[26] Zwingli, like Karlstadt and Hoen, emphasized the memorial aspect of the Lord's Supper, using the same symbolic mode of interpretation.

Luther was reluctant to let go of the "real presence." First, he argued against any tendency to split the physical versus the spiritual presence of Christ. Yet "Karlstadt, Zwingli, and Oecolampadius . . . had insisted that Christ was only spiritually present in the Lord's Supper."[27] Zwingli had gone even further by equating the symbol as figuratively representing the church.[28] Luther objected, writing that if there was a problem with the physical presence, then the physical incarnation of Christ would in turn also not make any sense. In a similar way, the Incarnation could not be separated. Christ's body was given not "in the same form or mode but in the same essence or nature."[29] Second, Luther addressed the attempts to separate the bread and the wine from the body and the blood of Christ in Jesus' statement, "This is my body" (Matthew 26:26). Karlstadt argued that "this" does not refer to the bread; Zwingli insisted that the words were representative; and Oecolampadius interpreted it as "This is a figure of my body." Luther, on the other hand, maintains that the words should speak for themselves. Luther viewed Zwingli's argument (along with Hoen and Karlstadt) as both theologically and grammatically suspect. Such a plain meaning should not be so readily dismissed. The third argument put forth by Zwingli was that since God is both at the right hand of God that He could not also be at the Supper at the very same time. Luther responded by stating that God is present everywhere because of His omnipotence and is active in the world. For Luther, Christ was present in the bread and the wine. He explained this mystery as an *unio sacramentalis* (sacramental union) between the bread and the wine and the body and the blood of Christ. He refused to explain *how* this actually happened. Such theories could only serve to distract from the spiritual benefits that were to be received.

Finally, after the Marburg Colloquy, Luther continued conversations with Martin Bucer. Bucer did come around and accept Luther's position of the "real presence" in terms of a sacramental presence. Yet there were two remaining issues that separated them. Bucer objected to the preposition used to describe the bread and the body of Christ. Whereas Luther was flexible, "Bucer insisted 'with the bread' (*cum pane*) be used because the preposition 'with' placed the bread and wine on a 'parallel' plane to the body and blood, without mixing the two together. It was this preposition that made it into the Wittenberg Concord of May 1536."[30] Luther and Bucer also continued to debate who ate the body of Christ in the meal. Basing his position on 1 Corinthians 11:29, Luther argued that the person who partakes of the sacraments eats the body of Christ. The faith of the godly or ungodly did not affect what was received. Luther does not allow for any obedience to cause Christ's body and blood to be present. Bucer insisted that faith was crucial in the reception of the sacrament. "The impasse was resolved when Luther, following a proposal offered by the Wittenberg pastor Bugenhagen, proposed a third category—'unworthy.'"[31] "Thus, the Wittenberg Concord stated that 'the body and blood of the Lord are truly extended also to the unworthy, and that the unworthy receive, where the words of institution of Christ are retained.'"[32]

One final Reformation development was the viewpoint of John Calvin, who steered a middle course between those in Wittenberg (i.e., Karlstadt and Oecolampadius) and Zurich. He maintained that the Eucharist was an external symbol that the finite and the physical were used to reveal invisible truths. This growth in understanding was a lifelong project and remained a mystery (*arcanum*) that extended beyond human reason. He taught that Christ was substantially present for those with proper faith. Thus, he comprehended two realities at once ("physical signs" that expressed invisible or spiritual truths).[33]

What is evident is that among the Protestant Reformers there was a clear *evangelical* or Protestant understanding of the Eucharist that developed. While there was still some variety, including the development, nuancing, and polarization among various Reformers, it is obvious that they believed it was God's life-changing presence and action that reached troubled people. For Luther, his views "underwent considerable development."[34] Yet what did not change was his pastoral concern against the Roman Catholic abuse of the Eucharist. Luther was consistent in emphasizing God's grace and gift expressed through the sacrament. "Thus by the mid-sixteenth century Protestant Christianity understood the Eucharist, and with it Christ and his relationship to the Church, in radically different terms to Catholicism."[35]

> Yet what did not change was his pastoral concern against the Roman Catholic abuse of the Eucharist. Luther was consistent in emphasizing God's grace and gift expressed through the sacrament.

Perspective

Early Seventh-day Adventists perpetuated the Protestant practice of the Lord's Supper. It is therefore significant that William Miller, a licensed Baptist preacher, advocated and observed the Lord's Supper.[36] The radical early Adventist commitment to Scripture and, in particular, to the return of the primitive purity of the early Christian church meant that this practice was readily adopted. During the formative period of early Adventism, there was no question whether or not the Lord's Supper should be preserved. In fact, early Sabbatarian Adventists readily appropriated their understanding of the Lord's Supper to the development of their views, especially their stance on the imminent return of Jesus Christ.[37]

Early debates were not centered on whether the Lord's Supper should be practiced or not, but whether this ordinance should also be connected to the practice of footwashing. This was carried over from the Baptists and other Restorationist groups in America. This is in contrast to other Advent groups who, like Joshua V. Himes and others at the 1845 Albany Conference, condemned "the act of promiscuous feet-washing" as both "unscriptural" and "subversive."[38] In 1858, Josiah Litch joined Himes in condemning the washing of feet.[39] In this way, footwashing became one of several markers separating Sabbatarian Adventism from the larger group of disappointed believers.

Early Adventists seemed to be enthusiastic about continuing the practice of the Lord's Supper and also footwashing. James White, in the first issue of *The Present Truth* (1849), explained that the meaning of the Sabbath was a sign between Christ and His church. He says that it is the same as the "communion of the body and blood of Christ was given for a memorial to the Church, that we may not forget the sufferings and death of the Lamb of God."[40] By far, the most enthusiastic adherent of the Lord's Supper was Joseph Bates, who repeatedly celebrated the rite in almost every church he visited. The earliest known reference to the Communion service by Ellen G. White comes from a letter where she urges that the ordinance "should be more frequently practiced by us." She opined that it was fanaticism connected to footwashing that at an early point caused some hesitancy and confusion about the ordinance. She made clear that the best solution was to make sure that men do not wash the "sisters' " feet or vice versa.[41] It appears this squelched any further objections and allowed for the continuation of both footwashing and the Lord's Supper. As a general rule, the practice of observing the Lord's Supper played a central role in early Adventist worship. It became a part of the monthly or quarterly meetings, thus perpetuating an early American practice among both Baptists and Methodists of celebrating this ordinance on a quarterly basis.

Seventh-day Adventists inherited, appropriated, and perpetuated the Lord's Supper. In most cases, Adventists were not too concerned about the intricate theological controversies of the Reformers of the past, even as they celebrated their legacies. At the same time, there are some important observations about the continuation of the Lord's Supper within Adventism. First of all, Luther's focus on transformed symbols remained an important theological concept that led early Adventists to continue to point to Christ's first and second advents as related to the Cross, salvation, and redemption. Adventists effectively perpetuated a largely moderate Calvinist position about the Lord's Supper as

> Seventh-day Adventists inherited, appropriated, and perpetuated the Lord's Supper.

a memorial of Christ's death. Some early Adventists also recognized a certain element of mystery about the rite and that the Lord's Supper is a recognition of both our sinfulness and the gift of forgiveness. Thus, for Seventh-day Adventists, the primary appropriation of the Lord's Supper is to focus on it as a memorial of Christ's death and the Second Advent.

---

1. One of a variety of names used to describe the sacred rite.

2. Quoted by C. Scott Dixon, *The Church in the Early Modern Age*, The I. B. Tauris History of the Christian Church (London: I. B. Tauris, 2016), 68.

3. Ibid. (italics in the original).

4. Hans J. Hillerbrand, *The Division of Christendom: Christianity in the Sixteenth Century* (Louisville, KY: Westminster John Knox Press, 2007), 299.

5. Dixon, *The Church in the Early Modern Age*, 70, 71.

6. Gregg R. Allison, *Historical Theology: An Introduction to Christian Doctrine* (Grand Rapids, MI: Zondervan, 2011), 635.

7. A recent example includes Lee Palmer Wandel, ed., *A Companion to the Eucharist in the Reformation*, Brill's Companions on the Christian Tradition (Leiden: Brill, 2013).

8. Allison, *Historical Theology*, 635, 636.

9. Gordon A. Jensen, "Luther and the Lord's Supper," in *The Oxford Handbook of Martin Luther's Theology*, ed. Robert Kolb, Irene Dingel, and L'ubomír Batka (New York: Oxford University Press, 2014), 323.

10. Donald K. McKim, ed., *The Cambridge Companion to Martin Luther* (Cambridge, UK: Cambridge University Press, 2003), 50.

11. Friedrich Gräbke, *Die Konstruktion der Abendmahlslehre Luthers in ihrer Entwicklung dargestellt* (Leipzig: Deichert, 1908). For a discussion on his views, see *The Oxford Handbook of Martin Luther's Theology*, 322, 323.

12. Susi Hausammann, "Realpräsenz in Luthers Abendmahlslehre," in *Studien zur Geschichte und Theologie, Festschrift für Ernst Bizer*, ed. L. Abramowski and J. F. G. Goeters (Neukirchen-Vluyn: Neukirchener Verlag, 1969), 157–173. See also modifications by John Alfred Faulkner, "Luther and the Real Presence," *American Journal of Theology* 21 (1917): 225–239; Ralph W. Quere, "Changes and Constants: Structure in Luther's Understanding of the Real Presence in the 1520's," *Sixteenth Century Journal* 16, no. 1 (Spring 1985): 45–78.

13. Martin Luther, *D. Martin Luthers Werke: Kritische Gesamtausgabe*, vol. 1 (Weimar: Hermann Böhlau, 1883), 329–335.

14. Martin Luther, *D. Martin Luthers Werke: Kritische Gesamtausgabe*, vol. 2 (Weimar: Hermann Böhlau, 1884), 742–758; Martin Luther, *Luther's Works*, vol. 35, *Word and Sacrament 1*, ed. E. Theodore Bachmann (St. Louis, MO: Concordia, 1960), 45–74.

15. Luther, *D. Martin Luthers Werke*, 2:751, line 18; Martin Luther, *Luther's Works*, vol. 36, *Word and Sacrament 2*, ed. Abdel R. Wentz (Philadelphia, PA: Fortress, 1959), 63, 64.

16. Martin Luther, *D. Martin Luthers Werke: Kritische Gesamtausgabe*, vol. 6 (Weimar: Hermann Böhlau, 1888), 353–378; Luther, *Luther's Works*, 35:79–112.

17. Jensen, "Luther and the Lord's Supper," 324.

18. Luther, *D. Martin Luthers Werke*, 6:364, line 20; Luther, *Luther's Works*, 36:93, cited in Jensen, "Luther and the Lord's Supper," 324.

19. Jensen, "Luther and the Lord's Supper," 324.

20. Luther, *D. Martin Luthers Werke*, 6:497–573; Luther, *Luther's Works*, 36:3–236.

21. Jensen, "Luther and the Lord's Supper," 325.

22. McKim, *The Cambridge Companion to Martin Luther*, 29, 30.

23. Dixon, *The Church in the Early Modern Age*, 72. See also Alister E. McGrath, *Reformation Thought: An Introduction*, 4th ed. (Oxford: Wiley-Blackwell, 2012), 177–179.

24. Dixon, *The Church in the Early Modern Age*, 72.

25. Ibid., 72, 73.

26. Ibid.

27. Jensen, "Luther and the Lord's Supper," 326.

28. Allison, *Historical Theology*, 650.

29. Martin Luther, *D. Martin Luthers Werke: Kritische Gesamtausgabe*, vol. 26 (Weimar: Hermann Böhlau, 1909), 299, lines 17–21; Martin Luther, *Luther's Works*, vol. 37, *Word and Sacrament 3*, ed. Robert H. Fischer (Minneapolis, MN: Fortress, 1970), 195, quoted in Jensen, "Luther and the Lord's Supper," 327.

30. Jensen, "Luther and the Lord's Supper," 329.

31. Ibid.

32. Martin Luther, *D. Martin Luthers Werke: Kritische Gesamtausgabe, Briefwechsel*, vol. 12 (Weimar: Hermann Böhlau, 1967), 207, lines 17–20; 209, lines 12–15, cited in Jensen, "Luther and the Lord's Supper," 329.

33. Dixon, *The Church in the Early Middle Age*, 74, 75.

34. McKim, *The Cambridge Companion to Martin Luther*, 50.

35. Dixon, *The Church in the Early Modern Age*, 75.

36. See William Miller, Diary for 1846, Jenks Memorial Collection of Adventual Materials, Aurora University.

37. [James White], "The Conference," *Review and Herald*, May 24, 1864, 204.

38. *Proceedings of the Mutual Conference of Adventists, Held in the City of Albany, the 29th and 30th of April, and 1st of May, 1845* (New York: Joshua V. Himes, 1845), 20.

39. Josiah Litch, "Feet-Washing" *Advent Herald*, August 7, 1858, 254.

40. James White, "The Sabbath a Perpetual Weekly Memorial," *Present Truth*, July 1849, 3.

41. Ellen G. White to Sister Kellogg, Rochester, New York, December 5, 1853, Lt. 9, 1853, Ellen G. White Writings, accessed July 25, 2017, https://m.egwwritings.org/en /book/2889.2000001#0. This letter was republished as part of *Experience and Views* (1854), and then later republished in Ellen G. White, *Early Writings of Ellen G. White* (Battle Creek, MI: Review and Herald® Pub. Assn., 1882), 116, 117, as Ellen White's first published reference to the Communion service.

CHAPTER 12

Martin Luther's View on the State of the Dead

Trevor O'Reggio

M artin Luther's theology was forged in the crucible of his struggle to find forgiveness and peace from his overwhelming sense of guilt. He felt as if he hung in the balance between life and death. The German word that captures Luther's emotional state is *Anfechtung*: one feels cut off from God and hope is suffocated. "*Anfechtung* is the foretaste of the peril of death."[1] Not only did the fear of death terrorize him, but it also was an intimate part of his life. It is not surprising that Luther wrote much about death; some of his writings about it are, at times, confusing, contradictory, and complicated.

How did Luther view the state of the dead? Did he believe in soul sleep or in an immortal soul that survives death? Generally, two views exist among Christians concerning the state of the dead. The first view argues that when people die, their bodies perish, but their souls survive and continue to exist. At death, the souls of those who are saved go directly into Paradise. Those not-so-righteous believers go to a halfway house called *purgatory* (a Roman Catholic view) where they are purified and made ready for Paradise. Rebellious and unrepentant sinners go directly to hell to suffer in the eternal flames.[2] For most Protestants, there is no intermediate place called purgatory; after death, one goes to hell or to heaven. The basic agreement here is that the soul—whether righteous or sinful—is immortal. The immortal righteous soul enjoys the everlasting bliss of Paradise, while the sinful soul suffers the eternal agony of hell.

On December 19, 1513, at the Fifth Lateran Council, Pope Leo X issued a bull (*Apostolici regiminis*) declaring, "We do condemn and reprobate all who assert that the intelligent soul is mortal." This was directed against the growing "heresy" of those who denied the natural immortality of the soul. The bull also decreed that those who adhere to the like "erroneous" assertions should be shunned and punished as heretics.[3] This view further suggests that at the resurrection of the righteous, the body and the soul are reconnected, and salvation is now complete in a glorified state. The Catholic Church affirms the immortality of the soul and condemns those teaching contrary to this view.

The alternate position, sometimes called *soul sleep*, asserts that the soul is not a separate entity from the body, but that the body is a soul. At death, there is no surviving entity called the soul as the soul is dead; it is not immortal. In other words, the soul is simply the person, not a part of the person. It does not and cannot survive death. A person in this state is unaware of anything because there is no surviving entity called the soul that survives death; the Bible calls it a sleep. The soul is not in hell, heaven, or purgatory because it does not exist. At the resurrection, the person is raised again from the dead and becomes a living soul.[4]

With which of these two positions did Luther agree? These are the questions that will be explored in this chapter.

In trying to get a better handle on Luther's teaching on this matter, I have categorized his views into two main areas: first, where he writes definitively on death as a sleep; second, where he appears to be ambiguous or seems to contradict his view of death as a sleep.

Philip Secker's article "Martin Luther's Views on the State of the Dead" quotes Francis Blackburne, an eighteenth-century Anglican theologian. He asserts that Luther "espoused the doctrine of the sleep of the soul, upon a scripture foundation, and then he made use of it as a confutation of purgatory and saint worship, and continued in that belief to the last moment of his life."[5]

LeRoy Froom, the noted Adventist historian, used Blackburne's words later as evidence to support his views that Luther taught soul sleep. Speaking of the Reformer, he writes, "He stated many times that the Christian dead are unaware of anything, for they see not, feel not, understand not. They are asleep, oblivious of all passing events. More than one hundred times, scattered over the years, Luther declared death to be a sleep, and repeatedly asserted that in death there is total unconsciousness, and consequent unawareness of the passage of time."[6] Froom further asserts, "He [Luther] presses the point that death is a sound, sweet sleep. And furthermore, the dead will remain asleep until the day of resurrection, which resurrection embraces both body and soul, when both will be brought together again."[7] It is possible that Froom wanted to use what he perceived to be Luther's position on this subject to support the Adventist views on the state of the dead.

Is this characterization of Luther's view an accurate and balanced picture? Did Luther emphatically teach soul sleep without any variance? Was Luther's position an ambiguous one that finds support in both camps? Was Luther himself confused about his views and therefore wrote contradictory statements? Did his views change over time as his theological position shifted?

Luther's understanding of death in his early years was fundamentally a late-medieval Catholic view. Bernhard Lohse asserts that "Luther appropriated something from the dominant medieval view of death and judgment."[8] How did Luther's world deal with death and what were some of the prevailing explanations about it? For late medieval and early modern Europeans, death was a very frequent visitor. The average life expectancy was thirty years. One in four died in infancy; another 25 percent died before their first year; and 50 percent died before they reached the age of ten. One historian writes, "Marriages were dissolved by death as frequently as they are today by divorce, and remarriage was common and expected. In a world without antibiotics or reliably effective sanitation, influenza, smallpox, typhoid, and dysentery were regular and lethal callers (particularly in towns)."[9] But nothing could be compared to the devastating Black Death pandemics that swept across Europe from 1348 to the late 1660s, carrying millions to their graves. The impact of disease was exacerbated by wars and famines. Death was everywhere.

How did ordinary people cope with such unrelenting tragedy? "If theology matters to ordinary people at any time, it must surely do so here, in the act of contemplating the fate of loved ones after their death or peering through the veil to try to catch a glimpse of one's own eternal destiny."[10] The Catholic Church provided the prescriptive advice for people facing the trauma of death and dying. The church offered the sacraments to those facing death. There was ritual anointing called *extreme unction* in which oil was placed on eyes, ears, nostrils, mouth, hands, and feet as a dedication of the senses to God. The other deathbed sacrament was a last confession of sins and the administration of Communion, here called the *viaticum* (literally, that taken on a journey).[11]

The event that propelled Luther into historic prominence on October 31, 1517, was his attack on the abuse of the doctrine of indulgences by the papal emissary Johann Tetzel. Indulgences cannot be understood without understanding purgatory. Purgatory was a Scholastic doctrine invented by the medieval church to explain how God deals with those who are good but not good enough to merit immediate entry into heaven. Catholicism taught that Christ's atonement on the cross (collectively) and the sacrament of baptism (individually) freed humans from "original" sin and made it possible to gain access to heaven.

However, because of human nature's continuing propensity to commit "mortal" sins, this created a further barrier. So the church was delegated authority to forgive sins through the sacrament of Penance.

Medieval authorities made a distinction between the guilt attached to a mortal sin versus the penalty or satisfaction that was still due to God, even when the guilt was removed. The priest, through Penance, could only remove a small fraction of that satisfaction due, so that the remainder (along with the punishment for less serious or venial sins) would have to be paid off after death in purgatory. The time in purgatory could be measured in tens, hundreds, or thousands of years. So when the church began to issue indulgences (certificates remitting part or all of the satisfaction due for sin), they were expressed in terms of "days" and "years" equivalent to earthy Penances so that the perception was that the experience of purgatory was a temporary one.[12] Indulgences were first made available to assist souls in purgatory by a papal bull of 1476.[13]

The medieval church also popularized "the notion of a 'communion of saints,' the compelling idea that all Christian souls, whether saints in heaven, sinners on earth, or suffering in purgatory, were inextricably linked to each other, and that the living had the ability, and the duty, to ease the sufferings of the dead."[14] Consequently, a living person could alleviate the suffering of their dead relatives by paying an indulgence fee.[15]

The immediate cause of Luther's stand on soul sleep was the issue of purgatory, with its focus on the sufferings of anguished souls. In his Ninety-Five Theses, Luther addresses purgatory from the viewpoint of a believing Catholic. His original intent was not to abolish the system but to address the abuses and challenge the church for a debate on the subject. Although the Ninety-Five Theses were written in the fall of 1517, this was not Luther's first exposure to the German public because he had already written a popular article that was well received by the German people. His first essay, "Die Sieben puszpsalm," appeared in the spring of 1517 and, according to Heinz Bluhm, was met with "instantaneous success."[16] Martin Luther became the most widely read and beloved German writer. Some even consider him to be the master of the modern German language.[17] His Ninety-Five Theses, although originally written in Latin, were translated into German and were widely dispersed. They soon captured the imagination of the people and sparked the flame that ignited the Reformation across Europe.

Luther's early view of death

According to Paul Althaus, one of the earliest descriptions of Luther's early views on death was a sermon titled "Preparing to Die," which he preached in 1519. He describes death as a "narrow gate and the small way to life," which corresponds with the narrow exit through which a child is born into this world from the mother's body.[18]

Luther considered that in death " 'a dying man must courageously enter into anxiety with the knowledge that there will be great space and much joy afterwards.'[19] This is dying as faith sees it in the light of the gospel. The voice of the law says, 'In the midst of life, we are in death.' The voice of the gospel says, 'In the midst of death, we are in life.' "[20] Thus, in his earliest days, Luther still shows his dependency on the Catholic understanding of life after death. He spoke in favor of prayer for the dead as late as 1521.[21]

Moving away from the Catholic view of death

Until the end of his life, Luther believed in the dualistic view of human nature. The belief that at death the soul separates from the body was characteristic of all Magisterial Reformers.[22] The difference between Luther and other Reformers was his assertion that the separation of body and soul results in death being a sleep when the body perishes in dust and the soul enters a "sweet sleep," where it does not "feel nor see anything." With few variations, Luther consistently held this position until his death. In a sermon preached a year before his death, Luther asserted:

> We should learn to view our death in the right light, so that we need not become alarmed on account of it, as unbelief does; because in Christ it is indeed not death, but a *fine, sweet and brief sleep*, which brings us release from this vale of tears, from sin and from the fear and extremity of real death and from all the misfortunes of this life, and we shall be secure and without care, rest sweetly and gently for a brief moment, as on a sofa, until the time when he shall call and awaken us together with all his dear children to his eternal glory and joy. For since we call it a sleep, we know that we shall not remain in it, but be again awakened and live, and that the time during which we sleep, shall seem no longer than if we had just fallen asleep. Hence, we shall censure ourselves that we were surprised or alarmed at such a sleep in the hour of death, and suddenly come alive out of the grave and from decomposition, and entirely well, fresh, with a pure, clear, glorified life, meet our Lord and Savior Jesus Christ in the clouds.[23]

For Luther, those who die in Christ experience a sweet unconscious sleep after which comes awakening at the resurrection. It seems that around 1521–1522 he started changing his Catholic view of "soul-awareness" into a position that can be described as soul sleep. In a January 13, 1522, letter to Nicholas von Amsdorf, Luther wrote the following:

I am inclined to agree with your opinion that the souls of the just are *asleep* and that *they do not know where they are* up to the Day of Judgment. . . . But I do not dare to affirm that this is true for *all souls* in general. . . . Who knows how God deals with the separated souls? Can He just as well make them sleep on and off or for as long as He wished? . . .

I think the same about those condemned; some may feel punishments immediately after death, but others may be spared until that Day. . . . *Therefore, it is my opinion that these things are uncertain.* It is most probable, however, that with few exceptions, *all of the departed sleep without possessing any capacity of feeling.*[24]

In this letter, Luther shows that he is not sure about the nature of death. He confesses to von Amsdorf that "these things are uncertain." However, he ventures an opinion that "with few exceptions, all of the departed sleep without possessing any capacity of feeling." Luther further explains who these "few exceptions" are: "I am inclined to agree with your opinion that the souls of the just are asleep. . . . But I do not dare to affirm that this is true for all souls in general, because of the taking up of Paul, of Elijah, and of Moses (who certainly did not appear as phantoms on Mount Tabor). . . . And that passage in Luke 16 about Abraham and Lazarus—although it does not attribute sensation to all of the departed, yet it does attribute sensation to Abraham and Lazarus."[25] Thus, although the majority of the souls are in an unconscious sleep where there is no "sensation," for Luther, the examples of Elijah, Moses, Paul, and Abraham, prove that some exceptional souls are aware of their surroundings. For him, all the righteous souls are asleep, but there may be exceptions and he identifies such exceptions. There is some confusion between his earlier assertions about the just souls that are sleeping, but he offers no reasons why there are exceptions.

It is uncertain whether Luther counted the damned souls among the exceptions from the unconscious soul sleep. On a number of occasions, Luther confessed that he is not absolutely certain what happens to the wicked after their death.[26] In the above quoted letter to Nicholas von Amsdorf, Luther asks his colleague, "Consider now, who were the spirits in prison to whom . . . Christ preached?" Luther wondered, "Were they not able to sleep in Him until the [Last] Day?"[27] In a sermon preached in 1522, Luther said that the rich man of Luke 16 suffered "in his conscience" after his death and "had no rest."[28] While in 1525, Luther asserted that "the damned fall asleep against and not through Christ," whatever that might mean.[29]

Through the correspondence with von Amsdorf, it is obvious that Luther accepted some notion of soul sleep; whereas, at the same time, he tried to harmonize this idea with biblical texts that appear to suggest otherwise. Between 1522 and 1532, Luther affirmed the belief that the "dead know nothing" (Ecclesiastes 9:5, NKJV). In 1523, Luther said that the "dead do not experience time, hours, days or years."[30] In 1524, Luther said that the "dead know nothing."[31] In 1525, he stated that the dead "do not praise God."[32] In his sermon for the funeral of Frederick III, the elector of Saxony, Luther concluded, "Frederick rests and is quiet. Those who acknowledged Christ here on earth are now sleeping. Do not worry if [whether or not] Frederick also suffers pains and grieves as you do, for he rests and is quiet."[33] In 1526, he said about the righteous, "I think they are in such a sleep that they *neither feel nor see anything*." In 1532, Luther is recorded as saying: "The sleep is so deep that the dead *do not even dream*."[34] It seems that Luther was quite positive that the righteous dead, at least most of them, are completely oblivious; they do not feel, see, or know anything; and finally, they do not even dream but abide in complete unconsciousness.[35] The vast majority of Luther's statements support this position.

Luther's ambiguous statements

If these statements were the only ones Luther ever made on the state of the dead, then Froom and other conditionalists who argued that Luther was a firm supporter of soul sleep (for the majority of souls, at least) would be correct. However, the Reformer also made some ambiguous and contradictory statements during his later years. The majority of these stem from his *Lectures on Genesis* (written between 1535 and 1545). In them, he asserts several times that dead souls are conscious. The most pertinent quote in the category of contradictory statements can be found in his comments on Genesis 25:7–10: "There is a difference between the sleep or rest of this life and that of the future life. For toward night a person who has become exhausted by his daily labor in this life enters into his chamber in peace, as it were, to sleep there; and during this night he enjoys rest and has no knowledge whatever of any evil caused either by fire or by murder. But the soul does not sleep in the same manner. It is *awake*. It *experiences visions* and the *discourses of the angels and of God*."[36]

At first glance, this statement seems to contradict those earlier statements made between 1522 and 1532. But it must be noted that in the following verse, Luther defends his statement when he mentions the examples of Elijah and Moses as proof for his assertion. "But after death, soul enters into its bedroom and rests in peace. There it sleeps *without knowing that it is asleep*, and yet it still serves God with *awaken soul*. Thus, God is able to wake up Moses and Elijah etc. and in such way he can control [them] that they may become alive. But how can that be? We do not know enough about bodily sleep and how God affirms that this [state] is a sleep, quiet and peaceful."[37] Thus, the question is, who are these "few, exceptional ones" whom God chose to keep awake and let experience visions and discourses of angels and of God? Or, is this the case with all souls?

In the next chapter of his lecture, Luther adds the argument about Abraham in Luke 16 as another proof of the soul being asleep, but at the same time it is also ready for God to awaken it at any time. "These things must be carefully noted: because it is divine truth that Abraham lives, serves, and reigns with God. But what sort of life that is, whether he is asleep or awake, that is another question. How the soul rests, we are not to know."[38]

Luther is attempting to bring into line the biblical texts that affirm soul sleep and the biblical texts that seem to affirm the conscious activities of souls, such as Moses, Elijah, and Abraham. In trying to harmonize them, Luther comes to an ambiguous conclusion that souls who are asleep are at the same time available for God to "awaken" even before the judgment. It is in this light that we need to understand this and other similar comments (especially in his *Lectures on Genesis*), where he affirms that "God talks with the dead."[39] The dead can "hear," "think," and "see, although we do not know how"[40] "God opens the eyes of the dead."[41] They, he states, see with "spiritual eyes after death."[42] These statements seem to suggest that Luther believes in the conscious state of the dead.

Luther's contradictory statements

During the last few years of his life, Luther made statements that seem to indicate that all souls (not just the few exceptions) are completely awake, conscious, and even rejoicing in heaven. Such statements were frequently made during his funeral sermons. For example, in 1542, Luther wrote to Justus Jonas: "After mourning for a season, we shall enter into joy unspeakable, where your Cathy and my Magdalene, together with many others, have preceded us and daily call, admonish, and beckon us to follow."[43] In the same year, Luther wrote the following about the deceased Urbanus Rhegius: "We know that he is blessed and has life and eternal joy in fellowship with Christ and the heavenly church, in which he now personally learns, sees, and hears of those things which he proclaimed here in the church in accordance with the Word of God."[44] In 1544, when George Hoesel's son died, Luther consoled the bereaved father with these words: "You must have no doubt that your son is rejoicing with our Saviour, Christ, and with all the saints."[45]

How should these statements be reconciled with his earlier ones about an unconscious soul sleep? Did Luther change his views toward the end of his life? Is it possible to understand these funeral speeches as merely emphatic statements that do not reflect his actual beliefs? Were these merely pastoral exhortations to encourage and comfort the family of the deceased? But if that is so, why would these funeral sermons be at odds with his more reasoned theological views?

Some of what Luther said points to the fact that he struggled with the idea of the soul being dead but still alive through the mysterious soul-sleep phenomenon. In a sermon written around 1542, Luther argued that from God's point of view, death is not death but life, because God is not a God of the dead but of those who are alive. Nevertheless, Luther asks, "How can people be in the same time alive while dead and not breathing?" The Bible answers, they sleep, says Luther. Here are his words:

Death in Christ is nothing more than a mere sleep. . . .

. . . "How can a person be said to sleep when he no longer has either breath or life, is buried under ground and is in [the] process of decomposition?" . . .

. . . Christ says that to him the dying of a person is not death, but a sleep, yea, from his point of view none of those who have lived and died before our time are dead, but are all alive, as those we see standing before us; for he has concluded that all shall live, yea, he holds their lives in their hands.[46]

Soul sleep or immortal soul sleep?

The great majority of Luther's clearest statements definitively support a doctrine of soul sleep. Yet at the same time, we must acknowledge that, for Luther, souls who sleep are still immortal. Luther is not a conditionalist. For him, souls are immortal. The souls of the righteous sleep before God and await resurrection (with a few souls already being awaken), while the damned souls lay in darkness, waiting for God.

Bernhard Lohse confidently asserts that Luther held to the immortality of the soul.[47] For Lohse, Luther's argument is strictly theological. Paraphrasing Luther, he states, "God creates the soul immortal in the womb."[48] Quoting from Luther, he continues, " 'He speaks with man alone. Accordingly, where and with whomever God speaks, whether in anger or in grace, that person is surely immortal. The Person of God, who speaks, and the Word point out that we are the kind of creatures with whom God would want to speak eternally and in an immortal manner.' "[49] Lohse continues to quote from Luther: " 'Those who believe in him, and acknowledge him from whom they have their being never die. Their natural life will be stretched out into life eternal, so that they never taste death.' " He then quotes John 8:51: " 'If any one keeps my word, he will never see death.' " Lohse quotes again from Luther: " 'When we are dead, we are not dead to [God]. For he is not a God of the dead but God of Abraham etc., who live; as it is said in Matthew 22 [v. 32] "they are not dead but live to me." ' "[50]

Although these quotes clearly talk about the immortality of the soul, none of them disprove of soul sleep. In these quotes, Luther did not address the issue of the state of the dead. He affirms the reality of Jesus' words that death has no power over those who believe in the gospel.

Conclusion

Writing for a funeral service in 1542, Luther penned these words:

But we Christians . . . should train and accustom ourselves in faith to despise death and regard it as a *deep, strong, sweet sleep*; to consider the coffin as nothing other than our Lord Jesus' bosom or Paradise, the grave as nothing other than a soft couch of ease or rest. As verily, before God, it truly is just this; for he testifies, John 11:21; Lazarus, our friend sleeps; Matthew 9:24: The maiden is not dead, she sleeps. Thus, too, St. Paul in 1 Corinthians 15, removes from sight all hateful aspects of death as related to our mortal body and brings forward nothing but charming and joyful aspects of the promised life. He says there [vv. 42ff.]: It is sown in corruption and will rise in incorruption; it is sown in dishonor (that is, a hateful, shameful form) and will rise in glory; it is sown in weakness and will rise in strength; it is sown in natural body and will rise a spiritual body.[51]

Throughout his life, Luther utilized the biblical metaphor of sleep to describe death. He called it "a deep, strong, sweet sleep." This is no ordinary sleep by virtue of the adjectives he used to describe this kind of sleep: it is "deep," "strong," and "sweet." Luther often affirmed that *the departed sleep without possessing any capacity of feeling*[52] and that the dead soul therefore has no consciousness, no sense of awareness, and so on.

Philip Secker suggests that Luther declares death to be a sleep more than 100 times. Luther also repeatedly asserts that in death there is total unconsciousness and no awareness of the passage of time.[53] The Lutheran scholar T. A. Kantonen refers to Luther's view of death in these terms: "Luther, with a greater emphasis on the resurrection, preferred to concentrate on the scriptural metaphor of sleep. 'For just as one who falls asleep and reaches morning unexpectedly when he awakes, without knowing what happened to him so we shall suddenly rise on the last day without knowing how we have come into death and through death.' 'We shall sleep, until He comes and knocks on the little grave and says, Doctor Martin, get up! Then I shall rise in a moment, and be happy with Him forever!' "[54]

Paul Althaus focuses primarily on Luther's theology of death and the resurrection rather than explaining Luther's view on the state of the dead. He asserts that Luther answers the question of where we are in death by referring to the Word of God. For Luther, the Word declares that Christians rest in the bosom of Christ.[55] What does Luther mean by this? Are Christians literally in heaven with Christ, or does Christ preserve the identity of Christians until the resurrection? Luther's bold, revolutionary statement "that the dead know nothing" stands in sharp contrast to the traditional teaching of his day in which Christian souls were placed in some intermediate state between Paradise and hell. For Luther, all who die in faith have their place in God's Word and Christ's promise. They "rest" and "sleep" in the bosom of Christ.[56]

Althaus concludes that while Luther retained a Hellenistic dualist definition of death as a separation of soul and body, the Reformer's thinking, however, is dominated by the New Testament insights on death, which he understood as a "deep and dreamless sleep without consciousness and feeling." In Luther's words, "For just as a man who falls asleep and sleeps soundly until morning does not know what has happened to him when he wakes up, so we shall suddenly rise on the Last Day; and we shall know neither what death has been like or how we have come through it."[57]

Althaus also acknowledged Luther's apparent inconsistency: for in trying to explain some difficult biblical passages, Luther argues, souls can "experience visions and hearing God and the angels speak."[58] This flatly contradicts his other statements on the unconsciousness at death. Thus, we must ask, Which is it, Luther? Are the souls unconscious at death or conscious; are they in heaven or are they in the grave? Did Luther, in his older years, yield to the pressure of other Reformers, who tried to avoid the concept of unconsciousness by emphasizing more of the living aspect of soul sleep? Or was Luther trying not to sound like some Anabaptist thinkers of his time, who were strong proponents of soul sleep? Unfortunately, the answers to these complex questions are not clear, and more study is needed to clarify them.

How does one explain Luther's apparent conflict on the state of the dead? One scholar proposes that Luther "was reluctant to speak of the total death of a person when at the same time strongly believing in the certainty of this person's being awakened by the voice of God at the last day."[59] It is not easy to understand Luther, for he defies labeling. Simplistic explanations about the state of the dead are problematic. There is no question that Luther wanted to remain faithful to the biblical record, and it is clear from the New Testament that such a focus was never simply on the dead and what they may or may not be doing. The New Testament emphasizes Christ's triumph over death and sin. The focus is on the certainty of the resurrection for the saints because of Christ's own resurrection. So Luther's essential focus is on the resurrection power over death, for now death holds no power over the believer, and it is never the last word. The believer can therefore live without fear of death or the grave, for both have been conquered in Christ Jesus, our Lord.

Luther's views on the state of the dead have important implications on the nature of humanity and the final disposition of the wicked. Adventists remain at odds with much of Christianity (both Catholics and Protestants) on these two vital subjects. Most of Christianity believes in the conscious state of the dead and in an immortal soul that survives death and therefore is never totally destroyed by hell. Are Luther's views, as Froom asserts, similar to that of Adventism? The answer is both Yes and No. The vast majority of his statements appears to support soul sleep, although he contradicts himself on some occasions, and he never fully abandoned the doctrine of the immortality of the soul. Adventists admire the best that Luther wrote on this subject but must go beyond him by crafting a doctrine that is biblically sound and in keeping with the character of God. The reason is that the doctrine of an immortal soul burning in hell eternally, casts a grave shadow upon the character of God and remains one of the most pernicious misrepresentations of a loving God. Adventists believe the doctrine of the soul's immortality will feature prominently in the final masterpiece of deception by the enemy just prior to Christ's return. It is therefore imperative to remain rooted in Scripture. Soul sleep as taught in Scripture affirms the benevolence and mercy of a loving heavenly Father and refutes false misrepresentations made by the devil concerning the character of God, which is ultimately the central issue of the cosmic conflict.

1. Gerhard Sauter, "Luther on the Resurrection," in *Harvesting Martin Luther's Reflections on Theology, Ethics, and the Church*, ed. Timothy J. Wengert (Grand Rapids, MI: Eerdmans, 2004), 107.

2. Heinrich Denzinger, ed., *The Sources of Catholic Dogma*, trans. Roy J. Deferrari (St. Louis, MO: Herder, 1957), 181, 184, 193, 197, 199, 206, 237, 238.

3. Ibid., 237, 238.

4. Such a concept was held in the time of Luther by the English Reformer William Tyndale, who argued against Thomas More in favor of soul sleep. See William Tyndale, *An Answer to Sir Thomas More's Dialogue* (Cambridge: Cambridge University Press, 1850), 180; see also Michael Watts, *The Dissenters: From the Reformation to the French Revolution* (Oxford: Oxford University Press, 1985), 119. In contemporary theology, the Seventh-day Adventists are the largest body of believers in soul sleep. This teaching is considered one of their fundamental teachings and marks one of the major differences that they have with mainline Protestantism. See "Death and Resurrection," in *Seventh-day Adventists Believe*, 2nd ed. (Silver Spring, MD: Ministerial Association, General Conference of Seventh-day Adventists, 2005), 387–401.

5. Francis Blackburne, *A Short Historical View of the Controversy Concerning an Intermediate State and the Separate Existence of the Soul Between Death and the General Resurrection Deduced From the Beginning of the Protestant Reformation to the Present Times* (London: T. Field, 1765), 14, quoted in Philip J. Secker, "Martin Luther's Views on the State of the Dead," *Concordia Theological Monthly* 38, no. 7 (July/August 1967): 422–435.

6. LeRoy Froom, *The Conditionalist Faith of Our Fathers*, vol. 2 (Washington, DC: Review and Herald® Pub. Assn., 1965), 76, 77.

7. Ibid., 2:77.

8. Bernhard Lohse, *Martin Luther's Theology: Its Historical and Systematic Development*, trans. and ed. Roy A. Harrisville (Minneapolis, MN: Fortress Press, 1999), 325, 326.

9. Peter Marshall, "Leaving the World," in *Reformation Christianity*, ed. Peter Matheson, vol.

5, A People's History of Christianity (Minneapolis, MN: Fortress Press, 2007), 168.

10. Ibid., 5:169.

11. Ibid., 5:170.

12. Ibid., 5:174.

13. "Our aim is that the salvation of souls may be secured above all at that time when they most need the intercession of others and are least able to help themselves. We wish by our Apostolic authority to draw on the treasury of the Church and to succour the souls in purgatory who died united with Christ through love and whose lives have merited that such intercessions should now be offered through an Indulgence of this kind. With the longings of such great paternal affection . . . we grant by concession and indulgence as follows:

"If any parents, friends or other Christians are moved by obligations of piety towards these very souls who are exposed to the fire of purgatory . . . let them during the stated period of ten years give a fixed amount or value of money, as laid down by its dean and chapter or by our own collector, for the repair of the church of Saints, paying either in person at the Church or by duly accredited messengers." Pope Sixtus IV, *Salvator Noster*, 1476, quoted in E. G. Rupp and Benjamin Drewery, eds., *Martin Luther*, Documents of Modern History (London: Edward Arnold, 1970), 14.

14. Marshall, "Leaving the World," 175.

15. The most famous indulgence preacher of the late-medieval period was Johann Tetzel, who went about Saxony, Germany, preaching the indulgence message while raising funds to repair Saint Peter's Basilica. Luther's Ninety-Five Theses were a response to what Luther saw as a blatant abuse and exploitation of the indulgence doctrine by this flamboyant and charismatic cleric. Carter Lindberg, *The European Reformations*, 2nd ed. (Oxford: Wiley-Blackwell, 2010), 71.

16. Heinz Bluhm, "Luther's View of Man in His Early German Writings," *Concordia Theological Monthly* 34, no. 10 (October 1963): 583.

17. Ibid.

18. Paul Althaus, *The Theology of Martin Luther* (Philadelphia, PA: Fortress Press, 1966), 408.

19. Martin Luther, *D. Martin Luthers Werke: Kritische Gesamtausgabe*, vol. 2 (Weimar: Hermann Böhlau, 1884), 685, quoted in ibid.

20. Martin Luther, *Luther's Works*, vol. 13, *Selected Psalms 2*, ed. Jaroslav Pelikan (St. Louis, MO: Concordia: 1956), 83, quoted in Althaus, *The Theology of Martin Luther*, 408. See also Martin Luther, *Luther's Works*, vol. 53, *Liturgy and Hymns*, ed. Ulrich S. Leupold (St. Louis, MO: Concordia, 1965), 275.

21. *Sermon* [1st printed ed.] (1520), in Martin Luther, *D. Martin Luthers Werke: Kritische Gesamtausgabe*, vol. 6 (Weimar: Hermann Böhlau, 1888), 372, lines 4–10; see Secker, "Martin Luther's Views on the State of the Dead," 433.

22. Luther's view of death was firmly embedded in the classic division between body and soul. In one of his last sermons before his death, Luther explains this division in these words: "It is not difficult for Christ, in the hour when body and soul are separated, to hold in his hand the soul and spirit of man, even though we ourselves neither feel nor see anything, yea, even though the body be entirely consumed. For, since he can preserve the breath of life and spirit, apart from the body, so he can again bring the body together out of dust and ashes. This he has proved in

this and similar examples, when he restored to life with one work those who had truly died and whose body and soul had been separated. Hence we must conclude that he holds in his hand the life of those who have died; for if this power did not belong to him, he could not restore life." Martin Luther, "On Matthew 9:16–25" (1544), in *The Complete Sermons of Martin Luther*, ed. John Nicholas Lenker, trans. John Nicholas Lenker et al., vol. 5 (Grand Rapids, MI: Baker Books, 2000), 358.

23. Ibid., 5:359 (emphasis added).

24. Martin Luther, "Letter to Nicholas von Amsdorf" (1522), in *D. Martin Luthers Werke: Kritische Gesamtausgabe, Briefwechsel*, vol. 2 (Weimar: Hermann Böhlau, 1931), 422, lines 4–6, 10–25; Martin Luther, *Luther's Works*, vol. 48, *Letters 1*, ed. Helmut T. Lehmann (St. Louis, MO: Concordia, 1963), 360, 361, with a few changes made by Secker, "Martin Luther's Views on the State of the Dead," 428 (emphasis added).

25. Ibid. According to the Bible, Moses' body was resurrected (Jude 1; Matthew 17:1–9) and Elijah's body was taken to heaven without seeing death. It seems that the Reformer thought that only their souls were taken to heaven and not their bodies.

26. Martin Luther, "Sermon" (1522), in *D. Martin Luthers Werke: Kritische Gesamtausgabe*, vol. 10, bk. 3 (Weimar: Hermann Böhlau, 1905), 194, lines 17–19; Martin Luther, "Sermon" (1523), printed ed., in *D. Martin Luthers Werke: Kritische Gesamtausgabe*, vol. 11 (Weimar: Hermann Böhlau, 1900), 127–131; Martin Luther, "Commentary on Genesis on 25:7–10" (1540), in *D. Martin Luthers Werke: Kritische Gesamtausgabe*, vol. 43 (Weimar: Hermann Böhlau, 1912), 361, lines 30–36. See also Martin Luther, *Luther's Works*, vol. 4, *Lectures on Genesis, Chapters 21–25*, ed. Jaroslav Pelikan (St. Louis, MO: Concordia, 1964), 314–316, 362, 363; Martin Luther, "Commentary on Genesis on 42:38" (1544), in *D. Martin Luthers Werke: Kritische Gesamtausgabe*, vol. 44 (Weimar: Hermann Böhlau, 1915), 517, lines 31–36; Martin Luther, *Luther's Works*, vol. 7, *Lectures on Genesis, Chapters 38–44*, ed. Jaroslav Pelikan (St. Louis, MO: Concordia, 1965), 294.

27. Luther, "Letter to Nicholas von Amsdorf," quoted in Secker, "Martin Luther's Views on the State of the Dead," 429.

28. Luther, "Sermon" (1522), Luther's ed., in *D. Martin Luthers Werke*, vol. 10, bk. 3, p. 192, lines 12–18, 28, 29; see Rörer's notes in Luther, "Sermon" (1523), in *D. Martin Luthers Werke*, 11:130, lines 13–17.

29. Unbelievers "entschlaffen nicht durch, sondern, wieder Jesus und sind verdampt." This comes from the 1539 Wittenberg edition of a sermon preached in 1525. Martin Luther, *D. Martin Luthers Werke: Kritische Gesamtausgabe*, vol. 17, bk. 1 (Weimar: Hermann Böhlau, 1907), 211, line 36.

30. Luther, "Sermon" (1523), Luther's ed., in *D. Martin Luthers Werke*, vol. 10, bk. 3, p. 194, line 17. He said this repeatedly; see Rörer's post notes in "Sermon" (1523), in *D. Martin Luthers Werke*, 11:130, lines 25–29; Martin Luther, "Annotations on the Book of Ecclesiastes" (1532), in *D. Martin Luthers Werke: Kritische Gesamtausgabe*, vol. 20 (Weimar: Hermann Böhlau, 1898), 162, lines 27–163.

31. Martin Luther, "Sermon" (1524), printed ed., in *D. Martin Luthers Werke: Kritische Gesamtausgabe*, vol. 14 (Weimar: Hermann Böhlau, 1895), 70, lines 14–19. See also Martin

Luther, "Anton Lauterbachs" (1538), in *D. Martin Luthers Werke: Kritische Gesamtausgabe, Tischreden*, vol. 3 (Weimar: Hermann Böhlau, 1898), 697, no. 3904, lines 3–7.

32. Martin Luther, *Die sieben Busspsalmen* (1525), in *D. Martin Luthers Werke: Kritische Gesamtausgabe*, vol. 18 (Weimar: Hermann Böhlau, 1908), 482, lines 4–7; Martin Luther, *Seven Penitential Psalms*, in *Luther's Works*, vol. 14, *Selected Psalms 3*, ed. Daniel E. Poellot (St. Louis, MO: Concordia, 1956), 143.

33. Martin Luther, "Sermon" (1525), in *D. Martin Luthers Werke: Kritische Gesamtausgabe*, vol. 17, bk. 1 (Weimar: Hermann Böhlau, 1907), 203, lines 13–17.

34. Martin Luther, *Der Prophet Jona ausgelegt* (1526), in *D. Martin Luthers Werke: Kritische Gesamtausgabe*, vol. 19 (Weimar: Hermann Böhlau, 1897), 221, lines 24–28 (emphasis added). See Rörer's notes in Martin Luther, "Sermon" (1532), in *D. Martin Luthers Werke: Kritische Gesamtausgabe*, vol. 36 (Weimar: Hermann Böhlau, 1909), 252, lines 8, 9; Martin Luther, *Luther's Works*, vol. 51, *Sermons 1*, ed. and trans. John W. Doberstein (Philadelphia, PA: Fortress Press, 1973), 241, 242. See also a letter to Luther's father in 1530: Martin Luther, *D. Martin Luthers Werke: Kritische Gesamtausgabe, Briefwechsel*, vol. 5 (Weimar: Hermann Böhlau, 1934), 240, lines 64–70, and Luther, "Annotations on the Book of Ecclesiastes" (1532), in *D. Martin Luthers Werke,* 20:162, lines 27–163.

35. I would like to acknowledge the contribution of my graduate assistant, Dojcin Zivadinovic for much of this section.

36. "Anima autem non sic dormit, sed vigilat, et patitur visiones, loquelas Angelorum et Dei." Martin Luther, "Lectures on Genesis on 25:7–10," in *D. Martin Luthers Werke*, 43:360, lines 24–33; Luther, *Luther's Works*, 4:313 (emphasis added).

37. Ibid. (emphasis added).

38. Martin Luther, "Commentary on Genesis 26:24–25" (1540), in *D. Martin Luthers Werke: Kritische Gesamtausgabe,* vol. 43 (Weimar: Hermann Böhlau, 1912), 480, lines 11–15 (author's translation).

39. "Loquitur Deus cum mortuis non aliter." Luther, "Commentary on Genesis on 26:24–25" (1540), in *D. Martin Luthers Werke*, 43:481, lines 24, 25, quoted in Secker, "Martin Luther's Views on the State of the Dead," 432.

40. "*Es ist war.* Animae audiunt, sentiunt, vident post mortem, *aber wie es zugeheit, vorsthen wir nicht.*" Martin Luther, "Heidenreich" (1542–1543), in *D. Martin Luthers Werke: Kritische Gesamtausgabe, Tischreden*, vol. 5 (Weimar: Hermann Böhlau, 1919), 219, no. 5534, lines 3–8. See also Martin Luther, *Luther's Works*, vol. 1, *Lectures on Genesis, Chapters 1–5*, ed. Jaroslav Pelikan (St. Louis, MO: Concordia, 1958), 287.

41. "Quando aliquis Sanctus mor[itur], deus aperit amb[o] oc[ulos]." Rörer's notes *in* Luther, "Sermon" (1532), *D. Martin Luthers Werke*, 36:260, line 6 (30 in the printed ed.); Luther, *Luther's Works*, 51:247.

42. "Oculos spirituales, quibus credentes in Christum videant, cum per mortem isti corporis oculi clausi, vel potius prorsus extincti sunt." Martin Luther, "Commentary on Genesis on 15:1" (1537–1538), in *D. Martin Luthers Werke: Kritische Gesamtausgabe*, vol. 42 (Weimar: Hermann Böhlau, 1911), 556, lines 8–10; Martin Luther, *Luther's Works*, vol. 3, *Lectures on Genesis, Chapters 15–20*, ed. Jaroslav Pelikan (St. Louis, MO: Concordia, 1961),11.

43. Martin Luther, "Letter to Justus Jonas" (1542), in *D. Martin Luthers Werke: Kritische Gesamtausgabe, Briefwechsel*, vol. 10 (Weimar: Hermann Böhlau, 1947), 227, no. 3829, lines 27–30; quoted in Martin Luther, *Luther: Letters of Spiritual Counsel*, ed. and trans. Theodore G. Tappert, vol. 18, Library of Christian Classics (Westminster: John Knox Press, 1955), 76.

44. Martin Luther, preface to *Urbanus Rhegius, Prophetiae veteris testamenti de Christo* (1542), in *D. Martin Luthers Werke: Kritische Gesamtausgabe*, vol. 53 (Weimar: Hermann Böhlau, 1920), 400, lines 17–19.

45. Martin Luther, "To George Hoesel" (1544), in Martin Luther, *Luther: Letters of Spiritual Counsel*, ed. and trans. Theodore G. Tappert, vol. 18, Library of Christian Classics (Westminster: John Knox Press, 1955), 79. See also Luther, *D. Martin Luthers Werke: Kritische Gesamtausgabe, Briefwechsel*, 10:699, lines 9–13.

46. Luther, *The Complete Sermons of Martin Luther*, 357, 358.

47. Lohse, *Martin Luther's Theology*, 326. The author suggests that the evidence for this has been furnished by Werner Thiede, "Nur ein ewiger Augenblick: Luthers Lehre vom Seelenschlaf zwischen Tod und Auferweckung," *Luther* 64, no. 3 (1993): 112–125.

48. Martin Luther, *D. Martin Luthers Werke: Kritische Gesamtausgabe*, vol. 39, bk. 2 (Weimar: Hermann Böhlau, 1926), 401, cited in Lohse, *Martin Luther's Theology*, 327.

49. Martin Luther, *Luther's Works*, vol. 5, *Lectures on Genesis, Chapters 26–30*, ed. Jaroslav Pelikan (St. Louis, MO: Concordia, 1968), 76, quoted in Lohse, *Martin Luther's Theology*, 327.

50. Martin Luther, *Luther's Works*, vol. 52, *Sermons 2*, ed. Hans. J. Hildebrand (St. Louis, MO: Concordia, 1973), 55, quoted in Lohse, *Martin Luther's Theology*, 326, 327.

51. Martin Luther, "Christian Song Latin and German, for Use at Funerals" (1542), in *Works of Martin Luther*, vol. 6 (Philadelphia, PA: Muhlenberg Press, 1932), 287, 288 (emphasis added).

52. See Luther, "Letter to Nicholas von Amsdorf," quoted in Secker, "Martin Luther's Views on the State of the Dead," 429.

53. Secker, "Martin Luther's Views on the State of the Dead," 422–435.

54. T. A. Kantonen, *The Christian Hope* (Philadelphia, PA: Muhlenberg Press, 1954), 37. For Luther's reference, see Martin Luther, *D. Martin Luthers Werke: Kritische Gesamtausgabe*, vol. 37 (Weimar: Hermann Böhlau, 1910), 151.

55. Althaus, *The Theology of Martin Luther*, 412. Luther, *D. Martin Luthers Werke*, 43:361; Luther, *Luther's Works*, 4:313.

56. Althaus, *The Theology of Martin Luther*, 412, 413.

57. Althaus, *The Theology of Martin Luther*, 414; Luther, *D. Martin Luthers Werke*, 17:11, 235.

58. Luther, *D. Martin Luthers Werke*, 43:360, lines 24–33; Luther, *Luther's Works*, 4:313, quoted on page 12.

59. Winfried Vogel, "The Eschatological Theology of Martin Luther; Part 1: Luther's Basic Concepts," *Andrews University Seminary Studies* 24. no. 3 (Autumn 1986): 263.

CHAPTER 13

Martin Luther and the Sabbath

Sergio Becerra

Why are Seventh-day Adventists interested in Martin Luther's view of the Sabbath? In his teaching on the Ten Commandments, he considers eight commandments still valid for Christians but not the commandments concerning the veneration of images and the Sabbath. Regardless, Luther had quite a few things to say about the Sabbath. Luther was very intuitive about God's original purpose for humanity when God, at the very beginning of Earth's history, gave us the weekly day of worship and rest.

This chapter presents Martin Luther's thinking on the biblical Sabbath and explores why he did not see the full validity of this divine institution for Christians. We will also look at God's purpose in giving a day of rest and its usefulness for today.

In order to better understand Luther's perspective, it is important to provide some background on the Ten Commandments, Sabbath, and Sunday observance, and then on Luther's perspective of the biblical Sabbath.

Mosaic law and Sunday observance during the Middle Ages

In general, Western Christians viewed the commandments, in particular the

Sabbath commandment, through the teachings of Augustine of Hippo and Thomas Aquinas. Augustine spiritualized the commandment of the Sabbath. He maintained that observance of the Sabbath did not mean ceasing from work but ceasing from sin and experiencing rest in the heart.[1] For Augustine, Sunday was a Christian holy day for worship and useful activity, and it consisted of a festive element not present in the Jewish Sabbath observance.[2]

Over time, Sunday observance became the Christian Sabbath, and for some, rest was the norm. The Mosaic law was a model for their legislation.[3] The medieval church considered Sunday observance a means for developing religiosity. It used the Old Testament, especially the Decalogue, as a tool to enforce Sunday observance. The church employed three approaches to attain this goal: "enacted ecclesiastical legislation derived from the Mosaic laws,"[4] assistance through civil authorities,[5] and the superstition of the masses.[6] The result was a preference for the interruption of physical work instead of the Augustinian ideal of a spiritual cessation from sinning, along with internal rest. Sunday became the Christian Sabbath that should be observed according to the Sabbath commandment of the Decalogue.[7]

Thomas Aquinas, the twelfth-century theologian, stated that the replacement of Sunday as the Sabbath was not by virtue of the law but through the authority of the church and the custom of the people.[8] He also maintained that the Sabbath commandment was partly moral and partly ceremonial. It was moral in that humans should set aside time to focus upon the things of God, but the particular time commanded was not meant to be binding upon Christians. As a result, the church could determine the appropriate time for religious gathering.[9]

The Reformers and the law

The Reformers radically inverted the late-medieval understanding about the Sabbath commandment in favor of "sabbatizing" Sunday observance. Although the Reformers disagreed with the Scholastic view of Sabbatarianism, such divergence was only superficial. The Protestant Reformers retained a certain number of medieval theological principles upon which Sunday sanctification was based. These principles included (1) having the Decalogue, according to Augustinian tradition, remain at the center of Christian morality. (2)

> During the Middle Ages, Sunday worship was based primarily upon church authority.

Reformers, like Scholastic theologians, identified the second table of the Decalogue as a synthesis of the revealed natural law. (3) They made a distinction between "moral" and "ceremonial" elements in the fourth commandment. (4) The Reformers did not argue in favor of Sunday worship based upon Scripture. During the Middle Ages, Sunday worship was based primarily upon church authority. By rejecting this authority, the Reformers turned Sunday into a social

institution. And (5) those Protestant Reformers who differentiated Sunday observance from the Mosaic Sabbath continued to stress the need to consecrate
one day out of seven for religious worship.[10]

Martin Luther's view of the law and the Sabbath

In essence, Luther's understanding of the Decalogue was Scholastic—"Moses
is dead."[11] "For not one little period in Moses pertains to us."[12] And finally,
"For God never led us out of Egypt, but only the Jews."[13] Luther rejected the
authority of the Decalogue as the law of Moses and claimed that it applied
only to the Jews. However, he stated that the Decalogue was natural law and is
therefore mandatory for all humans. "Why does one then keep and teach the
Ten Commandments? Answer: Because the natural laws were never so orderly
and well written as by Moses. Therefore it is reasonable to follow the example
of Moses."[14] Like Thomas Aquinas, Luther perceived ceremonial elements in
the Decalogue; those elements that would be abrogated by Christ. Thus, "Moses' legislation about images and the Sabbath, and what else goes beyond the
natural law, since it is not supported by the natural law, is free, null and void,
and is specifically given to the Jewish people alone."[15] It is clear that Luther, by
referring only to the natural law, did not distinguish which elements were moral
and which were ceremonial in the Decalogue. He maintained that the New
Testament supported neither of these commandments.[16]

Luther, for the most part, held a different view of the law and Sabbath
from that of the Roman Catholic Church and from other Reformers. Andreas
Karlstadt, once Luther's colleague and friend, distanced himself from Luther.
Karlstadt stated that the commandments about the Sabbath and prohibiting
the veneration of images were still valid.[17] Karlstadt's views were similar to later
Protestant positions, but Luther opposed him in the name of Christian liberty.
Edward Allen maintains Luther misunderstood Karlstadt's theology of the Sabbath.[18] Karlstadt was no Sabbatarian, although he favored a spiritual experience
of the Sabbath. Luther, in his writing against Karlstadt, denied that Christians
had any religious obligation to keep a day of rest or even to have a day for
worship.[19]

Yet the Sabbath commandment had spiritual and practical value for Luther.
People always need rest, time to recover from physical forces, and a consecrated
period for worship and religious instruction.[20] Luther considered physical rest as
the important element in the Sabbath commandment as it related to the natural
law. But he interpreted it in a very broad manner: "For where it [the Sabbath]
is kept for the sake of rest alone, it is clear that he who does not need rest may
break the sabbath and rest on some other day, as nature allows."[21] In other
words, for Luther, the natural law demanded that human beings separate some
time for physical rest and worship. It does not specifically prescribe how much
time or the precise moment this should be done. For him, human authority

should establish specific demands that make it possible to have a weekly rest day on Sunday as a legitimate and necessary rest for the common good.

Luther stated many positive things about the Sabbath. In his exposition of Genesis 2:2, he wrote, "The Sabbath, or the Sabbath rest, denotes that God ceased in such a way that He did not create another heaven and another earth."[22] But according to Luther, God's ceasing and rest does not imply that He ceased preserving and governing the earth He had created.[23] Christ said, "The Sabbath was made for man," but Moses said "that God blessed the Sabbath and that He sanctified it for Himself."[24] For Luther, this means the Sabbath should be devoted to worship and set aside for a specific sacred purpose. He wrote the following: "If Adam had remained in a state of innocence, he nevertheless would have held the seventh day sacred. That is, on this day he would have given thanks; he would have sacrificed, etc. On the other days he would have tilled his fields and tended his cattle. Indeed, even after the Fall he kept the seventh day sacred; that is, on this day he instructed his family. . . . Therefore, from the beginning of the world, the Sabbath was intended for the worship of God."[25] As a part of worship, the Sabbath would allow the worshiper to get to know God. "Then it is also shown here that man was especially created for the knowledge and worship of God; for the Sabbath was not ordained for sheep and cows but for men, that in them the knowledge of God might be developed and might increase."[26] This knowledge will help us to know that there is another life after this life and in order "to attain it we need the Word and the knowledge of God." So for Luther, this is what the Sabbath or the rest of God meant: it is a time in "which God speaks with us through His Word and we, in turn, speak with Him through prayer and faith." This is only possible between God and human beings; it occurs during the Sabbath and thus "clearly proves . . . that man was created not for this physical life only, like the other animals, but for eternal life, just as God."[27]

According to Luther, the sanctifying power of the Sabbath intended for Adam and his descendants (including after the Fall) has the ability to restore the spiritual life for Christians: "God wanted this command about sanctifying the Sabbath to remain in force." And also "because the Sabbath command remains for the church, it denotes that spiritual life is to be restored to us through Christ."[28] Although one must be careful in regard to what Luther meant when he applied the Sabbath to the church, he did allegorize Paradise and the Sabbath by stating that Christ rested in the tomb during the entire Sabbath and was

It seems puzzling that Luther, after offering a glowing description of the Sabbath for Adam and his descendants before and after the Fall, engaged himself in what William M. Landeen called "a theological odyssey of the Sabbath in human history."

resurrected on the eighth day. The Resurrection therefore brought forth a new spiritual reality in which days no longer counted. It was most important to observe one eternal day for God's elect—God's eternal Sabbath.[29]

It seems puzzling that Luther, after offering a glowing description of the Sabbath for Adam and his descendants before and after the Fall, engaged himself in what William M. Landeen called "a theological odyssey of the Sabbath in human history."[30] Luther believed Abraham associated the Sabbath with other rites, such as circumcision, making it a Hebrew tribal tradition. He explained that when Moses arrived as the Hebrew lawgiver he undertook this Sabbath tradition and included it in the Decalogue. He recognized that God or the angels spoke the commandments, but that the commandment God pronounced was probably "Remember the sabbath day, to keep it holy" (Exodus 20:8). Luther explained, "In itself it is a universal command for all the world. But the ornamentation that Moses gives it and makes it peculiar for his own people obligates no one especially except the Jews to keep."[31] Luther explained the "ornamentation" as a reference to Creation and the seventh day in the Sabbath commandment and that it was not meant to last forever.[32] But the idea behind "remember the sabbath day, to keep it holy" was based on the natural law, while the rest of the commandment was not.[33] He then explains why Christians keep Sunday: "Although all days are free and open, one like another, it is nevertheless useful, good, and necessary to observe one, be it Sabbath, Sunday, or any other day, because God wants to rule the world orderly and peacefully. Therefore, He gave six days over to labor, but on the seventh day servants, day laborers, and all labors, even horse, ox, and other working animals, must rest and recuperate according to the commandment."[34] Luther was quite liberal regarding Sunday rest as compared to later positions held by the second generation of Protestant Reformers. He was careful to relate Sunday rest to the Sabbath commandment in a minor way.

Why was Luther able to see so many benefits to the Sabbath before and after the Fall, while failing to preserve its value for Christians beyond a simple physical rest once a week or even a symbolic, spiritualized rest? This seems to be the weakest line of argumentation in his understanding of the Sabbath. An important source for Luther's position against the Sabbath was Augustine's spiritualization of the Sabbath commandment. Another reason for his rejection of the Sabbath for Christians may be due in part to anti-Semitism that began with the early church fathers. While much has been said about Luther's anti-Semitism, he did cherish real hopes about better relations with Jews and even their eventual conversion to a reformed Christianity. Nevertheless, Luther expressed a real concern for the fascination some Christians felt for the Jewish religion.[35] He saw Jewish proselytism in the Sabbatarian expressions in Moravia and Austria.[36] In the context of such conflicts (particularly during the years of 1523–1525) that pitted him against Erasmus, Karlstadt, Müntzer, and the peasants, he felt the need to confront what he considered expressions of heresy. The way he handled the law and the gospel also impacted his view of the Sabbath. Edward Allen points out that Karlstadt had a positive view of the law, teaching that it not only reveals God's will, but also arouses our "desire to become holy as God is holy." It was similar to John Calvin's third use of the law.[37] Luther, on the other hand, held a negative view of the law; he felt it opposed the gospel. While the law revealed sin, it was also an enemy that condemned and discouraged the believer. Only the gospel truly offered hope and grace and delivered the sinner from the bondage of sin. That is why Luther wrote, "We ought to proclaim the law and its works, not for the Christians, but for the crude and unbelieving."[38] He did not take Karlstadt's theology of the law and the Spirit seriously and therefore did not see any benefit to this interpretation of the Sabbath commandment.

Conclusion

Five centuries after Luther, Seventh-day Adventists relate to his statements about the importance of the Sabbath as a day for worshiping God. The Sabbath enables us to learn about God's character, and it allows for the development of the spiritual life as relating to the Creator in preparation for a sanctified life. This resonates well with the first angel's message of Revelation 14:6, 7, which calls for us to worship God, our Creator. Such motivations for the Sabbath are beyond a personal benefit through rest, leisure, and contentment. The Sabbath also gives us the time for works of mercy. Unfortunately, Luther did not connect the Sabbath with Creation. Seventh-day Adventists have the opportunity to show the relationship between God and the Sabbath that reminds us of God's salvation, rest, *and* Creation.

1. Augustine, *Tractates on the Gospel of John,* vol. 7 of *The Nicene and Post-Nicene Fathers* 1, ed. Philip Schaff (Buffalo, NY: Christian Literature Publishing Co., 1888), 133.

2. Augustine, "To His Beloved Son Januarius," in *Letters of St. Augustine,* trans. J. G. Cunningham, vol. 1 of *The Nicene and Post-Nicene Fathers* 1, ed. Philip Schaff (Buffalo, NY: Christian Literature Publishing Co., 1887), lt. 55, para. 23.

3. P. J. Verdam, *Mosaic Law in Practice and Study Throughout the Ages* (Kampen: J. H. Kok, 1959), 19.

4. See Daniel Augsburger, "The Sabbath and Lord's Day During the Middle Ages," in *The Sabbath in Scripture and History,* ed. Kenneth Strand (Washington, DC: Review and Herald Pub. Assn., 1982), 198.

5. Ibid.

6. Ibid., 198, 199.

7. Marie-Dominique Chenu, *Nature, Man, and Society in the Twelfth Century* (Chicago: University of Chicago Press, 1968), 160.

8. Thomas Aquinas, *Summa Theologiae* 2.2, question 122, art. 4.

9. Ibid.

10. D. A. Carson, ed., *From Sabbath to Lord's Day* (Grand Rapids, MI: Zondervan, 1982), 314.

11. Martin Luther, *Luther's Works*, vol. 35, *Word and Sacrament 1*, ed. Theodore Bachmann (St. Louis, MO: Concordia, 1955), 165.

12. Ibid., 35:166.

13. Ibid., 35:165.

14. Martin Luther, *Luther's Works*, vol. 40, *Church and Ministry 2*, ed. Conrad Bergendoff (St. Louis, MO: Concordia, 1958), 98.

15. Ibid., 40:97, 98.

16. Martin Luther, *D. Martin Luthers Werke: Kritische Gesamtausgabe*, vol. 16 (Weimar: Hermann Böhlau, 1899), 478, quoted in William M. Landeen, *Martin Luther's Religious Thought* (Mountain View, CA: Pacific Press® Pub. Assn., 1971), 195.

17. For a study on Karlstadt's position on the Sabbath commandment and observance, see Edward Allen, "Was Karlstadt a Proto-Sabbatarian?" *Adventist University Seminary Studies* 44, no. 1 (2006): 131–153.

18. Ibid., 151.

19. See especially Martin Luther, "Against the Heavenly Prophets in the Matter of Images and Sacraments," in *Luther's Works*, 40:93, 94, 96–98.

20. Martin Luther, *Luther's Works*, vol. 44, *The Christian in Society 1*, ed. Jaroslav Pelikan (St. Louis, MO: Concordia, 1966), 72, 198.

21. Luther, *Luther's Works*, 40:98.

22. Martin Luther, *Luther's Works*, vol. 1, *Lectures on Genesis, Chapters 1–5*, ed. Jaroslav Pelikan (St. Louis, MO: Concordia, 1958), 74, 75.

23. Ibid., 1:75.

24. Ibid., 1:79.

25. Ibid., 1:79, 80.

26. Ibid., 1:80.

27. Ibid., 1:81.

28. Ibid., 1:80.

29. Martin Luther, *Luther's Works*, vol. 3, *Lectures on Genesis, Chapters 15–20*, ed. Jaroslav Pelikan (St. Louis, MO: Concordia, 1961), 141.

30. Landeen, *Martin Luther's Religious Thought*, 195.

31. Luther, *D. Martin Luthers Werke*, 16:478, quoted in Landeen, *Martin Luther's Religious Thought*, 195.

32. Martin Luther, *Luther's Works*, vol. 2, *Lectures on Genesis, Chapters 6–14*, ed. Jaroslav Pelikan (St. Louis, MO: Concordia, 1960), 129, 130.

33. Martin Luther, *D. Martin Luthers Werke: Kritische Gesamtausgabe*, vol. 50 (Weimar:

Hermann Böhlau, 1914), 333, 334, quoted in Landeen, *Martin Luther's Religious Thought*, 196.

34. Luther, *D. Martin Luthers Werke*, 16:478, 479, quoted in Landeen, *Martin Luther's Religious Thought*, 197.

35. See French Lutheran historian Marc Lienhard's analysis of the relationship of Luther and the Jews in *Martin Luther*, 3rd ed. (Geneva: Labor et Fides, 1991), 259–274.

36. Daniel Liechty, *Sabbatarianism in the Sixteenth Century* (Berrien Springs, MI: Andrews University Press, 1993).

37. Allen, "Was Karlstadt a Proto-Sabbatarian?" 135.

38. Luther, *Luther's Works*, 40:83.

—————— CHAPTER 14 ——————

Reformation Ecclesiology and Adventism

Reinder Bruinsma

M ost current Protestant denominations emerged through secessions from their parent churches.* They usually began with an established *ecclesiology* (theology of the church), along with a well-defined system of church governance. The Seventh-day Adventist Church, however, did not develop from only one Christian tradition. It is indebted for its ecclesiology and its model of church governance to various traditions from which early Adventist leaders came. Adventist ecclesiology developed mostly in response to the practical organizational issues the movement faced.[1] Over time, the Seventh-day Adventist Church developed an intricate and strong governance structure, even though its ecclesiology developed more slowly. Other doctrines demanded more urgent attention at first.[2] In fact, only recently has the doctrine of the church come into sharper focus.[3]

> Over time, the Seventh-day Adventist Church developed an intricate and strong governance structure, even though its ecclesiology developed more slowly.

* This chapter is based on a paper presented at Perceptions of the Protestant Reformation in Seventh-day Adventism Symposium, Institute of Adventist Studies, Friedensau Adventist University, Germany, May 9–12, 2016.

Early Adventist thinking was deeply influenced by the Calvinist roots within American Protestantism. This also shows the influence of Lutheranism and the "free church" tradition, which were indebted, to a great extent, to the Radical Reformation. Both Methodism[4] and the Christian Connexion[5] played a significant role. This chapter focuses on Luther's contribution to Adventist ecclesiology. Before focusing on Luther, however, other Reformation figures and their heritage within various Protestant traditions are examined.[6]

Reformation ecclesiology

John Calvin. Whereas Luther was especially occupied with the doctrine of grace, John Calvin and his associates were responsible for the development of the Protestant understanding of the church.[7] A significant portion of Calvin's *Institutes of the Christian Religion*[8] was devoted to his views about the church. Like Luther (as demonstrated below), Calvin proposed a minimalist definition of the church: the church is where the Word of God is purely preached and heard and where the sacraments are administered according to Christ's instructions. Calvin differentiated between the perfect, yet invisible church of all the elect and the visible church within which are both the elect and reprobate members. It is not the condition of the members but the presence of the authorized means of grace that determines whether it is the true church. The visible church is a sign of the invisible church. Calvin strongly emphasized the need for discipline administered by the pastor.

Calvin also believed that the Bible teaches a fourfold church order: pastor, teacher, elder, and deacon. He based his views upon the principle that authority should arise from within the church's base. Nonetheless, he defended (like Luther and other Reformers) infant baptism. He argued that if faith must precede baptism, it in turn becomes a kind of work and is no longer a symbol of true grace.

Calvin's view of the Lord's Supper was somewhere between Luther and Zwingli. He contended that the real presence of Christ was not in the bread and the wine, but he also critiqued Zwingli's understanding of "mere" symbolism as too meager. He argued that the bread and the wine are signs that show how the blood and the body of Christ are available to believers.

Calvin defended an integral relationship between church and state. The state is subject to the church, and Christian statesmen are supposed to defend true doctrine. If necessary, the state can assist the church in disciplining its members. Calvin's emphasis on severe discipline, no doubt, was a factor in stimulating a legalist undercurrent within much of Calvinism, as it sought "to implement a specific and rather ascetic view of the norms of Christian conduct."[9]

Huldrych Zwingli. Like Luther, Zwingli recognized the existence of an invisible church, as well as a visible church. The visible church must be kept as pure as possible. The local church plays an important role by providing necessary discipline. Like Luther and Calvin, Zwingli defended infant baptism. He differed from Luther in his views of the Lord's Supper, which he regarded as purely symbolic. Zwingli saw a very close connection between the church and the state that came close to a form of theocracy.

The Radical Reformation. Some Reformers were more "radical" than Luther, Calvin, Zwingli, and their associates. The Anabaptists were the most important branch of the Radical Reformation.[10] They rejected the kind of relationship between church and state that would lead to the formation of state churches, or "established churches," in several European countries. They insisted on believer's baptism as the only valid mode of entrance into the church. For them, the church was a visible community of committed Christians.

The Christian Connexion and Methodism. The nineteenth-century Connexionists tended to be extremely biblicistic and claimed that the Bible was their only creed.[11] Two of the three founders of the Seventh-day Adventist Church—James White and Joseph Bates—were Connexionist ministers. For the early Connexionists, any form of organization was anathema. Yet practical considerations forced them to somewhat mitigate this initial antiorganization stance, and by 1830, state "conferences" were formed that met each year.[12]

Methodism originated within the Church of England but eventually became a separate movement. It was a latecomer to the United States, but eventually it dominated the American religious landscape.[13] By 1850, one in every three American Protestants was a Methodist.[14]

Methodism had far-reaching influences upon Adventism, and these are especially noticeable in the area of church organization. Methodism used conferences as umbrella organizations for local groups and churches, with a General Conference as its highest ecclesial body. In line with John Wesley's view of the church, American Methodism did not regard any form of church governance as fully right or wrong.[15] The focus was not on polity but instead on the spiritual fruits in the lives of believers.

Reformation ecclesiology and Adventism

Lutheranism had some definite influence upon Adventist ecclesiology. Yet in many ways, that influence was not as significant as that of some Radical Reformation adherents through their Methodist and Connexionist heirs. Despite the fact that Luther was highly esteemed among early Adventists (and continues to be in contemporary Adventism), Calvinism had a more distinct impact. Many of the denominations that developed in post-colonial times were Calvinist in origin, even though Arminian influences from Europe had already convinced many that the doctrine of predestination was unbiblical. The revivalist tradition, with its emphasis upon free will, did its work.[16] In many ways, Calvinism left its enduring imprint upon American religion through its ecclesiology.

Martin Luther, by and large, was received much more positively in the Adventist Church than John Calvin, even though Calvinism was a much stronger force than Lutheranism in nineteenth-century American religion. Clear evidence for this is found in the way the two Reformers are treated in Ellen G. White's book *The Great Controversy*.[17] Ellen White not only devoted many more pages to Luther than to Calvin, but she also appears to offer a much more positive assessment of Luther than of the Reformer from Geneva. With regard to Calvin, Ellen White states, "For nearly thirty years Calvin labored at Geneva, first to establish there a church adhering to the morality of the Bible, and then for the advancement of the Reformation throughout Europe. His course as a public leader was not faultless, nor were his doctrines free from error."[18] A little further in the same book, she writes in no uncertain terms about the "monstrous" Calvinist doctrine of predestination.[19] In comparison, she writes the following about Luther: "Foremost among those who were called to lead the church from the darkness of popery into the light of a purer faith, stood Martin Luther. . . . Knowing no fear but the fear of God, and acknowledging no foundation for religious faith but the Holy Scriptures, Luther was the man for his time."[20] When Ellen White describes Luther's appearance before the Diet of Worms, she states: "Thus stood this righteous man upon the sure foundation of the word of God. The light of heaven illuminated his countenance. His greatness and purity of character, his peace and joy of heart, were manifest to all as he testified against the power of error and witnessed to the superiority of that faith that overcomes the world."[21]

Luther's view of the church.[22] Several precursors of the Reformation existed that protested against erroneous ideas, including the notion that the Roman Church is the "mother church" replete with its hierarchical and sacerdotal structure, along with some serious abuses. Martin Luther was bold enough to eventually cut all ties with the Church of Rome. Through his study of Paul's letter to the Romans, he became convinced that humans are saved on the basis of grace and therefore are justified by God through faith. This had profound consequences for his view of the church. He returned to the Augustinian thesis that the church is always a mixed community, with those who are justified sinners at various stages of spiritual growth.[23] The communion of the saints is always simultaneously a communion of saints and of sinners. This idea is expressed in Luther's soteriological maxim that the believer is *simul iustus et peccator*—simultaneously righteous and sinful.

The church, Luther maintained, is where the Word of God is purely preached and heard and also where the sacraments (baptism and Communion) are properly administered. These are the only two *notae ecclesiae*, or "marks," of the church.

Luther placed great emphasis on the New Testament principle of the priesthood of all believers (as opposed to the sacerdotal system of Catholicism). Yet he recognized a special role for those who are called to preach and are ordained for public service. It is the task of the pastor and bishop to regard every diocese as a hospital where church members receive the treatment they need. Calvin, on the other hand, placed more emphasis upon correct faith and being an upright Christian.

For Luther, the church is both visible and invisible. He stressed the non-institutional aspect of the church and preferred the terms *Sammlung* (gathering) or *Gemeinde* (community) to the word *Kirche* (church). Luther defended infant baptism and rejected believer's baptism. Baptism is linked with faith, but faith does not have to precede baptism. He viewed the Lord's Supper as a compromise between Roman Catholic transubstantiation and other Reformers who defended a symbolic meaning. Luther's concept is often referred to as *consubstantiation*. This means that during the celebration of the sacrament, the fundamental "substance" of Christ's body and blood remain present alongside the substance of the bread and the wine.

Another important aspect about Luther's view of ecclesiology is his doctrine of two kingdoms—both created by God, yet each with a different role. Though the church and the state have separate spheres, Luther did not want a total separation. For example, he supported the princes against the peasants when the peasants revolted in 1525. In 1555, Lutheranism accepted the Augsburg settlement that determined that the religion of a region would follow that of its ruler.

Lutheran influences. The early Adventist believers' admiration of Luther and Lutheranism most certainly exerted an influence upon Adventism. Luther's courage to confront the church of his day with serious accusations of theological error and ecclesial abuse found an enthusiastic reception among Adventist believers of the nineteenth century. His insistence on the principle of *sola scriptura* and the New Testament idea of the justification of the sinner by faith, rather than by works, and his view of the priesthood of all believers were warmly welcomed.[24]

In many countries, Adventists reflect Martin Luther by their preference for terms such as *community, gathering,* or *meeting* as opposed to the word *church.* Adventists did, however, probably take this practice from other, more contemporary religious groups. And in a number of important areas, Adventism chose a route that differed significantly from Luther.[25]

Adventists define the church more narrowly than Luther. They stress the importance of the visible church as a community of committed Christians who enter the church through believer's baptism rather than infant baptism. Adventists, to a large extent, agree with Luther's definition of the church as a place where the Word is purely preached and the sacraments are administered properly. They place more emphasis on the *true* church—that is usually referred to as the *remnant* church (i.e., as the community of those who keep God's commandments and recognize "the Spirit of prophecy" as manifested in the ministry of Ellen White).[26]

Early Adventists also viewed Luther's understanding of consubstantiation as a tragic compromise with the Roman Catholic Mass and therefore as unacceptable. Similarly, Adventists also rejected Luther's doctrine of the two kingdoms and the close relationship between the church and the state. Instead, Adventists opted for a system of church governance that was not modeled after Lutheranism.

Calvinist influences. Calvinism—albeit mostly indirectly, through such movements as Methodism and the Christian Connexion—impacted Adventist ecclesiology more than Lutheranism. This is especially so in such areas as the offices in the local church and the structure of church governance. Although Adventists did not recognize the separate office of the teacher as Calvin did, early Adventists emphasized the role of ministers, elders, and deacons in the same way. The Adventist system of electing various officers for church organizations most definitely has a Calvinist flavor.

Other influences. Early Adventism is greatly indebted for many of its ideas to its Anabaptist roots, even though many other denominations also emerged from those same origins. It adopted the view of the church as a believers' church, in which members enter through believer's baptism, and holy living and a commitment to mission were paramount. Such convictions as the symbolic view of the Lord's Supper—with a rediscovery of the value of footwashing[27]—stem indirectly from the Radical Reformation, as does the insistence upon a full separation between church and state.[28]

The earliest steps toward the organization of the local church reflected the influence of the covenantal or federal theology of Puritanism. Early Adventist congregations during the first few decades after 1844 arranged themselves on the basis of a "covenant" between members. Such covenants were rather common in congregationally organized congregations and therefore could be expected to emerge in Adventist faith communities.[29] While creating the organizational umbrella structure, the Connexionists and Methodist models were adapted to the needs of the emerging Adventist movement.

Conclusion

Various Protestant denominations had varying degrees of influence on Seventh-day Adventists, though sometimes it was subconscious. Influential factors included the origins of the Millerite movement, with all its diversity, and the spiritual roots of its leaders. Calvinism was an important, often indirect, source of inspiration, as Adventists started and developed their own denomination; but with it came some specific Lutheran ideas about the church that are now fundamental to Adventist identity. As we reflect on Martin Luther, it is appropriate for Adventists to remind themselves that, with all of its peculiarities and "unique" ideas, Adventist theology and practice—especially its ecclesiology—must remain firmly embedded in the Christian past and its Reformation roots.

---

1. For the pragmatic nature of much of American thought, see, e.g., Henry Steele Commager, *The American Mind: An Interpretation of American Thought and Character Since the 1880's* (New Haven, CT: Yale University Press, 1950), 7–9. See also Bruce Kuklick, *A History of Philosophy in America, 1720–2000* (Oxford: Clarendon Press, 2001), 95–178.

2. For a concise but useful survey of the development of the Adventist doctrinal system, see George R. Knight, *A Search for Identity: The Development of Seventh-day Adventist Beliefs* (Hagerstown, MD: Review and Herald˙ Pub. Assn., 2000).

3. See Raoul Dederen, "The Church," in *Handbook of Seventh-day Adventist Theology*, ed. Raoul Dederen, Seventh-day Adventist Commentary Reference Series (Hagerstown, MD: Review and Herald® Pub. Assn., 2000), 538–581; Reinder Bruinsma, *The Body of Christ: A Biblical Understanding of the Church* (Hagerstown, MD: Review and Herald˙ Pub. Assn., 2009); Gerald A. Klingbeil, "Ecclesiology in Seventh-day Adventist Theological Research, 1995–2004," *Andrews University Seminary Studies* 43, no. 1 (2005): 11–29; and two publications of the Biblical Research Institute: Ángel Manuel Rodríguez, ed., *Toward a Theology of the Remnant: An Adventist Ecclesiological Perspective*, Studies in Adventist Ecclesiology 1 (Silver Spring, MD: Biblical Research Institute, 2009), and Ángel Manuel Rodríguez, ed., *Message, Mission, and Unity of the Church*, Studies in Adventist Ecclesiology 2 (Silver Spring, MD: Biblical Research Institute, 2013).

4. See Richard P. Heitzenrater, *Wesley and the People Called Methodists* (Nashville, TN: Abingdon Press, 1995), esp. chap. 4 and onwards; John H. Wigger, *Taking Heaven by Storm: Methodism and the Rise of Popular Christianity in America*, reprint ed. (Chicago: University of Illinois Press, 2001).

5. George R. Knight, "Christian Connexion," in *The Ellen G. White Encyclopedia*, ed. Dennis Fortin and Jerry Moon (Hagerstown, MD: Review and Herald® Pub. Assn., 2013), 702, 703.

6. There are, of course, a great number of books and scholarly articles that deal with the history of the doctrine of the church and the details of the ecclesiologies of the various traditions that emerged from the Reformation. There are also many useful summaries and comparisons of

these various views. I have found the summary provided by Veli-Matti Kärkkäinen especially helpful: *An Introduction to Ecclesiology: Ecumenical, Historical, and Global Perspectives* (Downers Grove, IL: InterVarsity Press, 2002), 17–91. But see also Dederen, "The Church," 569–575; Justo L. Gonzáles, *A History of Christian Thought*, 2nd ed. (Nashville, TN: Abingdon Press, 1987), 3:61–69, 79–85, 161–174; Alister E. McGrath, *Historical Theology: An Introduction to the History of Christian Thought* (Oxford: Blackwell, 1998), 200–207; and Mark Husbands and Daniel J. Treier, eds., *The Community of the Word: Toward an Evangelical Ecclesiology* (Downers Grove, IL: InterVarsity Press, 2005), 23–40.

7. McGrath, *Historical Theology*, 168.

8. John Calvin, *Institutes of the Christian Religion*, trans. Henry Beveridge (Peabody, MA: Hendrickson, 2012), bk. 4, 669–988.

9. Kärkkäinen, *An Introduction to Ecclesiology*, 51.

10. A good guide to the Radical Reformation is George H. Williams's *The Radical Reformation* (Philadelphia, PA: Westminster Press, 1962); also William R. Estep, *The Anabaptist Story: An Introduction to Sixteenth-Century Anabaptism,* 3rd ed. (Grand Rapids, MI: Eerdmans, 1996).

11. Some of the early Adventist leaders had belonged to the Christian Connexion. For a discussion of the main theological convictions of the Connexionists (such as their anti-Trinitarian position and their acceptance of conditional immortality), see George R. Knight, *Joseph Bates: The Real Founder of Seventh-day Adventism* (Hagerstown, MD: Review and Herald® Pub. Assn., 2004), 38–41.

12. Andrew G. Mustard, *James White and SDA Organization*, Andrews University Seminary Doctoral Dissertation Series (Berrien Springs, MI: Andrews University Press, 1988), 29–33; George R. Knight, *Organizing to Beat the Devil: The Development of Adventist Church Structure* (Hagerstown, MD: Review and Herald® Pub. Assn., 2001), 16, 17.

13. Roger Finke and Rodney Stark, *The Churching of America, 1776–1990: Winners and Losers in Our Religious Economy* (New Brunswick, NJ: Rutgers University Press, 1992), 25.

14. Ibid., 55.

15. Heitzenrater, *Wesley and the People Called Methodists*, 153.

16. Peter J. Thuesen, *Predestination: The American Career of a Contentious Doctrine* (Oxford: Oxford University Press, 2009).

17. Ellen G. White, *The Great Controversy* (Nampa, ID: Pacific Press® Pub. Assn., 2005).

18. Ibid., 236.

19. Ibid., 261.

20. Ibid., 120.

21. Ibid., 160.

22. Luther's theology of the church is found in its most complete form in his *D. Martin Luthers Werke*, a multivolume German series, usually referred to as the Weimar edition (WA), first published in 1883. An American edition was published as *Luther's Works*, by Fortress Press and Concordia (1957). Luther's writings on the church and ministry are found in vols. 39, 40, 41. For good summaries of Luther's ecclesiology, see Paul D. L. Avis, *The Church in the Theology of the Reformers* (London, UK: Marshall, Morgan, and Scott, 1982); and Timothy George, *Theology of the Reformers* (Nashville, TN: Broadman and Holman, 1988).

23. McGrath, *Historical Theology*, 34; Jaroslav Pelikan, *The Emergence of the Catholic Tradition (100–600)*, A History of the Development of Doctrine, vol. 1 (Chicago: University of Chicago Press, 1971), 302–312.

24. Adventistism certainly agreed with the Lutheran rediscovery of justification by faith and its insistence on *sola scriptura*, but in actual practice often found it difficult to live up to these essential Protestant principles, as is attested by Adventist history.

25. Dederen, "The Church," 569, 570; Gonzáles, *A History of Christian Thought*, 3:61–69.

26. The texts usually referred to are Revelation 12:17; 14:12; 19:10; and Joel 3:1–5.

27. Reinder Bruinsma, "Christ's Commandment of Humility," *Ministry*, July 1966, 24–26.

28. It should be noted that in many parts of the world current views about the relationship between church and state have, over time, significantly developed. See Ronald Lawson, "Church and State at Home and Abroad: The Evolution of Seventh-day Adventist Relations With Governments," *Journal of the American Academy of Religion* 64, no 2 (Summer 1996): 279–311.

29. Mustard, *James White and SDA Organization*, 154.

CHAPTER 15

Martin Luther and Education

Heidi Campbell

E ducation played a crucial role in the Protestant Reformation, enabling it to grow and thrive. Even earlier efforts at reform, such as those of the Waldenses and the Hussites, recognized the value of education in transmitting religious values. The Seventh-day Adventist Church builds upon this Reformation heritage by continuing in this rich spirit of reform that is closely aligned with and transmitted through education. With an education system that spans the globe and has almost two million students,[1] the Seventh-day Adventist Church maintains one of the largest religious education systems in the world. This system, as with many other aspects of the Seventh-day Adventist Church, is a beneficiary of the Protestant legacy of education, with deep roots that can be credited to Martin Luther and the Reformation.

Martin Luther transformed the world, especially Western culture, by writing his Ninety-Five Theses. He also changed the expectations about what an ideal government is, and this, in turn, had implications for the definition of what a good citizen should be. Through this process, Luther drastically altered all levels of education. Most governments today provide schooling and ensure the right of education for all citizens.[2] These rights are very much a part of Luther's enduring legacy. As R. Ward Holder writes, "Part of the story of the Reformation is a story of the foundation of schools."[3] This chapter explores why Luther developed his educational perspective and what his views of pedagogy were that have impacted Protestants, including Adventists.

Medieval foundations for education

Martin Luther was born at a time when the education system was not well coordinated and was unavailable to most. Education consisted of a mix of cathedral, parish, monastic, and palace schools, along with universities that emerged just prior to Luther's time.[4] These schools did not provide general instruction for all children, but rather trained students for certain careers, generally in government or the church. Monastic schools, for example, existed primarily to provide religious tutelage and literacy for novice monks and nuns. Occasionally, monasteries provided education for the laity, but that was rare and generally was viewed as a distraction from their primary focus. Instead, they trained monks, who in turn often became instructors in the newly developing universities.[5] The universities formed during the late medieval period were modeled upon Islamic universities[6] and gradually replaced the cathedral schools. These universities produced a rich flowering of intellectual achievement but only for the privileged few. Universities were too expensive, inaccessible to most, and had little impact on regular clergy.[7]

The education provided by these schools was also inconsistent. Many schools failed to provide even basic literacy. Children at parish schools, for example, were frequently taught only memorized prayers rather than how to read, and the teacher (generally the local priest) was not necessarily literate either.[8] Cathedral schools could be excellent; some of the most gifted intellectuals of the medieval period attended them, but the content and quality depended almost entirely on the master.[9] Even though schools and universities were tasked with producing an erudite clergy, the evidence indicates that the education for most clergy was generally neglected.[10]

With such a low level of learning among clergy, it is therefore not surprising that it was not highly valued among the laity. The late medieval period went through a rapid expansion of capitalism, and many in Germany saw education as a waste of time.[11] In the preface to Luther's *Small Catechism*, he reacts to the generally poor state of education and condemns the lack of knowledge on the part of the clergy.[12] The main focus of "A Sermon on Keeping Children in School" is to encourage parents to educate their children instead of hurrying them into the workforce. Luther states, "Common people appear to be quite indifferent to the matter of maintaining the schools. I see them withdrawing their children from instruction and turning them to the making of a living and to caring for their bellies."[13] Against this background of apathy toward education, Luther posted his Ninety-Five Theses.

The Reformers as educators

Martin Luther, along with most other Protestant Reformers, was university educated. Not only did they benefit from university educations, but also many, like Luther, who was a monk as well as a professor at the University of Wittenberg, were career teachers.[14] The Augustinians—Luther's monastic group—were known for producing theology professors.[15] Augustine's theology played a key role in the formation of Luther's thinking, including about educational reform. At the university, Luther had a reputation for being a meticulous and thorough professor who carefully prepared his lectures.[16] Even in the midst of the conflict following his dissemination of the Ninety-Five Theses, Luther continued his role as a university professor.

As Christian Reformers and professors, Luther and his co-Reformer Philip Melanchthon recognized the importance of education as a mechanism for implementing lasting values and changes. Additionally, both revered it and saw the need for universal Protestant schooling. A religion that focused on the need to return to Bible-based doctrine logically needed its adherents to be able to read the Bible. As Melanchthon noted, God wrote the Ten Commandments Himself for others to read; therefore, it followed that His believers needed the ability to read and understand the Bible.[17] They also recognized that Protestants needed a deep understanding of their faith and the biblical evidence supporting Protestant beliefs to withstand the arguments of the Catholic Church.[18]

Thus, Luther wrote extensively about the need to establish parish schools supported by the government. A tour of churches and schools in 1527 brought further impetus for reforms; this subsequently ensured that basic education was given to as many Protestants as possible, including all clergy. During the trip, Melanchthon was horrified to discover that many of the priests and monks who had accepted Protestantism still did not have any significant understanding of Protestant doctrine. Some of the priests and teachers could not even read.[19] As a result, Melanchthon wrote *Instructions for the Visitors of Parish Pastors in Electoral Saxony*.[20] The reforms that he and Luther encouraged were so instrumental in developing a German education system that, Melanchthon received the moniker "Educator of Germany."[21]

Melanchthon indeed deserves much of the credit for many of these educational efforts. Luther was a firm advocate of Melanchthon's work of reform and supported these endeavors through a series of pamphlets: *To the Councilmen of All Cities in Germany That They Establish and Maintain Christian Schools* (1524) and *A Sermon on Keeping Children in School* (1530).[22] In 1529, he wrote two catechisms with a specific instructional purpose: *Small Catechism* and *Large Catechism*. The *Small Catechism* was written as training material for both home and school. Together both catechisms were meant to ensure a basic knowledge of Christian beliefs for children and adults.[23] The *Small Catechism* proved incredibly popular at the time and remains so among Lutherans.[24]

Luther and Melanchthon's education ideals were profoundly influenced by humanism as well as Protestant theology.[25] When Luther began his career at the University of Wittenberg, scholasticism was the predominant philosophy in education. Those educators who differed in their philosophy, such as humanists, were pressured to conform to scholasticism.[26] Early in his career, recognizing the deficiencies of scholasticism, Luther was attracted to humanism. How he initially became interested in humanism is unknown;[27] it is clear that he appreciated the worth of the writings of humanist Faber Stapulensis and Erasmus's *New Testament*.[28] Although Luther never became a true humanist,[29] adopting the parts of humanism that resonated with his worldview and rejecting those that did not, along with his biblical worldview, impacted his views and eventually influenced Protestant and Adventist educational practices, especially in regard to theological training.

One way humanism shaped Luther's view of education was in teaching methods, particularly for children. As revealed by the catechisms, Luther believed that education must be more than rote memorization. Instead, he advocated that all church members should think deeply and understand their beliefs.[30] Furthermore, education should awaken an interest in learning.[31]

> Luther believed that education must be more than rote memorization. Instead, he advocated that all church members should think deeply and understand their beliefs.

As a consequence of this conviction, his *Small Catechism* was written in a question-and-answer format,[32] which made it easy for children to remember and reflected questions children might ask. His catechisms were written in German rather than Latin in order to be as widely read and understood as possible.[33] Additionally, he concurred with humanists that education should be presented to children in small components so that they could be easily grasped and built upon.[34] Teaching methods should be adapted to the age and abilities of the students. In fact, schooling should be made enjoyable for children and not be harsh and/or demanding. Most of these pedagogical methods now seem logical; but at the time, these were radical ideas and not embraced by the majority of society except for a few humanists, such as Erasmus.[35]

Luther and the Reformation also changed the focus as to *who* should be taught. Luther's belief in the priesthood of all believers had significant implications for who was to be educated. During the medieval period, boys who were intended for the priesthood and government positions or who came from wealthy families were educated.[36] Boys who were not intended for careers that required the ability to read or who were from lower classes were not generally educated. Luther argued that every child with the ability to do so should have at least a basic education in order to be able to read the Bible.[37] In *A Sermon on Keeping Children in School*, Luther urged parents to educate their children, even if, in the end, they worked in a career that did not require schooling, as it would prepare them for service to God and enable them to explain their beliefs.

More radically, Luther also pushed for girls to receive an education. Girls were not generally viewed as worthy of schooling. Only girls from a few rich and/or noble families could afford to hire a tutor for their daughters. Like monks, nuns, who generally also came from wealthy families, were, according to their charters, to be educated.[38] Of course, as with monks, education was the ideal and not necessarily the norm. One Italian proverb is representative of the predominant attitude about female education. It states, "A girl should be taught to sew and not to read, unless one wishes to make a nun of her."[39]

If, as Luther contended, all Christians were priests, then all Christians from across all social classes, including both boys and girls, must be able to read in order to understand the Bible. Although Luther still viewed wives as subordinate to their husbands, he recognized the importance of both fathers and mothers in the instruction of their children. To this end, Luther encouraged each parish to establish a school for boys and another for girls and to provide a female teacher financially supported by the parish.[40]

After centuries of neglecting female scholarship, Luther's emphasis on education for both genders did not bring immediate results. Nevertheless, between the efforts of the Reformation and the Catholic Counter-Reformation, there was an increase in female literacy. In England, a study shows that female literacy rose from 2 percent just prior to the Reformation in 1500 to 9 percent by 1600 after the Reformation and expanded to 32 percent by 1700. The literacy rate also increased among men from 10 percent in 1500 to almost 40 percent by 1700. Thus, the Reformation encouraged widespread education, particularly in northern Europe where Protestantism was dominant, in contrast to southern Europe where Catholicism remained dominant.[41]

In order to obtain an education, Luther originally emphasized the importance of the home as the primary religious training ground.[42] In his view, parents had a duty to educate their children in basic Christian tenants. He argued that one of the worst sins for parents was to neglect instructing their children, and he suggested that it might lead to eternal damnation.[43] However, when he wrote the catechisms, Luther recognized that many parents were uneducated and not able to train their own children effectively. As Luther saw the results that came from a lack of education, he supported schooling, which would be funded by the government through taxes, being available to all children and indicated that a basic compulsory education for children would be the ideal.[44] His view that the government, rather than the church, should organize education was due in part to his conflict with Catholic religious authorities and the support that he received from civil authorities.[45] In *To the Councilmen of All Cities in Germany That They Establish and Maintain Christian Schools*, Luther argued that if governments spent money on weapons and infrastructure, then they surely could spend an equal amount on the far more important task of educating their citizens.[46] Additionally, the rich and noble had a spiritual obligation to financially support impoverished children.[47] At that time, there was no separation between church and state; thus, public schools supported by the local government were focused on religious indoctrination, fulfilling Luther's ideal. Despite some resistance because of monetary concerns, the number of local schools grew substantially, and at least an elementary education and basic literacy became the norm.[48]

Luther's impact upon educational reform extended not only to who was educated, but it also changed what was studied. Luther's emphasis upon *sola scriptura* required a greater emphasis on the study of Greek and Hebrew instead of Latin, which was the dominant academic language at that time.[49] Melanchthon, a brilliant scholar and professor of Greek,[50] had a crucial influence in encouraging the study of biblical languages for clergy. In order to understand the Bible and develop a correct interpretation of it, Melanchthon believed the Bible should not be studied through a Latin translation that both Melanchthon and Luther recognized contained many translation errors.[51]

The humanist emphasis of *ad fontes*, or the need to return to the earliest possible source, meant a corresponding emphasis upon reading the Bible in the original languages.[52] In addition, the Bible should be translated from these original languages into the lingua franca of the people. To that end, Luther translated the New Testament while in confinement in Wartburg Castle. Education should also take place in the lingua franca so that all can have the opportunity to receive an education.[53] Influenced by humanists such as Erasmus, Luther advocated for a broader curriculum that not only focused on the classical languages and the Bible, but also included the liberal arts, in particular history, literature, rhetoric, moral philosophy, and mathematics.[54] The curriculum at the University of Wittenberg shifted under the guidance of Melanchthon to reflect this view. For clergy, education went from being recommended to being mandatory for ordination.[55]

Luther also advocated for changes in how school should be taught. From his childhood and early educational experience, Luther cited three incidents of harsh punishment: a caning by his mother,[56] a whipping by his father,[57] and a caning at school. These experiences probably affected his views of discipline.[58] In this respect, he was in good company with Erasmus and Augustine, who pondered whether fear of punishment actually made people behave even worse.[59] In *To the Councilmen of All Cities in Germany That They Establish and Maintain Christian Schools*, Luther compared schools where students were beaten for not learning lessons as a "hell and purgatory" and contrasted them to schools where children can "study with pleasure and in play."[60] Furthermore, he also advised parents to "avoid all cruelty lest he shake the child's faith in him."[61] This is not to say that Luther did not believe in discipline, even corporal discipline, as he also extolled the virtues of teachers disciplining their students.[62] Instead, Luther advocated for a more humane view of discipline. Although not completely successful at changing the harsh punishment that had become ingrained in society as a part of teaching, Luther sought to alter the system of discipline to a kinder and gentler system so that "the rod is accompanied by the apple" and "all children are to be treated with equal love."[63]

Legacy for Adventist education

Most Adventist schools, whether they recognize it or not, are the beneficiaries of the Reformation and its emphasis upon education. A glance at the theology program of most Adventist universities reveals Luther's influence upon them. The fact that most theology students are required to master the basics of Greek and Hebrew are some of the obvious evidences of Luther's educational legacy.

Adventist education was one of the last major organizational developments in the Seventh-day Adventist Church.[64] Initial attempts to develop an Adventist education system resulted in modeling the conventional forms of the day—particularly a focus on rote memorization and the study of Latin classics. A major revolution occurred during the 1890s, especially with the 1891 Harbor Springs, Michigan, education convention, when a broad philosophy of Adventist education was articulated that included the removal of Latin classics and made the Bible the center of the curriculum.[65] Adventists readily embraced and adapted the Sunday School movement, as part of a vigorous Sabbath School, as another avenue for providing religious instruction to children.[66]

In many ways, Adventist education is the continuation of educational initiatives made by Martin Luther and other Reformers, particularly Melanchthon. Ellen G. White, who articulated as early as 1872 her views about education, eventually paved the way for an Adventist system that resonated closely with Luther on schooling issues.[67] Like Luther, she argued that education was not merely for pecuniary gain or work skills, or even academic knowledge, but its primary focus should be spiritual instruction and the knowledge of God.[68] Although Ellen White's support led to the creation of the Adventist education system, she, too, saw the home as the foundation of spiritual education.[69]

Pedagogically, Ellen White's views also closely matched Luther's. She viewed education as more than mere rote memorization in that "the work of true education" is "to train the youth to be thinkers, and not mere reflectors of other men's thought."[70] Discipline, she argued, should be strict but redemptive and not harsh.[71] Furthermore, students needed to have adequate resources in order to study. Even libraries that are a part of every Adventist school, and every school in general, owe their existence in part to Luther, who greatly supported libraries.[72]

Conclusion

Martin Luther's vision of education finds much in common with the Seventh-day Adventist system and philosophy of education. Adventist education is primarily religious education with an emphasis on the liberal arts and the study of original sources, especially the Bible. Adventists support the belief of the priesthood of all believers; and that means that all children deserve an education that begins on this earth, focuses on the development of character, and ultimately, leads to a better understanding of the Bible and a personal relationship with Jesus Christ. The Reformation left a legacy that endures today through Seventh-day Adventist education.

1. "The General Conference Education Team," Department of Education, Seventh-day Adventist Church, accessed May 3, 2017, http://education.gc.adventist.org/about.html.

2. John Witte Jr., "From Gospel to Law: The Lutheran Reformation and Its Impact on Legal Culture," in *Protestantism After 500 Years*, ed. Thomas Albert Howard and Mark A. Noll (New York: Oxford University Press, 2016), 69.

3. R. Ward Holder, *Crisis and Renewal: The Era of the Reformations* (Louisville, KY: Westminster John Knox Press, 2009).

4. John J. Contreni, "Schools, Cathedral," in *Dictionary of the Middle Ages*, ed. Joseph R. Strayer (New York: Charles Scribner's Sons, 1988), 11:59–63.

5. Charles W. Jones, "Schools, Monastic," in *Dictionary of the Middle Ages*, ed. Joseph R. Strayer (New York: Charles Scribner's Sons, 1988), 11:72–78.

6. James E. Reed and Ronnie Prevost, *A History of Christian Education* (Nashville, TN: Broadman and Holman Publishers, 1993).

7. Justo L. González, *The History of Theological Education* (Nashville, TN: Abingdon Press, 2015). This was still a problem in 1527 after the Reformation.

8. Ibid., 53.

9. Contreni, "Schools, Cathedral," 59–63.

10. Jones, "Schools, Monastic," 72–78.

11. Charles M. Jacobs, introduction to *A Sermon on Keeping Children in School*, in Martin Luther, *Luther's Works*, vol. 46, *The Christian in Society 3*, ed. Robert Schultz III (St. Louis, MO: Concordia, 1966), 209.

12. Kevin P. Emmert, "Luther's Small Catechism," in *Encyclopedia of Christian Education*, vol. 2, ed. George Thomas Kurian and Mark A. Lamport (New York: Rowman and Littlefield, 2015), 770, 771.

13. Luther, *Luther's Works*, 46:219.

14. González, *The History of Theological Education*, 69–77.

15. Scott H. Hendrix, *Martin Luther: Visionary Reformer* (New Haven, CT: Yale University Press, 2015), 34.

16. Ibid., 39.

17. González, *The History of Theological Education*, 72.

18. Ibid., 74.

19. Ibid., 73.

20. The authorship of *Instructions for the Visitors of Parish Pastors in Electoral Saxony* is disputed, but Melanchthon is generally believed to be the primary author.

21. Charlotte Methuen, "Luther's Life," in *The Oxford Handbook of Martin Luther's Theology*, ed. Robert Kolb, Irene Dingel, and L'ubomír Batka (New York: Oxford University Press, 2016), 18.

22. Delbert Schulz, "Martin Luther's Influence," in *Harper's Encyclopedia of Religious Education*, ed. Iris V. Cully and Kendig Brubaker Cully (San Francisco, CA: Harper and Row, 1990), 388; Reed and Prevost, *A History of Christian Education*.

23. Emmert, "Luther's Small Catechism," 2:770, 771.

24. Schulz, "Martin Luther's Influence," 388.

25. Alister E. McGrath, *Reformation Thought: An Introduction*, 4th ed. (Malden, MA: Wiley-Blackwell, 2012), 56.

26. Robert Rosin, "Humanism, Luther, and the Wittenberg Reformation," in *The Oxford Handbook of Martin Luther's Theology*, ed. Robert Kolb, Irene Dingel, and L'ubomír Batka (New York: Oxford University Press, 2016), 93, 94.

27. Ibid., 96.

28. Ibid., 99.

29. Ibid., 101; McGrath, *Reformation Thought*, 54, 55.

30. Gerald Strauss, *Luther's House of Learning: Indoctrination of the Young in the German Reformation* (Baltimore, MD: Johns Hopkins University Press, 1978), 5.

31. Schulz, "Martin Luther's Influence," 388.

32. Emmert, "Luther's Small Catechism," 2:770, 771.

33. McGrath, *Reformation Thought*, 245.

34. Strauss, *Luther's House of Learning*, 5; and Delbert Schulz, "Martin Luther's Influence," 388.

35. González, *The History of Theological Education*, 66–68.

36. Luther's father, a pious miner and owner of foundries, wanted Luther to become a lawyer.

37. Jeff Mallinson, "Lutheran Church Christian Education," in *Encyclopedia of Christian Education*, vol 2, ed. George Thomas Kurian and Mark A. Lamport (New York: Rowman and Littlefield, 2015), 768, 769.

38. Although nuns were supposed to be taught to read and write, evidence indicates that this was unevenly applied.

39. T. L. Jarman, *Landmarks in the History of Education* (New York: Philosophical Library, 1952), 123, quoted in Reed and Prevost, *A History of Christian Education*, 159.

40. Martin Luther, *Ordinance of a Common Chest, Preface*, in *Luther's Works*, vol. 45, *The Christian in Society 2*, ed. Walther I. Brandt (Philadelphia, PA: Fortress Press, 1962), 188, 189.

41. Allan C. Ornstein, Daniel U. Levine, Gerald L. Gutek, and David E. Vocke, *Foundations of Education*, 11th ed. (Belmont, CA: Wadsworth, 2011), 85, 86.

42. Strauss, *Luther's House of Learning*, 5; Jeffrey P. Greenman, "Luther's Catechisms," in *Encyclopedia of Christian Education*, vol. 2, ed. George Thomas Kurian and Mark A. Lamport (New York: Rowman and Littlefield, 2015), 769, 770.

43. Martin Luther, *A Sermon on Keeping Children in School*, in *Luther's Works*, vol. 46, *The Christian in Society 3*, ed. Robert Schultz III (St. Louis, MO: Concordia, 1966), 243.

44. Ibid.

45. Martin Luther, *On War Against the Turks*, in *Luther's Works*, vol. 46, *The Christian in Society 3*, ed. Robert Schultz III (St. Louis, MO: Concordia, 1966), 187. This view is also expressed in Martin Luther's *To the Councilmen of All Cities in Germany That They Establish and Maintain Christian Schools*, in *Luther's Works*, vol. 45, *The Christian in Society 2*, ed. Walther I. Brandt (Philadelphia, PA: Fortress Press, 1962).

46. Luther, *Luther's Works*, 45:350.

47. Ibid.

48. Strauss, *Luther's House of Learning*, 200.

49. Luther did not, however, argue that Latin should be removed from the curriculum, as it still remained a common language for scholars and government officials to communicate in, but rather that Greek and Hebrew be added to it.

50. Hendrix, *Martin Luther*, 75–77.

51. González, *The History of Theological Education*, 72.

52. Rosin, "Humanism, Luther, and the Wittenberg Reformation," 96; McGrath, *Reformation Thought*, 35–58.

53. Luther, *Luther's Works*, 45:347–378.

54. Schulz, "Martin Luther's Influence," 388; González, *The History of Theological Education*, 66–74; Rosin, "Humanism, Luther, and the Wittenberg Reformation," 91–104.

55. González, *The History of Theological Education*, 74.

56. Martin Luther, *Luther's Works*, vol. 54, *Table Talk*, ed. Theodore G. Tappert (St. Louis, MO: Concordia, 1967), 235.

57. Ibid., 54:157.

58. Roland Bainton, *Here I Stand: A Life of Martin Luther* (Nashville, TN: Abingdon Press, 1950), 23.

59. Strauss, *Luther's House of Learning*, 38.

60. Luther, *Luther's Works*, 45:369.

61. Strauss, *Luther's House of Learning*, 37.

62. Martin Luther, *Luther's Works*, vol. 26, *Lectures on Galatians, 1535, Chapters 1–4*, ed. Walter A. Hansen (St. Louis, MO: Concordia, 1963), 417; Strauss, *Luther's House of Learning*, 180–182.

63. Luther, *Luther's Works*, 54:235.

64. For a survey of the history of Adventist education, see Floyd L. Greenleaf, *In Passion for the World: A History of Seventh-day Adventist Education* (Nampa, ID: Pacific Press® Pub. Assn., 2005).

65. George R. Knight, "Harbor Springs, Michigan," in *The Ellen G. White Encyclopedia*, ed. Denis Fortin and Jerry Moon (Hagerstown, MD: Review and Herald® Pub. Assn., 2014), 856.

66. *The Seventh-day Adventist Encyclopedia*, rev. ed., Seventh-day Adventist Commentary Reference Series (Hagerstown, MD: Review and Herald® Pub. Assn., 1996), s.v. "Sabbath School."

67. Her original 1872 statement can be found in Ellen G. White, *Testimonies for the Church* (Mountain View, CA: Pacific Press® Pub. Assn., 1948), 3:131–160. For a concise overview, see Herbert E. Douglass, "Education, Ellen G. White's Role in Adventist," in *The Ellen G. White Encyclopedia*, ed. Denis Fortin and Jerry Moon (Hagerstown, MD: Review and Herald® Pub. Assn., 2014), 794–796.

68. Ellen G. White, *Education* (Mountain View, CA: Pacific Press® Pub. Assn., 1952), 13.

69. Ibid., 275–286.

70. Ibid., 17.

71. Ibid., 287–297.

72. Luther regarded libraries as so essential to good education that he devotes a major portion of his *To the Councilmen of Germany* on how to properly set up libraries. See also Mallinson, "Lutheran Church Christian Education," 2:768, 769; Luther, *Luther's Works*, 45:373–377.

CHAPTER 16

Missiological Lessons From Martin Luther: An Adventist Perspective

Abner P. Dizon

Martin Luther positively altered the course of Western history with his thirty-two years of active ministry as well as his German translation of the Bible, hymn writing, and volumes of sermons and theological treatises. His influence is truly far reaching, and he is no stranger to Seventh-day Adventists. Ellen G. White, in her book *The Great Controversy*, introduced Luther as "foremost among those who were called to lead the church from the darkness of popery into the light of a purer faith."[1] For Adventists, who view themselves as "heirs of the great truths"[2] of the Reformation, a question remains, does Luther have anything to offer Adventists about world missions?

The debate about Luther's missiology

Missions do not usually come to mind when discussing the Protestant Reformation. The literature on sixteenth-century Protestant missions points out that, except for the Anabaptists, there is little missionary vision or missionary spirit evident during the

> Missions do not usually come to mind when discussing the Protestant Reformation.

Reformation.[3] Among the first to promote this notion was Gustav Warneck, the father of missiology. For him, not only was there no missionary action in the age of the Reformation, "even the idea of missions" was absent.[4] Twentieth-century missions historians (including Kenneth S. Latourette, Stephen C. Neill, J. Herbert Kane, Ralph Winter, and Ruth Tucker) perpetuated this claim that the Reformers were indifferent to mission.

Yet there is some evidence in Luther's writings that challenges this negative assumption about missions on the part of Luther and other Reformers. For instance, in Luther's commentary on Zechariah 10:9, he describes what missiologists call the centrifugal force of mission (i.e., the scattering of missionaries among unbelievers):[5] "They will be *scattered among the nations. . . . They will be sent by God among the nations as preachers* and thus draw many people to themselves and through themselves to Christ. . . . 'They shall remember Me *in far countries . . . they shall preach and teach of Me*, and thus they shall be increased and shall convert many others to Me.' "[6] In Luther's metaphorical interpretation of Zechariah 12:6, he not only points to the global scope of mission but also to the power for its accomplishment: "The Christians shall also, through the Word, harvest much fruit among all the Gentiles and shall convert and save many. . . . The fire of the Holy Spirit . . . shall devour the Gentiles . . . and prepare a place everywhere for the Gospel and the kingdom of Christ."[7]

Luther also had a grasp of the integration of ministry (internal) and mission (external). In his explanation of the Lord's Prayer (1529), Luther writes the following:

> We pray . . . *that all this may be realized in us* and that God's name may be praised through his holy Word and our Christian lives. . . . *That it may gain recognition and followers among other people and advance with power throughout the world.*
>
> God's kingdom comes to us . . . through the Word and faith, and . . . through the final revelation. Now, we pray for both of these, *that it may come to those who are not yet in it, and that it may come by daily growth here and in eternal life hereafter to us who have attained it.* All this is simply to say: "Dear father, . . . *give us thy Word, that the Gospel may be sincerely preached throughout the world* and that it may be received by faith and may work and live in us."[8]

Another evidence of Luther's missional vision is his recognition and attempt to interact with the Jews and the Muslim Turks. To reach the Jews, Luther published his treatise *That Jesus Christ Was Born a Jew* (1523). Luther did not believe in crusades against Muslims; instead, he suggested that they send evangelists to reach them. Luther studied Islam and wrote apologetic tracts for Muslim Turks. He also encouraged the study of the Koran.

Such evidence suggests that Luther recognized the missionary mandate of the church. So why do many scholars believe that Luther was not involved in missions?

A definition of *mission*

Scholars overlook the missional motif in Luther's writings because of a difference in defining the terms *mission, missionary,* and *mission field.* These words were not used during the time of the Reformation. The words *mission* and *missionary* were first used in English literature in 1598 and 1644 respectively in describing the work of the Jesuits.[9] The terms *world mission* and *mission* only became familiar in Protestant literature two centuries after Luther's death.[10] Apparently, Gustav Warneck and his successors were imposing late eighteenth-century terms on Luther and the other Reformers. As Michael Parsons observes, Luther is judged "guilty" for not following a definition of mission that did not exist during his lifetime.[11] Such an approach to the Reformers is understandable. Foreign missionary activity did not have a tangible form among Protestants in the sixteenth century—even among the Anabaptists.[12] The intention of mission historians to raise awareness about the importance and urgency of foreign missions is commendable.[13] But as David J. Bosch notes, "mission . . . should never be incarcerated in the narrow confines of our own predilections."[14]

> Scholars overlook the missional motif in Luther's writings because of a difference in defining the terms *mission, missionary,* and *mission field.*

Warneck advocated that *missions* should only be understood as the sending of missionaries to non-Christian nations. Yet that view is no longer how *missions* is defined today. In fact, there is a consensus among missiologists that *missions* should be understood widely or holistically. Missiologists no longer see *missions* as the activity of the church "overseas." Instead, they recognize that the frontiers of mission are not just geographical ones. They can also be religious, ethnic, or cultural boundaries.

The understanding of mission has radically changed during the past century.[15] The earliest change had to do with distinguishing between *mission* (singular) and *missions* (plural). Before the mid-1900s, there was no distinction between the two. Contemporary missiologists now describe *mission* as *missio Dei.* This Latin phrase refers to God's purposes and activities in and for the entire universe.[16] The central idea of *missio Dei* is that "God is the One who initiates and sustains mission. At most, then, the church is God's partner in what is God's agenda . . . mission is God-centered rather than human-centered, but without neglecting the important role that God has assigned to the church in that process."[17] Gailyn Van Rheenen further defines *mission* as "the work of God in reconciling sinful humankind to himself."[18] *Mission* is not limited to the activities of the church because God has been actively ministering to the world. God initiated His mission through patriarchs, prophets, priests, and judges in Old Testament times. In the New Testament, He reached out to the world through Jesus Christ and His disciples. Today God continues His mission through the church. *Mission refers to what the church is mandated to do*—starting right where the church is located. Another definition of *mission* is "the task, obligation or commission, adopted by the Church to spread the Christian faith throughout the world."[19]

> *Mission* refers to what the church is mandated to do—starting right where the church is located.

The idea of *missions* (plural) refers to the activities in which the church participates in the *missio Dei*.[20] It also refers to the plans of committed Christians to accomplish God's mission.[21] *Missions* is anchored in the mission of God, and it is the implementation of the mission of God. With this corrective lens, we may now look at the missiological lessons from Luther's thought and practice.

Missiological lessons for Adventist mission

At least seven lessons can be learned from the Reformation for the Seventh-day Adventist Church today.

First, mission must be God centered. Luther articulates three concepts as the starting point for mission: *missio Dei* (God's mission), *missio Christi* (Christ's mission), and *missio ecclesiae* (the church's mission). He believed that the church and mission are all ultimately *missio Dei*.

As Ruthven Roy points out, Adventists must remember that Adventist mission is "God's enterprise from beginning to end."[22] It does not belong to the Adventist denomination—it is God's mission. Adventists must simply recognize and seek opportunities to participate in it. Adventists must not let human pride get in the way, as if mission is about our plans and accomplishments. The success of mission does not merely depend on us. Nor is mission about statistics or missiometrics. Indeed, the "field is the world" (Matthew 13:38)[23] and we are "God's fellow workers" (1 Corinthians 3:9), but God is "the Lord of the Harvest"—not us (Matthew 9:38). It is He who "will finish the work, and cut it short in righteousness" (Romans 9:28, KJV).

Second, Adventists must understand their mission. Luther knew that his movement was a missionary movement.[24] He understood his mission, but not by the definition of nineteenth-century-mission historians. His mission was to re-Christianize Europe—a continent that, during his time, was no longer authentically Christian. Once Luther understood his lifelong mission, he never let go of it. Adventists believe they are a movement and are called out for a specific purpose. Adventist biblical scholar Jiří Moskala observes, "There is no election without a commission" because "God's call presupposes a call for action."[25] Adventists must understand what mission is because their answers to the many challenges of contemporary mission, such as the new forms of missions and strategies, depend on their understanding of their mission.[26]

Third, Adventists must understand their message. Despite his criticisms, Warneck admits that the Reformers helped the cause of missions by restoring the gospel message. Indeed, mission is incomplete without proclamation of that message. Luther understood his mission, and he also understood his message. His theology, with its emphasis on God's redemptive purpose, was ideally suited to mission. Adventists may differ from Luther on some doctrines, but one thing they have in common with him is the doctrine of justification by faith. The Adventist Church must proclaim that message. As Eric Webster observes, "Justification by faith is not a preamble to the third angel's message; it is not introductory or preparatory; it is the very heart and core of the [Adventist] message."[27] Understanding and proclaiming that message is crucial. Russell Burrill thus contends, "Adventists must not preach a new gospel. If we are to fulfill Revelation 14:6-12, then we must preach the eternal gospel of salvation by grace alone. We may do it in the setting of Christ's soon return, but we must not, dare not, add anything as the basis of salvation, which is faith in Christ alone."[28]

Fourth, theology must lead to mission. One valid criticism against the Reformers was that they did not engage in foreign missions. This lack of overseas missions is due to the many obstacles they faced.[29] The first obstacle is that most foreign countries were then under Roman Catholic monarchies. The second obstacle has to do with the Reformers rejecting monasticism without developing their own missionary-sending structure. The third obstacle may be attributed to the fact that the churches of the Reformation were under siege and were struggling just to survive. However, the worst obstacle was the internal conflicts that drained their energy and unintentionally impeded missionary outreach.[30] Because of endless theological disputes and dissensions, the Reformers had little energy left to turn to those outside the Christian fold.[31] They were too busy debating the "what is" and they lost sight of the "so what." As Gordon Doss points out, "What good is excellent theology if it does not produce strong mission?"[32] The Adventist Church must not allow issues to result in energy-draining disputes. Instead, Adventists must develop a commitment to the mission of God among non-Christian peoples that goes beyond mere intellectual assent to impact their time, influence, and resources.

Fifth, eschatology must fuel Adventist mission. Contrary to what some scholars suggest, Luther's eschatology did not hinder his missiology.[33] In the same way, Adventist eschatology is crucially linked to the missionary work of the church. At its core, Adventist theology is missional and belief in the Parousia should be a major motive for Adventist mission. As Rick McEdward suggests, missions should be "eschatology with feet."[34] Adventist eschatology should increase our motivation for mission, because while Revelation shows a beast that has authority over every tribe, people, language, and nation, it also depicts the redemption of "a great multitude that no one could number, from *every nation, from all tribes and peoples* and *languages*" (Revelation 7:9).

Sixth, the Adventist message and mission must be relevant. God's mission is the same throughout Earth's history. The mission task, however, depends on the time and place where churches and individuals live. Luther discerned his time, and he had a vision of the response required.[35] Understanding the context of his message and mission, he went about his task with zeal, planted a new faith, and denounced the obstacles that stood in his way. The Adventist message and mission must be contextualized to be relevant. Gottfried Oosterwal observes, "Each generation of believers . . . must reassess the task of presenting Christ to the world so that it can fulfill its mission in its own particular way."[36] Hence, Jon Dybdahl suggests that theologians "learn to read not only historic theology but also their Bibles and their society and then take steps to create out of their matrix a theology that allows Jesus to be seen and understood clearly in their setting."[37] Ellen White similarly notes, "There was a present truth in the days of Luther,—a truth at that time of special importance; there is a present truth for the church today."[38] We must understand the time and be seized by the urgency to accomplish our God-given task.

Seventh, every member must embrace Adventist mission. Luther believed that every believer is an evangelist who should teach the gospel to others.[39] Luther taught that the function of the priesthood, which includes the proclamation of the gospel and concern for the salvation of others, belongs to every Christian.[40] The danger is that churches buy into a "consumer" church model whereby pastors become performers or providers of a certain kind of service, while the people of God (the *laos*), as customers, sit back to be served.[41] It is essential that the Adventist Church fully implement a sound theology of the priesthood of all believers so that every member will become involved in mission.[42] As Oosterwal points out, such a "rediscovery of the Biblical role of the laity is essential . . . to the finishing of God's mission on earth."[43]

1. Ellen G. White, *The Great Controversy* (Nampa, ID: Pacific Press® Pub. Assn., 2009), 120.

2. Peter M. van Bemmelen, "Justification by Faith: An Adventist Understanding," *Journal of the Adventist Theological Society* 20, nos. 1–2 (2009): 177.

3. Glenn S. Sunshine, "Protestant Missions in the Sixteenth Century," in *The Great Commission: Evangelicals and the History of World Missions*, ed. Martin Klauber and Scott M. Manetsch (Nashville, TN: B & H Publishing, 2008), 12.

4. Gustav Warneck, *Outline of a History of Protestant Missions From the Reformation to the Present Time*, ed. George Robson (New York: Fleming H. Revell, 1901), 9.

5. Ingemar Öberg, *Luther and World Mission: A Historical and Systematic Study*, trans. Dean Apel (St. Louis, MO: Concordia, 2007), 123.

6. Martin Luther, *Luther's Works*, vol. 20, *Lectures on the Minor Prophets, 3: Zechariah*, ed. Hilton C. Oswald (St. Louis, MO: Concordia, 1973), 305, 306, quoted in Öberg, *Luther and World Mission*, 123 (emphasis added).

7. Luther, *Luther's Works*, 20:326, quoted in Öberg, *Luther and World Mission*, 123.

8. Öberg, *Luther and World Mission*, 132 (emphasis added).

9. Elias Medeiros, "The Reformers and 'Missions': Warneck, Latourette, Neill, Kane, Winter, and Tucker's Arguments—Part 1," *Fides Reformata* 18, no. 1 (2013): 121.

10. Pekka Huhtinen, "*Luther and World Missions*: A Review," *Concordia Theological Quarterly* 65, no. 1 (January 2001): 17n5.

11. Michael Parsons, ed., *Text and Task: Scripture and Mission* (Eugene, OR: Wipf and Stock, 2006), 66.

12. Sunshine, "Protestant Missions in the Sixteenth Century," 12 (emphasis added).

13. A. Chadwick Mauldin, *Fullerism as Opposed to Calvinism: A Historical and Theological Comparison of the Missiology of Andrew Fuller and John Calvin* (Eugene, OR: Wipf and Stock, 2011), 35.

14. David J. Bosch, *Transforming Mission: Paradigm Shifts in Theology of Mission*, 20th Anniversary ed. (Maryknoll, NY: Orbis Books, 2011), 9.

15. A. Scott Moreau, Gary R. Corwin, and Gary B. McGee, "Missions in the Modern World," in *Introducing World Missions: A Biblical, Historical, and Practical Survey*, 2nd ed. (Grand Rapids, MI: Baker Academic, 2013), 17.

16. J. Andrew Kirk, *What Is Mission? Theological Explorations* (Minneapolis, MN: Fortress Press, 2000), 25.

17. Moreau, Corwin, and McGee, "Missions in the Modern World," 18.

18. Gailyn Van Rheenen, *Missions: Biblical Foundations and Contemporary Strategies* (Grand Rapids, MI: Zondervan, 1996), 20.

19. David B. Barrett, George T. Kurian, and Todd M. Johnson, eds., *World Christian Encyclopedia: A Comparative Survey of Churches and Religions in the Modern World*, vol. 1 (New York: Oxford University Press, 2001), 29.

20. Bosch, *Transforming Mission*, 10.

21. Rheenen, *Missions: Biblical Foundations and Contemporary Strategies*, 20.

22. Ruthven Roy, *A Challenge to the Remnant! Designing Our Mission Strategy to Impact the Real World* (Frederick, MD: Network Discipling Ministries Books, 2002), 19.

23. Unless otherwise noted, all Scripture references in this chapter are from the English Standard Version.

24. Parsons, *Text and Task*, 66.

25. Jiří Moskala, "The Mission of God's People in the Old Testament," *Journal of the Adventist Theological Society* 19, nos. 1–2 (2008): 40.

26. Gottfried Oosterwal, *Mission: Possible; the Challenge of Mission Today* (Nashville, TN: Southern Publishing Association, 1975), 12.

27. Eric Webster, "The Third Angel's Message in Verity," *Ministry* 53, no. 8 (August 1980): 4.

28. Russell Burrill, *Radical Disciples for Revolutionary Churches* (Fallbrook, CA: Hart Research Center, 1996), 92.

29. Bosch, *Transforming Mission*, 250.

30. Abraham Kovacs, "Protestant Churches," in *Encyclopedia of Missions and Missionaries*, ed. Jonathan Bonk (New York: Routledge, 2007), 356.

31. Bosch, *Transforming Mission*, 250.

32. Gorden R. Doss, "Viewpoint: Reforming Christians or Converting Non-Christians?" *Journal of Adventist Mission Studies* 6, no. 2 (2010): 111.

33. Bosch, *Transforming Mission*, 246.

34. Rick McEdward. "Adventist Mission Theology: Developing a Biblical Foundation," *Journal of Adventist Mission Studies* 7, no. 1 (2011): 75.

35. Parsons, *Text and Task*, 67.

36. Oosterwal, *Mission: Possible*, 15.

37. Jon L. Dybdahl, "Adventist Responses to Mission Challenges Through Theology and Contextualization," *Journal of Adventist Mission Studies* 5, no. 2 (2009): 31.

38. White, *The Great Controversy*, 143.

39. From Luther's exposition on the "herald of good tidings" (Isaiah 40:9), *Luther's Works*, vol. 17, *Lectures on Isaiah, Chapter 40–66*, ed. Jaroslav Pelikan (St. Louis, MO: Concordia, 1972), 13, 14, quoted in Parsons, *Text and Task*, 74. All believers "have the right and duty to confess, to teach, and to spread God's Word." Martin Luther, *Luther's Works*, vol. 27, *Lectures on Galatians, 1535, Chapters 5–6*, ed. Jaroslav Pelikan (St. Louis, MO: Concordia, 1964), 394.

40. Parsons, *Text and Task*, 75.

41. Monte Sahlin, foreword to *Revolution in the Church*, by Russell Burrill (Fallbrook, CA: Hart Research Center, 1993), v.

42. Daniel Kewley and Sven Östring, "Can Church Planting Movements Emerge in the West? Case Studies of Three Church Planting Strategies in Western Australia," *Journal of Adventist Mission Studies* 8, no. 1 (2012): 29.

43. Oosterwal, *Mission: Possible*, 13.

CHAPTER 17

Luther and Romans:
Five Hundred Years Later

Sigve K. Tonstad

We do not need Martin Luther's Ninety-Five Theses to impress upon us the potential of *words* to create waves in the world.* For that, we have our own living mentors, whether in the form of a tweet, fake news, or the soaring "I Have a Dream" speech of another Martin—that is Martin Luther King Jr.

Yet we need the original Martin Luther to tell us of the importance of words more *eloquently* than anyone else. This year, five hundred years after the Reformation started, we will pay respect to Luther for a host of reasons. One obvious thing is to instill within us a renewed respect for words—words in general, and *the* Word

> One obvious thing is to instill within us a renewed respect for words—words in general, and *the* Word in particular.

in particular. In a sermon preached at Wittenberg on March 10, 1522, one year after his confrontation with the emperor in Worms, Luther's tribute to words stands out.

---

* An earlier draft of this chapter was presented as the Clinton Emmerson memorial address in the Loma Linda University Seventh-day Adventist Church on February 18, 2017, on the occasion of the author receiving the Charles E. Weniger Award for excellence.

For the Word created heaven and earth and all things [Ps. 33:6]; the Word must do this thing, and not we poor sinners.

In short, I will preach it, teach it, write it, but I will constrain no man by force, for faith must come freely without compulsion. Take myself as an example. I opposed indulgences and all the papists, but never with force. I simply taught, preached, and wrote God's Word; otherwise I did nothing. And while I slept [cf. Mark 3:26-29], or drank Wittenberg beer with my friends Philip and Amsdorf, the Word so greatly weakened the papacy that no prince or emperor ever inflicted such losses upon it. I did nothing; the Word did everything. Had I desired to foment trouble, I could have brought great bloodshed upon Germany; indeed, I could have started such a game that even the emperor would not have been safe. But what would it have been? Mere fool's play. I did nothing; I let the Word do its work. . . . For it is almighty, and takes captive the hearts, and when the hearts are captured the work will fall of itself.[1]

Luther compares words to other means of persuasion; and in particular, he contrasts the use of mere words with coercion. This is not a small matter, given that he was an Augustinian monk by vocation, both in terms of his way of thinking and in his love for Romans. Augustine bequeathed to the church the policy that coercion is legitimate whenever persuasion fails.[2] Luther, at least the young Luther, repudiated it.[3] Words, he says, have to do it. And the Word will do it, because it has the capacity to take the heart captive.

Words started the Reformation, and words carried it forward—an obvious example is Luther's translation of the Bible into German.[4] *Sola scriptura* may be an ideological and doctrinal slogan, but it is also a tribute to *words*—and to words *alone*—to make the difference in what we think and how we conduct our lives. Words carved out space for the rights of the individual conscience, impressing on Luther the necessity of defending the encounter between the individual and the Word over any other authority, secular or ecclesial.[5] Democracy and the notion of the consent of the governed owe more than a little to the Protestant Reformation.[6]

Although the Ninety-Five Theses are celebrated, not everyone remembers them. The first line states, "1. When our Lord and Master Jesus Christ said, 'Repent,' he willed the entire life of believers to be one of repentance."[7] This is a blunt corrective to the controversy over indulgences, but it also works as a mature theological statement. Luther's theology is introspective, and the first of the Ninety-Five Theses is a case in point. But this is not the whole story. The notion that Luther, not the apostle Paul, is the founding father of "the introspective conscience of the West" has drawn many prominent thinkers to the table, and the discussion is ongoing.[8] One outstanding reading of the evidence calls this emphasis a serious *mis*reading. Heiko A. Oberman writes, "It is precisely this conventional, conscience-oriented morality that man's innermost self struggles to fulfill, and that Luther, to the horror of all well-meaning, decent Christians, undermined."[9] In this perception, the forces without count for more than the defect within; and Luther is, by these criteria, a Reformer who understands the reality of a cosmic conflict. "The issue is not morality or immorality, it is God and the Devil," states Oberman.[10] In the preface to the English version of his book, he argues, "The Reformer can only be understood as a late medieval man for whom Satan is as real as God and mammon."[11] *This* forgotten (and embarrassing) Luther is the one that modernity is least likely to understand, but it is also this *forgotten* Luther that, in my view, is closest to Seventh-day Adventist theology.

We turn to Romans, for we are not ignorant of its role in Luther's experience. We know that Paul's letter marked the turning point in Luther's life story, and it became the cornerstone in his theology and legacy. Most of us have heard the story, even though the time line might be fuzzier than those who tell the story make it seem.[12] Luther takes from Romans what has been called *the material principle of the Reformation*—the doctrine of justification by faith.

Perhaps the most familiar version of the story (as told by Luther in 1545, shortly before his death) spells out what Gerhard Ebeling calls "the fundamental theological perception of the Reformation."[13]

A strange burning desire had seized me to understand Paul in the Epistle to the Romans; it was not coldness of heart which had stood in my way until then, but a single phrase in chapter I: "For in it the righteousness of God is revealed" [Rom. I:17]. For I hated this phrase, "the righteousness of God," which I had been taught to understand philosophically, from its normal usage by all who teach doctrine, as referring to the so-called formal or active righteousness, by means of which God is righteous and punishes sinners and the unrighteous. . . . Was it not enough that poor sinners, eternally lost as the result of original sin, should be cast down in pure wickedness through the law of the Decalogue, but that God should add one torment to another through the gospel, and even through the gospel should threaten us with his righteousness and his anger? So . . . I returned time and again to this very passage in Paul, burning with thirst to know what St. Paul meant. Finally, thanks to the mercy of God, and thinking ceaselessly of this matter one night, I recalled the context in which the words occur, namely: "In it the righteousness of God is revealed . . . as it is written, 'The righteous shall live by faith.' " Then I began to understand . . . that this is the meaning of the passage: through the gospel the righteousness of God is revealed, that is, passive righteousness, . . . through faith, as it is written: "The righteous shall live by faith." Then I had the feeling that straight away I was born again, and had entered through open doors into paradise itself.[14]

This is the familiar Luther that most people know. It is also Romans and the apostle Paul as interpreted by Luther. And this is Paul and Romans as they *should be* understood, the *Gospel* with a capital *G*. Paul, Augustine, Luther, John Wesley, and Karl Barth are a towering fivesome agreeing on the most important doctrine in Protestant Christianity.[15] Thus, there is in Luther's reading, then, something that approaches a *normative* reading of Paul.

One year later, in the year of his death in 1546, Luther gave Romans one last boost to ensure its position of preeminence in the Protestant tradition. "This letter is truly the most important piece in the New Testament. It is purest Gospel. It is well worth a Christian's while not only to memorize it word for word but also to occupy himself with it daily, as though it were the daily bread of the soul. It is impossible to read or to meditate on this letter too much or too well."[16]

Five hundred years later

Is it our task to revisit, reaffirm, and recommit to the tenets of the Protestant Reformation and to Luther's reading of Paul's most important letter? Among Seventh-day Adventists, many will respond affirmatively, even though the Seventh-day Adventist experience has had an uneasy relationship with Romans.[17] Adventist identity is rooted in *Daniel* and *Revelation*, not in Romans. Romans has been a challenge, as though it is a letter against which we need to defend ourselves instead of a message on which to build our identity. The central question concerns whether the task today is to revisit, reaffirm, and recommit to Luther's reading of Paul's most important letter. Or—without intending to diminish the importance of Luther—is it necessary to *revise, rethink,* and *commit* to a different reading of Paul's letter? If the second option describes our task, as I believe it does, why should we do it, and what will the result look like?

To answer the why question, I offer two main reasons: one exegetical and the other situational and historical. The exegetical part reexamines Luther's reading of Romans. It is not an easy task to challenge Luther's exegesis, but this is precisely what many scholars have been doing for the past thirty years.[18] Scholars who are "Lutheran," broadly speaking, have also been doing it.[19]

Romans 1:16, 17 is the text that serves as the battle cry for Protestant theology. What does the text say? What is the context? Which variables must the interpreter take into consideration? Luther's German translation does not differ much from the one we have in the NRSV: "For I am not ashamed of the gospel; it is the power of God for salvation to everyone who has faith, to the Jew first and also to the Greek. For in it the righteousness of God is revealed through faith for faith; as it is written, 'The one who is righteous will live by faith' " (Romans 1:16, 17).[20]

Faith is the theme word in this translation. There is even an Old Testament text to drive it home: "As it is written: *'The one who is righteous will live by faith'*" (verse 17; emphasis added).[21] Did Habakkuk write that the righteous shall live by faith, as translations of Romans make it seem?

The answer is No; he did not. We need a little context to understand what he did write.

First, what is the problem in Habakkuk?

O LORD, how long shall I cry for help,
　　and you will not listen?
Or cry to you "Violence!"
　　and you will not save?
Why do you make me see wrongdoing
　　and look at trouble?
Destruction and violence are before me;
　　strife and contention arise (Habakkuk 1:2, 3).

Is the problem in Habakkuk human sin—or is it the sense of God's absence? That is to say, is the problem the bad things humans do, or is it the good things God fails to do? Is the problem that humans fall short of the norm, or is it that God's actions fall short of expectations? Habakkuk's chief concern is failure on *God's* part.[22]

Second, will God respond to Habakkuk's complaint? (I have devoted a whole book, *God of Sense and Traditions of Non-Sense*, to this subject—whether God cares about our questions.[23]) Does God care about Habakkuk's question, and does Habakkuk expect an answer?

I will stand at my watchpost,
　　and station myself on the rampart;
I will keep watch to see what he will say to me,
　　and what he will answer concerning my complaint (Habakkuk 2:1).

Does Habakkuk get an answer? If the answer is Yes, what is God's answer? Before we read it, let us put two options on the table. Is God's answer to Habakkuk to live by faith, no matter how bleak things may look? That is option 1. Option 2 is this: Will God address the critical concern in his question, God's seeming failure to make good on His promises? Is God's answer found in the realm of *faith*—in here, in our heads—or is it found out there, in the world, in the form of a demonstration of God's faithfulness?

Then the LORD answered me and said:
Write the *vision* [Hebrew *hazon*; Greek *horasis*];
　　make *it* [the vision] plain on tablets,
　　so that a runner may read *it* [the vision].

For there is still a *vision* [Hebrew *hazon*; Greek *horasis*] for the appointed time;
  it [the vision] speaks of the end, and [*it*] does not lie.
If *it* [the vision] seems to tarry, wait for *it* [the vision];
    it [the vision] will surely come, *it* [the vision] will not delay (verses 2, 3; emphasis added).

Option 2 wins this one. God's primary answer is *not* found in the realm of faith. God's answer is found in the promise that He will do something; it is found in the realm of *faithfulness*. "Wait for it; it will surely come," God tells Habakkuk (verse 3). This is the promise. I believe that the line in Habakkuk runs from *problem* to *promise* to *summons*.[24] What is the summons?

In the Hebrew text, it is this: "the Righteous One by *his faithfulness* shall live" (verse 4, author's translation). In the Greek translation (Septuagint), which Paul most likely used, the text in Habakkuk reads, "but the righteous one by *my faithfulness* shall live" (verse 4, LXX).

There are minor issues in the text that deserve further discussion, but we have enough information to answer my test question. In the summons to Habakkuk, did we hear the word *faith*? In the summons to Habakkuk, whether in Hebrew or Greek, did we hear the word *faithfulness*? On what basis, now, shall the righteous one live?

In summary, the *problem* for Habakkuk is God's apparent absence. The *promise* to Habakkuk is that something will happen to put God's faithfulness on display. The *summons* to Habakkuk, in a (non-Messianic) translation of the Septuagint, is that "the righteous will live by my faithfulness."[25] This is what is written, in the context within which it is written. When we go back to Romans with this understanding, what is written?

I am not ashamed of the gospel.
For in it the right-making of God is revealed
    from faithfulness for faithfulness,
      as it is written,
"The righteous shall live by [My] faithfulness" (Romans 1:16, 17, author's translation).

This is different than Luther's reading. How can I be saved? Luther's faith message answers *that* question. Can God be trusted? The line that runs from Habakkuk to Romans answers *that* question.[26] The exegetical arguments tilt toward the second option. Faith has not disappeared, but God's faithfulness occupies the theological center: here in Romans 1; in the great exposition in chapter 3, verses 21–26; in chapter 5; in chapter 8; in the difficult chapters 9–11, where Luther's exposition fails dismally; and in chapter 15, the chapter that confirms that we were not taking things out of thin air in our exposition of chapter 1. God's *compassion* occupies the center in these chapters, with tremendous and underappreciated consequences for how we read the wrath passage in Romans 1:18–32, the groaning of creation in Romans 8:18–23, and the misunderstood story of Israel and the Gentile world in Romans 9–11.

What is perhaps even more important is the *cosmic* perspective that emerges in what some call a *widescreen* reading of Romans. In the cosmic perspective, the message in Romans runs from *misrepresentation* to *revelation* and not simply from *sin* to *salvation*. A case in point is Romans 7, usually seen as the place where Paul is most introspective. What if, instead, we hear the voice of Eve in this chapter and allusions to the conversation between Eve and the serpent in Genesis? This is what recent and careful expositions of Romans argue.[27]

Before going to the second reason why a different reading of Romans is due, I will mention briefly other elements of support for our understanding of Paul. For Luther, good theology begins with doctrine.[28] For many leading scholars on Paul today, the tenor of his thought is *story*, not doctrine. To Luther, Judaism is a religion of works. To the "new perspective" on Paul, Judaism is a religion of grace.[29] Many New Testament scholars recognize that the New Testament in general, and Paul in particular, are steeped in apocalyptic conceptions.[30] According to Oberman, Luther is also apocalyptic, but the Protestant tradition is not. This means that the *apocalyptic* Luther, the Luther who knows and feels the cosmic conflict, has been lost. To Luther, Paul's use of the Old Testament is opportunistic. To Richard Hays and others, Paul's use of the Old Testament is sensitive to context. To Luther, divine sovereignty and arbitrary election are key teachings in Romans. By contrast, the key message in Romans is divine compassion, and there is no arbitrariness. Protestant readings of Romans in the Augustinian and Lutheran traditions fail the compassion test laid down by Paul in Romans. This is the textual case, if only a glimpse.

Reading Romans in context (1543 and 1943)

The second reason for reading Romans different than the way Luther read it is historical and contextual. It, too, begins with Luther.

In 1543, Luther wrote a booklet whose English title is *On the Jews and Their Lies*.[31] Luther devotes a big part of it to alleged mistakes in Jewish readings of the Bible. Seventh-day Adventists will applaud his lengthy exposition of Daniel 9, especially his defense of a time line that fits our Messianic understanding of Daniel 9:24–27. We have to bypass that and skip ahead to Luther's prescription for how Christians in Germany should relate to Jews. He asks, "What shall we Christians do with this rejected and condemned people, the Jews?"[32]

His answer has seven points.

- First, to set fire to their synagogues or schools and to bury and cover with dirt whatever will not burn, so that no man will ever again see a stone or cinder of them. This is to be done in honor of our Lord and of Christendom, so that God might see that we are Christians, and do not condone or knowingly tolerate such public lying, cursing, and blaspheming of his Son and of his Christians.

Luther maintains that our civilization is incompatible with Jewish houses of worship. My question is, does Luther's recommendation pass the compassion test and the vision of inclusion that we find in Romans?

- Second, I advise that their houses also be razed and destroyed. For they pursue in them the same aims as in their synagogues. Instead they might be lodged under a roof or in a barn, like the gypsies.

According to Luther we do not want Jews to live in our neighborhoods. Does this pass the compassion test, with no room in the inn for the Jews?

- Third, I advise that all their prayer books and Talmudic writings, in which such idolatry, lies, cursing, and blasphemy are taught, be taken from them.

Luther's position is that the sacred books of the Jews should not be circulated or read. They should be confiscated, by force, if necessary. Does he not realize that the very existence and identity of a people to a large extent depend on their books?

- Fourth, I advise that their rabbis be forbidden to teach henceforth on pain of loss of life and limb.

Luther maintains that we do not want a religion in our midst that is incompatible with our values. He advocates the death penalty for those found to violate the ban.

- Fifth, I advise that safe-conduct on the highways be abolished completely for the Jews. For they have no business in the countryside, since they are not lords, officials, tradesmen, or the like. Let them stay at home.

Luther advocates a travel ban for all Jews, whether we see them as an ethnic group or as a faith community. According to Luther, ordinary rights and civil protections do not apply to this group.

- Sixth, I advise that usury be prohibited to them, and that all cash and treasure of silver and gold be taken from them and put aside for safekeeping.

Luther proposes an economic boycott of the Jews that is reminiscent of the prophecy in Revelation 13:7.

- Seventh, I recommend putting a flail, an ax, a hoe, a spade, a distaff, or a spindle into the hands of young, strong Jews and Jewesses and letting them earn their bread in the sweat of their brow, as was imposed on the children of Adam (Gen. 3[:19]).

Luther does not say it quite this way, but the remaining option for the Jews, the career choice open to their young, is forced labor. This is not a return to Adam but to slavery in Egypt. From that slavery, as we know, from that state of being unwanted and oppressed resident aliens, God intervened to set them free.

Finally, Luther concludes with this:

- But if the authorities are reluctant to use force and restrain the Jews' devilish wantonness, the latter should, as we said, be expelled from the country and be told to return to their land and their possessions in Jerusalem, where they may lie, curse, blaspheme, defame, murder, steal, rob, practice usury, mock, and indulge in all those infamous abominations which they practice among us, and leave us our government, our country, our life, and our property, much more leave our Lord the Messiah, our faith, and our church undefiled and uncontaminated with their devilish tyranny and malice.[33]

Do we have a situational and historical reason for reading Romans in a different way, assuming that the exegetical case has been successful? We do, and not only a case, half-heartedly pursued, but an obligation; not only an academic exercise left to a few, but a communal enterprise obligating and consuming the many. Luther's reading of Romans is inadequate exegetically and theologically, and his legacy has an enormous compassion deficit. If the two are linked—and they may be linked more than marginally—shall we be at risk, too, of a similar compassion deficit?

On September 4, 1942, Chaim Rumkowski, the head of the Jewish Council in Lodz, Poland, addressed thousands of Jews and informed them that they would have to surrender their children under the age of ten on that day.

I understand you, mothers, I see the tears in your eyes; I feel what you feel in your hearts, you fathers who are obliged to go to your work even on the morning after your children have been taken from you, your darling little ones whom you were playing with only yesterday. All this I know and feel. Since four o'clock yesterday, when the order was first conveyed to me, I have been prostrate; I share your pain, I suffer your anguish, and I do not know how I shall survive this—where I shall find the strength to do it. I must let you into a secret: they [the Nazi authorities] demanded 24,000 sacrifices, 3,000 a day for eight days. I was able to reduce that to 20,000, but only on condition that all children under ten be included. Children of ten and older are safe. Since the children and old people together amount to only 13,000 souls, the gap must be filled with the sick.[34]

I stated at the beginning that there are two reasons—one exegetical and the other situational or historical—for reading Romans differently five hundred years after Luther. Our exegetical warrant relies on the line that runs from Habakkuk to Romans. Habakkuk is a post-Holocaust voice, heard in pre-Holocaust times: *he speaks to the problem of God's apparent absence.* Romans stays on topic: its main affirmations are the compassion of God and the faithfulness of God—faith or no faith on our part. The situational and historical warrant is found in the Holocaust and in the mind-numbing absence of compassion in the world. Words are powerful weapons. Words sometimes assert themselves late, as did Luther's words when, on the eve of Luther's birthday, the Nazis launched the Kristallnacht in 1938.[35] In the light of history, Luther's words of 1543 may count for more than the words of 1517 or the words of 1522. Recent scholarship on Romans improves on Luther's understanding. It shows a profound understanding of the cosmic conflict and restores to Romans the capacity to speak to the needs of our time more forcefully than traditional readings. For what it is worth, it is my conviction that the revised readings will enrich and improve distinctive emphases in Seventh-day Adventist theology.

> Romans stays on topic: its main affirmations are the compassion of God and the faithfulness of God—faith or no faith on our part.

Conclusion

I want to introduce Phoebe to you. She was a deacon in the church in Cenchreae, mentioned first in the greeting section of Romans 16. Scholars agree that she carried Paul's letter to Rome. At the first reading of the letter, she read it out loud in house churches in Rome in A.D. 56, during the reign of Nero. It has richly nourished my reading of Romans to imagine that Phoebe mastered the rhetorical twists and turns of the letter that are often lost on us. *Our* "Phoebe" comes to us in 2017, almost two thousand years after the letter was first read, five hundred years after Luther, and seventy years after the Holocaust. She will read two excerpts from Romans (Romans 1:16, 17 and 3:21–26 in my translation). When this chapter was first presented in lecture form, I had Faith Calaminos, a third-year student in the School of Medicine in the role of Phoebe. She helped make it a memorable event. This is what she read:

> For I am not ashamed of the gospel,
>> for it is the power of God for salvation
>> to everyone who trusts,
>> to the Jews first and also to the Greek.
> For God's right-making is revealed in it
>> from faithfulness for faithfulness,
> as it is written,
>> The righteous shall live by [My] faithfulness (Romans 1:16, 17, author's translation).

> But now apart from law
> the right-making of God
>> has been disclosed,
>> witnessed by the law and by the prophets,
> the right-making of God
>> through the faithfulness of Jesus Christ
>> to all who believe.
> For there is no difference,
>> for all have missed the mark
>> and lack the glory of God.
> They have been set right freely by His grace
>> through the liberation which is in Christ Jesus.
> God set Him forth publicly
>> as a means of reconciliation
>> through the faithfulness of His bloody death.
> He did this in order to show His right-making
>> in view of the fact
>> that He had passed over the sins previously committed
>> in the forbearance of God;
>> that is,
> in order to demonstrate His right-making
>> at the present time,
> that God may be right
>> in the very act of setting right
>> the one who lives
>> on the basis of the faithfulness of Jesus (Romans 3:21–26, author's translation).

Romans and Seventh-day Adventists in 2017 and beyond: we can do wondrous things in the world if we read anew Paul's most important letter.

Romans and Seventh-day Adventists in 2017 and beyond: we can do wondrous things in the world if we read anew Paul's most important letter.

1. Martin Luther, "The Second Sermon, March 10, 1522, Monday After Invocavit," in *Luther's Works*, vol. 51, *Sermons 1*, ed. John W. Doberstein (St. Louis, MO: Concordia, 1959), 77, 78.

2. Peter Brown, *Augustine of Hippo* (London: Faber and Faber, 1967), 235. See also Sigve K. Tonstad, *The Letter to the Romans: Paul Among the Ecologists* (Sheffield: Sheffield Phoenix, 2016), 28–30.

3. When the Reformation turned political, Luther abandoned his earlier conviction. See John Emerich Edward Dalberg-Acton, "The Protestant Theory of Persecution," in *Essays on Freedom and Power*, ed. Gertrude Himmelfarb (Gloucester, MA: Peter Smith, 1972), 113–140.

4. See the chapter in this book by Nikolaus Satelmajer on Bible translations.

5. Daniel Olivier, *The Trial of Luther*, trans. John Tonkin (St. Louis, MO: Concordia, 1978), 166.

6. This is a large and complex subject. Luther was neither a political philosopher nor a political reformer, but his writings have political implications. See Martin Luther, "Temporal Authority: To What Extent It Should Be Obeyed" (1523), trans. J. J. Schindel, in *Luther's Works*, vol. 45, *The Christian and Society 2*, ed. Walther I. Brandt (Philadelphia, PA: Fortress, 1962); Markus Wriedt, "Luthers Verhältnis zu Demokratie und individueller Freiheit," *Luther* 85 (2014): 149–163. According to Roland Bainton, the religious controversy of the sixteenth century contributes to democracy by denying state absolutism. See Roland Bainton, *The Reformation of the Sixteenth Century* (Boston, MA: Beacon Press, 1952), 228–243.

7. Martin Luther, *Luther's Works*, vol. 31, *Career of the Reformer 1*, ed. Jaroslav Pelikan, Hilton C. Oswald, and Helmut T. Lehmann (Philadelphia, PA: Fortress Press, 1999), 25, 26.

8. Krister Stendahl, "The Apostle Paul and the Introspective Conscience of the West," *Harvard Theological Review* 56, no. 3 (July 1963): 199–215; Krister Stendahl, *Final Account: Paul's Letter to the Romans* (Minneapolis, MN: Fortress Press, 1995).

9. Heiko A. Oberman, *Luther: Man Between God and the Devil*, trans. Eileen Walliser-Schwarzbart (New Haven, CT: Yale University Press, 1989), 155.

10. Ibid.

11. Ibid., xv.

12. Some scholars point out that Luther does not start talking about his "tower experience" until after 1530, and his most complete account dates to 1545. See Gerhard Ebeling, *Luther:*

An Introduction to His Thought, trans. R.A. Wilson (London: Collins, 1970), 39–42; William M. Landeen, *Martin Luther's Religious Thought* (Mountain View, CA: Pacific Press® Pub. Assn., 1971), 42–51. Roland Bainton smooths out the wrinkles by locating all of the most important elements in the story before 1517. Roland Bainton, *Here I Stand: A Life of Martin Luther* (Nashville, TN: Abingdon, 1978), 39–64.

13. Ebeling, *Luther,* 39.

14. Martin Luther, "Preface to the *Complete Edition of Luther's Latin Writings,*" in *D. Martin Luthers Werke: Kritische Gesamtausgabe,* vol. 54 (Weimar: Hermann Böhlau, 1928), 185, 186, translation by R. A. Wilson, in Ebeling, *Luther,* 39, 40.

15. For a brief overview of the subject, see Tonstad, *The Letter to the Romans,* 23–48.

16. Martin Luther, *D. Martin Luther: Die gantze Heilige Schrifft Deudsch 1545 aufs new zurericht,* ed. Hans Volz and Heinz Blanke (Munich: Roger and Bernhard, 1972), vol. 2, 2254–2268, in Martin Luther, *Preface to the Letter of St. Paul to the Romans,* trans. Andrew Thornton, Christian Classics Ethereal Library, accessed July 30, 2017, http://www.ccel.org/l/luther/romans/pref_romans.html.

17. Seventh-day Adventist works on Romans are few and far between, and none has had a truly formative influence on Adventist thought. A. Graham Maxwell's comments on Romans in *The Seventh-day Adventist Bible Commentary* might be seen as a slight exception—and not because Maxwell took a Lutheran reading to heart. See also John C. Brunt's book, *Romans: Mercy for All,* Abundant Life Bible Amplifier (Nampa, ID: Pacific Press® Pub. Assn., 1996).

18. Richard B. Hays, *The Faith of Jesus Christ: The Narrative Substructure of Galatians 3:1–4:11,* 2nd ed. (Grand Rapids, MI: Eerdmans, 2002). This is the seminal work on the topic.

19. For the historical perspective, see Sigve K. Tonstad, "*Pistis Kristou*: Reading Paul in a New Paradigm," *Andrews University Seminary Studies* 40, no. 1 (2002): 37–59. More recently, views *pro* and *con* are represented in Michael F. Bird and Preston M. Sprinkle, eds., *The Faith of Jesus Christ: Exegetical, Biblical, and Theological Studies* (Peabody, MA: Hendrickson, 2009).

20. Unless otherwise noted, all Scripture references in this chapter are from the New Revised Standard Version.

21. Paul is quoting Habakkuk 2:4 in this verse.

22. To Francis I. Andersen, Habakkuk's outcry is "the passionate prayer of a desperate man," a person who is anguished by "moral outrage and perplexity." Francis I. Andersen, *Habakkuk: A New Translation With Introduction and Commentary,* Anchor Bible (New York: Doubleday, 2001), 123, 125.

23. Sigve K. Tonstad, *God of Sense and Traditions of Non-Sense* (Eugene, OR: Wipf and Stock, 2016).

24. Tonstad, *The Letter to the Romans,* 14.

25. For help in grasping the nuances of this text, see Richard B. Hays, " 'The Righteous One' as Eschatological Deliverer: A Case Study in Paul's Apocalyptic Hermeneutics," in *Apocalyptic and the New Testament: Essays in Honor of J. Louis Martyn,* ed. Joel Marcus and Marion L. Soards, *Journal for the Study of the New Testament* Supplement Series 24 (Sheffield: Sheffield Academic Press, 1989), 191–215.

26. Thus, Richard Hays states, "The driving question in Romans is not 'How can I find a

gracious God?' but 'How can we trust in this allegedly gracious God if he abandons his promises to Israel?' " Richard Hays, *Echoes of Scripture in the Letters of Paul* (New Haven, CT: Yale University Press, 1989), 53.

27. See Tonstad, *The Letter to the Romans*, 207–220.

28. Martin Luther, *Luther's Works*, vol. 26, *Lectures on Galatians, 1535, Chapters 1–4*, ed. Walter A. Hansen (St. Louis, MO: Concordia, 1999). The doctrine to be mastered is the distinction between the law and the gospel. To Luther, "Whoever knows well how to distinguish the Gospel from the Law should give thanks to God and know that he is a real theologian." Ibid., 115.

29. E. P. Sanders, *Paul and Palestinian Judaism: A Comparison of Patterns of Religion* (Minneapolis, MN: Fortress Press, 1979); see also James Dunn, *The New Perspective on Paul* (Grand Rapids, MI: Eerdmans, 2005).

30. To me, the reappraisal of the apocalyptic is the most important "new perspective" on Paul. See J. Christiaan Beker, *Paul the Apostle: The Triumph of God in Life and Thought* (Philadelphia, PA: Fortress Press, 1980); J. Louis Martyn, *Galatians: A New Translation With Introduction and Commentary*, Anchor Bible (New York: Doubleday, 1997). Martyn's commentary has the best grasp of the apocalyptic tenor in Galatians and is one of the best commentaries in print.

31. Martin Luther, *On the Jews and Their Lies*, in *Luther's Works*, vol. 47, *The Christian in Society 4*, ed. Franklin Sherman (Philadelphia, PA: Fortress Press, 1999), 123–306.

32. Ibid., 268.

33. Ibid., 268–276.

34. Göran Rosenberg, *A Brief Stop on the Road From Auschwitz*, trans. Sarah Death (New York: Other Press, 2015), 57.

35. The line from Luther to Hitler is stippled, but the anti-Semitism of Luther's later years cannot be explained away. What also cannot be explained away is the effect of toxic speech even if the toxic speech was not intended the way later generations used it. Books on the subject tend to bend over backward to put Luther in the best possible light; cf. Eric W. Gritsch, *Martin Luther's Anti-Semitism: Against His Better Judgment* (Grand Rapids, MI: Eerdmans, 2012); Christopher J. Probst, *Demonizing the Jews: Luther and the Protestant Church in Nazi Germany* (Bloomington, IN: Indiana University Press, 2012). The second of these books is published in association with the United States Holocaust Memorial Museum.

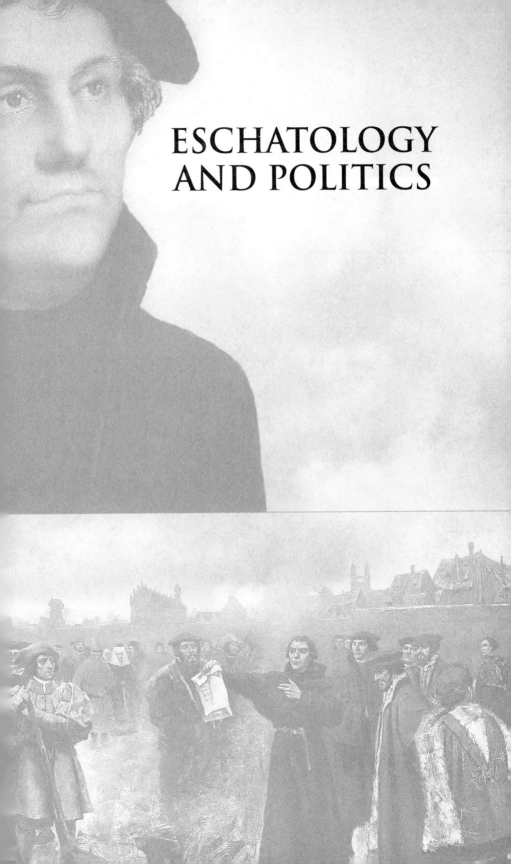

ESCHATOLOGY
AND POLITICS

The "Adventist" Luther: Signs of the Times, Apocalyptic Hope, and the Future Kingdom

Daniel Heinz

In his 1531 sermon on Luke 21, Martin Luther was not content to merely lament the pitiful condition of the world and castigate the ineptitude of those in power.* He opened up to his hearers the comforting perspective of faith in God's new and different world.[1] Christians, according to Luther, bite into the sour apple of life and drink a bitter drink, after which sweetness shall come.[2] Therefore, Christ tells those who belong to Him to stand up and rejoice.[3] Even if the proclamation of the gospel yields nothing among most, the Reformer feels called to speak up so the remnant may understand.[4]

Luther is convicted that "no sermons, calls, warnings, threats, or pleadings"[5] can help the world any longer. It remains a "den of thieves,"[6] and "there is no hope that it will get any better."[7] One should therefore expect nothing from the world, but rather look forward with longing and joy to the day that Christ has promised, and speak, "Come this very hour, if possible, and put an end to this misery."[8] So many have already perished for the sake of the faith, and their fate remains unatoned. The day, therefore, must come when the dead believers and the living followers of Christ are glorified.[9] Nothing "better and more precious"

---

* This chapter was translated from German by Jamie Boucher.

could befall the Christian than the coming of Christ "in power and great glory" in order to receive the believing church "unto Himself."[10]

The Reformer suggests that his opponents choose to place their hope in politics. The emperor, he maintains, will advance upon Germany with his troops in order to "exterminate the Lutherans." This is Luther's adversaries' *venit salvator*—coming of the redeemer. But the emperor is a false redeemer; for in Psalm 146, the believers are warned already not to put their trust in princes: "Put not your trust in princes, nor in the son[s] of man, in whom there is no help" (Psalm 146:3, KJV).[11]

While Luther is convinced that Charles V is a "pious emperor," his advisors have made him into a *Feiland*;[12] that is, someone who has been constantly downsized (or filed down) in order to meet their expectations. But in so doing, they merely celebrate a man, from whom they have no promise. Christians should trust and rejoice in the one who is the true Savior, because He has never failed or lied. He "most solemnly promised" His coming, so that they can expect it "with great confidence."[13]

The signs: Comfort and warning

In order to strengthen His church in this "Adventist" expectation—that is, the literal return of Christ—Christ pointed to certain signs. Just as there are often signs for insignificant things, so there must also be signs for the *Parousia* (the coming Christ), which is the most important event yet to come.[14] These signs have multiple meanings for Luther. They are evident in heaven and on earth and serve to strengthen the believers while proclaiming judgment to unbelievers.[15] For Christians, the signs are promises of the coming liberation; but for unbelievers, they announce the coming judgment. The latter—people with "hard heads and iron hearts"—are blissfully ignorant and have false security, while in the signs Christians already recognize God's wrath.[16] However, these evil signs will not harm the believers, for God sustains His own.[17]

Furthermore, signs announce the time of the return of Christ and comfort Christians so that they joyfully await His return.[18] Luther's appeal to the signs of the end of the world—such as natural disasters, the Turkish threat, or the emergence of the papacy as the antichrist—did not arise from a widespread, apocalyptic-colored panic as was typical for the Middle Ages. Rather, the signs were grounded in such biblical messages as Jesus' speech on the end times (Luke 21) that, for Luther, were clearer and less ambiguous than the statements in Revelation.

The Reformer does not argue whether or not most of the signs have already occurred, but rather leaves it to the judgment of the believers. Personally, however, he is convinced that the signs "have for the most part already occurred."[19] But even if not all of the signs have yet taken place, the increase, prevalence, and frequency of those that have already occurred are an important indication of the imminence of the end.[20] The coming of Christ itself will happen suddenly.[21] Because so many signs have already appeared, hope lies in the fact that the Redeemer "is at the door and that someone will still exist, who will experience it."[22] In exchange for these warnings (sermons, pleas, advice), the believers receive from the world only scornfulness, ungratefulness, hate, envy, and malice, because it holds Christ in contempt.[23] But those who live with such a feeling of security and smugly hold everything in disdain should take God's warning to heart.[24]

Luther maintains that the believers need to have strong faith in God's Word. Without such faith, the signs in nature and human history are cast to the wind. The astronomers—Luther is thinking of the widespread astrology of his day[25]—view the signs as natural and threatening events.[26] They do not have the comforting promise that Christ's redemption draws near. Therefore, only the believing Christian can behold the natural and historical disasters with joyful eyes.[27]

Luther refers to storms, floods, and earthquakes of his day as well as religiopolitical events, such as the disintegration of the Christian faith and the Turkish threat. The Turks and Rome both appear to him, at different stages in his life, to be the biblically prophesied antichrist.[28] And yet, despite this sense of crisis, Luther never tired of constantly announcing to believers that the biblical apocalyptic goes beyond mere horror scenarios. He announces in his sermons that the day of Christ will be a day of sweetness for the believers, who are now in a den of thieves.[29] He tells the believers that sorrowfulness makes life waste away like consumption,[30] while a merry heart holds the head up high.[31] Therefore, a pious Christian joyfully longs for that day of the Lord in daily prayers, for on this earth the believer has no other help or comfort.[32]

Whoever does not long for that day does not understand the Lord's Prayer and therefore cannot pray it.[33] For according to Luther, the request "Thy kingdom come" (Matthew 6:10, KJV) is aimed toward the *Parousia*, through which the world and everything that is contrary to the good Lord must be destroyed and annihilated.[34]

The request for the future kingdom is *the* prayer of the Christian. In this vein, Luther plays on the words of the apostle Paul concerning the resurrection in 1 Corinthians 15:19: "If only for this life we have hope in Christ, we are of all people most to be pitied" (NIV). For whoever does not have this hope can only wish he or she were never born and that there was no God.[35] Human life means mishaps, illness, pestilence, famine, and war—the daily bitter cup that the believers must drink so that they can maintain their longing for another and better life. Without this bitter cup, they would become cold and numb; they would no longer sense their misfortune and overlook how the unrepentant world is drowning in the lust and desire of this life.[36] Therefore, Christ now calls His own to stand up and rejoice, for our redemption means victory over death

206 | HERE WE STAND

and the gift of eternal life. It also means the end of all horrors, entrance to the kingdom, and thus eternal comfort and joy.[37]

In view of this hope, Christians should not regret the passing of this world nor lose themselves in mourning the dead.[38] Rather they should say, "Winter has been long enough. Now I wish a more beautiful summer to come, such a summer that will never end."[39]

Longing and preparation for the kingdom

Luther believed that he had a prophetic mission to the German people.[40] He did not, however, claim to be an inspired visionary like the Old Testament prophets or the New Testament apostles. He did not see himself as a true prophet, for God had not given him the gift of prophecy;[41] and yet he did understand his position to be that of a watchman, preacher, teacher, advisor, and admonisher. "As such," Paul Joachimsen states, "he [Luther] ultimately acquired a status like that of no German before him, nor of any after him."[42] In the light of the anticipated redemption, Luther understood his message to be the final call of warning: "Come, come! Dear people, learn!"[43] Thus, he stood before the people as an admonisher and a comforter—giving them time to prepare to meet the Coming One.

Just like every true disciple of Christ, Luther longed for the soon end of the time period that God has placed between the first and the second coming of Christ at the end of time, referred to as the "last hour" in the New Testament (1 John 2:18, NIV). Because no one—except God Himself—knows when this end will be, it is necessary to live and act as if today were the last day. For the Reformer, this meant having a yearning desire for restoration. For "whoever desires to be a true member of the Lord Christ, poor in this world and despised, will earnestly plead that the time of His judgment and His visitation, together with His kingdom, will come soon and redeem us."[44]

But this also means a call to repentance. Just as this call belonged to the message of the One who came (Mark 1:15), so also does it belong to the preparation for the Coming One: "Repent, Germany, during the time of probation. It is time!"[45] Whoever understands the "signs of the times" to be cries of warning and caution will live on high alert. Those people who listen to the warnings do not anticipate an "ideal" world, but rather are aware of the world's disintegration and decline.

Luther was not deceived by the awakening civilization and culture of his time. He did not doubt the moral decline of the world, with its godless, hedonistic, materialistic mind-set. The whole world is nothing more than the opposite of the Decalogue,[46] for "there is no end to gluttony, wretched avarice, usury, and other sins."[47] The histories of the Jews, the Greeks, and the Romans set examples that judgments do not just appear without a reason. Even Christian cultures can come to an end. These punishments are a microcosm of God's last great act—when He will bring human history to an end forever.

What Luther in his day impressed upon the hearts of people in order to be prepared for the end is still relevant for the Second Advent hope today.

The necessity of God's Word as a compass

When the Reformer produced his Bible translation (1522–1534), he not only accomplished a great literary feat but also created the centerpiece of his Reformation work. Prior to this translation, there were already eighteen German Bible translations,[48] but they were translations of the Latin Vulgate and therefore were translations of a translation. They exerted no formative influence on the spiritual life of the people.

The central role in faith and life that Luther conferred upon the Bible made all the difference. For him, the Bible was the book of life for those on earth who need a reliable compass to point the way through the times to Christ and thus to the present and future redemption: "They are not mere words for reading, but sweet words of real life, that are written for actions and conduct."[49]

Luther understood his Bible translation to be a gift to the people. Shortly before his death, he wrote, "For I received nothing for it, I gave it for nothing, and desire nothing for it."[50] In his work, producing a Bible in the language of the people for all German regions; giving the Bible a central place in questions of faith, of lifestyle, and of hope, he saw the divine *kairos*—the moment of grace—to hold on to and not let go. With this work, he had led the people out of the darkness of spiritual error and superstition: "I think that Germany has never heard so much of God's Word as it has now."[51]

Luther foresaw, with trepidation, the coming ungratefulness and contempt for the Word. He reminded his contemporaries what God had bestowed upon them. Therefore, he urged whoever could reach out and hold on to the Word to do so, because the wisdom, speculations, and viewpoints of "natural men" are dispensable. Only the Bible speaks of real and true life: "First, you should know that the Holy Scripture turns the wisdom of all other books into foolishness, for none of them teach of eternal life as does this book alone."[52]

Since we as human beings of the twenty-first century have largely lost this awareness, we are lacking a final and sure compass. And so we stand here, perplexed by the question of where the world is headed. The "Adventist" Luther shows us the way, in that he makes the Bible the center of faith and life. It contains the wonderful promises of the imminent Second Advent, the fact that the Creator will not abandon His creation, and in the end He will bring us home to Himself.

The necessity of a steadfast faith in God

The assurance of God's faithfulness—demonstrated by the first coming of Jesus Christ—is a great encouragement for the belief that God will also stand true in the future. Luther calls upon us to trust this promise of God. God has thousands of ways to strengthen our faith even during the trials and tribulations of this world. Luther had such a faith experience that should be seen as exemplary for every Christian in the end time.

Luther's faith was put on trial many times. Between 1518 and 1525, the threat of death hung over him like the sword of Damocles. When in 1518, Cardinal Cajetan called him to Augsburg for a hearing, Luther was aware of his desperate condition—death was a real possibility. He felt helpless because he realized that his territorial sovereign, Frederick the Wise, would probably not go to war for him. Nevertheless, Luther maintained an unshakable faith in his God.

When Luther was pressured in 1521 to recant before the emperor at the Diet of Worms, he held fast to his trust in God. This trust gave him the strength, despite his life being at risk, to set his conscience in opposition to centuries of tradition: "For those who do not trust in God, trust in creation—the papists in their works, the heathen in their idols, the miserly in their possessions, others in rulers. The world desires and must have idols."[53] A true Christian, however, puts all faith in God Almighty.

We in our time, a time of atheism, ecumenical apathy, and of culture clash, are challenged to have this confessing faith of the Reformer. Luther called for resistance in his day to the papacy, emperor, Catholic rulers, and Islam. He thus challenges us not to capitulate to the threats of modern time, including the secularization of the Christian hope and the disintegration of the Christian world. In 1530, Luther wrote these words to Philip Melanchthon, who was overwhelmed at the Diet of Augsburg: "From the bottom of my heart, I hate the great anxieties with which you . . . are consumed. That they so much dominate your heart is not the fault of the size of the danger, but rather of the size of our unbelief."[54]

The Advent hope implies Advent joy

Unbelief plummets the Christian into anxiety and despair, but hope makes one certain and happy: that is a way to summarize Martin Luther's end-time faith. A Christian must be a joyful person because joy consists of faith and hope. Faith is about the eternal and true God, and thus it cannot fail. Hope will not disappoint, because it is based on divine promises.

The "panic of nihilism" and the resignation of having no future should not cause us to despair.[55] Few have understood so well as Luther that Christianity is a religion of hope: "I hope in the Lord" is the sum all of Christian doctrine.[56]

The coming of the Messiah was the hope of Israel. The coming of the kingdom of God was the message of hope of the Messiah. The second coming of the Messiah was the hope of the early Christians. Everything in the Christian message points forward to the future, to a new existence in a different world.

This hope for the future kingdom reaches from the time of the apostles ("Maranatha": Come, Lord Jesus [1 Corinthians 16:22, KJV]) through the Reformer ("Come, dear Last Day!") to all who are ready today to hear the Advent call. Without this hope, the gospel shrivels into moral teaching—into a social message and earthly life philosophy.

There is reason to fear today, in the very place where Luther is still highly regarded and his memory celebrated, that this essential aspect of his theology remains ignored. For example, in the publication *Rechtfertigung und Freiheit: 500 Jahre Reformation 2017* (*Justification and Freedom: Celebrating 500 Years of the Reformation in 2017*), by the Lutheran Church in Germany, the *Parousia* of Christ is only mentioned once, and only because the authors of this publication cite the Heidelberg Catechism.[57] What Luther said and wrote about Christian hope and the second coming of Christ remains unnoticed.

Luther, the liberator from spiritual despotism; Luther, the trailblazer of freedom of conscience; Luther, the pioneer of intellectual freedom; Luther, the literary sensation—certainly, some of these ideas and positions did come from him, and they continue to influence the modern world. Yet he himself would not be pleased with this. He did not wish to be a champion for the autonomy of the mind, but rather he saw himself as a champion for the Word of God and the assurance and joy of salvation revealed therein.

Thus, Martin Luther stands before us, even five hundred years later, as the herald of salvation that has come and *is* to come to us in Christ. As such, he knew about the futility of all human plans and future hopes. For him, the future ultimately means the future as redemption!

According to Peter, the creation of "a new heaven and a new earth" (2 Peter 3:13, NIV) does not lie in human hands but alone in the hands of Him who makes "all things new" (Revelation 21:5, NKJV). This was the hope and joy of the first Christians, and this also remains the legacy of the Reformer. He proclaimed, "God has promised the day when He will deliver us from all evil. So let it come even in this hour."[58] Christ's coming is our sure and only hope so that all Christians may joyfully await the future.

---

1. The term *Adventist* is not meant primarily to point to a demonination but rather to an event—the second coming of Christ.

2. Martin Luther, *D. Martin Luthers Werke: Kritische Gesamtausgabe*, vol. 34, bk. 2 (Weimar: Hermann Böhlau, 1908), 472.

3. Ibid., 34:478.

4. Ibid., 34:479.

5. Ibid., 34:466.

6. Ibid., 34:475.

7. Ibid., 34:476.

8. Ibid., 34:466.

9. Ibid., 34:477.

10. Ibid., 34:473.

11. Ibid., 34:467.

12. Ibid., 34:468. This is a play on words. In German, *Heiland* means "redeemer," while *feilen* means "to file or hone."

13. Ibid.

14. Ibid., 34:459.

15. Ibid., 34:460, 461.

16. Ibid., 34:460.

17. Ibid., 34:464.

18. Ibid., 34:461.

19. Ibid.

20. Ibid., 34:463.

21. Ibid., 34:479.

22. Ibid.

23. Ibid., 34:473.

24. Ibid., 34:464.

25. Ibid., 34:482.

26. Ibid., 34:462.

27. Ibid., 34:470.

28. Ibid., 34:463, 478.

29. Ibid., 34:460, 478.

30. Ibid., 34:465.

31. Ibid., 34:469.

32. Ibid., 34:474, 475.

33. Ibid., 34:475.

34. Ibid., 34:474.

35. Ibid., 34:472.

36. Ibid.

37. Ibid., 34:478.

38. Ibid., 34:469, 471, 479, 482.

39. Ibid., 34:481.

40. Martin Luther, *D. Martin Luthers Werke: Kritische Gesamtausgabe*, vol. 30, bk. 3 (Weimar: Hermann Böhlau, 1910), 290.

41. Martin Luther, *D. Martin Luthers Werke: Kritische Gesamtausgabe, Tischreden*, vol. 2 (Weimar: Hermann Böhlau, 1913), no. 1796.

42. Paul Joachimsen, quoted in Heinrich Bornkamm, *Luther im Spiegel der deutschen*

Geistesgeschichte (Heidelberg: Quelle und Meyer, 1955), 320.

43. Martin Luther, *D. Martin Luthers Werke: Kritische Gesamtausgabe, Tischreden*, vol. 6 (Weimar: Hermann Böhlau, 1921), no. 6893.

44. Martin Luther, *D. Martin Luthers Werke: Kritische Gesamtausgabe, Tischreden*, vol. 5 (Weimar: Hermann Böhlau, 1919), no. 5776.

45. Martin Luther, *D. Martin Luthers Werke: Kritische Gesamtausgabe, Tischreden*, vol. 4 (Weimar: Hermann Böhlau, 1916), no. 4096.

46. Ibid., vol. 4, no. 4011.

47. Ibid., vol. 6, no. 6546.

48. Cf. Oscar Paret, *Die Überlieferung der Bibel*, 4th ed. (Stuttgart: Württembergische Bibelanstalt, 1966), 23, 24.

49. Martin Luther, *D. Martin Luthers Werke: Kritische Gesamtausgabe*, vol. 31, bk. 1 (Weimar: Hermann Böhlau, 1913), 67.

50. Quoted in Ernst von Dobschütz, *Die Bibel im Leben der Völker*, 3rd ed. (Witten: Luther-Verlag, 1952), 146.

51. Martin Luther, *D. Martin Luthers Werke: Kritische Gesamtausgabe*, vol. 15 (Weimar: Hermann Böhlau, 1899), 32.

52. Martin Luther, *D. Martin Luthers Werke: Kritische Gesamtausgabe*, vol. 50 (Weimar: Hermann Böhlau, 1914), 659.

53. Martin Luther, *D. Martin Luthers Werke: Kritische Gesamtausgabe, Tischreden*, vol. 3 (Weimar: Hermann Böhlau, 1914), no. 3407.

54. Martin Luther, *D. Martin Luthers Werke: Kritische Gesamtausgabe, Briefwechsel*, vol. 5 (Weimar: Hermann Böhlau, 1934), 399.

55. Emil Brunner, *Eternal Hope*, trans. Harold Knight (Philadelphia, PA: Westminster Press, 1954), 23.

56. Martin Luther, *D. Martin Luthers Werke: Kritische Gesamtausgabe*, vol. 25 (Weimar: Hermann Böhlau, 1902), 119.

57. Evangelische Kirche in Deutschland, *Rechtfertigung und Freiheit: 500 Jahre Reformation 2017* (Gütersloh: Gütersloher Verlagshaus, 2014), 69. See also Evangelische Kirche in Deutschland, *Justification and Freedom: Celebrating 500 Years of the Reformation in 2017*, trans. Stephen Buckwalter, Evangelische Kirche in Deutschland, accessed August 1, 2017, https://www.ekd.de/ekd_de/ds_doc/2014_justification_and_freedom.pdf.

58. Luther, *D. Martin Luthers Werke*, vol. 34, bk. 2, 466.

CHAPTER 19

State Power and Loyalty: Luther and the Adventists

Lisa Clark Diller

Martin Luther's famous "Here I stand" at the Diet of Worms is both the iconic Luther moment and perhaps the last thing he did that we still think about today. And to be fair, for many of his sympathizers or followers, there was also a fear that this would be his last prophetic performance. It was assumed that the emperor's edict against him after his defiance at the diet would result in his death. But in the words of Ellen White, "God gave wisdom to Frederick of Saxony to devise a plan for the Reformer's preservation."[1] It was a prince, a governmental leader, who saved the Reformer's life and made a way for Luther's work in the decades afterward.

> The Reformation took the form it did because of the role of the state—governments and princes *chose* to protect and celebrate the Protestant leaders and movement.

The Reformation took the form it did because of the role of the state—governments and princes *chose* to protect and celebrate the Protestant leaders and movement. Most of the Reformation took place under the auspices of such "magisterial" or state-based movements.[2] However, it was also states that persecuted; it was princes who attempted to coerce believers in the valley of decision to join one side or another in the conflict.

Seventh-day Adventists have often traced their strongest Reformation roots and influence to the Anabaptists; the Anabaptists were pacifist communities recognized primarily because they were attacked on all sides by princes and states—both Protestant and Catholic. Luther himself articulated some of his strongest statements about the role of the magistrate in his conflict with the Anabaptists. So it is not surprising that his views on the power and place of government would be out of keeping with much of what Seventh-day Adventists

> S o how might Adventists position themselves with respect to their views on the role of government within the Reformation heritage?

have claimed or thought about concerning the state. So how might Adventists position themselves with respect to their views on the role of government within the Reformation heritage?

State power in medieval times and beyond

There are significant differences between Luther and modern Adventists, and the primary variation comes from his location in the sixteenth century. In western Europe, this time period is known for laying the foundation for what historians call "state formation." Kings and princes known as the "New Monarchs" in England, France, Italy, Spain, and the German territories were beginning to take on roles and ideals that moved away from feudalism. Luther, however, was very much a medieval man, and his world was the world of Christendom—where the church and state worked together to accomplish God's work. Luther and his peers assumed that all the states they lived in, whether imperial or national, were formed by and for Christians and led by Christian monarchs, who were trying to do God's calling.

But things were changing, for "state-building" coincided with confessionalization in sixteenth-century Christian Europe. Bureaucracy and territorial boundedness went along with the development of the idea of the sovereignty of the prince. Christendom was fragmented into territorial churches that, along with their princely lords, organized norms and ideals into something that looked more national. For instance, in England, the Church of England became the state church; in Scotland, the Calvinist faith; in France and Spain, the monarchs directly ran the Catholic Church without much input from the pope. In Germany, the small size of the states assumed face-to-face relations between citizens and rulers and competition between sovereignties. Some scholars argue that it was actually the very power to protect and govern their *churches* that ended up giving these princes their sovereign authority.[3]

In fact, as the Reformation moved on, the formation of early national state-building happened through expanding bureaucracies, such as the officials controlled and hired by the state to enforce ecclesiastical law. Additionally, the fiscal complexity developed because of the state control of church finances and the sacralization of the ruler's person as the head of the church, in charge of the sacred life of the community, completed the thorough expansion of what we today take for granted as normal state power.[4] Thus, our modern states owe much of their current forms to the process of the Reformation.

The clergy and local administrator or magistrate shared the increasing centralization of the government. Church registers kept track of information, and pastoral relationships and reports helped build state authority and power. They also allowed for uniformity of relationships to the state instead of the disparate groups that had been the norm previously. In the medieval world, merchants, peasants, and knights all had different rules and identities with respect to their government.[5] Sovereign control over the church came before those other two monopolies of state-building—control over taxation and the military—that are usually considered foundations of the modern state. This developing system also included education of civil servants and a more comprehensive thinking about law and order.[6]

Luther's discussion of the state never took the shape of an inclusive political theory. He was a medieval man, and power was not broad or theoretical but deeply personal and immediate.[7] Luther did not want to pronounce on laws or the politics of his day; he saw himself as a theologian.[8] He believed in and promoted the medieval Augustinian characterization of the two kingdoms. There was a temporal one that did God's work in this world; and there was the kingdom of God that was eternal and was the work of the church.

Even when Luther made ad hoc suggestions for reforms for the state, they were religious in nature and in keeping with his spiritual reformation. Changing institutions was not really part of his plan for bad governments; it was changing immoral people. He was mostly worried about spiritual liberty, not temporal freedom; and he did not know he would become the leader of a revolutionary movement.[9] Nevertheless, as Douglas Morgan's chapter in this book argues, Luther's emphasis on freedom was often used, especially by peasants—eventually groups such as those at Münster, who were more "radical" in their reformation commitments—to justify rebellion. The freedom he was most worried about was the freedom to obey God without the constraints of human authority. There was spiritual equality, but this did not have anything to do with the authority of this world.[10]

Luther never thought of the state as an impersonal force but as personal relationships. God set up the government to save people from anarchy. Yet Luther was more positive about the possibilities for earthly powers than Augustine, and Luther viewed the government as a blessing. The state was a coercive power, but that was because of sin. Like Augustine, Luther thought an important difference between spiritual and temporal authority is that the latter could use physical force.[11] Luther believed that secular powers were ordained by God to punish evil, and sometimes that included evil in the church, which is a role that would concern Adventists.[12]

Almost all of Luther's advice regarding the state or governance was a response to current events, and sometimes it appears at variance with itself (as is true with much of Luther's thought!). For instance, in 1520, early in Luther's ministry, he wrote *To the Christian Nobility*: "Since those who exercise secular authority have been baptized with the same baptism, and have the same faith and the same gospel as the rest of us, we must admit that they are priests and bishops and we must regard their office as one which has a proper and useful place in the Christian community."[13]

In 1523, however, following his excommunication and conflict with the emperor, he seems to have backed away from assuming that the entire polity was Christian, partly by focusing on biblical admonitions in Romans 13 and 1 Peter 2. Laws were needed because not everyone was truly Christian, and thus governments could not make assumptions about the faith of the subjects. So there could not be any truly Christian government, consisting only of such laws as Jesus gave about good behavior. Jesus' command to turn the other cheek, Luther argued, was indeed the rule for how Christians should treat each other; but the government could not enforce this because not all citizens were actually Christians.[14] Therefore, just as with Seventh-day Adventists today, policy and ideas about government evolved as changing facts on the ground provoked new realities and responses.

Ideals for government

From a twenty-first-century perspective, it may seem odd that Luther did not advocate for any particular form of government as being better than another. He lived in a "princely" kingdom, effectively under a monarchy, but he seemed to think that God gave all forms of government. He never questioned the validity of the republican forms of government, such as those held by the Swiss states and the imperial free city-states. Furthermore, he did not think that non-Christian rulers were necessarily worse than others; using the example of Alexander the Great, he even argued that sometimes they governed better than believers. At one point, he said that most princes were not good Christians, and they were almost all weak and corrupt. Luther was also comfortable referencing pagan authorities on subjects such as the law and justice. He believed God had given them wisdom.[15] Just like Luther, Adventists today are also comfortable with forms of government that may not have been developed specifically from a biblical perspective. We, too, occasionally quote from or use non-Christian scholars as we form our own notions regarding politics, if those scholars do not contradict our biblical understanding.

Luther's view of government was layered because he lived in a small princely state that was part of a larger empire. Local princes were often in tension with their lord, the emperor. One of the Protestant views on the state that was most innovative (and defiant of the emperor) was the notion that individual or local provinces should be run by their own laws rather than the imperial edict. Luther argued that this had to do with the locales having their own peculiar characteristics. Each territory, he said, had its own laws and customs, and rulers were bound by them. All those variances could still be seen as valid under the law of nature.[16]

This is certainly a viewpoint with which modern Adventists are comfortable. Although located in a post-Enlightenment world, we have, for the most part, articulated goals for government that are in keeping with representative, liberal republics and democracies, not monarchies or empires.[17] The notion that there may be variability in our human form of government and that cultural changes might result in new policies or structures is one of Luther's pioneering ideas with which we usually find ourselves in agreement.

Luther's embrace of freedom in spiritual things occasionally meant that he reminded people that legalism in politics could also be a bad thing. Luther was no fundamentalist about written constitutions. Instead, he thought princes should rule justly and not simply by the law.

> A good and just decision . . . must come from a free mind, as though there were no books. . . .
> . . . Therefore, we should keep written laws subject to reason, from which they originally welled forth as from the spring of justice. We should not make the spring dependent on its rivulets, or make reason a captive of letters.[18]

Justice was more important than the details of particular legal systems, and such laws could and should change as reason and justice deemed necessary. Seventh-day Adventists have also affirmed the continual development of humane laws and the evolution of legal justice.[19]

In economics, Luther was an agrarian traditionalist. He pointed out that God had not wanted the Israelites to be traders, but farmers, and that too much wealth came from debt and international trade. He thought the state should intervene to prevent the power of bankers and the wealthy. This is probably a notion that would not sit as well with twenty-first-century capitalists, but it was not at all unusual for a late-medieval thinker. The temporal sword, he argued, should be used to prevent exploitation, promote the tilling of the ground, and avoid poverty of the people. Such laws should be "rigidly enforced."[20] The purpose of government was to protect the poor and provide education and support of the good morals and teachings of the church. This was a state with more power than the church, but it did not do things too differently than it had in medieval times.[21] What had changed with Luther and the Reformation was the very reduced power of the church.

Seventh-day Adventists live in a wide range of polities—from states that exploit their people to ones that provide socialist welfare systems to others that see themselves as relying primarily on the free market to supply the needs of their citizens. Nevertheless, they have consistently called on governments to do the sorts of things Luther also assumed good states would engage in. According to the Seventh-day Adventist Church's Department of Public Affairs and Religious Liberty: "The state must also endeavor to build communities with public order, public health, a clean environment, and an atmosphere that does not unduly inhibit its citizens' ability to raise families and freely explore the facets of their humanity."[22]

> Seventh-day Adventists live in a wide range of polities— from states that exploit their people to ones that provide socialist welfare systems to others that see themselves as relying primarily on the free market to supply the needs of their citizens.

Serving or resisting the government

Luther believed that Christians could and should serve in government when there was a need—even if their jobs required them to do something that was normally prohibited to Christians: "Therefore, if you see that there is a lack of hangmen, constables, judges, lords, or princes, and you find that you are qualified, you should offer your services and seek the position, that the essential governmental authority may not be despised and become enfeebled or perish. The world cannot and dare not dispense with it."[23] Christians were not to use the sword for themselves but for others.[24] And the idea here was that there was a separation between the office, which was part of the earthly kingdom in this world, and the person of the Christian himself. God ordained that secular rulers would ensure righteous behavior in this life—and that power in this world has nothing to do with eternal life.[25]

Seventh-day Adventists and Luther diverge from each other the most regarding how much obedience should be owed to governments. While he wanted liberty of conscience, Luther demanded much more submission to political authority than many modern Adventists are comfortable with. Even under Catholic rulers, rebellion was not countenanced. Under tyrants, Luther said to rely on prayer when citizens wanted change, unless the laws of the land allowed for resistance in specific contexts.[26]

When he finally discussed the possibility of legitimate resistance to magistrates, he spoke to Protestant princes or "lower magistrates" who were opposing the Catholic emperor. He and other Protestant thinkers seemed to have developed a notion that there could be resistance to evil rulers, *but only the lower magistrates could do this*—people who were in official capacities already, not the average citizen who felt oppressed. This was a very specific form of resistance and prevented ordinary people from being able to legitimize any rebellion.[27]

Luther's views were pragmatic and were formed in the context of state polities in which most people were Christian, including the monarchs. He did not assume that either the church or the Christian community at large consisted mainly of pure people. He accepted the existence of state churches. This was a continuation of the two-kingdoms theory: the church was to preach the gospel and oversee the sacraments, and the state was to punish evil. Over time, however, Luther appeared to move from a position that only bishops could punish heresy. He advocated that sins such as blasphemy and heresy were crimes against natural law (as part of the moral code of the Ten Commandments) and as such should be suppressed by the magistrate.[28]

The Anabaptists around him, however, were more concerned with purity. They did not want to cooperate with any behavior that caused them to sin. They were more concerned with creating a pure community that was separate from the world. They refused to countenance or support the policies of the state with which they disagreed. They criticized state interference in the church community and for this (and other refusals to cooperate with their governments) they were persecuted. It was against Anabaptists that much of Luther's concern about rebellion was directed, and he comes across as especially harsh to modern ears.[29]

Adventists have traditionally taken a quieter approach to rebellion or resistance to the state; one that would have been appreciated by Luther. His first concern was the spread of the gospel, and he did not think much of political practices unless they impinged on the freedom to evangelize and preach. Adventists, too, have committed first of all to the preaching of the three angels' messages and only tend to become involved in opposition to state policies when they see injustice as preventing the spread of the gospel. Yet, like Luther, Adventists have never been entirely quiet and have participated in actions rebuking state power when they believed that their consciences called them to do so, in both pacifist and more political ways.[30]

Seventh-day Adventists live in societies where the theory of pluralism and the possibility for secular government mean that we are able to imagine worlds where Christians can flourish under completely atheist or non-Christian political leaders. We no longer have primarily an Augustinian two-kingdoms model for how society works. We are much more suspicious of state power. We consider freedoms beyond the merely religious as part of what we hope for in government.

And yet, like Luther, we know that God can work in spite of what is happening in politics—even though there is a sort of "veiling" of how He is working in the state realm. This world is fleeting and fragile, and it is unlikely that the political system reflects God's will. It is not possible to use reason, Luther said, to determine if God is here or there in the political system. Reason is primarily the worry of the powers of this world, and those of us who live by faith have knowledge of God's activity through the Word.[31]

We are even more skeptical of the role of states to establish moral communities, and our prophetic model places the responsibility for persecution on governments. We also have a stronger mandate to care for the body and the soul and so our attempt to live out Jesus' model means that we are often involved in the welfare and justice work that our civil society allows us to have (and Luther's did not) in ways he could not have imagined. Our political systems often allow for participation and influence that were not possible for Luther. And while we do not expect our government to turn the other cheek, as the beloved community, we both model this among ourselves and work to create a society in which forgiveness and grace are more possible because of our presence.

1. Ellen White, *The Great Controversy* (Mountain View, CA: Pacific Press® Pub. Assn., 1950), 168.

2. David Whitford, "Religious Violence and Martyrdom" (2016), 2. This article was given to the author in an unpublished manuscript but is available from the author or David Whitford. I am grateful to Dr. Whitford for conversations on Luther's views of state power and violence. I have also benefited from conversations and resources at the National Endowment for the Humanities Summer Institute on Teaching the Reformation After Five Hundred Years (2016) and the H. Henry Meeter Center at Calvin College. Nevertheless, all opinions, conclusions, and Heinz Schilling, "The Reformation and the Rise of the Early Modern State," in *Luther and the Modern State in Germany*, ed. James D. Tracy, vol. 7, Sixteenth Century Essays and Schilling, "The Reformation and the Rise of the Early Modern State," 25, 26. This can easily be seen as laying the foundation for "civil religion," with the rituals and materials of the state replacing the church as the focus for total loyalty and sacredness.

3. Ibid., 28.

4. Ibid., 29, 30.

5. W. D. J. Cargill Thompson, *The Political Thought of Martin Luther* (Totowa, NJ: Barnes and Noble Books, 1984), 62.

6. Robert N. Crossley, *Luther and the Peasants' War* (New York: Exposition Press, 1974), 88.

7. Thompson, *The Political Thought of Martin Luther*, 138, 139, 69.

8. David Whitford, *Tyranny and Resistance: The Magdeburg Confession and the Lutheran Tradition* (St. Louis, MO: Concordia, 2001), 31–34.

9. Crossley, *Luther and the Peasants' War*, 94, 95; Thompson, *The Political Thought of Martin Luther*, 62.

10. Crossley, *Luther and the Peasants' War*, 83. Adventists might agree that the state should make sure such crimes as stealing, rape, or other violations of the law should be enforced even when they are committed by church entities or the organization as a whole. But they tend to be concerned when theological ideas (heresy, blasphemy, etc.) are called crimes and are prosecuted by the state. In fact, our Public Affairs and Religious Liberty Department looks out for precisely these issues.

11. Martin Luther, *To the Christian Nobility of the German Nation Concerning the Reform of the Christian Estate*, in *Luther: Selected Political Writings*, ed. J. M. Porter (Philadelphia, PA: Fortress Press, 1971), 41.

12. Martin Luther, *Temporal Authority: To What Extent It Should Be Obeyed* (1523), in *Luther: Selected Political Writings*, ed. J. M. Porter (Philadelphia, PA: Fortress Press, 1971), 55, 56.

13. Thompson, *The Political Thought of Martin Luther*, 70, 71.

14. Crossley, *Luther and the Peasants' War*, 88; Thompson, *The Political Thought of Martin Luther*, 70.

15. Council of Interchurch/Interfaith Faith Relations of the General Conference of the Seventh-day Adventist Church, "Church-State Relations," Seventh-day Adventist Church, March 1, 2002, accessed August 1, 2017, https://www.adventist.org/en/information/official-statements /documents/article/go/-/church-state-relations/.

16. Luther, *Temporal Authority*, 68, 69.

17. Seventh-day Adventist Church, "Church-State Relations."

18. Crossley, *Luther and the Peasants' War*, 83, 88, 90.

19. Ibid., 94, 95.

20. Seventh-day Adventist Church, "Church-State Relations."

21. Luther, *Temporal Authority*, 58.

22. Ibid., 59.

23. Martin Luther, *Whether Soldiers, Too, Can be Saved* (1526), in *Luther: Selected Political Writings*, ed. J. M. Porter (Philadelphia, PA: Fortress Press, 1971), 105.

24. Thompson, *The Political Thought of Martin Luther*, 62, 68, 69.

25. Whitford, *Tyranny and Resistance*, 83.

26. Luther, *Temporal Authority*, 63; Thompson, *The Political Thought of Martin Luther*, 158, 159.

27. Whitford, *Tyranny and Resistance*, 56.

28. The documents assembled in *The Peacemaking Remnant*, ed. Douglas Morgan (Silver Spring, MD: Adventist Peace Fellowship, 2005) highlight specific moments in our history when this has been true: Joseph Bates, "A War for Slavery" (1846), 93, 94; George Amadon, "Why Seventh-day Adventists Cannot Engage in War" (1865), 95, 96; Ellen G. White, "The Kingdom of Christ" (1896), 98–101; General Conference Executive Committee, "A Seventh-day Adventist Call for Peace" (2002), 109–115.

29. Whitford, *Tyranny and Resistance*, 35.

CHAPTER 20

Martin Luther, Antichrist, and Seventh-day Adventists

Dennis Pettibone

I n the ecumenical afterglow of Vatican II, Martin Luther's identification of the papacy as the antichrist of Bible prophecy is often seen as narrow-minded and bigoted.* It is no longer socially acceptable to describe the papacy as the fulfillment of a collection of prophecies regarding a powerful spiritual tyranny.

Since Protestantism owes its very existence to Luther's conviction that the papacy was the antichrist,[1] it might be instructive to inquire why Luther held this view and under what circumstances he reached this conclusion. We will see that he came to this view slowly and reluctantly, driven by historical circumstances and theological reflection.

> I n the ecumenical afterglow of Vatican II, Martin Luther's identification of the papacy as the antichrist of Bible prophecy is often seen as narrow-minded and bigoted.

Luther was probably unaware of the previous attacks on the papacy made by John Hus, John Wycliffe, and others[2] when, in 1517, he drafted his Ninety-Five

---

* Much of this chapter has been condensed and adapted from the author's article, "Martin Luther's Views on the Antichrist," *Journal of the Adventist Theological Society* 18, no. 1 (Spring 2007): 81–100.

Theses.[3] Moreover, his target at that time was not the papacy; it was the greedy Dominican monk Johann Tetzel, who was distorting Catholic doctrine by exaggerating the benefits of indulgences.[4] Sylvester Prierias, the papal court's chief theologian, transformed the debate from a question of policy to one of authority.[5] He wrote, "He who does not accept the doctrine of the Church of Rome and pontiff of Rome as an infallible rule of faith, from which the Holy Scriptures, too, draw their strength, is a heretic," and "Whoever says that the Church of Rome may not do what it is actually doing in the matter of indulgences is a heretic."[6] Thomas Cardinal Cajetan demanded that Luther recant. Luther asked for scriptural reasons to do so, but none were given him.[7]

After reading Prierias's assertions of papal infallibility and Cajetan's reliance upon tradition, Luther considered the possibility that these men might be serving the antichrist. He shared this suspicion privately with several like-minded believers.[8]

In July 1519, Luther took the position that both popes and church councils could err.[9] Now, for Luther, "everything stood under the judgment of scripture."[10] He soon used Scripture to pass judgment on the pope.

Two things that Luther read the following year, however, weakened his hesitation about calling the pope antichrist: (1) Lorenzo Valla's demonstration that the Donation of Constantine—the basis for Rome's "claim to supremacy over the Western world"[11]—was a forgery,[12] and (2) Prierias's second treatise against Luther's teachings. Repeating his claim that the pope had more authority than either Scriptures or church councils, Prierias quoted a passage of canon law that horrified Luther: the pope could not be deposed from office[13] even if he "were so scandalously bad that he led multitudes of souls to the devil."[14] Shocked at this extreme statement from Rome's chief theologian, Luther wrote to a friend, "I think . . . that everyone in Rome has gone crazy."[15]

1520 publications

Luther's treatise *To the Christian Nobility of the German Nation Concerning the Reform of the Christian Estate* (June 13, 1520)[16] repeatedly linked the papacy and the antichrist. Referring to Prierias's appalling statement, he wrote,

> It must . . . have been the very prince of devils who said what is written in canon law: "If the pope were so scandalously bad as to lead souls in crowds to the devil, yet he could not be deposed." . . .
>
> . . . It is to be feared that this is a game of Antichrist or a sign that he is close at hand.[17]

Luther also attacked as "works of the . . . Antichrist" papal claims to have power over earthly authorities and even angels. Luther bluntly said, "No vicar's rule can go beyond his lord's."[18]

In August 1520, Luther learned that Leo was sending a bull that threatened him with excommunication. With this bull, Richard Marius observes, "All ambiguity about the Antichrist evaporated from his [Luther's] mind."[19] These views culminated in *The Babylonian Captivity of the Church*, which mentions several reasons for calling the papacy antichrist: the claim that the pope had the power to make laws; withholding the Communion cup from the laity;[20] and the annulment of legitimate marriages.[21]

Luther's response to the bull

The threatening bull, *Exsurge Domine*, denounced forty-one of Luther's published statements. It condemned anyone holding or defending these positions and warned Luther that he must return "to the bosom of the church" within sixty days.[22] After its arrival, Luther burned the bull, along with books of canon law.[23]

Luther replied to *Exsurge Domine*'s charges in his *Defense and Explanation of All the Articles*, repeatedly depicting the pope as antichrist.[24] Arguing that Christ was the rock of Matthew 16:18, Luther wrote that interpreting this text to suggest "papal authority" was "a lying device," perverting God's Word.[25] He called the pope antichrist for giving people false assurance through indulgences, denying that belief was required for forgiveness of sins, spreading "errors throughout the world" in exchange for monetary wealth, and imposing on people the penitential system.[26]

Luther also responded that papists had burned the "good Christians" John Hus and Jerome of Prague, as well as the "godly man of Florence, . . . Girolamo Savonarola," thus "fulfilling the prophecy concerning the Antichrist that he will cast Christians into the oven."[27]

To Worms and Wartburg (1521)

Luther promised that the Word would crush the antichrist "without violence."[28] Yet he fully expected that he would lose his life before this happened because, as he wrote to Georg Spalatin, "Antichrist holds the kingdoms and this world captive."[29] Nevertheless, at Worms, he courageously refused to retract anything he had written unless "convinced by the testimony of the Scriptures or by clear reason."[30] Consequently, he was declared an outlaw. The fact that he survived despite the imperial ban was due to the intervention of Frederick of Saxony.[31]

The chief reason the mature Luther described the pope as antichrist was because, in Luther's opinion, he had usurped God's place as Lawmaker, adding his own rules to those in the Bible, burdening consciences with human traditions, infringing on Christian freedom, sitting in judgment on God's Word, nullifying the texts assuring of forgiveness of sins, and giving people a distorted picture of God.

The chief reason the mature Luther described the pope as antichrist was because, in Luther's opinion, he had usurped God's place as Lawmaker, adding his own rules to those in the Bible, burdening consciences with human traditions, infringing on Christian freedom,[32] sitting in judgment on God's Word, nullifying the texts assuring of forgiveness of sins, and giving people a distorted picture of God.[33] The pope also supplanted God's place by teaching that the Scriptures derived their authority from the church rather than vice versa[34] and by claiming authority not only over the church but also over the whole world.[35] According to Luther, persecuting people for following God's Word was another way the pope was assuming God's authority. "The false church is always the persecutor of the true church," he wrote.[36]

Central to Luther's understanding of the pope as the antichrist seizing God's place was 2 Thessalonians 2:3, 4.[37] Noting that the villain in 2 Thessalonians 2 sits in God's temple and exalts himself above God, Luther said, "The Antichrist took his seat in the church, yet not to govern it with divine laws"[38] but "with human commandments."[39]

Interpreting Daniel 7, Luther wrote that the little horn arising out of the Roman Empire after its division[40] was the papal antichrist.[41] He believed that Daniel 8, 11, and 12 contained blended prophecies applying to both Antiochus IV and the antichrist.[42]

Luther also found predictions of the antichrist in the book of Revelation, especially chapters 13 and 17. In Revelation 13, it was the lamblike beast, appearing "to be Christian," yet preaching the doctrines of "the dragon from hell."[43] Usurping Christ's role as High Priest, Luther said, the pope had set up his own clergy, claiming that he was "imprinting on their souls an indelible character," when in actuality he was imprinting them with "the mark of the beast."[44]

Using the symbolism in Revelation 14, 17, and 18, Luther frequently referred to Rome as Babylon and the "scarlet whore of Babylon." He "praised and thanked" the Lord for rescuing him from "the scarlet whore."[45]

Negating Christ's sacrifice

The Roman antichrist, according to Luther, in effect negated Christ's sacrifice and mediation.[46] The doctrine of merit, he said, nullified God's grace and made "Christ die to no purpose."[47] Luther said that the papacy also negated Christ's sacrifice by proclaiming the Mass to be "a sacrifice" for obtaining "forgiveness of sins," as if Christ's "sacrifice . . . were of no value."[48]

Luther insisted that Christ is still our only Mediator. Jesus had not abdicated His High Priestly office, nor had He transferred it to the pope.[49]

Eschatology

Luther suggested that the time of judgment predicted in Daniel 7:8, 9 was taking place during his lifetime. He found comfort in the prophecies that the last days would "be shortened for the sake of the godly" and "that the church" would "be preserved and Antichrist . . . [would] not encompass everything with error and falsehood."[50]

He noted that, in the second angel's message of Revelation 14, "the gospel" was followed by a voice predicting that Babylon, "the spiritual papacy," would be destroyed. At that time, "those who cling to the papacy against the gospel shall be cast . . . into the wine press of God's wrath."[51]

Luther's final year

During the final year of his life,[52] Luther described the pope not only as antichrist but also as the devil's vicar.[53] In his "last and most bitter attack on the pope,"[54] *Against the Roman Papacy, an Institution of the Devil,* Luther referred to the pope as "the most hellish father" three times.[55] He denounced him as a teacher of lies, blasphemies, and idolatries, an inciter to all kinds of bloodshed,[56] and "a brothel-keeper over all brothel-keepers and all vermin"—and even "a true werewolf."[57]

Were such attacks un-Christian? Luther did not think so. He said, "We are incited to anger against him not by personal ambition but by righteous jealousy and fervor of conscience to vindicate and protect the glory of God."[58] Paul's attacks on "the false apostles" were not slander: he was "judging them by his apostolic authority." Likewise, when Luther called the pope antichrist, he said he was "judging . . . by divine authority" on the basis of Galatians 1:8.[59]

> During the final year of his life, Luther described the pope not only as antichrist but also as the devil's vicar.

Although Luther was antipapal, he was not anti-Catholic. As Jaroslav Pelikan puts it, "Although the pope was the Antichrist 'seated in the temple of God,' the church in which he was seated was still the temple of God."[60]

Seventh-day Adventists

By the time of William Miller (1782–1849), Luther's concept of the papacy as the antichrist was widely shared throughout Protestantism. Like Luther, Miller identified the little horn arising out of the Roman Empire as the papal antichrist.[61] Key leaders in the Millerite movement agreed that this little horn, Babylon, and the man of sin were all symbols of the antichrist—the papacy.[62]

In July 1843, one Millerite, Charles Fitch, broadened the definition of Babylon to include not just the papacy, but also any Protestant churches that rejected the impending pre-millennial advent of Jesus Christ. He urged true Christians to "*come out of Babylon.*"[63] As more and more Millerites were expelled from their churches because of their Advent beliefs, a chorus of Adventist preachers joined Fitch in calling for God's people to come out of the newly identified Protestant Babylon.[64]

Other Adventist theologians refined this theological trajectory. Joseph Bates brought a new dimension to the identification of the little horn as the papal antichrist: applying the phrase "he shall think to change times and laws" (see Daniel 7:25) to Rome's role in the change of the Sabbath.[65] Like Fitch, Bates gave the symbol of Babylon a broader interpretation than the traditional Protestant view. He saw it as "the professed Christian churches, with a form of godliness."[66] James White, in line with Luther, argued that the papal little horn had trodden the sanctuary underfoot (Daniel 8:13) by assuming power that "belongs alone to Christ."[67]

Ellen G. White[68] agreed with Luther and Miller that the little horn of Daniel 7 was the papacy,[69] called by Paul "the man of sin."[70] Like Fitch and Bates, she considered that Babylon included the papacy, but it was much more than the papacy, using such expressions as "the fallen denominational churches"[71] and "the world-loving churches of the last days."[72] She said, "Babylon has been fostering poisonous doctrines, . . . such as the natural immortality of the soul, the eternal torment of the wicked, the denial of the preexistence of Christ prior to His birth in Bethlehem, and advocating and exalting the first day of the week above God's holy, sanctified day."[73]

Ellen White, in the same way as Luther, was antipapal but not anti-Catholic. She opposed Protestant apostasy but not the *people* who belonged to the other Protestant churches. She declared, "The great body of Christ's true followers are still to be found in [Babylon]."[74] Similar to Luther,[75] Ellen White offered multiple interpretations for the word *antichrist*. She stated, "The pope . . . is, in reality, the viceregent of Satan—he is antichrist."[76] She did not stop there but defined *antichrist* as "all who exalt themselves against the will and work of God."[77] She even declared, "Whoever presumes to judge the motives of others is again usurping the prerogative of the Son of God. These would-be judges and critics are placing themselves on the side of antichrist."[78] Ellen White also used the term to describe Satan himself impersonating Christ and performing miracles.[79] "Antichrist will appear as the true Christ. . . . Men will be deceived and will exalt him [Satan] to the place of God, and deify him."[80]

Later mainstream Seventh-day Adventist expositors tended to follow in the footsteps of the early denominational pioneers with regard to interpreting the various antichrist symbols. They echoed Ellen White's expanded definition of Babylon.[81] Some spoke specifically of more than one antichrist,[82] while others focused their attention on "papal power" when discussing the antichrist.[83] Nevertheless, there does seem to be general agreement that the "man of sin" described in 2 Thessalonians 2:3, 4[84] is equated with the little horn of Daniel 7 to refer to the papacy.[85]

Conclusion

Luther's position on the antichrist is no longer politically correct. It is out of sync with the groupthink of the twenty-first century. As Heiko Oberman says, "Luther's way of speaking about the Antichrist has become alien to us."[86] Yet the question for us should not be, is this position embarrassing, politically correct, or socially acceptable? Rather, it should instead be, is it biblically correct? This view was *not* politically correct in Luther's day—it was very incorrect politically. In the same way, just as it was in Luther's time, this opinion could be potentially fatal for the person who adheres to such a view, just as it was for John Hus.

1. Phillip Cary, *Luther: Gospel, Law, and Reformation*, The Great Courses (Chantilly, VA: Teaching Company, 2004), 1:155.

2. This idea also circulated among the Waldensians, the Albigensians, and the Fraticelli, who were a group of Franciscans with more regard for the rule of St. Francis than for papal authority. LeRoy Edwin Froom, *The Prophetic Faith of Our Fathers: The Historical Development of Prophetic Interpretation*, vol. 1 (Washington, DC: Review and Herald® Pub. Assn., 1950), 884; Joseph R. Strayer, *The Albigensian Crusades* (Ann Arbor, MI: University of Michigan Press, 1992), 22; Roland Bainton, *Christianity* (Boston: Houghton Mifflin, 2000), 212.

3. If he had been, he would have been unsympathetic. At the time, he regarded John Hus as a heretic. Martin Luther, *Luther's Works*, vol. 26, *Lectures on Galatians, 1535, Chapters 1–4*, ed. Walter A. Hansen (St. Louis, MO: Concordia, 1963), 70; Martin Luther, *Luther's Works*, vol. 28, *Commentaries on 1 Corinthians 7, 1 Corinthians 15, Lectures on 1 Timothy*, ed. Jaroslav Pelikan (St. Louis, MO: Concordia, 1973), 242.

4. Martin Marty, *Martin Luther* (New York: Viking, 2004), 29–31; Jaroslav Pelikan, *Reformation of Church and Dogma (1300–1700)*, vol. 4 of *The Christian Tradition: A History of the Development of Doctrine* (Chicago: University of Chicago Press, 1984), 136; Cary, *Luther*, 1:135; Richard Marius, *Martin Luther: The Christian Between God and Death* (Cambridge, MA: Belknap Press, 1999), 135; Patrick Collinson, *The Reformation: A History* (New York: Modern Library, 2004), 54.

5. Marty, *Martin Luther*, 33; Cary, *Luther*, 139; Martin Luther, *Works of Martin Luther With Introductions and Notes* (Philadelphia, PA: A. J. Holman, 1915), 2:73.

6. Heiko A. Oberman, *Luther: Man Between God and the Devil*, trans. Eileen Walliser-Schwarzbart (New York: Doubleday Image Books, 1992), 193, 194.

7. Rome had ordered that Luther be arrested if he refused to recant, but Luther—mindful of the fate of John Huss—avoided arrest by stealing away from Augsburg on the night of October 16, 1518. Oberman, *Luther*, 195–197; Marius, *Martin Luther*, 159–164, 209; Robert Herndon Fife, *The Revolt of Martin Luther* (New York: Columbia University Press, 1957), 283, 308, 309.

8. George Waddington, *A History of the Reformation on the Continent* (London: Duncan and Malcolm, 1841), 1:201; Will Durant, *The Reformation: A History of European Civilization From*

Wyclif to Calvin: 1300–1564, vol. 6 of *The Story of Civilization* (New York: Simon and Schuster, 1957), 349; Marius, *Martin Luther*, 188; Martin Luther, *Luther's Works*, vol. 8, *Lectures on Genesis, Chapters 45–50*, ed. Jaroslav Pelikan (St. Louis: Concordia; 1966), 114.

9. Collinson, *The Reformation*, 30.

10. Marius, *Martin Luther*, 179.

11. Oberman, *Luther*, 42.

12. This seems to have inspired a letter to Georg Spalatin (February 24, 1520): "I . . . can hardly doubt any more, that the Pope is really the Antichrist . . . because everything so exactly corresponds to the way of his life, action, words, and commandments." LeRoy Edwin Froom, *The Prophetic Faith of Our Fathers: The Historical Development of Prophetic Interpretation*, vol. 2 (Washington, DC: Review and Herald® Pub. Assn., 1948), 255.

13. Oberman, *Luther*, 42; Marius, *Martin Luther*, 237; Luther, *Works of Martin Luther*, 2:72.

14. Cary, *Luther*, 1:140.

15. Oberman, *Luther*, 43.

16. Marius, *Martin Luther*, 237.

17. Luther, *Works of Martin Luther*, 2:72, 73.

18. Ibid., 2:81. He pointed out that Jesus had said, "My kingdom is not of this world." Ibid., 2:81; see also ibid., 2:108, 109. Rome's corruption and immorality—"buying, selling, bartering, trading, trafficking, lying, deceiving, robbing, stealing, luxury, harlotry, knavery and every sort of contempt of God"—and the pope's accepting money for annulling oaths were suggested as two other indications of antichristlike behavior. Ibid., 2:95, 140.

19. Marius, *Martin Luther*, 248.

20. Luther, *Works of Martin Luther*, 2:236, 247.

21. Ibid., 2:268. Luther wrote three other tracts that year that linked the papacy and antichrist: *Treatise on Christian Liberty*; *Sermon on Usury*; and *Treatise on the New Testament*. Ibid., 1:320–322, 2:346; 4:450.

22. Meanwhile, it ordered that he keep silent and that his books be burned. Martin Luther, *Luther's Works*, vol. 32, *Career of the Reformer 1*, ed. Jaroslav Pelikan (St. Louis, MO: Concordia, 1957), ix, x.

23. Marty, *Martin Luther*, 57; Froom, *The Prophetic Faith of Our Fathers*, 1:21.

24. Luther, *Works of Martin Luther*, 3:51, 84, 85.

25. Luther, *Luther's Works*, 32:42.

26. Ibid., 32:36, 44–47; Luther, *Works of Martin Luther*, 3:53, 57.

27. Luther, *Luther's Works*, 32:82, 87, 88. One of the statements Leo had condemned in *Exsurge Domine* was, "The burning of heretics is contrary to the will of the Holy Spirit." In his *Defense and Explanation of All the Articles*, Luther also condemned "the error about the free will" as "a peculiar teaching of Antichrist" and denounced the creation of mendicant orders as "one of Antichrist's tricks" for increasing his own power. Luther, *Works of Martin Luther*, 3:111, 113.

28. Luther, *Luther's Works*, 32:xii. See also Philip Schaff, *History of the Christian Church*, vol. 7, 3rd rev. ed. (Grand Rapids, MI: Eerdmans, 1986), 201, 202.

29. Luther, *Luther's Works*, 32:xiv, xv.

30. Ibid., 32:112.

31. Bainton, *Christianity*, 250; Schaff, *History of the Christian Church*, 7:332.

32. Martin Luther, *Luther's Works*, vol. 13, *Selected Psalms 2*, ed. Jaroslav Pelikan (St. Louis, MO: Concordia, 1956), 281; Martin Luther, *Luther's Works*, vol. 41, *Church and Ministry 3*, ed. Eric W. Gritsch (St. Louis, MO: Concordia, 1966), 364; Luther, *Luther's Works*, 26:385; Martin Luther, *Luther's Works*, vol. 52, *Sermons 2*, ed. Hans J. Hildebrand (St. Louis, MO: Concordia, 1973), 137; Martin Luther, *Luther's Works*, vol. 4, *Lectures on Genesis, Chapters 21–25*, ed. Jaroslav Pelikan (St. Louis, MO: Concordia, 1964), 141; Luther, *Luther's Works*, 8:282, 185; Martin Luther, *Luther's Works*, vol. 3, *Lectures on Genesis, Chapters 15–20*, ed. Jaroslav Pelikan (St. Louis, MO: Concordia, 1961), 349; Martin Luther, *Luther's Works*, vol. 30, *The Catholic Epistles*, ed. Jaroslav Pelikan (St. Louis, MO: Concordia, 1967), 107; Martin Luther, *Luther's Works*, vol. 51, *Sermons 1*, ed. and trans. John W. Doberstein (St. Louis, MO: Concordia, 1966), 364; Luther, *Luther's Works*, 28:23, 24.

33. Luther, *Luther's Works*, 52:81; 8:312; Martin Luther, *Luther's Works*, vol. 24, *Sermons on the Gospel of St. John, Chapters 14–16*, ed. Jaroslav Pelikan (St. Louis, MO: Concordia, 1961), 355; 52:21; Martin Luther, *Luther's Works*, vol. 27, *Lectures on Galatians, 1535, Chapters 5–6*, ed. Jaroslav Pelikan (St. Louis, MO: Concordia, 1964), 89; Luther, *Works of Martin Luther*, 4:77; 5:116.

34. Martin Luther, *Luther's Works*, vol. 2, *Lectures on Genesis, Chapters 6–14*, ed. Jaroslav Pelikan (St. Louis, MO: Concordia, 1960), 101; Pelikan, *Reformation of Church and Dogma*, 175.

35. Martin Luther, *Luther's Works*, vol. 22, *Sermons on the Gospel of St. John, Chapters 1–4*, ed. Jaroslav Pelikan (St. Louis, MO: Concordia, 1957), 82; 27:342; Martin Luther, *Luther's Works*, vol. 29, *Lectures on Titus, Philemon, and the Hebrews*, ed. Hilton C. Oswald (St. Louis, MO: Concordia, 1968), 42; 13:281, 282; Martin Luther, *Luther's Works*, vol. 14, *Selected Psalms 3*, ed. Daniel E. Poellot (St. Louis, MO: Concordia, 1956), 12, 13; Martin Luther, *A Commentary on St. Paul's Epistle to the Galatians*, ed. Erasmus Middleton (London: B. Blake 1833), quoted in Philip S. Watson, *Let God Be God: An Interpretation of the Theology of Martin Luther* (London: Epworth Press, 1947), 96. Luther cited both Scripture and history to show that neither Peter himself nor the bishop of Rome at the time of the Council of Nicaea ruled over the whole church. Luther, *Luther's Works*, 41:299, 357.

36. Luther, *Luther's Works*, 2:214. See also ibid., 2:34, 101, 316; 22:61; 24:308; Luther, *Works of Martin Luther*, 5:26.

37. Phrases he borrowed from this passage to describe the pope include "man of sin," "the lawless one" (two different translations of the same words), and "son of perdition." Luther, *Works of Martin Luther*, 2:102; Luther, *Luther's Works*, 28:357; Martin Luther, *Luther's Works*, vol. 31, *Career of the Reformer 1*, ed. Jaroslav Pelikan (St. Louis, MO: Concordia, 1957), 391, 392.

38. Luther, *Luther's Works*, 8:283. Cf. ibid., 31:393; 41:209; Martin Luther, *Luther's Works*, vol. 46, *The Christian in Society 3*, ed. Robert Schultz (St. Louis, MO: Concordia, 1967), 408.

39. Martin Luther, *Luther's Works*, vol. 37, *Word and Sacrament 3*, ed. Robert H. Fischer (St. Louis, MO: Concordia, 1961), 367.

40. Ibid., 13:342; 28:119, 131; Martin Luther, *Luther's Works*, vol. 35, *Word and Sacrament 1*, ed. E. Theodore Bachmann (St. Louis, MO: Concordia, 1960), 314, 387; Martin Luther, *Luther's Works*, vol. 39, *Church and Ministry 1*, ed. Jaroslav Pelikan (St. Louis, MO: Concordia, 1970),

191; Martin Luther, *Luther's Works*, vol. 20, *Lectures on the Minor Prophets 3*, ed. Jaroslav Pelikan (St. Louis, MO: Concordia, 1973), 192.

41. Martin Luther, *Luther's Works*, vol. 10, *Lectures on the Psalms, Chapters 1–75*, ed. Jaroslav Pelikan (St. Louis, MO: Concordia, 1974), 114; Martin Luther, *Luther's Works*, vol. 18, *Lectures on the Minor Prophets 1*, ed. Jaroslav Pelikan (St. Louis, MO: Concordia, 1975), 120; 41:198; 35:106, 107.

42. Ibid., 35:306, 313, 351.

43. Ibid., 35:405; Martin Luther, *Luther's Works*, vol. 38, *Word and Sacrament 4*, ed. Martin E. Lehmann (St. Louis, MO: Concordia, 1971), 102; 39:195.

44. Martin Luther, *Luther's Works*, vol. 36, *Word and Sacrament 2*, ed. Abdel Ross Wentz (St. Louis, MO: Concordia, 1959), 201. In another passage, Luther identified as the papacy "that loathsome beast (Rev. 13:1) which has blasphemous names on its forehead." Ibid., 4:31. He also identified the beast of Revelation 15 and 16 as the papacy. Ibid., 35:407.

45. Ibid., 39:102; 32:89; 41:206. Cf. ibid., 8:282, 283; 13:327; 35:402.

46. Ibid., 26:180.

47. Ibid., 26:200, 201. Cf. ibid., 35:393.

48. Martin Luther, *Luther's Works*, vol. 7, *Lectures on Genesis, Chapters 38–44*, ed. Jaroslav Pelikan (St. Louis, MO: Concordia, 1965), 297; 13:313. See also Martin Luther, *Luther's Works*, vol. 40, *Church and Ministry 2*, ed. Conrad Bergendoff (St. Louis, MO: Concordia, 1958), 15.

49. "God preserve us from having any other priest but Christ!" he said. Ibid., 13:330.

50. Ibid., 2:229. See also ibid., 24:367; 41:198.

51. Ibid., 35:407, 408. Cf. ibid., 13:258; 24:366; 35:258, 405; 39:279; 41:198.

52. As Will Durant puts it, "Luther's temper became hot lava as he neared the grave." Durant, *The Reformation*, 450.

53. Luther, *Works of Martin Luther*, 1:11.

54. William M. Landeen, *Martin Luther's Religious Thought* (Mountain View, CA: Pacific Press® Pub. Assn., 1971), 82.

55. Preserved Smith, *The Life and Letters of Martin Luther* (New York: Barnes and Noble, 1968), 399.

56. Marty, *Martin Luther*, 163; Luther, *Luther's Works*, 41:263, 264, 336.

57. Luther, *Luther's Works*, 41:357.

58. Martin Luther, *Luther's Works*, vol. 6, *Lectures on Genesis, Chapters 31–37*, ed. Jaroslav Pelikan (St. Louis, MO: Concordia, 1970), 63.

59. Ibid., 27:129.

60. Pelikan, *Reformation of Church and Dogma*, 173.

61. LeRoy Edwin Froom, *The Prophetic Faith of Our Fathers: The Historical Development of Prophetic Interpretation*, vol.4 (Washington, DC: Review and Herald® Pub. Assn., 1954), 463.

62. Ibid., 4:574, 575, 580.

63. George R. Knight, *William Miller and the Rise of Adventism* (Nampa, ID: Pacific Press® Pub. Assn., 2010), 94, 130.

64. Arthur Whitefield Spalding, *Origin and History of Seventh-day Adventists*, vol. 1 (Washington, DC: Review and Herald® Pub. Assn., 1961), 89. Miller disassociated himself from

this development. Knight, *William Miller and the Rise of Adventism*, 131, 193; David T. Arthur, in Edwin S. Gaustad, ed., *The Rise of Adventism* (New York: Harper and Row, 1974), 170.

65. Froom, *The Prophetic Faith of Our Fathers*, 4:957, 1118. Regarding Rome's role in the change of the Sabbath, see Robert L. Odom, *Sabbath and Sunday in Early Christianity* (Washington, DC: Review and Herald® Pub. Assn., 1977), 107, 108, 215, 248; Victorinus, *On the Creation of the World*, vol. 7, in *The Ante-Nicene Fathers*, ed. Alexander Roberts and James Donaldson (Peabody, MA: Hendrickson Publishers, 1994), 341–343; Samuele Bacchiocchi, *From Sabbath to Sunday: A Historical Investigation of the Rise of Sunday Observance in Early Christianity* (Rome: Pontifical Gregorian University, 1977), 291, 294, 295.

66. Froom, *The Prophetic Faith of Our Fathers*, 4:1079.

67. Ibid., 4:1063, 1155n1. This argument was echoed by many later Seventh-day Adventist expositors. See, e.g., Raymond F. Cottrell, *Beyond Tomorrow* (Nashville, TN: Southern Pub. Assn., 1963), 243–246.

68. She is believed by Seventh-day Adventists to have "exercised the biblical gift of prophecy." Ellen G. White, "Mission Accomplished: Working to Hasten That Glorious Day," *Adventist World*, September 2016, 39.

69. Ellen G. White, *The Great Controversy* (Mountain View, CA: Pacific Press® Pub. Assn., 1911), 439, 446.

70. Ibid., 446.

71. Ellen G. White, *Testimonies to Ministers and Gospel Workers* (Mountain View, CA: Pacific Press® Pub. Assn., 1923), 61.

72. Ellen G. White, *Patriarchs and Prophets* (Mountain View, CA: Pacific Press® Pub. Assn., 1890), 124.

73. Ellen G. White to Brother Stanton, Napier, New Zealand, March 22, 1893, Lt. 57, 1893, quoted in Arthur L. White, *Ellen G. White*, vol. 4, *The Australian Years, 1891–1900* (Washington, DC: Review and Herald® Pub. Assn., 1983), 81. Sometimes she referred to these churches as daughters of Babylon who followed Rome's "example of sacrificing the truth and the approval of God, in order to form an unlawful alliance with the world." White, *The Great Controversy*, 382, 383.

74. White, *The Great Controversy*, 390.

75. Luther, *Luther's Works*, 2:181. But see also ibid., 3:122; 36:216.

76. Ellen G. White, *The Great Controversy* (Oakland, CA: Pacific Press® Pub. Assn., 1888), 680.

77. Ellen G. White, "Ellen G. White Comments," in *The Seventh-day Adventist Bible Commentary*, ed. Francis D. Nichol, rev. ed. (Washington, DC: Review and Herald® Pub. Assn., 1980), 7:950.

78. Ellen G. White, *Thoughts From the Mount of Blessing* (Mountain View, CA: Pacific Press® Pub. Assn., 1909), 125, 126

79. White, *The Great Controversy* (1888), 680.

80. White, *Testimonies to Ministers and Gospel Workers*, 62, quoted in White, "Ellen G. White Comments," 7:911.

81. See Nichol, *The Seventh-day Adventist Bible Commentary*, 7:830; Hans K. LaRondelle, "The Remnant and the Three Angels' Messages," in *Handbook of Seventh-day Adventist Theology*, ed.

Raoul Dederen, Commentary Reference Series, vol. 12 (Hagerstown, MD: Review and Herald® Pub. Assn., 2000), 888; *Bible Readings for the Home* (Washington, DC: Review and Herald® Pub. Assn., 1958), 250–252; Uriah Smith, *The Prophecies of Daniel and the Revelation*, 2nd ed. (Hagerstown, MD: Review and Herald® Pub. Assn., 1972), 653, 715.

82. Nichol, *The Seventh-day Adventist Bible Commentary*, 7:272, 273; C. Mervyn Maxwell, *God Cares*, vol. 1 (Mountain View, CA: Pacific Press® Pub. Assn., 1981), 122.

83. *Bible Readings*, 211–217; LaRondelle, "The Remnant and the Three Angels' Messages," 867, 869.

84. Smith, *The Prophecies of Daniel*, 372, 522; *Bible Readings*, 212; LaRondelle, "The Remnant and the Three Angels' Messages," 866–869. Nichol, *The Seventh-day Adventist Bible Commentary*, 7:271, 273.

85. Smith, *The Prophecies of Daniel*, 119, 521; *Seventh-day Adventists Believe . . . : A Biblical Exposition of 27 Fundamental Beliefs* (Hagerstown, MD: Review and Herald® Pub. Assn., 1988), 261; Maxwell, *God Cares*, 1:131–132; Mark Finley, *The Next Superpower: Ancient Prophecies, Global Events, and Your Future* (Washington, DC: Review and Herald® Pub. Assn., 2005), 135–141; *Bible Readings*, 212; Maxwell, *God Cares*, 1:127–131; Francis D. Nichol, ed., *The Seventh-day Adventist Bible Commentary*, rev. ed. (Washington, DC: Review and Herald® Pub. Assn., 1980), 4:826–828. Most Seventh-day Adventist expositors considered the little horn of Daniel 8 to be both imperial Rome and papal Rome. Martin Pröbstle, in Gerhard Pfandl, ed., *Interpreting Scripture: Bible Questions and Answers*, Biblical Research Institute Studies, vol. 2 (Silver Spring, MD: Biblical Research Institute, 2010), 245–247; *Seventh-day Adventists Answer Questions on Doctrine* (Washington, DC: Review and Herald® Pub. Assn., 1957), 256–258; Maxwell, *God Cares*, 1:158–161; Nichol, *The Seventh-day Adventist Bible Commentary*, 4:841–843.

86. Oberman, *Luther*, 67.

CHAPTER 21

Luther, Adventists, Anabaptists, and Liberty

Douglas Morgan

I n 1548, two years after the death of Martin Luther, Fritz Erbe, a successful farmer from the town of Herda, near Eisenach, died at Wartburg Castle. More than a quarter of a century before, the castle had been a refuge to Luther, under the auspices of Duke Frederick the Wise, after the Reformer's heroic stand at the Diet of Worms made him an outlaw in the Holy Roman Empire. Like Luther, Erbe had withstood the demands of earthly authorities and refused to recant his convictions based on the clear testimony of God's Word. Unlike Luther, Erbe's stand earned him imprisonment, not protective custody, at the Wartburg Castle. He held out through sixteen years of incarceration that led to his death.[1]

Fritz Erbe's martyrdom came at the hands of *Protestant* authorities, not Catholic. In fact, had it been up to the Wittenberg Reformers Martin Luther and Philip

> Fritz Erbe's martyrdom came at the hands of *Protestant* authorities, not Catholic.

Melanchthon, Erbe would not have had the opportunity to give quite so remarkable a demonstration of the "patient endurance . . . of the people of God" (Revelation 14:12, NIV). He would have been executed a dozen years earlier, in 1536, rather than receiving what turned out to be a life sentence.

233

Erbe committed no crime that brought physical or material harm to others. He neither participated in nor advocated resistance to civil authority. He was deemed guilty of blasphemy and sedition for his persistence in openly proclaiming and acting upon his conviction that entry into God's church requires separation from the world signified by the believer's baptism. He regarded the baptism of infants—incapable of making such a choice—as useless, even though it was a near-universal practice in Christendom for approximately a millennium. He was thus identified with a highly diffuse and variegated movement on the radical fringes of the Protestant Reformation, pejoratively called "Anabaptists" (rebaptizers).

Erbe was also a rather fervent Second "Adventist." He believed Christ was about to return and execute final judgment on the world. To be ready, one needed to be truly baptized. Yet he seems to have been an unusually irenic radical. He did not presume to judge the consciences of other Christians. For himself, however, there was no question—following Jesus required believer's baptism.

In 1531, the first time he was apprehended, Erbe's resolve had weakened. He recanted and was released. But then he refused to have his newborn child baptized and within a year was again in prison. He had the relative good fortune, though, of being in the jurisdiction of Landgrave Philip of Hesse, who among the German Protestant princes was the most reluctant to exact harsh punishments on the Anabaptists. In 1536, he decided to seek a wide range of expert opinions as he wrestled with the dilemma of what to do with Erbe and thirty other Anabaptists languishing in his custody. Among the replies from the cities and university faculties Philip queried, one of the most severe came from Wittenberg, composed by Melanchthon and signed by Luther. "We judge," declared the Wittenberg Reformers regarding persons engaged in the crime of opposing the baptism of infants, that "the obstinate are to be put to death."[2]

Raising the question of Luther and religious liberty quickly leads to a second question, Which Luther? The Luther who risked death to defy pope and emperor, thereby breaking the shackles of medieval conformity and opening a new era of freedom for humanity? Or the Luther who wanted to see synagogues burned and the Jews banished and who, on two occasions, explicitly endorsed the death penalty for peaceful Anabaptists? And those questions are preliminary to a third—the central question in what follows: what significance does Luther's complex career hold for Adventists, who have made religious liberty a prominent cause for nearly 150 years?

> What significance does Luther's complex career hold for Adventists, who have made religious liberty a prominent cause for nearly 150 years?

Luther the liberator

"To go against conscience is neither right nor safe," Luther declared to the imperial Diet held at Worms in 1521.[3] In his biography of the Reformer, Heiko Oberman notes that this "appeal to conscience as the highest authority made an extraordinary impression on later generations." But, he contends, the widespread impression is misleading when couched in the language of individual rights. Such terminology connotes the Enlightenment concept of natural rights that, on the basis of human reason, are held by all people, independent of any higher authority. Those who equate Luther's bold statement "Here I stand, I can do no other" with "the principle of freedom of conscience" are "missing the whole point," according to Oberman. Luther did not declare that his conscience was free. Rather, he testified that it was "captive to the Word of God." In sum, Oberman writes, "Luther liberated the Christian conscience, liberated it from papal decree and canon law. But he also took it captive through the Word of God and imposed on it the responsibility to render service to the world."[4]

At times, Adventist writers seem to have been among those who missed the point. Take, for example, Alonzo T. Jones, who spearheaded Adventism's foray into activism for religious liberty in the late nineteenth century and spawned lines of argument that would serve Adventist polemics on the relationship between church and state for decades to come. Some passages in *The Two Republics* (1891), Jones's sweeping tome on history in the light of prophecy, present Luther as virtually espousing the political philosophy of America's founders, such as Thomas Jefferson and James Madison.[5] For example, Jones introduces Luther not only as an apostle of individual rights but also of "separation between Church and State."[6] We have already seen enough to suggest how far off the mark that claim is.

A more careful look, however, reveals much that harmonizes with Oberman's insight as well. Jones actually does not attempt to make Luther into a flawless exemplar of religious freedom or human rights as defined by modern liberal democracy. Rather, Jones pictures Luther "opening up the contest" that others later would press to new fronts, requiring refined weaponry in pursuit of the same objectives.[7]

The freedom-generating Word of God

The title of Oberman's biography of Luther, *Luther: Man Between God and the Devil*, in itself signals a deeper resonance—that between the historian's analysis of Luther's outlook and Ellen G. White's interpretation of the significance of the Reformer's career in the book *The Great Controversy*. Adventists, with Ellen White at the lead, have seen the great controversy, not the triumphant progress of liberal human rights, as the critical dynamic at work in history. Oberman observes that for Luther influence over the human conscience is "hotly contested by God and the Devil." The conscience thus "is not the autonomous center of man's personality" but is instead "always guided and is free only once God has freed and 'captured' it."[8]

That struggle indeed is the context in which Ellen White extols the influence of Luther's stand on individual conscience: "Had the Reformer yielded a single point, Satan and his hosts would have gained the victory. But his unwavering firmness was the means of emancipating the church."[9] Given the forces at work, the Word of God was the indispensable foundation and springboard for Luther's free assertion of conviction in the face of human authority. Luther thus stood "upon the sure foundation of the word of God" and thereby "testified against the power of error and witnessed to the superiority of that faith that overcomes the world."[10]

Though at first glance it may seem otherwise, a similar perspective on the source of liberty informs Alonzo T. Jones's conclusion that the freedom struggle initiated by Luther reached its culmination in the formation of the American republic. The Declaration of Independence and the Constitution established "the first national government upon the earth that accords with the principles announced by Jesus Christ for mankind and for civil government," Jones pronounced.[11]

Despite its chauvinistic ring, Jones did not use this claim to argue that the United States was a Christian nation or the bearer of God's redemptive purposes for history. Quite the opposite; it was the basis for refuting such notions. In Jones's analysis, secular government—that is, complete separation of church and state—is God's idea, revealed in the Bible.

Rigorous analysis might show Jones's reading of American history oversimplified and unduly idealistic and some of his scriptural arguments tendentious. Yet the more significant point here is that he really believed that the freedom Luther stood for, and gained its fullest implementation in the American experiment, was grounded in God's Word—both written and made flesh—and not on enlightened human reason liberated from religious authority. He substantiated his claim that Jesus Christ was the "author of religious liberty" from the New Testament gospel, not the gospel of Americanism.[12]

Christ came in to the world, wrote Jones, to implant in human souls "the genuine principle of liberty." This was "liberty led by a conscience enlightened by the Spirit of God,—liberty in which man may be free from all men, yet made so gentle by love that he would willingly become the servant of all, in order to bring them to the enjoyment of this same liberty." More than simply a matter of teaching and example, the gift of freedom came about through God's work of reconciliation in Christ. It was a freedom that also bound His followers "in everlasting, unquestioning, unswerving allegiance to him as the royal benefactor of the race" and empowered them to preach the gospel of freedom throughout the earth.[13]

In the view of Ellen White, the freedom that animated Luther and other

Reformers to challenge misdirected authority with the truth of God's Word has a dynamic quality. She compared those who resisted Luther's message with "many at the present day" who refuse "additional light" because their religious forebears did not accept it, rather than "searching the word of truth" for themselves.[14] The covenant that the English Separatists of the early seventeenth century made "as the Lord's free people, 'to walk together in all His ways made known or to be made known to them,' " exemplified "the true spirit of reform, the vital principle of Protestantism." Ellen White affirmed the confidence of their pastor, John Robinson, that "more truth and light" was yet to "break forth" from God's Word. That process would be an ever-renewable source of constructive dissent against the status quo. Suppression of that freedom—rejection of the "great principle" that "truth is progressive" and failure to "press forward in the path of reform"—had, in her view, such a deadening impact among the Protestant churches of nineteenth-century America that "there was almost as great need of reform . . . as in the Roman Church in the time of Luther."[15]

From an Adventist perspective, then, Luther was a champion of religious liberty, first of all, by virtue of his *witness to the freedom-generating Word of God*, not by asserting a self-generated natural right. The riveting showdown with imperial power in 1521 remains history's definitive drama of freedom, inspired and informed by God's Word, standing unconstrained against the highest earthly powers that oppress humanity and suppress the truth. Its impact comes not only by way of example but by virtue initiating a process of liberating reform that will persist and widen "to the close of time."[16]

The faith-denying implications of reliance on coercion

The predominant governing authority in Luther's world at the outset of the Reformation was the duke of electoral Saxony, Frederick the Wise. The papacy claimed centralized authority over all of Christendom, but it could no longer dominate the temporal rulers of Europe as it had during the High Middle Ages. And the Holy Roman emperors strove mightily to unite the large swath of central Europe in their domain, but it was a protracted, losing battle against the three hundred or so feudal territories, city-states, and other political jurisdictions within the empire who wanted to keep power in their hands.

As one of just seven members of the imperial diet (or assembly) who held the title *elector* (empowering them with a vote when it became necessary to elect a new emperor), Frederick was one of the most powerful of the nobles within the empire. From a political standpoint, Luther was in Frederick's hands. Through a strategy of delaying maneuvers, Frederick prevented the papacy from apprehending Luther after the pope's legate, Cardinal Cajetan, failed in 1518 to bring Luther into submission. Then, when the Edict of Worms in 1521 declared Luther an outlaw in the Holy Roman Empire, Frederick devised a scheme to keep him in friendly confinement in Wartburg Castle.[17]

Luther welcomed the protection and even more the genuine embrace of the reformed faith on the part of godly princes. But he was deeply sensitive to the incongruity of using "carnal" weapons to defend the faith and was deeply resistant to the notion that the protection or advance of the gospel cause required such unseemly means.

In 1522, Luther, without seeking the elector's permission, returned to Wittenberg at the invitation of the town council. Frederick advised holding off, at least until after the conflicts anticipated at the upcoming Diet of Nuremberg died down. The elector believed it his duty to protect Luther but warned that it could get messy, even violent, if the Reformer returned then. Luther's reply, in a tone that suggests genuine gratitude and respect, was nonetheless forthright about the placement of his trust: "I would have you know that I am come to Wittenberg with a higher protection than that of Your Grace. I do not ask you to protect me. I will protect you more than you will protect me. If I thought you would protect me, I would not come. This is not a case for the sword but for God, and since you are weak in the faith you cannot protect me. . . . If Your Grace had eyes, you would see the glory of God."[18]

Yet in the swirl of politics, Luther's fate in fact had become inextricably bound with that of his temporal lord. Similarly, the fate of the Reformation became linked with the efforts of the German Protestant princes to resist Charles V's relentless pursuit of his dream for reunification of Catholic Christendom under the rule of the Holy Roman emperor. Luther's position that the church could not look to the violence and coercion of the state for protection of the faith became increasingly difficult to hold. Yet for nearly a decade, he did so.

In 1530, when the Protestant princes moved to form a defensive alliance, Luther wrote to Elector John of Saxony, as he had written his predecessor, Frederick, eight years before: "We cannot on our conscience approve the proposed alliance. We would rather die ten times than see our gospel cause one drop of blood to be shed. Our part is to be like lambs of the slaughter. The cross of Christ must be borne."[19]

Ellen White applauded Luther's adherence to the principle that "there should be no resort to secular power in support of the Reformation, and no appeal to arms for its defense." The source of "the power that shook the world in the Great Reformation," she pointed out, was the "secret place of prayer." Luther's insistence about *the faith-denying implications of reliance on force to defend the church* is a second facet of his legacy for religious liberty that holds value for Adventists.[20]

The impotence and inhumanity of coercive suppression of dissent

The same principle, but now applied to the "heresy" of dissenting, often vulnerable minorities within, rather than to opposition from without, constitutes a third aspect of that legacy. A gamut of radicals and extremists complicated

Luther's life and endangered the progress of the Reformation, all the way from his break with Rome until his death. Despite his well-known penchant for verbal assault, Luther was, until 1531, essentially consistent in contending that violence and coercion are inappropriate and ineffectual means for combating erroneous beliefs.

Despite his well-known penchant for verbal assault, Luther was, until 1531, essentially consistent in contending that violence and coercion are inappropriate and ineffectual means for combating erroneous beliefs.

In his tract *On Civil Government*, published in 1523, the Reformer laid down the following maxims:

> "Faith is a free work to which no one can be forced. It is a divine work in the Spirit, let alone then that outward force should compel or create it." . . .
>
> "Heresy is a spiritual thing, which cannot be cut with steel nor burned with fire nor drowned with water."[21]

Luther rebuked the radicals who, while he was in seclusion at Wartburg Castle, sought to impose sudden and total change on worship forms and practices of the faith at Wittenberg. Mob violence broke out against priests as they celebrated Mass, forcibly ejecting them from altars and destroying the liturgical books. Though not involving lethal violence, Luther saw at work the principle of coerced change that he opposed. He advised the zealots:

> "In a word I will preach, speak, write, but I will force and drive no one, for faith must be willing and unconstrained."
>
> "Christians fight only with the Word against the devil's teaching and work. First take hearts and consciences away from him and then all will fall of itself."[22]

> "Were I to employ force, what should I gain? Grimace, formality, apings, human ordinances, and hypocrisy. . . . But there would be no sincerity of heart, nor faith, nor charity. Where these three are wanting, all is wanting, and I would not give a pear stalk for such a result."[23]

Again in this connection, though, the political reality bore down on the gospel principle. The intermittent and inconclusive thirty-year war between Catholic and Protestant forces in the Holy Roman Empire led to an arrangement in which the religion of the ruler (or ruling authority) in each territory was the sole religion granted legal status in that territory. This arrangement did not permit religious freedom *within* a given territory. And it left out completely the Anabaptists and other marginalized dissenters.

In 1527, Luther bent to the territorial principle and endorsed the penalty of banishment. But that was the severest stricture he could countenance. He was taken aback by the Swiss Reformer Huldrych Zwingli's rapid implementation of the death penalty for Anabaptists in 1526, and was haunted by the thought of emulating "the papists and the Jews before Christ" in killing "false prophets." More than four hundred years before Martin Niemöller, Luther seemed to have had an inkling that everyone's liberty is put on shaky ground if the principle of targeting any particular group because of their beliefs is put into law. He observed that "when there was a statute for the killing of false prophets and heretics, in time it came about that only the most saintly and innocent were killed."[24]

Another comment in 1528 seems to reflect a heart still pushing in the direction of liberty: "It is not right and I am deeply troubled that the poor people are so pitifully put to death, burned, and cruelly slain," Luther wrote of the Anabaptists. "Let everyone believe what he likes. If he is wrong, he will have punishment enough in hell fire." They should be opposed "with Scripture and God's Word," said Luther. "With the fire one will get nowhere."[25]

With his limitations acknowledged, Luther, through the 1520s at least, bore compelling witness concerning *the inefficacy and inhumanity of using force to suppress religious dissent.* As with the previous two points, this aspect of his contribution to religious liberty has, in the twenty-first century, lost none of its resonance with Adventists nor its relevance to the church's message for all people.

Luther the persecutor

How, then, to account for, and what to do with, the change from Luther's apparently heartfelt horror at violent punishment of "heretics" to his reluctant yet firm endorsement of the death penalty for nonresistant Anabaptists—the likes of Fritz Erbe—in 1531 and thereafter? Though he did not mention Luther's eventual support for the death penalty, Alonzo T. Jones acknowledged that "even Luther swerved from the genuine Christian and Protestant principle" in advocating "the banishment of 'false teachers' and the utter rooting out of the Jews from 'Christian' lands." Jones attributed this deviation to Luther's refusal "to walk in the advancing light," which left him with "less of the word of God and therefore less faith."[26]

In another sense, however—narrower, perhaps, yet historically significant—Luther did not swerve in the 1530s but rather continued further in a direction of the clear distinctions he had articulated between the roles of civil and ecclesiastical governance. Jones overpraised this distinction as exemplifying complete separation of church and state because he seems not to have grasped the extent to which Luther retained the assumptions of the medieval fusion of church and society. The pertinent assumption here is that the church had authority to judge *behavior* based on religious heresy to be injurious to civil society and thus subject to criminal punishment to be carried out by civil authorities.

Within this framework, Luther distinguished between heresy and blasphemy. He could be permissive about *heresy*, a privately held unorthodox belief, recognizing the ineffectiveness of force against inner conviction. On the other hand, *blasphemy*—the public advocacy for denial of a doctrine central to Christian faith, such as those affirmed in the Apostles' Creed—was an action that served to "upset society" and thus was punishable with civil penalties. The *exercise* of heretical religion could not be free if it entailed blasphemy and/or sedition.[27]

The sequence of events as the Protestant revolution unfolded created a context that predisposed Luther to see opponents of infant baptism in the colors of blasphemy and sedition. Thomas Müntzer, the prophet of apocalyptic warfare, was the dominant figure in Luther's first brush with radicals opposed to infant baptism. Müntzer's incendiary rhetoric did much to stir the ill-fated German Peasants' War of 1524. The slaughter of up to one hundred thousand poorly armed, disorganized peasants was exacerbated by the ill-timed publication of one of Luther's most intemperate tracts, which seemed to encourage the nobles to a level of cruelty Luther did not intend. A decade later apocalyptic extremists seized control of the city of Münster and abandoned the usual Anabaptist pacifism for a Davidic monarchy, complete with polygamy for the rulers. This, too, ended in a bloody nightmare.[28]

The two debacles featured religion-based revolutionary violence that modern liberal democracies would have no difficulty categorizing as sedition that must be stopped and punished by force. These tragedies distorted perceptions of Anabaptism not only during the Reformation era but also well into the twentieth century. Citizens of the twenty-first century should have no difficulty understanding how the actions of violent extremists can cast a pervasive atmosphere of suspicion over an entire faith whose adherents, by an overwhelming majority, are law abiding.

Yet awareness of this factor in the cultural context of the Wittenberg Reformers also magnifies the significance of the fact that the Melanchthon-Luther memoranda of 1531 and 1536 do make a clear distinction between the revolutionary and peaceful Anabaptists and judge both classes deserving of execution. All who reject the "ministerial office" were guilty of blasphemy, a crime that Luther, in his addendum to the 1531 memorandum, characterized as a greater atrocity than the seeming cruelty of punishing them with the sword.

The 1536 memorandum details, as grounds for charging the Anabaptists with sedition, their teachings that Christians

• should not use a sword,

- should not serve as a magistrate,
- should not swear or hold property, and
- may desert an unbelieving wife.

Their claim that they do not cause anyone harm should be disregarded "because if they persuaded everyone there would be no government." And that leads to the most dangerous element of their seditious persuasiveness: the effect of their opposition to infant baptism was to "cast children out of Christendom," and the spread of that doctrine ultimately threatened to make society "openly heathen." For "obstinate" advocates of this doctrine, the death penalty, not simply punishment by the sword, is specified.[29]

Another step in 1531 took Luther further than he had previously been willing to go. When the Lutheran princes of the Holy Roman Empire formed the Schmalkaldic League in February 1531, Luther overcame his reluctance to utilize human weapons in defending the gospel. He gave the endorsement he had refused to give not long before to the concept of an alliance for the military defense of political territories defined by adherence to the Protestant faith. When the league added territory through a blatantly offensive campaign just three years later, Luther condemned the move, but the die was cast.[30]

The Reformation church: A search for identity

The steps Luther took in 1531 were momentous but did not lead in new directions. The channels had already been set at a level deeper than debate over how to define individual rights or criteria that may justify Christians in using force. The decisive questions were about the character of the Reformation church and the meaning of the sacraments that defined its identity and worshiping life.

In the early phase of his conflict with the papal church, Luther spoke of the true church as a *remnant* of consecrated believers. It would necessarily be a persecuted minority because the Word of God runs so fundamentally counter to the pride and desires natural to humanity. As he personally encountered the backlash of earthly powers to his own stand for the gospel in 1521, Luther took comfort in the testimony of all the Scriptures that the "majority always supports the lie and the minority the truth."[31]

As the Reformation got underway in the early 1520s, Luther sought to create an organizational framework for the physical gathering and nurture of this spiritual remnant, separate from the nominal church at large. As late as 1527 he encouraged formation of cells of genuine believers that would meet together in houses. They would pray and read scripture together, but that was not all. Baptism and reception of the sacraments would take place at these gatherings, making them virtually churches within the church at large.[32]

Though he finally gave up on it as impractical, this was not merely a passing suggestion on Luther's part. Rather, it was based on his recognition that "the world and the mass of men are and remain unchristian, though they have all been baptized and are called Christians." Luther continued this line of thought, written in 1523, with the even more striking observation that because true Christians are scattered, "it is impossible that a Christian regime should extend over the world or even over the country or a large group."[33]

Yet, in 1527, Luther finalized his commitment to a form of church premised on that very impossibility. Roland Bainton points out that as Luther began envisioning a new order of things in 1520, he had fundamental choices to make from a limited range of options. Papal abuses of temporal power had been one of the main targets of his protest as it emerged in the indulgence controversy. Thus, theocracy was never an option. His statements about the inadmissibility of coercion in matters of faith and interest in the church as a gathered minority of true believers suggested the possibility of separating church and state. But the reality in 1520 was that Luther had already embarked on a third option that, says Bainton, "left the door open for caesaropapism" (i.e., the church under the control of state authority).[34]

In *To the Christian Nobility*, Luther called up the nobles who embraced the reform movement to serve as "emergency bishops" to lead the reconstruction of the reformed church in their territories. He argued that the move was theologically appropriate because princes and magistrates, as members of the church, shared in the priesthood of all believers. He called upon them to step up as faithful Christians and meet the emergency.[35]

In 1527, the "visitation" was put into place as the mechanism for this reconstitution of the church under the supervision of the emergency bishops. Though this role was to be temporary—a transitional one for the princes—it set the precedent that in Lutheran lands the church would be under the authority of civil government. This would not be the church as a "remnant," shaped by adherence to the Word of God in contrast to society at large. Rather, this would be the "territorial" church in which the society a person entered at birth coincided with the church into which all were baptized as infants.[36]

In his reformed theology of the sacraments, Luther taught that a sacrament could only be valid if accompanied by faith on the part of the recipient. But this did not lead him to repudiate the practice of infant baptism. In responding to questions about this seeming inconsistency, Luther developed two lines of thought over the years: (1) the faith of the whole church applied to the baptized infant, and (2) the faith required was incipient in the infant—it was not yet apparent or consciously held but would later grow to full form.[37]

Serious theological commitments lay behind these rationales, including the value Luther placed on baptism as the sign of assurance to which a believer could cling when assailed by guilt or doubt. The fact that one was baptized as a helpless baby underscored, in this thinking, the fact that hope for salvation rested outside the believer in Christ alone, not in any fallible human act, not

244 | HERE WE STAND

even the exercise of faith.[38] Thus, according to Adventist scholar William M. Landeen, infant baptism was the *alpha* of Luther's theology. Without it, "Luther's whole religious thought would be impossible."[39]

When push came to shove, then, Luther felt compelled to follow the implications of infant baptism with regard to the nature of the church. Bainton called infant baptism the "sociological sacrament" because it is integral to the concept of the "territorial church." And the Melanchthon-Luther memorandum of 1536 vividly shows how the survival of this sociological construct depended on infant baptism.[40]

The Anabaptist corrective

Despite the tendency to downplay Luther's shortcomings, Adventist writers have been clear in diagnosing the failure of the magisterial or territorial church of the leading Protestant Reformers to break the corrupting links between the church and political power formed by the Constantinian revolution in the fourth century. The pattern of "attempting to build up the church by the aid of the state, of appealing to the secular power in support of the gospel," as Ellen White put it, continued to produce "evil results," so that the Protestant churches not only failed to progress further in the path of reform but lost much of what had been gained in the sixteenth-century Reformation.[41]

Adventists have traced the persistence of Constantinian evils after the Reformation to colonial North America. A breakthrough finally came in the person of Roger Williams who, in his dissent from the New England Puritan way and founding of the Rhode Island colony, finally got it right. Williams's corrective to the long history of religious persecution, in essence, was to apply the golden rule. He saw that one cannot claim religious liberty without recognizing that all people have the same right, whatever their beliefs. "Civil and religious liberty," the "foundation principles" of his small colony, "became cornerstones of the American Republic."[42]

Only with Williams does the saga of Luther and religious liberty come to a conclusion, as summarized by Alonzo T. Jones: "In the promulgation of the principles of Protestantism, and in the work of the Reformation, the names of Martin Luther and Roger Williams can never rightly be separated. Williams completed what Luther began; and together they gave anew to the world, and for all time, the principles originally announced by Him who was the Author and Finisher of the faith of both—JESUS CHRIST, THE AUTHOR OF RELIGIOUS LIBERTY."[43]

Anabaptists are virtually absent from nineteenth-century Adventist narratives of the Luther-to-Williams recovery of religious liberty. Yet more than a century before Williams, at enormous cost, the Anabaptist movement decisively severed the Constantinian links between the church and society and thereby pioneered religious freedom and the separation of church and state. This absence of Anabaptists from the writings of our nineteenth-century forebears should be noted without blame or condescension. By the time that the Protestant historical accounts most accessible to them were written, the Anabaptist story had long been obscured and distorted in the writing of church history.[44]

However, a five-hundredth anniversary reassessment of Luther and religious liberty would be deeply deficient without due consideration of the Anabaptist witness, with which Luther himself contended. The election of Mennonite historian Harold Bender, as president of the American Society of Church History in 1943, was a landmark in the process leading to open-minded study and writing of Anabaptist history. As a result, an abundance of resources meeting every level and type of interest are now easily accessible.

In his presidential address to the society, Bender showed that the core of Anabaptist reform was not unhinged apocalyptic fanaticism but rather could be summarized in these three points:

1. "A new conception of the essence of Christianity as discipleship": all of life was to be fashioned after the teachings and example of Jesus.
2. "A new conception of the church as a brotherhood": a community of voluntary commitment to the way of Christ, suffering, and sharing of possessions, which is separate from and a challenge to worldly society.
3. "A new ethic of love and nonresistance": rejection of warfare and violence in human relationships.[45]

During the past forty years, Adventist scholars have made a start at evaluating the significance of Anabaptist history. Nevertheless, if being part of a creative vanguard in the cause of religious liberty is a desirable goal for twenty-first-century Adventism, the significance of the second characteristic of Bender's summary—a *community* of voluntary commitment to the way of Christ—in particular, needs further exploration. Without it, the risk is turning the *victory* for individual rights, for which Roger Williams and the heritage of dissenting Protestantism must receive a large share of credit, into the *foundation* of our commitment and guide for our discernment. With reference to the specifically American context, the liberal ideals profoundly expressed in the nation's founding documents should be cherished and used as the basis for advocacy of specific policies in the public arena. Yet making American ideals about individual rights the main wellspring of thought and action means losing the critical distance, the creative edge, and the resilient energy that comes when public witness for liberty is generated by the gospel of the kingdom.[46]

A *church* is needed for that—a voluntary community of faithfulness. The pioneers of Adventism realized that in order for there to be such a church, something had to change. The stalled Reformation needed a jump-start and a renewed connection with its authentic source of power. The Anabaptist heritage can help us recover, refine, and extend the renewal vision that powered the rise of Adventism.

Roland Bainton, the Reformation scholar to whose insights this essay is heavily indebted, contended that, in a sense, Luther could be regarded "as the father alike of Anabaptism and of Lutheranism." The testimony of Fritz Erbe's enduring faithfulness is but one reason for seeing the former as a progression beyond the latter and an indispensable resource for an Adventist project of renewing the Reformation quest to advance the freedom enclosed in the promise of the gospel.[47]

1. Information on Erbe in this and the immediately following paragraphs is from John S. Oyer, *Lutheran Reformers Against Anabaptists: Luther, Melanchthon and Menius and the Anabaptists of Central Germany* (The Hague, Netherlands: Martinus Nijhoff, 1964), 68, 69, 85.

2. Roland H. Bainton, *Studies on the Reformation* (Boston, MA: Beacon Press, 1963), 41, 42.

3. Roland H. Bainton, *Here I Stand: A Life of Martin Luther* (Nashville, TN: Abingdon Press, 1978), 182.

4. Heiko A. Oberman, *Luther: Man Between God and the Devil* (New York: Doubleday, 1992), 203, 204.

5. Alonzo T. Jones, *The Two Republics; or, Rome and the United States of America* (Battle Creek, MI: Review and Herald Pub. Co., 1891), 569–576.

6. Ibid., 569.

7. Ibid.

8. Oberman, *Luther*, 204.

9. Ellen G. White, *The Great Controversy* (Mountain View, CA: Pacific Press® Pub. Assn., 1911), 166.

10. Ibid., 160.

11. Jones, *The Two Republics*, 663.

12. Ibid., 662.

13. Ibid., 139.

14. White, *The Great Controversy*, 164.

15. Ibid., 291, 292, 297, 298.

16. Ibid., 126.

17. Bainton, *Here I Stand*, 147–149.

18. Ibid., 163, 164.

19. Martin Luther, quoted in J. H. Merle D'Aubigne, *History of the Reformation of the Sixteenth Century*, London ed., bk. 14, chap. 1, quoted in White, *The Great Controversy*, 209.

20. White, *The Great Controversy*, 209, 210.

21. Martin Luther, quoted in Bainton, *Studies on the Reformation*, 22, 23.

22. Luther, quoted in ibid., 31.

23. Martin Luther, quoted in D'Aubigne, *History of the Reformation*, bk. 9, chap. 8, quoted in White, *The Great Controversy*, 189, 190.

24. Martin Luther, quoted in Bainton, *Studies on the Reformation*, 38, 39.

25. Luther, quoted in ibid., 39.

26. Jones, *The Two Republics*, 576.

27. Bainton, *Studies on the Reformation*, 40, 41.

28. Bainton, *Here I Stand*, 199, 200, 216–221; Diarmaid MacCulloch, *The Reformation: A History* (New York: Penguin Books, 2003), 204–207.

29. Bainton, *Studies on the Reformation*, 41, 42.

30. Steven Ozment, *The Age of Reform, 1250–1550: An Intellectual and Religious History of Late Medieval and Reformation Europe* (New Haven, CT: Yale University Press, 1980), 256, 257; Oberman, *Luther*, 238–240.

31. Bainton, *Studies on the Reformation*, 25.

32. Ibid., 37.

33. Ibid.

34. Bainton, *Here I Stand*, 188.

35. Ibid., 117–119.

36. Bainton, *Studies on the Reformation*, 38.

37. Bainton, *Here I Stand*, 109, 110.

38. Oberman, *Luther*, 230.

39. William M. Landeen, *Martin Luther's Religious Thought* (Mountain View, CA: Pacific Press® Pub. Assn., 1971), 104.

40. Bainton, *Here I Stand*, 109, 110.

41. White, *The Great Controversy*, 297.

42. Ibid., 295.

43. Jones, *The Two Republics*, 662.

44. Ellen White includes favorable discussion of the career of Menno Simons in a chapter on the Reformation in the Netherlands in *The Great Controversy*, 238, 239. She commends his rejection of infant baptism but does not present him as the leader of a distinct type of reformation that was severely persecuted by other Protestants.

45. Harold S. Bender, "The Anabaptist Vision," in Guy F. Hershberger, ed., *The Recovery of the Anabaptist Vision: A Sixtieth Anniversary Tribute to Harold S. Bender* (Eugene: Wipf and Stock, 2001), 42.

46. In *The Reformation and the Advent Movement* (Washington, DC: Review and Herald® Pub. Assn., 1983), W. L. Emmerson showed how it was in fact the Anabaptist strand of Reformation history that figures most directly in the Adventist heritage. More recently, Nicholas P. Miller (in *The Religious Roots of the First Amendment* [New York: Oxford University Press, 2012], an admirable analysis that has received much favorable recognition in the wider intellectual community), gives prominent place to the contribution of Anabaptists.

47. Bainton, *Studies on the Reformation*, 27.

CHAPTER 22

Islam in Luther and Seventh-day Adventism

Nikolaus Satelmajer

Europe faced many challenges in the 1500s. Martin Luther was a major headache to the Holy Roman Empire, specifically to Emperor Charles V and the papacy. Luther and his followers refused to submit to the emperor and the pope. Yet there was a challenge faced by all—the emperor, the pope, Luther, and, in fact, all of Europe—and there was no agreement what to do. This challenge was the ongoing aggression from the Ottoman Empire.

The Ottoman Empire—Turks,[1] as Luther refers to them—threatened the very existence of Europe. For Luther, it was not only an issue of invasion by another empire, it was the fact that another faith, Islam, challenged Europe and Christianity. Luther, as on many other topics, had much to say and said it in his characteristic strong language.

We will explore Luther's response to Islam and then look at the Seventh-day Adventist response to it. Furthermore, how have Adventists tried to fulfill their mission to bring their message to the whole world, including Islam?

> Furthermore, how have Adventists tried to fulfill their mission to bring their message to the whole world, including Islam?

Europe under siege

In the 1300s, Europe lost many to the Black Death, and its consequences impacted the continent for many years. On the other hand, there were positive events in the next century. For example, Johann Gutenberg, around 1440, developed movable type for the printing press. The printing press was a major and lasting innovation. Several years after the Gutenberg event, Constantinople, the capital of the Byzantine Empire, fell in 1453 to the Ottoman Turks. By 1463, Bosnia[2] was conquered, and Hercegovina fell in 1482.[3]

While Luther was at the Imperial Diet of Worms in April 1521, Ottoman ruler Süleyman I (r. 1520–1566), also known as Süleyman the Magnificent, marched westward and, by August 1521, had taken Belgrade. That conquest exposed Vojvodina, Hungary, Slavonia, and Croatia to the Turks. Süleyman focused on the rest of Europe and in 1526, at the Battle of Mohács, killed King Louis II of Hungary. Only three years later, in September and October 1529, Süleyman went even further west and attacked Vienna, Austria.[4] The Holy Roman emperor, Charles V (r. 1519–1556); the pope; and Francis I of France (r. 1515–1547) were busy fighting each other. Ferdinand I (r. 1558–1564), brother of Charles V, held Vienna against the Turks,[5] otherwise Vienna would have been lost.

How serious were these Ottoman incursions into Europe for its political and religious situation? Ahmed Essa, writing with Otham Ali, attempts to minimize the scope of these invasions: "After Spain and Sicily, the Muslims made no further efforts at major conquest and expansion. This is important when judging the ensuing events involving the Muslims in Europe and the distorted views of their history."[6] The same writers maintain that the Europeans benefited from these invasions: "History is full of ironies. The European Christians, who most wanted to destroy Islam and the Muslim world, were the same people who benefited most from the achievements of Islamic civilization."[7] Although it is outside the scope of this chapter to ascertain whether and how European Christians benefited from Islamic civilization, at least some of the invaders saw their mission as something other than spreading Islamic civilization. At the University of Oxford's Ashmolean Museum, the following description is found on a talismanic shirt: "In an often-quoted letter written in the 1530s Hürrem Sultan urged her husband, the Ottoman Sultan Süleyman [r.1520–66], to wear the shirt she had dispatched to the battlefield as it would 'turn aside bullets' and protect him from death. Fabricated by a holy man inspired by a vision of the Prophet Muhammad himself, this powerful garment was explicitly intended to be worn in the cause of Islam, deriving its efficacy from the sacred names that decorated it."[8] Certainly these individuals saw the military expeditions as more than attempts to share culture with the Europeans.

Another source implies the Ottoman invasions of Europe were joint operations between Muslims and Christians. The title of the book *Two Faiths, One Banner: When Muslims Marched With Christians Across Europe's Battlegrounds*[9] argues that the Ottoman military forays were joint operations between Muslims and Christians. The author, Ian Almond, states the following:

> The whole point of this chapter will be to dismantle some of the myths concerning the Turkish march on Vienna, especially the manner in which it is enrolled into some form of East-West conflict between a Christian Europe and a Muslim Orient—an interpretation which is, in the end, nothing more than a Disney version of history. . . . Thousands of Greeks, Armenians and Slavs in the Ottomans' own armies who loyally fought for the sultan to the Transylvanian Protestants and disaffected peasants who, tired of the Catholic Habsburgs' yoke (or their own Hungarian aristocracy) moved over to the Turkish side.[10]

In most wars, armies pick up mercenaries and others, who may, at times, even fight against their own country. That, however, does not adequately explain Almond's point as if these military actions were joint operations. Croatian historian Rudolf Horvat points out that the Ottomans took back with them many prisoners. According to Horvat, in 1532 the sultan took fifty thousand Croats to Turkey and a few years later another sixty thousand prisoners from Slavonia (the region east of Zagreb and north of Bosnia).[11] Often the prisoners were youth who were trained as soldiers for the Ottoman Empire, and some became part of future invading armies.

Luther and his contemporaries lived in a Europe where the religious situation was unstable and, at the same time, was facing a powerful external adversary. When the Ottoman armies tried to take Vienna, they were only about 345 miles from Luther's city of Wittenberg. Luther's pilgrimage to Rome was nearly 900 miles. If he could travel that distance, surely Süleyman the Magnificent, should he succeed in taking Vienna, could travel another 375 miles to Wittenberg and other parts of Germany. Further invasions were real possibilities faced by Luther and his contemporaries.

Luther and Islam

With this background in mind, what did Luther write about the ongoing threat posed by the Ottoman Empire? As early as 1518, Luther stated, " 'To fight against the Turk is the same as resisting God, who visits our sin upon us with this rod.' "[12] Some held him "responsible both for the Turkish advance itself as well as for the unwillingness of many to resist the foe of Christendom."[13]

While Luther was concerned about the Turkish invasions, he was in some ways an indirect beneficiary of their military action. Emperor Charles V needed the support of the fragmented empire—the kings, the princes, the electors, and the bishops in order to mount a defense. Some of these rulers supported Luther, and he, to some extent, benefited from the Turkish invasions. Charles V, for example, needed the support of Frederick III (r. 1486–1525), the elector of Saxony and Luther's protector. If Charles V did not need the support of Frederick, Luther's fate at the Diet of Worms in 1521 may have been different. Francis I of France did not help the situation

> While Luther was concerned about the Turkish invasions, he was in some ways an indirect beneficiary of their military action.

and eventually entered into an alliance with the Turks. These were some of the complex issues facing Europe, and Luther specifically.

Luther's friends urged him to write on the topic; but other than making brief comments, he did not do so until 1528, which was two years after the decisive victory by the Ottoman forces at Mohács, Hungary. His most extensive piece on the topic, *On War Against the Turk*, was written by October 9, 1528, and printed on April 23, 1529,[14] just six months before Süleyman's siege on Vienna started. Luther addressed his treatise to Philip I of Hesse (1504–1567), who as a youthful ruler of seventeen supported Luther at Worms in 1521. This is the same Philip whose later bigamous marriage caused problems for Luther and the Protestant movement.[15] What are the main points of Luther's message?

It is not Luther's fault. Luther knows the urgency and is also upset that "some stupid preachers among us Germans . . . are making people believe that we ought not and must not fight against the Turks."[16] Luther rails against those who want the Turks to come and "rule because they think our German people are wild and uncivilized—indeed, that they are half-devil and half-man."[17] Without a doubt, Luther would not agree with a recent source, already quoted in this chapter, who states that "the European Christians . . . were the same people who benefited most from the achievements of Islamic civilization."[18] Finally, Luther lashes out against those who blame him "for every bad thing that happens in the world."[19]

The pope was not doing his work. Luther is upset because Pope Leo X (r. 1513–1521), who put Luther under the ban, condemned him for writing that fighting the Turk was the same as resisting God.[20] Luther acknowledges such a statement but claims that it was not fair to use it against him because the situation was different when he took the position.[21] At the time he wrote the pamphlet, Luther had no sympathy for the Turkish invasion for "the Turk certainly has no right or command to begin war and to attack lands that are not his."[22]

While the pope was criticizing Luther for his position about the Turks, Luther charges that the pope only "pretended to make war on the Turk."[23] According to Luther, the popes "used the Turkish war as a cover for their game and robbed Germany of money by means of indulgences."[24] As far as Luther was concerned, the pope and cardinals had many sources of income, such as vacant benefices, if they were serious about fighting the Turks.[25]

Luther not only criticizes the pope for not doing anything about the Turks, he also passes judgment on the character of the popes. According to Luther,

Pope Julius II (r. 1503–1513), the pontiff when Luther made his 1511 pilgrimage to Rome, was "a wicked iron-eater," and "half devil."[26] Some considered Pope Clement VII (r. 1523–1534), the pope at the time Luther wrote his treatise, "almost a god of war,"[27] but not Luther. As far as Luther is concerned, the "pope pays as little heed to the gospel or Christian faith as the Turk, and knows it as little."[28]

Who should fight the Turks? The editors of the English translation of *On War Against the Turk* provide a helpful summary. According to them, it is the "Christian, who by prayer, repentance, and reform of life takes the rod of anger out of God's hand and compels the Turk to stand on his own strength."[29] Luther writes that the Christian is to fight under the banner of the emperor and not under the banner of the bishop, the cardinal, or the pope.[30] He does not urge anyone to go against the Turks; but if they do, they first must repent "and be reconciled to God."[31]

The Christian is the first man to fight against the Turks, and the second is the emperor. Luther writes, "The second man who ought to fight against the Turk is Emperor Charles, or whoever may be emperor; for the Turk is attacking his subjects and his empire, and it is his duty, as a regular ruler appointed by God, to defend his own."[32] The emperor's role is to protect his people, and the fighting should be under the "emperor's command, under his banner, and in his name."[33] Luther laments that the emperor has been seen as the head of Christendom

> While there is not even a hint of theological approval of Islam, Luther is willing for them to believe and live as they wish.

and the protector of the church and the faith. He vehemently objects to this concept: "Not so! The emperor is not the head of Christendom or defender of the gospel or the faith. The church and the faith must have a defender other than emperor and kings. They are usually the worst enemies of Christendom and of the faith, as Psalm 2 [:2] says and as the church constantly laments."[34]

If the emperor was the defender of the faith and was to destroy non-Christians and unbelievers, the emperor "would have to begin with the pope, bishops, and clergy, and perhaps not spare us or himself."[35] The emperor should not fight the Turks because of their idolatry, for idolatry exists in his own empire. And then, to make certain that he does not leave out anyone, Luther takes a broad swipe because "there are entirely too many Turks, Jews, heathen, and non-Christians among us with open false doctrine and with offensive, shameful lives."[36] He wants the emperor to protect the people from the invading Turks; but as far as the faith of the Turks is concerned, Luther gives them freedom: "Let the Turk believe and live as he will, just as one lets the papacy and other false Christians live."[37] While there is not even a hint of theological approval of Islam, Luther is willing for them to believe and live as they wish.

Luther's view of Islam. In his treatise, Luther addresses the question of how to deal with the invasion by the Turks and who should respond to those invasions. In more detail and in stronger language, he gives an assessment of Islam, the Turkish faith.

Luther is familiar with the Koran, and he would like to translate it into German so that "everyone may see what a foul and shameful book it is."[38] While Christ is presented as a holy prophet, Christ is not recognized as the Savior of the world,[39] and that is not acceptable to Luther.

Luther objects strongly to Islam's view of government and marriage. According to him, the Turkish man is a destroyer and blasphemer who "ruins all temporal government and home life or marriage."[40] In his strongest indictment on marriage, he not only condemns the Turks but for good measure also includes the pope: "Since they [the pope and the Turks] think lightly of marriage, it serves them right that there are dog-marriages (and would to God they were dog-marriages), indeed, also 'Italian marriages' and 'Florentine brides' among them; and they think these things are good."[41]

Luther is never shy in expressing his views. What makes him use such strong and judgmental expressions about the Turks and at times adding the papacy? For Luther, it is not sufficient that the Turks praise "Christ and Mary as being the only ones without sin" and that Christ "is a holy prophet." The Turks, according to Luther, believe that Christ is *nothing* more than a prophet and that is not acceptable to him.[42] He acknowledges that the Turks allow the Christian belief in the resurrection to stand, but that is not enough for him. If that is the only article of belief allowed, then "Christ is no redeemer, savior, or king; there is no forgiveness of sins, no grace, no Holy Ghost." Everything is destroyed, he maintains, because "Christ is beneath Mohammed."[43]

Did Luther understand Islam's view of Christ? It seems that his assessments are accurate and that Islam's views of Christ have not changed. In a recent interview, Muslim theologian Zeki Saritoprak calls Jesus "one of the five [Noah, Abraham, Moses, Jesus, Muhammad] greatest messengers of God." Nevertheless, Saritoprak states, "But for Muslims, Jesus is neither God nor the Son of God." Saritoprak sees some hope: "By understanding who Jesus is in Islam, Christians might find common ground with Muslims."[44] It seems that Luther *did* understand Islam's view of Christ, and that view, according to Saritoprak, is still the same. It is because Luther understood Islam's view of Christ that he rejected it. It was not acceptable to him.

Luther's response to the Turks and Islam was theological, not political. The emperor had the responsibility to defend the empire, but Luther was interested in sharing the Christian faith with the Turks.

Luther's response to the Turks and Islam was theological, not political. The emperor had the responsibility to defend the empire, but Luther was interested in sharing the Christian faith with the Turks. He "seemed to have envisioned missionary work amongst Muslims being carried out discreetly through Christian prisoners and slaves of the Ottomans."[45] Yet, interestingly, about two years after he wrote his treatise on the Turks, Luther did not pursue "an opportunity for an audience with Süleyman in 1530 when a former member of the Habsburg ambassadorial party informed him that the Turkish sultan made friendly inquiries about the German Professor."[46] More than thirty years later, Hans von Ungnad, a convert to the Reformation faith, also wanted to bring Christianity to the Turks. His approach was a Serbian New Testament translation that was printed in Cyrillic. His goal was to distribute it to the Turks as far as Constantinople. Some contacts, though limited and few, were made with the Turks.[47]

Seventh-day Adventists and Islam

This book is a testimony to the fact that Luther has had a significant impact on Seventh-day Adventists. Adventists have a high view of Luther even though there are areas of disagreement. Luther is mentioned in Adventist literature more than any other Reformer. It is thus natural to compare the Adventist view on Islam with those of Luther. We will look at the Adventist view of Islam from two perspectives—the prophetic view and the mission view.

Prophetic view of Islam. From the earliest days, Seventh-day Adventists have emphasized biblical prophecies, especially those in Daniel and Revelation. While two of the denomination's websites, the Adventist Digital Library[48] and *Ministry,*[49] list numerous entries on Islam or Turkey in prophecy, we will review only two sources. W. A. Spicer (1865–1952), a church leader and author, addresses the issue of Turkey in one of his books. In reference to Daniel 11 and 12, Spicer rather cautiously refers to Turkey in connection with these prophecies.[50] Uriah Smith (1832–1903), a long-term editor and writer, authored interpretations on Revelation (1867) and Daniel (1873).[51] His commentaries on these apocalyptic books have been republished numerous times. His views on Turkey are more specific than those of Spicer. Smith, for example, held the position that the king of the north in Daniel 11:40 is Turkey.[52] According to Adam S. Francisco, Luther also referred to the prophecies of Daniel. According to Luther, the little "horn's [Daniel 7:8] blasphemous mouth was synonymous for the false teachings of Islam."[53]

Mission view of Islam. The missional response of Seventh-day Adventists to Islam reaches back to the earliest days of the church. W. A. Spicer gives a positive review of William Goodell's mission activity to Turkey in the early 1800s, even though Goodell was not an Adventist. According to a Boston University Web page, Goodell was ordained in 1822 and sent to Syria and the Holy Land under the auspices of the American Board of Commissioners for Foreign Missions. In 1831, he published an Armeno-Turkish New Testament. He moved to Constantinople, where he served until 1865.[54] According to Spicer, Goodell encountered major difficulties in Constantinople: "In 1839 the rage of the opposition had reached the point of uncontrollable fury. The Greek patriarch, the Armenian bishop, and the sultan, as caliph of the Moslem religion, joined to quench the little light of Protestant truth being kindled."[55]

Since the 1870s, Adventists have provided enormous human and financial resources to proclaim their message to the world, and that proclamation includes Muslims. In 1989, the church established the Seventh-day Adventist Global Centre for Islamic Studies. The first objective is "to study ways, means, methods, and approaches meaningful for willing Muslims in their varied cultural and social contexts."[56] The implementation has been governed by available opportunities in light of the fact that many areas are not open to Christianity or where Christianity faces major limitations.

Conclusion

Martin Luther left the matter of military incursions by the Turks for the emperor. Seventh-day Adventists are not facing the same situation, yet generally the church has not attempted to influence government functions, unless it or certain principles are directly impacted.

Martin Luther and Seventh-day Adventists have looked at Islam from a faith perspective. Luther was not willing to compromise theologically, and Seventh-day Adventists uphold their theological perspectives. They continue to believe that the Seventh-day Adventist message must be presented to all, and that includes Muslims. Luther hoped that Christian captives or slaves would share the gospel with the Turks. Adventists have attempted, through friendship and service, to share their message with Muslims. Mission is key to understanding Luther's response to Islam, and that is also true for Seventh-day Adventists.

---

1. It is difficult to be consistent in the use of the terms *Ottoman*, *Turk*, and *Islam*. Luther usually referred to the Turks; and for him, their faith was Islam. Even today, in some parts of Europe the word *Turk* is used for Muslims, even though these individuals are not Turks.

2. The conquest was complete even though Bosnia is rather mountainous and has numerous secluded villages. During a lecture tour in Bosnia in the fall of 2016, my wife, Ruth I. Satelmajer, and I toured some of these secluded villages that were supposedly the last ones to be conquered. The villages are located near Konjic, a small city between Mostar and Sarajevo. Some of these villages are only accessible via small one-lane mountain roads.

3. Today both areas are part of Bosnia and Herzegovina, with about 50 percent Muslims, 30

percent Serbs, and about 15 percent Croats. "Largest Ethnic Groups of Bosnia and Herzegovina," *World Atlas*, last modified March 16, 2017, http://www.worldatlas.com/articles/largest-ethnic -groups-of-bosnia-and-herzegovina.html.

4. *New World Encyclopedia*, s.v. "Siege of Vienna," accessed May 28, 2017, http://www.new worldencyclopedia.org/entry/Siege_of_Vienna.

5. Paula Sutter Fichtner, *Emperor Maximilian II* (New Haven, CT: Yale University Press, 2001), 2.

6. Ahmed Essa with Othman Ali, *Studies in Islamic Civilization: The Muslim Contribution to the Renaissance* (Herndon, VA: International Institute of Islam Thought, 2010), 37.

7. Essa and Ali, *Studies in Islamic Civilization*, 243.

8. Francesca Leoni and Christiane Gruber, *Power and Protection: Islamic Art and the Supernatural* (Oxford: Ashmolean Museum, 2016), 58.

9. Ian Almond, *Two Faiths, One Banner: When Muslims Marched With Christians Across Europe's Battlegrounds* (Cambridge, MA: Harvard University Press, 2009).

10. Ibid., 140.

11. Rudolf Horvat, *Povijest Grada Varaždin* (Varaždin: Hrvatska Akademija Znanosti I Umjetnosti, 1993), 67–69.

12. Martin Luther, introduction to *On War Against the Turk*, in *Luther's Works*, vol. 46, *The Christian in Society 3*, ed. Robert Schultz (St. Louis, MO: Concordia, 1967), 158. For the German text, see Martin Luther, *Vom Kriege wider den Türken*, in *D. Martin Luthers Werke: Kritische Gesamtausgabe*, vol. 30, bk. 2 (Weimar: Hermann Böhlau, 1909), 107–148. (My primary source and focus is this tract.)

13. Luther, *Luther's Works*, 46:158.

14. Ibid., 46:159.

15. Ibid., 46:161.

16. Ibid.

17. Ibid.

18. Essa and Ali, *Studies in Islamic Civilization*, 243.

19. Luther, *Luther's Works*, 46:161.

20. Ibid., 46:162.

21. Ibid.

22. Ibid., 46:170.

23. Ibid., 46:163.

24. Ibid., 46:164.

25. Ibid.

26. Ibid., 46:168.

27. Ibid., 46:169.

28. Ibid., 46:199.

29. Ibid., 46:159.

30. Ibid., 46:169.

31. Ibid., 46:184.

32. Ibid.

33. Ibid., 46:185.

34. Ibid.

35. Ibid., 46:186.

36. Ibid.

37. Ibid.

38. Ibid., 46:176.

39. Ibid.

40. Ibid., 46:195.

41. Ibid., 46:198. Luther is referring to homosexual unions.

42. Ibid., 46:176.

43. Ibid., 46:177.

44. Zeki Saritoprak, interview by Amy Frykholm, "Who Is Jesus for Muslims?" *Christian Century,* May 23, 2017, https://www.christiancentury.org/article/who-jesus-muslims.

45. Adam S. Francisco, *Martin Luther and Islam: A Study in Sixteenth-Century Polemics and Apologetics* (Leiden: Brill, 2007), 93.

46. Ibid., 94.

47. Nikolaus Satelmajer, "A Bold Sixteenth-Century Mission: The First New Testaments for Croats, Bosnians, Serbs, Bulgarians, and Turks" (STM thesis, Lutheran Theological Seminary at Philadelphia, 2014), 85ff. See also the other chapter in this book by the same author.

48. The Adventist Digital Library is available at https://www.adventistdigitallibrary.org.

49. *Ministry* is available at https://www.ministrymagazine.org. E. Robert Reynolds's seven-part series titled "The Challenge of Islam" was published in June–December 1972 in *Ministry, International Journal for Pastors.* This is just one example of the ongoing effort of Seventh-day Adventists to find ways of reaching the Muslim world with the Adventist message.

50. W. A. Spicer, *Beacon Lights of Prophecy* (Washington, DC: Review and Herald® Pub. Assn., 1935), 132, 133.

51. *The Seventh-day Adventist Encyclopedia,* Seventh-day Adventist Commentary Reference Series (Hagerstown, MD: Review and Herald® Pub. Assn., 1996), s.v. "Smith, Uriah."

52. Uriah Smith, *Daniel and the Revelation* (Nashville, TN: Southern Pub. Assn., 1944), 307.

53. Francisco, *Martin Luther and Islam,* 82.

54. David M. Stowe, "Goodell, William," in *Biographical Dictionary of Christian Missions,* ed. Gerald H. Anderson (New York: Macmillan Reference, 1998), 250, 251, quoted in "Goodell, William (1792–1867)," Boston University School of Theology, accessed May 30, 2017, http://www.bu.edu/missiology/missionary-biography/g-h/goodell-william-1792-1867/.

55. W. A. Spicer, *The Hand That Intervenes* (Washington, DC: Review and Herald® Pub. Assn., 1918), 327.

56. *The Seventh-day Adventist Encyclopedia,* Seventh-day Adventist Commentary Reference Series (Hagerstown, MD: Review and Herald® Pub. Assn., 1996), s.v. "Seventh-day Adventist Global Centre for Islamic Studies." In order to understand Islam and not relate to it in the context of mission, other resources have been made available. See, e.g., Hans Heinz and Daniel Heinz, *Das Christentum begegnet dem Islam: Eine relgiöse Herausforderung* (Zurich: Advent-Verlag, 2007).

CHAPTER 23

Anabaptists—the Forgotten People of the Reformation

Richard W. Müller

When talking about the Reformation, many remember three individuals—Luther, Calvin, and Zwingli. The Reformation was more than these individuals; it was a Reformation *movement* consisting of many individuals and groups. One of these groups, or realistically a number of groups, was the Anabaptist movement,[1] also known as the left wing of the Reformation or the Radical Reformation. Space does not permit an in-depth discussion on the "radicals" in this chapter. There were radicals who did not just want to change doctrines and religious practices but wanted to change medieval society, especially the serfdom of the peasants. These radical groups have little to do with the Anabaptist movement, which was a rather peaceful Reformation movement. There is, however, one radical incident associated with the Anabaptists, which I call the "Münster episode": in 1534–1535, some fanatical Anabaptists wanted to erect, even by force, the New Jerusalem in Münster, Westphalia. This group was defeated by joint Catholic and Lutheran forces.

Luther, unfortunately, did not distinguish between the radical groups who opposed his reform or other more peaceful Reformers.[2] He was also opposed to groups that, perhaps in a more consistent way, followed his dictum of *sola scriptura*—the Bible only. Luther's views were influenced by a confrontation he had with one of the more radical groups in 1521. After the famous Diet of Worms, he was hidden as a "prisoner" in the famous Wartburg Castle at the request of Luther's protector, Frederick the Wise. During his seclusion at the castle, "prophets" from the city of Zwickau arrived in Wittenberg to reform the town and the church in a radical way. Luther disguised himself and returned to Wittenberg (some 135 miles) to confront these "prophets" who appealed directly to divine revelation. Luther, on the other hand, appealed to the Word of God, the Bible. His experience with these individuals, who were not Anabaptists, made a lasting impression on him. Most Anabaptists did not have this revolutionary spirit. In general, they were much more peaceful; some even rejected all participation in war, and some were pacifists and believed in nonresistance.[3]

Anabaptist beginnings

Anabaptism started a few years after Luther's confrontation with the Zwickau prophets. On Saturday, January 21, 1525, at the house of Felix Mantz in Zurich, Switzerland, Georg Blaurock, a former priest, confessed his sins and then was baptized by Conrad Grebel, a layman. During the following week, thirty-five people were baptized in the nearby village of Zollikon. Shortly after, Wilhelm Reublin went to Waldshut, some twenty-five miles north of Zurich, and baptized one who became a famous Anabaptist leader, Balthasar Hubmaier, and sixty others. During the Easter season that same year, Hubmaier, in turn, baptized three hundred new converts. These events marked the beginning of the Anabaptist movement.

On Saturday, January 21, 1525, at the house of Felix Mantz in Zurich, Switzerland, Georg Blaurock, a former priest, confessed his sins and then was baptized by Conrad Grebel, a layman.

Anabaptists spread throughout western Europe, although they were concentrated in northern Switzerland, southern Germany, the Netherlands, Moravia, and Silesia. Increasingly, however, we have evidence that Anabaptism also had followers in other places, such as central Germany (especially Hesse and Thuringia), northern Germany (Emden, Hamburg, Glückstadt), and along the Baltic Sea (Lübeck, Wismar, Danzig, Elbing, Königsberg). Anabaptists eventually spread into Romania and Russia and, because of persecution, many emigrated to North America.

After Zwingli's fruitless disputations in 1525 with the future Anabaptists did not bear fruit, the Zurich magistrate came out against the Anabaptists. An order was issued that infants should be baptized as was done before, and parents who did not have their children baptized should leave the city and the canton.

Anabaptists refused to leave their homeland, and arrests followed. One slogan of the day expressed this with ghoulish humor: "The one who dips [baptizing believers] shall be dipped [by drowning]."

Felix Mantz, a Hebrew scholar in whose house the first baptism had taken place, was the first victim. In 1527, he was bound, taken in a boat out into the river Limmat near Lake Zurich, and thrown overboard. Conrad Grebel escaped a similar fate by dying a natural death in 1526. Balthasar Hubmaier, the early Anabaptist leader who was instrumental in baptizing three hundred people shortly after his own baptism, was burned at the stake in Vienna in 1528. Three days later his wife was drowned in the Danube. Georg Blaurock, the former priest and first to be baptized, died at the stake in 1529. Many others could be added to this list. These severe persecutions did not only happen in Catholic areas but also where sympathizers of Zwingli, Calvin, and Luther were in the majority. Even in Luther's city, Wittenberg, great pressure was put on those who did not let their babies be baptized. One such case was that of Luther's former co-Reformer and colleague Andreas Karlstadt. [4]

Anabaptists beliefs

Although often referred to as the Anabaptist movement, there is no central figure, like Luther, Zwingli, or Calvin, among Anabaptists. There were many leaders and many groups. Yet already in 1527, some Anabaptists met at Schleitheim in the canton of Schaffhausen, Switzerland, and agreed on seven basic articles of faith. These articles indicate not only the beliefs they held in common but also, to some degree, point to doctrines in which they differed from the other Reformers.

The first article concerned baptism. Anabaptists agreed that only those who believe, who have repented, and are willing to live a life of active discipleship should be baptized. This excluded all infant baptism.

The second article dealt with the "ban," or excommunication. Anabaptists believed that they were not perfect after they decided to follow Jesus and that a believer indeed could fall into sin. They believed that in such a case, as Jesus Christ Himself outlined (Matthew 18), the church should administer discipline.

The third article encapsulated their understanding of the Lord's Supper. They believed that the Lord's Supper was celebrated in remembrance of Christ's broken body. They objected to the Roman Catholic idea of the Mass—the changing of the bread and the wine into the real body and blood of Christ at the ministration of the priest. They also felt that Luther erred in placing so much emphasis on the real bodily presence of Christ in the elements.

The fourth article laid out their agreement that the believer should separate from the evil and the wickedness of this world. To them, this meant a withdrawal from "Babylon" and "earthly Egypt," under which designation they included "all popish and anti-popish works and church services, meetings and church attendance, drinking houses, civic affairs."[5]

The fifth article stated that pastors should be men of good report. Pastors should admonish and teach, warn and discipline, administer the Lord's Supper, and care for the members of the church.

The sixth article revealed that early Anabaptists believed in discipline. But Christians should go no further than administrating the ban—in other words, excommunicating people from their fellowship. They opposed the use of the sword against erring members. They opposed capital punishment as well, even in civil matters. This article also pointed out how difficult it was for a Christian to serve as a magistrate.

The seventh article dealt with the oath. Anabaptists believed that Christ forbade all swearing and oath taking. The Christian's word, Yes or No, should be enough.[6]

While various Anabaptist groups developed different confessions, the Schleitheim Confession is the best known and most widely used or adapted. It encapsulates in a nutshell the main beliefs that united Anabaptists together.

Identifying the true church

What is the church? Who belongs to the church, and what marks identify the true church? Early Anabaptists asked these questions even before they dealt with the matter of baptism. Their concept of baptism arose as a consequence of their understanding of the church.

The Anabaptists' belief about the church is often misapprehended. A correct understanding of the Anabaptists' concept of church is necessary in order to understand them. This chapter highlights one particular concept that slowly entered the church: the idea that whole groups of people—including whole nations—constitute the church. This was the basic understanding at the time of the Reformation. For example, Zwingli, in whose country the Anabaptists first appeared, wished to reform all of society, with its many different institutions. He wanted to establish a kind of theocratic "Alpine Israel" that would include every member of society. It was against this idea that the Anabaptists protested. For Anabaptists, the church should consist of individuals who repented and experienced conversion. These individuals were then baptized and joined the church as a voluntary act.

Unfortunately, the Peace of Augsburg in 1555 removed the importance of this connection within the Reformation. After that point, the prevailing position was *cujus regio, ejus religio*, or "whose realm, his religion." Not even the Calvinists were included in this agreement, let alone the Anabaptists.

Marks of the fallen church

The Anabaptists stood under the conviction that the church had fallen away from the truth and had to be radically reformed. According to their understanding, the major signs of the fallen church were as follows:

Church and state are unified in the fallen church. Religion became compulsory, but according to Anabaptists, churches are voluntary associations. Anabaptists were thus among the first to uphold religious liberty.

The fallen church engages in war. Church history is filled with accounts of Christians killing Christians; a thought unthinkable to most Anabaptists and hopefully also to Seventh-day Adventists. Anabaptists believed that Christians should be peacemakers and not engage in armed struggles of any kind. Many Anabaptists were therefore pacifists.

The fallen church celebrates the Mass. The Anabaptists were opposed to the Roman Catholic understanding that the bread and wine, by the words of the priest, changed into the real body and blood of Christ (transubstantiation). Neither did they accept that the Mass was a repetition of the offer of Christ. They were also opposed to the real presence of Christ in the Lord's Supper and thereby collided head-on with Martin Luther. For the Anabaptists, Christ offered Himself once and for all at the cross. The Lord's Supper for them was a commemoration of that unrepeatable event.

The baptism of infants. The Anabaptists maintained that the state church stands or falls with infant baptism. That is why they so vehemently opposed the state or fallen church.

The rise of the hierarchy. Anabaptists especially attacked the lust for power and wealth by church leaders. They wanted the freedom for believers to come together to worship God inwardly, instead of being engaged in long liturgies, outward ceremonies, and formal processions.

Marks of the true church

The Anabaptists wished to return to the apostolic church. They also considered the true church to be identifiable. Some of the signs are the opposites of the fallen church, and I will not repeat them. The following additional characteristics reveal the true church:

Scripture. The true church will always follow the example and teaching of the Scriptures, especially the New Testament.

Community. The Anabaptists held that the material goods that God had given should be shared freely with other believers, especially those who did not have anything because they were persecuted. Only some groups of Anabaptists, such as the Hutterites, went so far as to practice a kind of Christian communism, not only sharing everything with each other but also having a common production in established farms, the *Brüderhöfe* (Brethren Farms), as they called them.

Magistrates. Magistrates are called to chasten evil, even destroy the enemies of society, while Christians should love their enemies and pray for their persecutors. The Anabaptists' noninvolvement in politics and their aloofness from social life in general created many difficulties.

Great Commission. The true church fulfills the commission to go into the entire world and proclaim the gospel to all creatures. This was central to the Anabaptists' understanding of the true church. They believed that all Christians have received this commission, so they considered all as teachers and preachers. No provincial, national, or ecclesiastical boundaries should stop a person from fulfilling this command of the risen Lord. With the Anabaptists, as with other reform movements before them, we find a reawakening of the missionary spirit of the early church. On the other hand, the Lutheran Reformation in central Europe came more or less to a halt by the Peace of Augsburg in 1555, as mentioned above.[7]

Faith must precede baptism

The genuine Anabaptists considered it of fundamental importance that their understanding of baptism was founded on Jesus' teachings and example. They frequently quoted the text in which the resurrected Lord commissioned the disciples to proclaim the gospel throughout the world and baptize believers (Matthew 28:19).[8] The text makes it clear that one should teach before one baptizes. The Anabaptists felt that the sequence Jesus established should not be reversed. It was obvious to them that infants could not be taught the Christian truth, so quite naturally the Anabaptists believed that infants should not be baptized. They also appealed repeatedly to Mark 16:16: "He who believes and is baptized will be saved" (RSV). Here again they pointed to the order established: first faith, then baptism.

Martin Luther argued with the Anabaptists, asking how they could be sure that infants did not have faith. He felt rather strongly about this. He actually believed that he could prove from Scripture that infants have faith. In one of his treatises on rebaptism, he writes the following:

There are Scripture passages that tell us that children . . . can believe, though they do not speak or understand. So, Psalm 72 [106:37f.] describes how the Jews offered their sons and daughters to idols, shedding innocent blood. If, as the text says, it was innocent blood, then the children have to be considered pure and holy—this they could not be without spirit and faith. Likewise the innocent children whom Herod had murdered were not over two years of age [Matt. 2:16]. Admittedly they could not speak or understand. Yet they were holy and blessed. Christ himself says in Matt. 18 [19:14], "The kingdom of heaven belongs to children." And St. John was a child in his mother's womb [Luke 1:14] but, as I believe, could have faith.

. . . I am giving proof that your foundation for rebaptism is uncertain and false inasmuch as you cannot prove that there may not be faith in children. Inasmuch as John had faith, though he could not speak or understand, your argument fails, that children are not able to believe. To hold that a child believes, as St. John is an example, is not contrary to Scripture. If it is not contrary to the Scripture to hold that children believe, but rather in accord with Scripture, then your argument, that children cannot believe, must be unscriptural.[9]

Much time was used either to prove or defeat the argument of whether infants have faith or not. The Anabaptists even addressed the difficult question of original sin and infant baptism. Some Reformers argued that we receive forgiveness of original sin through the sacrament of baptism. If infants are not baptized, they will not be saved. Menno Simons responded with these words: "To teach and believe thus, my brethren, is first of all a dangerous idolatry and an abominable blasphemy against the blood of Christ. There is no remedy in heaven nor on earth for our sins, whether original or actual, other than the blood of Christ."[10]

According to Anabaptists, children who die before they are baptized are under the grace of God. Before they reach the age of discretion, even though they partake of Adam's transgression and sinful nature, God reckons them as being without sin. Forgiveness does not come through water but through the blood of Christ.

Sabbath reform

From the first book of the Bible to the last, the seventh day as a day of rest and worship should be celebrated. The Ten Commandments of God should be upheld as God's ideal for our lives. Unfortunately, changes to the Sabbath came after the apostolic church. Some historians attribute this change to the early to middle second century. Sunday—the day of the sun, the first day of the week, later called the day of the Lord, the day of Christ's resurrection—replaced the Sabbath, the seventh day of the week. With the civil Sunday law of Constantine the Great (A.D. 321), in honor of the venerable day of the sun, Sunday became a day of rest. During the whole of the Middle Ages, ecclesiastical and civil laws were added to protect the sacredness of Sunday, and they even forbade rest and worship on the biblical Sabbath. Sunday was seen more and more as the Sabbath, and both the religious and civil authorities tried to protect it.

At the famous debate in Leipzig in 1519 between Martin Luther and Catholic theologian Johann Eck, one of the points was about authority. Eck challenged Luther on the question of authority. Luther maintained that the Bible was the authority in questions of faith. Eck used the Sabbath-Sunday issue as an example: Luther with his *sola scriptura* had no right to keep Sunday since the Scripture only speaks about Sabbath. The church had, according to Eck, introduced Sunday and other holy days, including days in honor of the saints, without Scripture. They were introduced only by tradition, based on the authority that the Holy Spirit bestowed upon the church.[11]

This issue of authority by elevating tradition over Scripture was again discussed during the Council of Trent (1545–1563). A prime example concerned the Sabbath-Sunday issue. Participants at Trent argued that the authority of the church and tradition, even if against the clear instruction of Christ, introduced Sunday. The result of the council was made available in the famous catechism of the Catholic Church, *Catechismus Romanus* (the Roman Catechism).[12] On the basis of this catechism, the same argument can be found in later catechisms.

With Luther's *sola scriptura*, some Anabaptists tried to be consistent and started a Sabbath reform; that is, introducing, according to the Bible, the seventh-day Sabbath.[13] They were convinced that the Roman Catholic Church introduced Sunday. This church, both for Luther and the Anabaptists, was an anti-Christian institution and therefore, according to some Anabaptists, one should keep the biblical Sabbath and not Sunday.

Oswald Glait and Andreas Fischer, two Sabbatarian leaders who were former priests and scholars, wrote books on the subject, although unfortunately none are extant. The only reason these books are known to exist is because of the books written against them. Clear historical evidence exists that Glait and Fischer worked in Nikolsburg (Moravia), Austerlitz (Bohemia), Liegnitz (Silesia), and other cities and villages. These Sabbath-celebrating Anabaptist leaders died for their faith. Fischer was taken prisoner to the castle of Hôrka (Moravia) and thrown over the high wall of the castle (1539–1540). Glait met his

> These Sabbath-celebrating Anabaptist leaders died for their faith.

demise by drowning in the Danube after having been incarcerated for more than a year in Vienna (1546). These two leaders and many others lost their lives because they were bound by their conscience to be true to the Word of God rather than the words of men.[14]

Conclusion

Although Luther opposed the Anabaptists in general and also Sabbath keeping (for him, all days are equal), Luther did originate the principle of *sola scriptura* (the Bible only). Based upon this foundation, the Anabaptists set out to reform the church even further: with regard to the view of the church, believer's baptism, and for some, introducing Sabbath worship among other areas of faith. The Reformation must always continue because it is always a progressing movement.

1. Many books have been written about the Anabaptists. Some classic treatments include C. Henry Smith, *The Story of the Mennonites*, 4th ed., rev. and enl. ed., ed. C. Krahn (Newton, KS: Faith and Life Press, 1957); H. Penner, *Weltweite Bruderschaft: Ein Mennonitisches Geschichtsbuch*, 2nd ed. (Karlsruhe, Germay: Schneider, 1960); William R. Estep, *The Anabaptist Story* (Grand Rapids, MI: Eerdmans, 1963).

2. See, e.g., Walter Elliger, *Aussenseiter der Reformation: Thomas Müntzer* (Göttingen: Vandenhoeck and Ruprecht, 1975).

3. This is clearly expressed in a letter written in 1524 by the later Anabaptist leader Conrad Grebel and friends to Thomas Müntzer. This letter can be found in G. H. Williams and Angel M. Mergal, eds., *Spiritual and Anabaptist Writers: Documents Illustrative of the Radical Reformation*, Library of Christian Classics (London: SCM Press, 1957), 73–85. An extensive treatment of this problem can be found in John S. Oyer, *Lutheran Reformers Against Anabaptists: Luther, Melanchthon and Menius and the Anabaptists of Central Germany* (The Hague: Martinus Nijhoff, 1964).

4. You will find more details in the extensive works on Anabaptist sources: H. Böhmer, ed., *Urkunden zur Geschichte des Bauernkrieges und der Wiedertäufer* (Bonn: n.p., 1921); Gustav Bossert, *Quellen zur Geschichte der Wiedertäufer, vol. 1, Herzogtum Württemberg* (Leipzig: M. Heinsius Nachfolger, 1930); G. Franz, ed., *Wiedertäuferakten, 1527–1626* (Marburg: N.G. Elwert, 1951); Horst W. Schraepler, *Die rechtliche Behandlung der Täufer in der deutschen Schweiz, Südwestdeutschland und Hessen, 1525–1618* (Tübingen: E. Fabian-Verlag, 1957); R. Wolkan, *Geschichtsbuch der Hutterischen Brüder* (Vienna: n.p., 1923).

5. J. C. Wenger, trans., "The Schleitheim Confession of Faith, 1527," *Mennonite Quarterly Review*, 19, no. 4 (October 1945): 247–253.

6. John H. Leith, ed., *Creeds of the Churches: A Reader in Christian Doctrine From the Bible to the Present* (Louisville, KY: John Knox Press, 1973), 281ff.

7. For those who want to study the understanding of the church among Anabaptists in more detail, see F. H. Littell, *The Anabaptist View of the Church: A Study in the Origins of Sectarian Protestantism*, 2nd ed. (Boston, MA: Beacon Hill, 1958). I have depended on this book for much of my description of the Anabaptist view of the church. Also helpful for this chapter were J. L. Burkholder, "The Anabaptist Vision of Discipleship," in *The Recovery of the Anabaptist Vision: A Sixtieth Anniversary Tribute to Harold S. Bender*, ed. G. F. Hershberger (Scottdale, PA: Herald Press, 1957), 135–137; J. D. Graber, "Anabaptism Expressed in Missions and Social Service," in *The Recovery of the Anabaptist Vision: A Sixtieth Anniversary Tribute to Harold S. Bender*, ed. G. F. Hershberger (Scottdale, PA: Herald Press, 1957), 152–166; and Robert Kreider, "The Anabaptists and the State," *The Recovery of the Anabaptist Vision: A Sixtieth Anniversary Tribute to Harold S. Bender*, ed. G. F. Hershberger (Scottdale, PA: Herald Press, 1957), 180–193. Also of great interest is Menno Simons's *Reply to Gellius Faber*, especially chap. 4, "The Church," in *The Complete Writings of Menno Simons, c. 1496–1561*, trans. Leonard Verduin, ed. John C. Wenger (Scottdale, PA: Herald Press, 1966), 734–759

8. All of the major Reformers wrote on the subject of baptism, mostly in order to defend infant baptism and oppose believer's baptism. Many Anabaptists also wrote on the topic. Balthasar Hubmaier was persuasive, and his writings influenced many. His main tracts on baptism are *Von*

der christlichen Taufe der Gläubigen (1526); *Ein Gespräch auf Zwinglis Taufbüchlein* (1525–1526); *Von dem Kindertauf* (1525–1526; *Eine Form zu Taufen* (1526–1527). He also speaks about baptism in other writings, especially in his last work, *Eine Rechenschaft des Glaubens* (1528). All these tracts are published in Gunnar Westin and Torsten Bergsten, eds., *Balthasar Hubmaier: Schriften*, vol. 9, Quellen zur Geschichte der Täufer (Gütersloh: Gerd Mohn, 1962).

Menno Simons's works *On Christian Baptism* (1539) and chap. 3, "Baptism," in *Reply to Gellius Faber* are also important. They can be found in *The Complete Writings of Menno Simons*. A more extended discussion on the Anabaptists' understanding of baptism can be found in Estep, *The Anabaptist Story*, 150–178. This is, of course, only one chapter of the extensive literature that is available.

9. Martin Luther, "Concerning Rebaptism" (1528), in *Luther's Works*, vol. 40, *Church and Ministry 2*, trans. and ed. Conrad Bergendoff (Philadelphia, PA: Fortress, 1958), 242.

10. *The Complete Writings of Menno Simons*, 244.

11. See the works of Johann Eck, *Enchiridion, Handbüchlinn gemayner stell un[d] Artickel, der yetz schwebenden neuwen leeren* (1530); *Vierhundertundvier Artikel zum Reichstag von Augsburg* (1530).

12. See *Catechismus Romanus* (first Latin ed.: 1566); *Römischer Katechismus* (first German ed.: Dillengen, 1568); *The Catechism for the Curats, Compos'd by the Decree of the Council of Trent, and Published by Command of Pope Pius the Fifth* (first English ed.: London, 1687).

13. The presence of Sabbatarian Anabaptists during the time of the Reformation is attested by Erasmus, Luther, and Calvin. See the original sources in Daniel Augsburger, "The Sabbath and Lord's Day During the Middle Ages," in *The Sabbath in Scripture and History*, ed. Kenneth Strand (Washington, DC: Review and Herald® Pub. Assn., 1982), 209, 214n149. Of interest are also "four lists of so-called sects" from the last part of the sixteenth century. The list contains up to forty groups who differed in faith with the Roman Church. Here are those who keep the Sabbath, the so-called Sabbatarians, listed as number three after "Lutherans" and "Calvinists" and on a list of Anabaptist groups as the fourth in number. See Gerhard F. Hasel, "Sabbatarian Anabaptists of the Sixteenth Century: Part 1," *Andrews University Seminary Studies* 5, no. 2 (1967): 101, 102, 107.

14. For an extensive discussion of the Sabbath-Sunday issue by Luther, Calvin, Karlstadt, and the Anabaptists, please refer to my doctoral dissertation where you will also find references to primary sources. Richard Müller, *Adventisten—Sabbat—Reformation* (Lund: Gleerup, 1979); Richard Müller, *Adventisten—Sabbat—Reformation*, 2nd rev. ed. (Daugaard: Lux Lucet, 2014), 45–145.

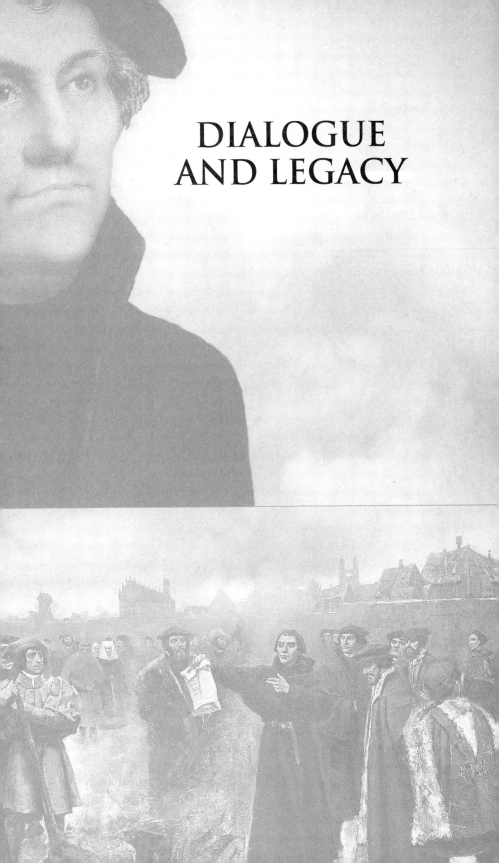

DIALOGUE
AND LEGACY

CHAPTER 24

Luther and Images

Daniel Wildemann

M artin Luther was a man of the Word: the Word of God was the driving force and the very center of his theology. "That word above all earthy powers," he composed in his famous hymn, "A Mighty Fortress" (1529). His famous *sola scriptura* principle is well documented in the 127 volumes and 80,000 pages of the Weimar (German) edition of his writings. It is, therefore, not a surprise that comparatively little has been written about Luther's approach to images. Nevertheless, his approach can inform those who wrestle with the proclamation of the Word in a *sola pictura* society dominated by visual media. How do we balance, if at all, the Word and image? Luther's approach, unparalleled by Zwingli or Calvin, was developed out of his controversy with Andreas Bodenstein von Karlstadt (1486–1541), and it provides some intriguing answers.

> M artin Luther was a man of the Word: the Word of God was the driving force and the very center of his theology.

Iconoclasm at Wittenberg

While Luther wrestled with the German translation of the New Testament during his Wartburg Castle exile in early 1522, he received word that in his beloved city of Wittenberg iconoclasm was under way. The destruction of images was spearheaded by Karlstadt, Luther's friend and colleague, who was a "substitute" Reformer during Luther's seclusion at Wartburg Castle. Under Karlstadt's leadership, the followers of the Wittenberg Reformation stormed into the churches and destroyed the images.

It was Karlstadt's moment of glory, and he felt compelled to push forward the Reformation in Wittenberg with great speed. On Christmas 1521, he held the Communion service in German and not Latin; he handed the cup to "unworthy" laity and did not reserve it for the priest only; and finally, did not wear the priestly cassock. All three of these practices were unheard of at the time. On January 19, 1522, he broke his celibacy and married Anna of Mochau, the daughter of a poor nobleman.[1] A month later, in February 1522, he published his programmatic tract *On the Removal of Images*,[2] which was a call for revolution. Its radical ideas were not only heard and felt in Wittenberg but soon spread over Germany and were even echoed in Switzerland,[3] where Zwingli and later Calvin encouraged the removal of religious images by invoking that they were forbidden by God.

Before the publication of *On the Removal of Images*, Karlstadt appealed, without success, to the authorities of Wittenberg in this matter. Bemoaning that "there was no execution,"[4] he concluded he had to take matters into his own hands. According to him, the believer should free the house of God of the "*Ölgötzen*" (painted idols), as he called the statues. His aim was to remove *all* images—wood, stone, crucifixes, altarpieces, and paintings. In his exegesis on Exodus 20:1–5, he concludes, "Our images have no foundation in God, for God forbade them."[5] He lets God Himself ask the believers: "How can you be so bold and cheeky, that you bow down and bend yourself in front of images in My house, which were created by the hand of a man?"[6] The "idol kisser" has no support in the Bible for this practice; and Gregory the Great (c. 540–604) erred by stating, "Pictures were the layman's Bible."[7] Karlstadt points out that Christ did not say, "My sheep see My pictures," for the true sheep follow the voice of their Shepherd (John 10:27). These "false Gods" cannot accomplish anything that benefits the Christian. Therefore, these "devils' heads" need to be "pulverized, knocked off . . . and be broken,"[8] just as they were during the times of the prophets. Karlstadt's words were not unanswered. Just about the time the Wittenberg Council reached out to Luther at Wartburg Castle, iconoclasm exploded in Wittenberg.

Luther restores order through a series of sermons

Luther—very much against the advice of his protector, Frederick the Wise (1463–1525)—returned to Wittenberg during the first week of March 1522. He left his "last conclave"[9] and returned to Wittenberg as the minister and pastor, thus answering the call to take care of the "sheep without a shepherd" (Isaiah 13:14, NIV) and guide them "along the right paths" (Psalm 23:3, NIV). Miraculously, Luther was able to calm the people's spirits, reach their hearts, de-escalate the state of affairs, and restore order in Wittenberg within a week. How did he do it? He did it through the preaching of the Word. He preached a series of sermons during the week of March 9–16, 1522, that became known as the Invocavit sermons. Luther addressed all of Karlstadt's reform ideas. The second and the fourth sermons addressed the issue of images.

Karlstadt was banned from the pulpit, and Luther enforced a censorship and forfeiture of his writings. At first, Luther tried to win back his friend Karlstadt, but he parted with him at the latest in 1525, when he addressed his book *Against the Heavenly Prophets in the Matter of Images and Sacraments* directly at the "pretentious prophet,"[10] as he then called Karlstadt. The Reformer was quite surprised that he needed to address these issues again after 1522: "There has been a change in the weather. I had almost relaxed and thought the matter was finished; but then it suddenly arises anew."[11] Luther challenges Karlstadt to write freely and attack Luther boldly, if he had anything to say for himself.[12] Karlstadt did not attack back; Luther triumphed in 1528, proclaiming that his treatise was still "unbitten," as he wrote in a marginal note of his copy.

What then was Luther's position on images?

What then was Luther's position on images? To answer this question we turn to his Invocavit sermons of March 1522 and *Against the Heavenly Prophets in the Matter of Images and Sacraments* from the year 1525.

Luther on images

Luther felt forced to develop a theological answer to the issue of images and idolatry. It is a pattern that repeated itself with the Reformer in other theological questions as well (e.g., the Eucharist). In this sense, it is true that Luther was not a systematic, but rather a pragmatic theologian. His theology was born from concrete situations, be they internal or external. He addressed Karlstadt's reforms and, in particular, the issue of whether images should be allowed, whether they should be banned, and/or whether they pose a threat to the believer.

The *Wörterbuch zu Martin Luthers deutschen Schriften* (dictionary of Dr. Martin Luther's German writings) lists several usages of *image*. Most prominent is the three-dimensional artwork (statue or ornamental column). The painting, as a flat, two-dimensional drawing, follows this. Then comes the metaphoric "outward and inward appearance" (cf. Genesis 5:3; 1 Corinthians 15:49), the type or the parable, and finally the theological anthropological "likeness" and "counterpart" of God (Genesis 1:26). Luther was certain that "man must be an image, either God's or the devil's."[13]

Somewhat surprisingly, Luther actually complimented Karlstadt's concern: "I would not have gone so far as you have done, if I had been here. What you did was good, but you have gone too fast. For there are also brothers and sisters on the other side who belong to us, and must still be won."[14] But at the same time, Luther was concerned about the order of things and asked Karlstadt, "You say it was right according to the Scriptures. I agree, but what becomes of order? For it was done in wantonness, with no regard to proper order and with offense to your neighbor."[15] The *how* mattered a great deal to Luther, and in his sermons he urges believers not to forget that "love is the captain"[16] or they will behave as the "children of wrath" (Ephesians 2:3). Furthermore, he stated that before God every believer is responsible for himself and to his or her neighbor. The believer must be patient with the weak, whom God wants to redeem too. He stated that two things were necessary: "Thus there are two things: the one, which is the most needful, and which must be done in one way and no other; the other, which is a matter of choice and not of necessity, which may be kept or not, without endangering faith or incurring hell. In both, love must deal with our neighbor in the same manner as God has dealt with us."[17] Images to Luther were clearly included in the second category. He regarded them as "a matter of choice and not of necessity." Although Luther did not develop a "theology" regarding images, he clearly established a principle that may be considered a *pragmatic* approach in dealing with religious imagery. And this was rather brilliant, because it took the wind out of Karlstadt's arguments, which focused on the "must not" only. Luther argued that the medium itself was neutral of any theological leaning: it was "neither evil nor good, we may have them or not, as we please."[18] Therefore, one must leave the conscience free from these "made-up sins."[19] He states, "The Scriptures set the consciences of men free, and forbid that they be taken captive with the doctrines of men. The doctrines of men take captive the conscience."[20]

Against constraint and the use of force

For Luther, the issue of using images was about balance. He warned the believers to stray "neither to the left nor to the right"[21] and passionately fought against Karlstadt's banning of the images. "In conclusion: I will preach it, teach it, write it, but I will constrain no man by force, for faith must come freely without compulsion."[22]

Not even the Reformer could coerce people to turn their hearts to God: "For I can drive no man to heaven with a club."[23] "I cannot, nor should I, force any one to have faith. That is God's work alone, who causes faith to live in the heart. Therefore we should give free course to the Word, and not add our works to it."[24] God cannot tolerate that "they wished to make a 'must' out of that which is free."[25] After all, even when Saint Paul was in Athens amid the pagan idols, he "did not destroy one of them by force."[26] (See Acts 17:16–34.) Paul, according to Luther, "did not touch any one of them even with his foot."[27] How much more should the Christian act accordingly? On a different occasion, Luther depicted Paul as the "true painter and carver,"[28] for he was able to capture the hearts of his audience through the Word, and the images lost their harm for humankind.[29]

In regard to the same matter, Luther concludes, images must be destroyed in the hearts and minds through the proper means of preaching and should not merely be removed: "For when they are no longer in the heart, they can do no harm when seen with the eyes."[30] "I approached the task of destroying images by first tearing them out of the heart through God's Word and making them worthless and despised."[31] Karlstadt, Luther maintains, put the emphasis on formalities: "And this forcing and commanding results in a mere mockery, an external show, a fool's play, man-made ordinances, sham-saints and hypocrites."[32]

In 1525, Luther concluded that Karlstadt had deserted the movement and had become the movement's "worst enemy."[33] Luther called him a false spirit, because he and his followers replaced "the highest with the lowest, the best with the least, the first with the last."[34] All should recognize Karlstadt's true intentions because he was "silent concerning the great and significant articles" and instead he inflated "the least significant ones as if the salvation of the world depended more on them than on Christ himself."[35] And this was Luther's key point, that he was able to put things back into proportion by focusing on the *necessary* (salvation of Christ, the Word), while at the same time not turning a blind eye on the actual abuse of images—a practice of which he was very aware: "I wish they were abolished everywhere because they are abused,—it is useless to deny it. For whoever places an image in a church, imagines he has performed a service unto God and a good work, which is downright idolatry."[36] He took on the fight eagerly—"I who do destroy images outwardly and inwardly"[37]— but strongly objected to any kind of prohibition. He argued, "Again, wine and women bring many a man to misery and make a fool of him. Shall we, therefore, kill all the women and pour out all the wine? Again, gold and silver cause much evil, shall we, therefore, condemn them? Nay, if we would drive away our one worst enemy, who does us the most harm, we would have to kill ourselves, for we have no greater enemy than our own heart. . . . And what good would that do us?"[38] Luther opposes condemnation as it may be of no use to others: "For I cannot deny that it is possible to find some one to whom images are useful."[39]

Luther's response to Karlstadt and the iconoclasts is deeper though than offering a quick and pragmatic solution. For him, the basic problem is this: *the one who prohibits images, sets up new images.* "Such legalism results in putting away outward images while filling the heart with idols."[40] Karlstadt, Luther maintains, actually provoked the opposite of what he was intending. Luther mocked that Karlstadt wanted "to paint the devil black, but forgot the charcoal and used chalk."[41]

The teaching and preaching image

Thomas Erne points out that the Reformation did not develop any "new symbols" but rather a "new approach towards the symbols."[42] According to Werner Hofmann, this approach impacted all art that followed: "What an image is all about, what it tells, what it means, is decided within the recipient. The artwork becomes an offer that completes itself within the viewer, if it is not at all constructed there. . . . All this started with Luther."[43] Church historian Hellmut Zschoch made the profound observation that Luther ultimately moved the place of the images "from the church into the book . . . and thus into the homes and schools."[44] This was true for the September Testament, which was published in 1522 with twenty-one full-page woodcuts in Revelation. In the complete Luther Bible of 1534, Lucas Cranach the Elder (1472–1553), the "founder of protestant iconography,"[45] provided the woodcuts.

Luther sensed the importance of images and the invention of the printing press in particular. In one of his *Table Talks*, he labeled the art of book printing as God's "final and greatest gift" and an "inextinguishable flame" through which the true faith will be proclaimed in every language to all the world.[46] No wonder that "everything Luther wrote was printed, down to the most trivial leaflet."[47] According to a recent source, Luther collaborated with numerous Wittenberg printers.[48] As for images, the Reformer saw great educational potential in the use of images: "What harm would it do if one would have the most important stories of the Bible, one after the other, painted into a small booklet?"[49] That might explain why his little *Prayer Book* of 1529 had fifty woodcuts, so that the children might learn from it. But Luther's use of pictures did not stop there.

Propagandistic images in the Reformation

During the Reformer's lifetime, many portraits of Luther circulated that were designed by numerous artists. This was impressively demonstrated in the 2015 exhibition, *Cranach, Luther und die Bildnisse*, at Wartburg Castle.[50] The youngest depiction of Luther by Wolfgang Stöckel is from 1519.[51] From 1520 on, Luther was portrayed in a variety of situations: one time as a fasting monk, another as an academic wearing the professor's cap, then as the bearded knight "Junker Jörg," as Saint George in his study, or with a halo and a descending dove over his head. Hans Holbein's woodcut from around 1519 even showed Luther as the infamous *Hercules Germanicus,* beating to death his enemies with a club.

Then there is an entire, and in many respects, distasteful body of artwork of mocking caricatures against the papacy and other personal enemies of Luther, which were occasionally commissioned by Luther.[52] He was very much aware that the image was no less effective than the tract.[53]

One of the most prominent Protestant examples of iconography is the *Passional Christi und Antichristi* of 1521 (*Passion Book of Christ and Antichrist*). It was illustrated with twenty-six woodcuts, and it had comments by Philip

Melanchthon. The passion book contrasted Christ's humility and meekness on one hand with the pride and presumptuousness of the papacy. With its publication, the Reformers clearly had in mind to tear down the kingdom of the antichrist and thus to establish the kingdom of Christ.[54]

Summary and Adventist legacy

In moving the image "from the church into the book,"[55] the Wittenberg Reformers also merged the medium of the Word with the image. However, the Word of God remained the organizing principle to *any* use of images. Luther was aware of the possibility of abuse; but at the same time, he maintained that images must remain free because they can be used rightly too.

Luther used images—and the new technology of the printing press—to preach, teach, and write, as he put it, albeit without constraint and any force, "for faith must come freely without compulsion."[56] At best, the Reformer used images as "graphical sermons"; at worst, he spread religious propaganda. Luther's condoning of propagandistic uses of images for his own cause could also be seen as characteristic for his "age of ruffians."

The founding fathers of the Reformed church, Zwingli and Calvin, went beyond Luther. They saw only idolatry in the use of images and thus rejected all images, arguing that there was no scriptural foundation for this practice. This fundamental distrust toward images is hardwired into the DNA of most denominations influenced by the Reformed tradition and remains influential even among Seventh-day Adventists.

Although Seventh-day Adventists were never prone to iconoclasm, they did not see the need to develop a systematic approach to the use of images. Adventists have been following the Reformed-Calvinistic tradition, whose "empty altar table, empty apse, empty walls are demonstrating the consequences of a Reformed zeal against images."[57]

On the other hand, Adventists agree with Luther's emphasis on the Word (*sola scriptura*) and certainly in their use of pictures and graphics for educational purposes. They share Luther's intuition to illustrate the symbolic language of the book of Revelation, as Luther did in his September Testament of 1522. Adventists, of course, extended this approach to the symbols in the book of Daniel and thus developed a rather idiosyncratic, but unique apocalyptic iconography. The question for Seventh-day Adventism today is this: will Adventists be able

Adventists, of course, extended this approach to the symbols in the book of Daniel and thus developed a rather idiosyncratic, but unique apocalyptic iconography. The question for Seventh-day Adventism today is this: will Adventists be able to update their repertoire of visual communication for a twenty-first-century *sola pictura* society?

to update their repertoire of visual communication for a twenty-first-century *sola pictura* society? Or will they remain steadfast in their decorative approach, which hardly exceeds what Francis A. Schaeffer called, in regard to evangelical art, "a very romantic Sunday school art"?[58] There is a far greater potential for religious visual communication than the church imagines—for *images are free.*

1. Luther married the runaway nun Katharina von Bora (1499–1552) on June 13, 1525.

2. The German title is *Von der Abthung der Bilder* (Wittenberg, 1522).

3. There were two major iconoclastic riots in Switzerland: one in 1523 in Zwingli's Zurich, and the other in 1535 in Calvin's Geneva.

4. Andreas Bodenstein von Karlstadt, *Von abtuhung der Bylder* (Wittenberg, 1522), 24 (translation by author), last modified June 18, 2014, https://de.wikisource.org/wiki/Von_abtuhung_der_Bylder.

5. Ibid., 12 (translation by author).

6. Ibid., 4 (translation by author).

7. Ibid., 8 (translation by author).

8. Ibid., 23, 24 (translation by author).

9. Richard Friedenthal, *Luther: Sein Leben und seine Zeit* (Munich: Piper, 2005), 361 (translation by author).

10. Martin Luther, *D. Martin Luthers Werke: Kritische Gesamtausgabe*, vol. 18 (Weimar: Hermann Böhlau, 1908), 63.

11. Martin Luther, *Luther's Works*, vol. 40, *Church and Ministry 2*, ed. Conrad Bergendoff (St. Louis, MO: Concordia, 1958), 79. Luther, *D. Martin Luthers Werke*, 18:62. The German text reads, "Da geht ein neu Wetter her. Ich hatte mich schier zur Ruhe gesetzt und gemeint, es wäre ausgestritten, da hebts überhaupt erst an."

12. Luther, *D. Martin Luthers Werke*, 18:37. The German text reads, "Frisch her, habt ihr etwas, so schreibt's frei heraus. . . . Je tapferer ihr mich angreift, je lieber ihr mir sein sollt."

13. *Wörterbuch zu Martin Luthers deutschen Schriften*, comp. Philipp Dietz (Hildesheim: Olms, 1997), s.v. "Bild" (translation by author).

14. Martin Luther, *Works of Martin Luther With Introductions and Notes*, vol. 2 (Philadelphia, PA: A. J. Holman, 1915), 393. Martin Luther, *D. Martin Luthers Werke: Kritische Gesamtausgabe*, vol. 10, bk. 3 (Weimar: Hermann Böhlau, 1905), 7.

15. Luther, *Works of Martin Luther*, 394. Luther, *D. Martin Luthers Werke*, vol. 10, bk. 3, 9.

16. Luther, *Works of Martin Luther*, 407. Luther, *D. Martin Luthers Werke*, vol. 10, bk. 3, 30. The German text reads, "Dass Liebe der Hauptmann ist."

17. Luther, *Works of Martin Luther*, 397.

18. Luther, *Works of Martin Luther*, 409. Luther, *D. Martin Luthers Werke*, vol. 10, bk. 3, 35.

19. Luther, *D. Martin Luthers Werke*, 18:74.

20. Luther, *Works of Martin Luther*, 454.

21. Luther, *Works of Martin Luther*, 397. Luther, *D. Martin Luthers Werke*, vol. 10, bk. 3, 14.

22. Luther, *Works of Martin Luther*, 399. Luther, *D. Martin Luthers Werke*, vol. 10, bk. 3, 18.

23. Luther, *Works of Martin Luther*, 401. Luther, *D. Martin Luthers Werke*, vol. 10, bk. 3, 21.

24. Luther, *Works of Martin Luther*, 398.

25. Luther, *Works of Martin Luther*, 404. Luther, *D. Martin Luthers Werke*, vol. 10, bk. 3, 26.

26. Luther, *Works of Martin Luther*, 399. Luther, *D. Martin Luthers Werke*, vol. 10, bk. 3, 17.

27. Luther, *Works of Martin Luther*, 399. Luther, *D. Martin Luthers Werke*, vol. 10, bk. 3, 17.

28. *Wörterbuch zu Martin Luthers deutschen Schriften*, s.v. "Bildschnitzer" (translation by author).

29. Luther, *D. Martin Luthers Werke*, vol. 10, bk. 3, 17.

30. Luther, *Luther's Works*, 40:84. Luther, *D. Martin Luthers Werke*, 18:67.

31. Luther, *Luther's Works*, 40:84. Luther, *D. Martin Luthers Werke*, 18:67.

32. Luther, *Works of Martin Luther*, 398. Luther, *D. Martin Luthers Werke*, vol. 10, bk. 3, 15, 16.

33. Luther, *Luther's Works*, 40:79. Luther, *D. Martin Luthers Werke*, 18:62.

34. Luther, *Luther's Works*, 40:83. Luther, *D. Martin Luthers Werke*, 18:67.

35. Luther, *Luther's Works*, 40:84. Luther, *D. Martin Luthers Werke*, 18:66, 67.

36. Luther, *Works of Martin Luther*, 407. Luther, *D. Martin Luthers Werke*, vol. 10, bk. 3, 31.

37. Luther, *Luther's Works*, 40:85.

38. Luther, *Works of Martin Luther*, 408. Luther, *D. Martin Luthers Werke*, vol. 10, bk. 3, 33, 34.

39. Luther, *Works of Martin Luther*, 409. Luther, *D. Martin Luthers Werke*, vol. 10, bk. 3, 34.

40. Luther, *Luther's Works*, 40:85. Luther, *D. Martin Luthers Werke*, 18:68.

41. Luther, *Works of Martin Luther*, 409. Luther, *D. Martin Luthers Werke*, vol. 10, bk. 3, 36.

42. Thomas Erne, "Ikonische Performanz: Luther und die Folgen für die Kunst der Gegenwart," *Luther* 82, no. 1 (2011): 6 (translation by author).

43. Werner Hofmann, *Luther und die Folgen für die Kunst* (Munich: Prestel-Verlag, 1983), 46 (translation by author). The original German text reads, "Was ein Bild ist, was es aussagt, was es bedeutet, entscheidet sich im Betrachter. Das Kunstwerk wird zu einem Angebot, das sich im Rezipienten vollendet, wenn nicht überhaupt erst konstituiert. . . . Alles das hat mit Luther begonnen."

44. Hellmut Zschoch, "Gefahr und Nutzen der Bilder," *Luther* 86, no. 1 (2015): 6 (translation by author).

45. Berthold Hinz, *Lucas Cranach der Ältere* (Reinbek: Rowohlt, 1993), 170, quoted in P. H. Unterreiner, *Reformation und Medien: Propaganda in Zeiten des Buchdrucks* (Norderstedt: GRIN Verlag, 2013), 20 (translation by author).

46. Martin Luther, quoted in *Buch und Reformation: Beiträge zur Buch—und Bibliotheksgeschichte Mitteldeutschlands im 16. Jahrhundert*, ed. Enno Bünz, (Leipzig: Evangelische Verlagsanstalt, 2014), 25 (translation by author). The original German text reads, "Die Buchdruckerkunst ist die letzte und zugleich größte Gabe, denn durch sie sollte nach Gottes Willen dem ganzen

Erdkreis die Sache der wahren Religion am Ende der Welt bekannt und in allen Sprachen verbreitet werden. Sie ist die letzte unauslöschliche Flamme der Welt."

47. Richard Friedenthal, *Luther: His Life and Times* (New York: Harcourt, Brace, and Jovanovich, 1970), 213.

48. Cf. Stefan Oehmig, ed., *Buchdruck und Buchkultur im Wittenberg der Reformationszeit* (Leipzig: Evangelische Verlagsanstalt, 2016).

49. Martin Luther, *D. Martin Luthers Werke: Kritische Gesamtausgabe*, vol. 10, bk. 2 (Weimar: Hermann Böhlau, 1907), 458 (translation by author). The original German text reads, "Was könnte es also schaden, wenn jemand die wichtigsten Geschichten der ganzen Bibel nacheinander in ein Büchlein malen ließe?"

50. Günter Schuchardt, *Cranach, Luther und die Bildnisse: Thüringer Themenjahr "Bild und Botschaft"* (Regensburg: Schnell and Steiner, 2015). This exhibition was held at Wartburg Castle, April 2–July 10, 2015.

51. Ibid., 55.

52. See also Daniel Wildemann, "The Use of Images in a Sola Scriptura Movement: Single Leaf Woodcuts in the German Reformation" (MA thesis, Andrews University, 2005), 50–101.

53. Friedenthal, *Luther: Sein Leben und seine Zeit*, 355.

54. The contrasting juxtaposition (comparison of the new and the old faith, of the right and the wrong one) can be seen as a prototype of Protestant iconography. A prominent example, for instance, is the popular nineteenth-century depiction of *Der breite und der schmale Weg* (The broad way and the narrow way), originally designed in 1866 by Charlotte Reihlen, a German Pietist. The pedagogical panorama was ornamented with quotes from the Luther Bible. Even early Adventist imagery, such as the picture *Christ, the Way of Life* (the initial version was commissioned in 1876; the revised version was commissioned in 1883), is another example of the iconography of contrast. In *The Way of Life*, Adventist pioneer James White graphically laid out the plan of salvation, by contrasting Old Testament faith with the way of the New Testament church of Christ.

55. Zschoch, "Gefahr und Nutzen der Bilder," 4–7 (translation by author).

56. Luther, *Works of Martin Luther*, 399. Luther, *D. Martin Luthers Werke*, vol. 10, bk. 3, 18.

57. Erne, "Ikonische Performanz," 8 (translation by author).

58. Francis A. Schaeffer, *Art and the Bible* (Downers Grove, IL: InterVarsity Press, 2009), 17. See also Claus Bernet's recent comparative study of the Adventist depictions of the New Jerusalem: Claus Bernet, *Das Himmlische Jerusalem bei Adventisten* (Berlin: Norderstedt, 2015).

CHAPTER 25

Bible Translations as a Catalyst

Nikolaus Satelmajer

The posting of the Ninety-Five Theses by Martin Luther in 1517 is probably the best-known event of Luther's life. As important as that is, this event may have only led to academic debates and arguments, possibly ending as a historical footnote. But Luther's writings, primarily composed in German, allowed everyday people to hear his message. On a much broader scale, his translation and publication of the 1522 New Testament (the complete Bible was published in 1534) had a profound impact across Germany and provided the central tool for later missionary movements. Without this Bible translation, there would have been no Reformation. In the same way, without Bible translations the Seventh-day Adventist missionary outreach of the late 1800s and the 1900s would have been merely good intentions without significant results. Bible translations were a catalyst for the Reformation and for the Adventist missionary movement.

Luther opens the door

Luther's 1522 translation created a firestorm in Europe. Bible translation was a revolutionary act—resulting in debates, intervention by rulers, book burning, and persecution. After surviving the Diet of Worms in 1521, Luther took a life-saving

Bible translations were a catalyst for the Reformation and for the Adventist missionary movement.

detour to Wartburg Castle. During his stay there, he battled health issues, depression, and demonic attacks. In spite of serious distractions, he managed to translate the New Testament within three months. This translation, published in September 1522,[1] is known as the September Bible. It was, however, not the first German translation, as some eighteen editions of the German Bible were completed before Luther's New Testament. Johannes Mentelin published the first German Bible in Strasbourg in 1466, some seventeen years before Luther was born.[2]

The first printing of Luther's New Testament had an estimated three thousand to five thousand copies.[3] That was an extraordinarily large print run for its day; and yet it sold out in three months. The second printing was in December 1522. Kenneth A. Strand points out that between 1522 and 1534 (when the complete Bible was printed) there were "no few[er] than 87 editions of his New Testament in High German plus some 19 in Low German." According to Strand, Erich Zimmerman estimated that during that period some 200,000 copies of Luther's New Testament were distributed.[4] Germany was not unified at that time, but the population of the "German" states was probably just over ten million.[5] Germany's current population is just over eighty million, thus the 200,000 copies would be an equivalent of about 1.6 million copies today.

What was it about Luther's New Testament that made it very popular? There are at least three reasons for its enthusiastic acceptance.

First, in 1516, Desiderius Erasmus (1466–1536) issued his Greek New Testament with his own Latin translation. This publication, just one year before the Ninety-Five Theses, was revolutionary. A source states, "Though based on insufficient MS [manuscript] material and not without bias, it exercised a profound influence on theological studies and was several times revised during Erasmus' lifetime, most notably in 1519."[6] The Erasmus Greek New Testament came at the right time and is one of the reasons for the success of Luther's German translation. Luther was immersed in the Vulgate Bible, but Erasmus made it possible for Luther to use the text in the original language. The Erasmus Greek New Testament is the start of the Textus Receptus, but it is most important because translators used the original Greek rather than some other language, such as the Latin Vulgate. Today translators have more and earlier Greek manuscripts; but what Luther did was revolutionary and challenged the accepted pattern. Strand maintains that in his lectures on Romans, Luther used Erasmus's 1516 edition and that Luther used both the 1516 and the 1519 Erasmus editions for the 1522 German New Testament.[7]

The second reason why the Luther New Testament became popular is the language of the translation. German translations of the Bible were already done in the eighth century. By the time of the printing revolution in the mid-1400s, a number of German translations existed. What was the basis of the first printed version? "The first printed German Bible employed the text of one of these early versions. Thought to have been composed around the end of the 14th century, it contained many words that were already unintelligible to the mid-15th century reader. The other 13 pre-Lutheran High German Bibles were, nonetheless, based on the same text."[8]

Johannes Gutenberg (c. 1398–1468), an innovative printer and publisher, gave the German people a printed Bible, but because of its antiquated language the impact was limited. Yet without the Gutenberg press, Martin Luther's 1522 translation would have had only limited impact. Luther made the Bible readable and the Gutenberg press made it available.

Luther's translation is readable because he chose the words carefully. Even a person with minimal reading ability understood his translation. In the translation, Luther used the words spoken by the people. Roland Bainton points to "the sweep of vocabulary, the native earthiness, and the religious profundity of [Luther's translation]."[9] Most readers did not have to do a word search to understand the translation. On the other hand, the language used by Luther was not only contemporary, it was also rather timeless. A German reader today can understand Luther's 1522 translation with minimal difficulty.[10]

Another reason for the acceptance and endurance is because of the type of translation he did. It was a formal translation devoid of personal interpretation and interjection, unless the text called for interpretation. Older German translations slavishly attempted a word-for-word translation from the Latin. Word-for-word translation is neither possible nor understandable. The goal of Luther's translation was to convey the original in language understood by the reader. But it *was* a translation and not a paraphrase. Though paraphrases are popular with many, they are interpretations and not translations.[11] Luther's translation method became a model for others.

The third reason for the popularity of Luther's translation is because it became "the foundation of the Reformation spirit in Germany."[12] Bainton calls Luther's translation his "noblest achievement,"[13] and it was the major force of the Reformation. Without the translation, Luther may have only encouraged reform[14] in the Roman Catholic Church; with the translation, he brought about the *Reformation*. The Bible

> The baker, the butcher, and the brewer now had their own Bible.

became a part of people's lives and discussions. The baker, the butcher, and the brewer now had their own Bible. Prior to that, even most priests, because of their limited education, did not utilize the Bible. Before Luther's translation, the Bible was a historic document used by a few—now it became everyone's book. Theological discussions shifted from the few to the many, from the monastery to the streets of Wittenberg and other cities and villages.

The words of the Luther translation were powerful, and yet they were reinforced with illustrations. The book of Revelation had twenty-one woodcuts.[15]

Revelation 11:1–7, the passage about the two witnesses, is one of these wood-cuts. The September Bible depicts the beast with "the papal triple crown."[16] The word and the picture together made the message easy to understand.

Others followed

Bainton, the same individual who describes Luther's Bible as his "noblest achievement," also states that it is "unfortunately untranslatable because every nation has its own direct version."[17] Bainton is correct; while Luther did not translate into other languages, he was a powerful example. He opened the floodgates of translation possibilities—what he did others could also do. We will look at others who, in one way or another, either followed Luther or used his approach as a model.

Dutch. In 1522, a New Testament by an unknown translator, based on the Vulgate but with an awareness of Greek readings, appeared. In 1523, a New Testament, based on Luther's translation, was published.[18]

Danish. In 1524, King Christian II asked his counselor Hans Mikkelsen to translate the New Testament. Mikkelsen, with Christiern Vinter's help, completed the project, and it was published in Wittenberg in 1524. It was partly based on Luther's translation.[19]

English. After church leaders opposed William Tyndale's proposal for an English translation, he fled to Hamburg, then to Cologne, and finally to Worms, where in 1525 his English New Testament was published. The English Bible "was born in exile. . . . Although the ecclesiastical authorities had forbidden the importation of Tyndale's work, copies were speedily smuggled into England."[20]

Swedish. It is believed that in 1526 Olaus Petri was responsible for the first New Testament.[21] A complete Bible was published in 1541, and it followed Luther more closely.[22]

Icelandic. The New Testament was translated by Oddur Gottskálksson and was published in Denmark in 1540. It was based on Luther's version, but the Vulgate and Erasmus's Greek were also used.[23]

Slovenian. The Gospel of Matthew, translated by Primož Trubar, a former Roman Catholic priest who became a Protestant pastor, was published in 1555. The New Testament was completed by 1577.[24]

Following Luther's example

Martin Luther died in 1546, but the concept of translating the Bible into the vernacular lived on. Some of the projects were completed in areas with little influence from the Reformation. One such translation project was a Bible for the Croats, Serbs, Bosnians, Bulgarians, and Turks. The Ottomans—or Turks as Luther referred to them—launched numerous military campaigns against Europe. This particular Bible translation project was unusual in many ways, but providing a Bible for the Turks, a non-Christian people, is a concrete example of the Reformation reaching outside Christian borders.[25]

The force behind this project was Hans von Ungnad (1493–1564), an official of the Holy Roman Empire and a Reformation convert.[26] Hans von Ungnad served in the court of Maximilian I (r. 1493–1519) and was made a baron by Charles V (r. 1519–1556) in 1522. Most of his service was under Ferdinand I who, in 1543, appointed him governor of lower Austria. Additionally, von Ungnad was a military leader against the invading Ottomans.

In spite of his close relationship to Ferdinand I, in 1555 von Ungnad had to vacate his castle at Sonnegg, Austria, located some twenty-five to thirty miles from Klagenfurt. Additionally he lost Waldenstein Castle near Wolfsberg, Austria, and castles in Varaždin and Samobor, Croatia. After spending several years in Wittenberg, Germany (he stayed with Philip Melanchton part of the time), in 1558, at the invitation of Duke Christoph of Württemberg, he moved to Bad Urach, Germany (near Tübingen). He lived in Bad Urach until he died in 1564, during a trip in Bohemia.

While von Ungnad had a notable career with the Holy Roman Empire, he is best known for what he did the last six years of his life. He assembled a team of translators and published Bibles for Balkan residents with the goal of reaching Constantinople itself. Even though von Ungnad had extensive contact with Slavic people—his wife was Croatian—his primary language was German. A pivotal figure in the project was Primož Trubar, a Slovenian convert to the Reformation, who had a limited understanding of Croatian. He provided valuable input on the project because, as mentioned previously, he translated portions of the New Testament into Slovenian. A number of individuals from Croatia, Dalmatia, Istria, Bosnia, and nearby areas were translators. The best-known translators—and the ones who received most of the credit—were Stephan Konzul and Antun Dalmatin. Konzul, Dalmatin, and some of the other translators were former Roman Catholic priests who joined the Reformation.[27]

Hans von Ungnad and his colaborers embarked upon a complex project. They had to translate and then print the Bible in two alphabets—Glagolitic and Cyrillic. Glagolitic, most likely developed by Cyril and Methodius, was for the Croats. The Cyrillic version (somewhat modified from the Croatian) was for Croats who used this alphabet; Serbs in Bosnia, Serbia, and Bulgaria; and for those Turks who used this alphabet and understood the language. In addition to the challenges of translation, the team had to develop the letters and then print the Bibles. It was a costly project. Hans von Ungnad, even though he had to leave the court of Ferdinand I, managed to get financial support from the royal family. Von Ungnad convinced Maximilian, the son of Ferdinand I and later Emperor Maximilian II (r. 1564–1576), to financially support the translation project. It was unusual for a Roman Catholic emperor to support a Protestant translation project, and that is why historians continue debating if Maximilian II was a public Catholic and a private Protestant.

The Hans von Ungnad project was unusual in at least two ways. First of all, the idea of providing a translation for the Slavic people did not fit the pattern of previous Protestant translations. Usually Bible translations were done in areas with a Protestant presence or at least where there was interest in the new faith. There were some Protestants in Slovenia, along the Austrian[28] border, and some in Istria, probably because of contact with Venice. Additionally, there was some Protestant activity in Vojvodina, the region north of Novi Sad and Belgrade and bordering Hungary on the north. All these Protestant pockets were small. The purpose of the translations was to provide the Bible in the vernacular *and* to introduce the Protestant faith. It was a missionary project—something usually not associated with the Reformation.

Secondly, Hans von Ungnad and his team had an even more ambitious goal. They thought that through a Bible translation they could convert the Turks to Christianity. As already mentioned, the Serbian version (in Cyrillic) was to be distributed to the Turks; some of whom read that alphabet and understood Serbian. The team also planned to translate the Bible into Turkish and thus make it available to many more. One of the team visionaries, Grgur Vlahović, collaborated with a Bosnian priest, Ivan Maleševac (Mileševac), with the goal of printing the Bible in Turkish.[29] They planned to obtain their own Turkish printing press. While there is no evidence of success for their project, they planned to spread Christianity to non-Christians.

Missionary movements and the Bible

Major Protestant missionary movements started in the 1700s and expanded in the coming decades. In light of the central role of the Bible in Protestant theology, it not surprising that as missionaries went to various parts of the world, Bible translations increased significantly. The need for Bible translations was met by Bible societies, starting with the founding of the British and Foreign Bible Society (now known as the Bible Society) in 1804. Other societies followed, and together they provided translations in numerous languages for distribution by the missionaries. In some instances, the missionaries asked for translations; in others, the Bible societies provided translations on their own. The Bible societies provided the Bibles, and the missionaries gave their interpretations of the Bible. Today while most people have access to a Bible in their language, the Bible societies continue to translate the Bible for languages used by small groups.[30]

Seventh-day Adventist missionaries and Bible translations

The Seventh-day Adventist Church was formally organized in 1863, though the movement traces its history to the Millerite movement of the 1830s and 1840s. While Adventists did not see missionary activity as their calling at first, by the 1870s they started sending missionaries to other countries. The initial focus was on Europe, but it did not take long for Adventists to send missionaries to other parts of the world. If there were no Adventists in a country, the church felt the need to send missionaries. The late 1800s and early 1900s were a time when a large number of missionaries were sent to every part of the world.[31]

Seventh-day Adventists saw themselves as people of the Word. Adventists maintained that their beliefs and practices were based on the Bible and not upon creedal statements. In 1853, even before the denomination was organized, James White (one of the founders of the church) wrote, "And while standing here, with the aid of no other creed than the Word of God . . . "[32] Adventist fundamental beliefs were articulated but were not drafted until 1931, but even after that the Bible was and is the final authority. At the 1946 General Conference Session of Seventh-day Adventists, it was voted that the beliefs could be only voted and revised by the world church in session.

In light of this position on doctrinal beliefs, Adventist missionaries had to have Bibles in the languages of the people. Bible translations were key to the success of Adventist mission, and the Bible societies were often the source. While Adventists did not join ecumenical missionary bodies, the Bible societies—which are ecumenical bodies—were critical to the success of Adventist mission.[33] In addition to using the translations of the Bible societies, Adventist missionaries and converts also participated in Bible translating. Here is a sampling of Adventist participation in Bible translation projects.[34]

- *Arthur Asa Grandville Carscallen (1879–1964).* The Canadian Carscallen was a missionary in Scotland, various African countries, and Guyana. While stationed in Kenya, he mastered the Luo language and reduced it to writing. He translated portions of the New Testament for the British and Foreign Bible Society. Additionally, in Guyana, "he produced a dictionary and grammar in the local language."[35]
- *Grace Agnes Clark (1898–1955).* Born in England, Clark went to Kenya, where she served in various leadership roles. Because of her expertise in the Luo language, the British and Foreign Bible Society asked her to participate in translating the Bible into that language. In appreciation for her work, the society made her a lifelong member of that organization.[36]
- *Orno Follett (1882–1960).* In spite of health issues, Follett was a missionary to the Navajo in the western United States. He lived among the Navajo and "aided in translating part of the Bible into Navajo."[37]
- *David Kalaka (c. 1844–1904).* Kalaka is listed as the first convert to Adventism in Basutoland, South Africa, and thereafter worked on various mission projects. He assisted in the translation of the Bible in the Sesuto (South Africa) language.[38]
- *Henri Monnier (1896–1944).* Born in Switzerland, Monnier went

to Africa, where his wife died five months after giving birth to their child. He eventually remarried and worked in various parts of Africa. He was proficient in the Ruanda language and translated a portion of the Bible into it.[39]

- *Kata Rangoso (1902–1964).* A native of the Solomon Islands, Rangoso served in various ministerial roles, especially during World War II when missionaries had to leave. He was one of the translators of the Bible into Marovo.[40] Another source lists A. R. Barrett, H. B. P. Wicks, J. T. Howse, and Mr. and Mrs. J. D. Anderson, of the Seventh-day Adventist Mission, as Marovo translators for the British and Foreign Bible Society translation project in 1956.[41]

These individuals, and others not listed, made it possible for the Adventist message to go international. Because the Bible was available in many languages, the Adventist message has gone to nearly every country in the world.

Conclusion

Luther's Bible translation gave the Reformation depth and endurance. He preached from the Bible and gave the Bible to the people in the language they understood. Without this Bible translation, Luther's movement may have ended shortly after it began, and today it would be just a historical footnote. His translation served his people, but his example inspired many others to provide the Bible in various languages.

Early Adventists were immersed in their Bibles. The Bible was central in the theological development and proclamation of the message. The Adventist message spread worldwide because the missionaries presented the Bible to people in languages they understood. Without the Bible in their vernacular, the Adventist Church would not be the international movement that it is today.

What about now? Are we fragmented into theological cliques, talking and listening to like-minded individuals? Or is the Bible as central in the theology and the life of the church as it was in the early years and when the Adventist message went global? The answers to these questions will determine the future of Seventh-day Adventism.

What about now? Are we fragmented into theological cliques, talking and listening to like-minded individuals? Or is the Bible as central in the theology and the life of the church as it was in the early years and when the Adventist message went global? The answers to these questions will determine the future of Seventh-day Adventism.

1. The complete Bible was published in 1534.

2. Paul Ellingworth, "From Martin Luther to the English Revised Version," in *A History of Bible Translation*, ed. Philip A. Noss, (Rome: Edizioni Di Storia E Letteratura, 2007), 110.

3. Kenneth A. Strand, "Brief Historical Introduction," in *Luther's "September Bible" in Facsimile* (Ann Arbor, MI: Ann Arbor Publishers, 1972), 3.

4. Strand, "Brief Historical Introduction," 3. A helpful source for pre-Luther translation is Kenneth A. Strand, *German Bibles Before Luther: The Story of 14 High-German Editions* (Grand Rapids, MI: Eerdmans, 1966).

5. See Örjan Martinsson, "Population of Germany," Tacitus.NU, accessed August 8, 2017, http://www.tacitus.nu/historical-atlas/population/germany.htm.

6. *The Oxford Dictionary of the Christian Church*, 3rd ed. (New York: Oxford University Press, 2005), s.v. "Erasmus, Desiderius."

7. Strand, "Brief Historical Introduction," 5.

8. Eric M. North and Eugene A. Nida, eds., *The Book of a Thousand Tongues*, rev. ed. (London: United Bible Societies, 1972), 442.

9. Roland Bainton, *Here I Stand: A Life of Martin Luther* (New York: Abingdon Press, 1950), 327.

10. I have on a regular basis read portions of Luther's 1522 translation (See Strand, "Brief Historical Introduction,"), and I am surprised by its readability. Language changes over time, yet the 1522 edition is not too different from a more recent Luther Bible edition. Readers of a dynamic translation, such as *Gute Nachricht für Sie*, will also read the 1522 translation with minimal difficulty.

11. Today we have access to many translations, and most of them are quality translations. Paraphrases have also become popular, though readers need to use them with caution. Paraphrases are interpretations and thus are close to being Bible commentaries. For additional information about translations and paraphrases, see Nikolaus Satelmajer, "The Joys and Challenges of Choosing a Bible Translation," *Journal of Adventist Education*, December 2011/January 2012, 29–33.

12. North and Nida, *The Book of a Thousand Tongues*, 154.

13. Bainton, *Here I Stand*, 326.

14. There were already signs of operational reformation within the Roman Catholic Church, but they were limited in scope and mission.

15. In spite of Luther's criticism of Revelation, it is interesting that it was chosen to have the woodcuts.

16. Kenneth A. Strand, *Woodcuts to the Apocalypse in Dürer's Time: Albrecht Dürer's Woodcuts Plus Five Other Sets From the 15th and 16th Century* (Ann Arbor, MI: Ann Arbor Publishers, 1968), 37.

17. Bainton, *Here I Stand*, 326.

18. North and Nida, *The Book of a Thousand Tongues*, 112.

19. Ellingworth, "From Martin Luther to the English Revised Version," 111, 112

20. North and Nida, *The Book of a Thousand Tongues*, 116, 117. For additional information about Tyndale and other English versions, see Nikolaus Satelmajer, ed., *The Book That Changed the World: The Story of the King James Version* (Nampa, ID: Pacific Press® Pub. Assn., 2012).

21. North and Nida, *The Book of a Thousand Tongues*, 411.

22. Ellingworth, "From Martin Luther to the English Revised Version," 112.

23. Ibid.

24. North and Nida, *The Book of a Thousand Tongues*, 398.

25. *Turks*, the term most often used by Luther, refers to the Muslims in the Ottoman Empire. The Ottoman Empire also had Christians in the invaded Balkans and Hungary. Ottomans also temporarily invaded even Austria, thus becoming a threat to the German lands. There were Christian groups within the empire, and thousands of Christians were taken prisoner or as slaves in what is now Turkey. For a helpful source about the Reformation in Croatia, see Stanko Jambrek, *Reformacija u hrvatskim zemljama u europskom kontekstu* (Zagreb: Bibliski Insitut, 2013).

26. For more details, see Nikolaus Satelmajer, "A Bold Sixteenth-Century Mission: The First New Testaments for Croats, Bosnians, Serbs, Bulgarians, and Turks" (STM thesis, Lutheran Theological Seminary at Philadelphia, 2014).

27. For a comprehensive list of translators, see Satelmajer, "A Bold Sixteenth-Century Mission," 33ff.

28. Austria had a significant Protestant presence until the early 1600s when Jesuits and others managed to make Roman Catholicism the dominant and controlling religion. E.g., Ignatius of Loyola (1491–1556), the founder of the Jesuits, wrote detailed instructions to Peter Canisius (1521–1597), the leader of the German Jesuits, outlining how Emperor Ferdinand I should treat the Protestants. In part, Loyola stated that some should be punished "with the expropriation of their life or goods or with exile." See John Patrick Donnelly, ed. and trans., *Jesuit Writings of the Early Modern Period, 1540–1640* (Indianapolis, IN: Hackett Publishing, 2006), 134.

29. For additional details, see Satelmajer, "A Bold Sixteenth-Century Mission," 40.

30. For an overview of Bible translations, see North and Nida, *The Book of a Thousand Tongues*.

31. In 1886, the general church paper *Advent Review and Sabbath Herald* "carried a drawing of the world labeled 'Our Field.' " Eugene F. Durand, *Yours in the Blessed Hope, Uriah Smith* (Washington, DC: Review and Herald® Pub. Assn., 1980), 133.

32. *The Seventh-day Adventist Encyclopedia*, rev. ed. Seventh-day Adventist Commentary Reference Series (Washington, DC: Review and Herald® Pub. Assn., 1996), s.v. "Doctrinal Statements, Seventh-day Adventists."

33. Bible societies have been held in high regard by Seventh-day Adventists. From personal experience, I know that many Adventists are active members of Bible societies. Additionally, Adventists have financially supported Bible societies. The American Bible Society in 1970 gave me a research grant. During my work at the society, there were public displays of giving by denominations, and Seventh-day Adventists were about the highest per capita donors.

34. I owe special thanks to my wife, Ruth I. Satelmajer (née Nutter), for spending many hours identifying Seventh-day Adventist Bible translators listed in the *The Seventh-day Adventist Encyclopedia*.

35. *The Seventh-day Adventist Encyclopedia*, rev. ed. Seventh-day Adventist Commentary Reference Series (Washington, DC: Review and Herald® Pub. Assn., 1996), s.v. "Carscalle, Arthur Asa Grandville."

36. *The Seventh-day Adventist Encyclopedia*, rev. ed. Seventh-day Adventist Commentary

Reference Series (Washington, DC: Review and Herald® Pub. Assn., 1996), s.v. "Clark, Grace Agnes."

37. *The Seventh-day Adventist Encyclopedia*, rev. ed. Seventh-day Adventist Commentary Reference Series (Washington, DC: Review and Herald® Pub. Assn., 1996), s.v. "Follett, Orno."

38. *The Seventh-day Adventist Encyclopedia*, rev. ed. Seventh-day Adventist Commentary Reference Series (Washington, DC: Review and Herald® Pub. Assn., 1996), s.v. "Kalaka, David."

39. *The Seventh-day Adventist Encyclopedia*, rev. ed. Seventh-day Adventist Commentary Reference Series (Washington, DC: Review and Herald® Pub. Assn., 1996), s.v. "Monnier, Henri."

40. *The Seventh-day Adventist Encyclopedia*, rev. ed. Seventh-day Adventist Commentary Reference Series (Washington, DC: Review and Herald® Pub. Assn., 1996), s.v. "Rangoso, Kata."

41. North and Nida, *The Book of a Thousand Tongues*, 284.

CHAPTER 26

Luther's Legacy in Music

Dan Shultz

B oth Martin Luther and the founders of the Seventh-day Adventist Church
valued music. They especially recognized the role hymns have in the life of
the Christian. Although Luther's music background differed dramatically from
that of the founders of the Adventist Church, in both instances their use of
music facilitated the acceptance of new beliefs.

Luther's musical talent was recognized early in his life. By the time he pursued his education at the University of Erfurt, he had received enough musical
training that his talent as a tenor gained him room and board from an elderly
woman near the university. He was a natural musician who enjoyed singing and
was a proficient lute player and flutist.[1]

A fter Luther's excommunication, he drew upon his
knowledge of music in the rituals and hymns associated with
the church to effectively present
his new theology to the masses.

When he became a monk at the
age of twenty-two, part of his life in
the monastery, and later as a priest,
included participating in music associated with church rituals. He was
ordained to the priesthood in 1507;
and in 1508, he was invited to teach
theology at the recently established
University of Wittenberg. Four years
later Luther became the chair of the theology department and spent the rest of
his career at the university.[2]

His Ninety-Five Theses were translated into German, printed and distributed, and because of the challenges they and his subsequent writings and preaching presented to the Catholic Church, he was excommunicated in 1521. After Luther's excommunication, he drew upon his knowledge of music in the rituals and hymns associated with the church to effectively present his new theology to the masses.

In Luther's time, cantors, choirs, and priests provided the worship-service music in Latin. While worshipers were passive observers, the settings they worshiped in and the beauty of the music moved them, particularly in large city churches. The whole experience was impressive and contrasted sharply with the difficulties of their daily lives, but it lacked the intimacy that an understanding of the words or meaningful participation in music could have created.

Luther, an experienced choir member and priest leading in the rituals and services of the church, respected the heritage of music that had developed over the centuries. While he hesitated to lessen the beauty of liturgy sung in Latin, he knew that hymns (chorales) in the language of the people, and sung by them as part of the religious service, increased the meaning of the service for them. Music also conveyed the importance of sharing the message that they could have salvation through faith without relying on the church.

He used scales and church modes (scalelike but with more complex construction and connotations) when possible and wrote music with both Latin and German texts that supported his new theological beliefs. He believed that the skillful joining of text and melody spoke to both Catholics and members of the newly forming church. Music served as an important part of a transforming message.

> Music served as an important part of a transforming message.

Luther wrote his first hymn in 1523, one year after translating the New Testament into German. He then published a hymnbook in 1524 in collaboration with his musician friend Johann Walter. The book had only eight hymns—half of which were Luther's. He continued writing hymns until two years before his death, composing altogether thirty-seven hymns, twenty-one of them in 1523 and 1524. Only nine were regarded as original. The remainder were translations from Latin, revisions of pre-Reformation hymns, versifications of psalms, with six being paraphrases of scriptural passages.[3] In the introduction to his first hymnbook, he wrote that the hymns should be sung with enthusiasm "so that God's Word and Christian teaching might be instilled and implanted in many ways."[4]

Luther believed that music was next to theology in importance and should be taught in schools where students would learn to sing the new music and then share it in their homes, as street singers, or in groups. Extended rehearsals of groups of varying ability were also held in schools to prepare music with both German and Latin texts suitable for church services.[5]

While some of the hymns were harmonized with chords, many were sung in unison, generally without accompaniment. Luther preferred vocal music and encouraged the singing of his new hymns in homes and churches, regarding it as a "beautiful and gracious gift from God since it drove away the devil and made people joyful."[6] He endorsed the use of plucked string instruments as an accompaniment or to provide instrumental interludes between verses.[7] He also agreed with counter-melodies or polyphony being sung by trained singers to create florid settings for straightforward unison singing of the chorale by the congregation.

> While the words to the best known of Luther's hymns—"A Mighty Fortress Is Our God," first published in a 1529 hymnbook—were written by Luther, there is uncertainty about the source of its melody.

While the words to the best known of Luther's hymns—"A Mighty Fortress Is Our God," first published in a 1529 hymnbook—were written by Luther, there is uncertainty about the source of its melody. The surviving hymn (a paraphrase of Psalm 46) with its verses, melody, and later chordal harmonized setting remains a majestic and dynamic statement of God's presence, power, and role in the Christian experience. When it was first introduced, it served as a rallying cry for the Reformation and survives today, five centuries later, as an important hymn in many Protestant churches.

Most hymns of that era drew on newly composed melodies or those previously associated with worship (including ancient plainsong). A few writers used melodies from secular and sacred folk music and current nonreligious songs. The use of current secular songs was an infrequent practice, but it made hymns more accessible and easily remembered by worshipers.

Also, active participation created ownership for the individual. Hymns became an important legacy from the work of Luther and others who followed, evolving into the strophic form and the four-part harmonization we now take for granted.

In succeeding years, the strength of Luther's hymns and those of his contemporaries and later Reformers and musicians became the inspiration for music written by major composers. Johann S. Bach, a Lutheran, drew on that heritage in composing music two centuries later, creating a vast musical legacy that continues to inspire. His chordal and polyphonic writing established rules in music harmonization that prevail today.

Isaac Watts and George F. Handel, two other composers from Bach's time, were inspired by Luther's heritage and created legacies of their own. Watts in his writing of music and verses for hundreds of hymns set a standard in message and melody that revolutionized hymn singing around the world. His *Hymns and Spiritual Songs* was the first real collection of hymns in English. Many are still in hymnals today.

Handel's *Messiah*, first performed in 1742, reflected a theological legacy that flowed from Luther's liberating beliefs. It has continued as a meaningful and enduring seasonal masterpiece for nearly three centuries.

In the five hundred years following Luther, other Protestant churches were formed that either accepted or distanced themselves from Luther's musical heritage. Some embraced the power of music in ministry; some limited the use of music; and others rejected the use of music in worship. While differing beliefs and practices developed in certain areas, shared articles of faith were celebrated in countless hymns in many other churches.

Music in the Seventh-day Adventist Church

Led primarily by James and Ellen White and Joseph Bates, the Seventh-day Adventist Church was formed in 1863 and was named for its emphasis on the seventh-day Sabbath and the imminent return of Christ. It provided a refinement to and departure from the beliefs that had evolved in the mainstream Protestant churches founded in the centuries following Luther's successful challenge to the Roman Catholic Church.

The Reformation started at a dispirited time for society. This was the result of profound and systemic problems arising from centuries of control and abuse by the Catholic Church. The Seventh-day Adventist Church in America was officially organized during the Civil War. It was an uncertain time as the country dealt with both the war and the effects of a transformation from an agrarian to an industrial society. At the same time, a significant portion of Americans lived and worked in dehumanizing circumstances.

In the United States, many welcomed the message of reassurance about a more hopeful future and the promise of a better life. Well-known, talented musicians, such as Ira D. Sankey, and later Homer Rodeheaver, worked with such charismatic preachers as Dwight L. Moody and William "Billy" Sunday. The churches experienced significant growth. It was an era when the new Seventh-day Adventist Church, with its emphasis on the Sabbath, biblical prophecy, and healthful living, won converts. The Seventh-day Adventist message met the needs of many.

Ellen G. White came out of the Methodist tradition where congregational singing was an important part of worship. James White's father was a singing teacher and had trained his children to sing.[8] Their musical backgrounds and the talent in their larger family made music an important part of presenting this new message in a memorable way, as it had in Luther's time.

Luther's musical background was more sophisticated than that of the Whites. It served him well in his time, with the challenges he faced, as a bridge from one way of belief and worship to another. The Whites' background, while at a more basic level, enabled them to speak to a less sophisticated American culture by integrating popular gospel hymns that were the musical choice for most Americans.

Gospel music dominated evangelistic meetings in both mainstream Protestant and Seventh-day Adventist churches and was more intimate music than traditional hymns. Its appeal lay in easily remembered messages and refrains that often centered on the needs and hopes of those who listened and sang. The effect was enhanced by tuneful melodies, some drawn from popular music sources; straightforward harmonies; repeated refrains; and often catchy rhythms.[9]

James White, one of the church's earliest evangelists, used his musical talents and those of his immediate and extended family[10] to assist in spreading the new message. His son Edson and nephew Franklin Edson "F. E." Belden—a prolific songwriter who became an important force in Seventh-day Adventism evangelism and worship—wrote gospel songs featuring the unique beliefs of the church. They also printed songbooks that were widely used in sharing the message with the public and also in worship services.

In its first four decades, the church published several collections of new, as well as familiar, gospel songs and hymns. These collections included words or music by the Seventh-day Adventist songwriters and composers Annie R. Smith, F. E. Belden, Edwin Barnes, and Edson White, in addition to other well-known writers of the era, such as Frances "Fanny" J. Crosby, William H. Doane, and Ira D. Sankey. They also included hymns from Martin Luther, John and Charles Wesley, Isaac Watts, Samuel Wesley, Lowell Mason, and others.

These collections were an essential part of an evangelism that relied heavily on the enthusiastic singing of familiar music to attract and hold crowds. In the tradition of Luther, who used music to create receptive minds for a message of change, the Whites and other Seventh-day Adventist evangelists used music to introduce practices and beliefs that were different from those of other denominations.

The enthusiasm for newfound beliefs and the limited cultural background of the early converts sometimes resulted in excesses in singing and emotion that led to a cautionary observation by Ellen White in the early 1880s: "We should endeavor in our songs of praise to approach as nearly as possible to the harmony of the heavenly choirs. I have often been pained to hear untrained voices, pitched to the highest key, literally shrieking the sacred words of some hymn of praise. How inappropriate those sharp, rasping voices for the solemn, joyous worship of God. I long to stop my ears, or flee from the place, and I rejoice when the painful exercise is ended."[11]

Like Luther, the Whites and other Adventist leaders believed in the importance of music in education. From the beginning of the first Seventh-day Adventist college—Battle Creek College in Michigan—music was part of the curriculum; it was valued for training students to teach or effectively assist in evangelism and worship. Edwin Barnes, a gifted singer and organist from England, who taught at the college, periodically returned to Europe for additional training. He oversaw a respected music program during his seventeen years of leadership at the college. Barnes also composed hymns in the English tradition and worked with Edson White and F. E. Belden in compiling early hymnbooks for the church.

Barnes's students were key providers of music for evangelism and worship and helped to establish music programs as additional Seventh-day Adventist schools were started in North America and abroad. Those early efforts in music education led to a school system that today is the second-largest church-sponsored system in the world, training musicians for a full spectrum of musical careers, including teaching and evangelism. These people have positively affected worship music as the Adventist Church has matured and adapted to changes in society and musical tastes.

While Lutheran churches often have paid ministers of music, Seventh-day Adventist churches usually rely on their music teachers and students. Also, a significant number of musical touring groups have provided music for Adventist congregations. The result is a church noted both for its theology and its music, including extensive, sophisticated choral and instrumental programs; accomplished keyboard performers; numerous soloists; and significant keyboard resources in pipe organs and pianos.

Many of the student participants in these school programs become active in their churches upon graduation and willingly volunteer their services. They are important contributors in the worship service. Numerous Seventh-day Adventist musicians also provide music in churches of other denominations.

The writings and collections of the church's early musicians inspired subsequent generations of composers and songwriters. This is similar to the musicians that followed Luther, who created a distinctive legacy in hymns and major musical works.[12] *The Seventh-day Adventist Hymnal*, published by the church in 1985, preserves the more durable works of those older Seventh-day Adventist gospel songs (although their numbers have been reduced by the passage of time and changing tastes) as well as timeless hymns in the Protestant heritage. The hymnal also contains distinctive hymns written by recent Seventh-day Adventist composers.

Conclusion

New insights on biblical teachings and the importance of communal worship were at the heart of both the Reformation and the Seventh-day Adventist Church. In both instances, music played a critical role in presenting new beliefs in a memorable way and creating unity and enthusiasm among the believers. Music continues to fulfill the same purposes, while evolving to meet changing tastes in both Western society and the spread of the message to other cultures.

While hymns continue to be an important part of evangelism and worship in Seventh-day Adventist and other Protestant churches, many changes occurred in sacred music in the last half of the twentieth century. In this new millennium, the church's diverse population needs to explore ways of having music be an inspiring and unifying part of worship.

1. Stanley Sadie, ed., *The New Grove Dictionary of Music and Musicians*, vol. 11 (New York: Macmillan, 1980), 366.

2. LeRoy Edwin Froom, *The Prophetic Faith of Our Fathers*, vol. 2 (Washington, DC: Review and Herald® Pub. Assn., 1948), 248–251.

3. William Jensen Reynolds, *A Survey of Christian Hymnody* (New York: Holt, Rinehart and Winston, 1963), 17. Other sources credit Luther with thirty-six hymns.

4. Martin Luther, *Preface to the Wittenberg Hymnal* (1524), in *Luther's Works*, vol. 53, *Liturgy and Hymns*, ed. Ulrich S. Leupold (Philadelphia, PA: Fortress Press, 1965), 315.

5. For an extended presentation on this subject, see Herbert R. Pankratz, "Luther's Utilization of Music in School and Town in the Early Reformation," *Andrews University Seminary Studies* 22, no. 1 (Spring 1984): 99–112.

6. Denis Arnold, ed., *The New Oxford Companion to Music* (New York: Oxford University Press, 1996), 1549.

7. Sadie, *The New Grove Dictionary of Music and Musicians*, 11:368.

8. James White, "Life Sketches: Chapter III—Continued," *Signs of the Times*, February 21, 1878, 58.

9. Reynolds, *A Survey of Christian Hymnody*, 107, 108; Sadie, *The New Grove Dictionary of Music and Musicians*, 7:549.

10. Ellen and James White as well as their sons were musical and sang as they did their chores, worshiped at home or publicly, and as they ministered for the church. More details about the White family's involvement in music can be found in Stanley D. Hickerson, "An Unutterable Sense of Glory," *Notes: International Adventist Musicians Association*, Winter/Spring 2007, 6, 7, accessed August 9, 2017, http://www.iamaonline.com/Notes/Notes_Winter_Spring_07.pdf.

11. Ellen G. White, " 'The Schools of the Prophets,' " *Signs of the Times*, June 22, 1882, 277.

12. Dozens of Adventist composers have written hundreds of works, including hymns and major works. A listing of Seventh-day Adventist composers and their works can be found in Dan Shultz, *Adventist Musicians Biographical Resource* (College Place, WA: International Adventist Musicians Association, 2014).

CHAPTER 27

Lutheran–Roman Catholic Dialogues and the Future of the Protestant Reformation

Denis Fortin

The Augustinian monk Martin Luther had no idea that his Ninety-Five Theses to protest, or more accurately to debate, the sale of indulgences in his town would lead to what happened next in Europe. His desire to reform the Catholic Church, which was shared by many people, did not intend to create a separate ecclesial structure or cause wars and political turmoil. But in the end it did. His original protest and the many more that followed in the form of treatises and sermons gave birth to a movement that rapidly went beyond Luther's control. Reform movements that had been dormant in many other countries erupted across Europe. Within a generation, the Protestant Reformation became a new religious and political reality.

> For five hundred years, Lutherans and other Protestants have grown their religious traditions in contrast to and apart from the Roman Catholic Church.

For five hundred years, Lutherans and other Protestants have grown their religious traditions in contrast to and apart from the Roman Catholic Church.

Much has happened in these five hundred years, but the most important event to impact Lutheran churches may not have been a Lutheran event. Rather, I maintain that it was the Roman Catholic Second Vatican Council (1962–1965). Pope John XXIII's call for the council in January 1959 surprised the Christian world. Since the proclamation of the infallibility of the pope at the First Vatican Council (1870), many Protestants believed the Catholic Church would no longer need any councils to establish or change religious beliefs and practices. Protestants had forgotten that the Catholic Church had always believed, more or less, in the principles of collegiality between bishops and to some forms of conciliar approach to the life of the church.[1] Among the many documents adopted by the council, the promulgation of the Decree on Ecumenism at the end of the third session in November 1964 surprised Protestants as well as Catholics.[2]

After the momentous World Missionary Conference of 1910 in Edinburgh, Scotland, the ecumenical movement grew during the first half of the twentieth century. The Roman Catholic leadership's initial reaction to the movement was one of antipathy and aversion. It considered itself as the only expression of the true church of Christ and did not intend to discuss the unity of the church with religious groups that had caused its rupture. Between 1910 and the early 1950s, popes repeatedly refused to even consider sending observers to the meetings of the Commission on Faith and Order and to the first two assemblies of the World Council of Churches.[3] But Pope John XXIII (1958–1963) and many cardinals and bishops saw things differently. If the Holy Spirit was guiding Protestant Christians to discuss the unity of the church, how could the Catholic Church, if it claims to be led by the Holy Spirit, not be part of this conversation?

The Decree on Ecumenism marked a conversion moment in the Catholic Church and forever changed the face of the ecumenical movement. From apathy toward the movement, the Catholic Church came to see the movement as an opportunity for witnessing and fulfilling the will of God for the church. In an encyclical in 1995, Pope John Paul II stated forcefully that, for Catholics, engagement in the ecumenical movement is imperative. "At the Second Vatican Council, the Catholic Church committed herself irrevocably to following the path of the ecumenical venture, thus heeding the Spirit of the Lord, who teaches people to interpret carefully the 'signs of the times.' "[4] The decree made many important points: it recognized that the Holy Spirit had been active in the lives of other ecclesial communities and that many elements of the gospel are found in Protestant churches.[5] Thus, Protestants were no longer heretics but "separated brethren."[6] The decree recommended a number of principles and steps for active participation in the ecumenical movement. One step was an encouragement to enter into dialogue with Protestant communities. The first "separated brethren" to benefit from this new overture were the Lutherans. Official dialogues between Lutherans and Catholics in the United States began in 1965 (barely a few months after the decree was voted) and between the

Lutheran World Federation and the Pontifical Secretariat for Promoting Christian Unity[7] in 1967. In the last fifty years, all of these dialogues at international and national levels have produced many remarkable documents.[8]

In the last two decades, a few documents from the Lutheran World Federation and the Pontifical Council for Promoting Christian Unity have helped bridge the gap between the two Christian traditions. Among the most prominent, in my opinion, are the *Joint Declaration on the Doctrine of Justification* (1999),[9] *The Apostolicity of the Church* (2006),[10] and the recent *From Conflict to Communion: Lutheran-Catholic Common Commemoration of the Reformation in 2017* (2013).[11] Added to this list of international documents is the recent American document *Declaration on the Way: Church, Ministry and Eucharist* (2015)[12] prepared by representatives of the United States Conference of Catholic Bishops and the Evangelical Lutheran Church in America. Some have commented that, given what these documents have accomplished, the Reformation is over.[13] In this chapter, I will explore what I consider as the most important theological and ecumenical developments these documents have accomplished. I will also identify some of the implications of the ecumenical dialogues between Lutherans and Roman Catholics. In some areas, the protest of the Reformation is over; but in other areas, the Reformation produced some historically conditioned and biblically grounded realities and experiences that will remain, and in time, may be embraced by all sides.

> In the last two decades, a few documents from the Lutheran World Federation and the Pontifical Council for Promoting Christian Unity have helped bridge the gap between the two Christian traditions.

Joint Declaration on the Doctrine of Justification (1999)

Protestant historians and theologians claim that "the doctrine of justification is *the* doctrine of the Reformation, that doctrine which—more than any other—gave to sixteenth-century Protestantism its character as Protestant."[14]

As the Catholic Church emerged from the Middle Ages into the Renaissance, the study of the Bible in its original languages and the discovery of the original meaning of some concepts gave rise to new interrogations and produced a flurry of discussions, debates, and writings.[15] It is in this context that Martin Luther challenged the practice of indulgences. His reading of the Greek New Testament led him to understand that the verb *metanoeō* in Matthew 4:17 should be translated "to repent" or "to change one's mind" rather than "to do penance" as Jerome implied in the Vulgate. Luther's first thesis underscored that fundamental point, and it was further elaborated in his *Explanations of the Ninety-Five Theses* the following year.[16] The same kind of insight transpired when he and others considered the verb *dikaioō* and its cognates in the epistle of Paul to the

Romans. Luther preferred to translate it "to declare righteous," with its forensic connotation, rather than the Vulgate's "to be made righteous," which implied a process of salvation with the accompanying sacramental infusion of righteousness.[17] In Bruce McCormack's opinion, "the Reformers' *forensic* understanding of justification had precisely that kind of wide-reaching influence. For the idea of an *immediate* divine imputation renders superfluous the entire Catholic system of the priestly mediation of grace by the Church."[18] Thus began one of the most divisive disputes of the Reformation.

Things basically remained the same between Catholics and Lutherans until the 1950s. Catholic theologian Hans Küng published a book on the doctrine of justification in which he argued for a fundamental agreement between the Swiss Reformed theologian Karl Barth's understanding of justification and the Roman Catholic perspective.[19] The book was a surprising and unexpected comparison and assessment, and it astonished Catholics as much as it did Barth. Yet Barth endorsed the assessment in a letter to Küng: "I here gladly, gratefully, and publicly testify not only that you have adequately covered all significant aspects of justification treated in the ten volumes of my *Church Dogmatics* published so far, and that you have fully and accurately reproduced my views as I myself understand them. . . . Your readers may rest assured . . . that you have me say what I actually do say and that I mean it in the way you have me say it." Barth went one step further in his assessment of Küng's conclusions. "If what you have presented in Part Two of this book is actually the teaching of the Roman Catholic Church, then I must certainly admit that my view of justification agrees with the Roman Catholic view; if only for the reason that the Roman Catholic teaching would then be most strikingly in accord with mine!"[20] At the beginning of the second edition, Küng claimed that justification as "the fundamental question at issue between the Roman Catholic Church and the Reformation may now be regarded as settled."[21] And Kenneth Green, in a review of the second edition of Küng's book in the *Catholic Herald*, stated that as a result of this book "a considerable breach has been made in the ugly walls dividing Christendom."[22] No doubt it did, and Alister McGrath claims, "It is no exaggeration to suggest that Küng's book marked the dawn of a new era of positive ecumenical discussion of a doctrine which had hitherto been seen largely as an insuperable obstacle to such dialogue."[23]

Once the Second Vatican Council encouraged ecumenical dialogues, the Pontifical Secretariat for Promoting Christian Unity reached out to the Lutheran World Federation for dialogue. The first phase of this international dialogue (1967–1972) produced the "Malta Report," *The Gospel and the Church*, in which Luther's "doctrine of justification is recognised and accepted."[24] Six documents were produced during the second phase of dialogue (1973–1984), including a new assessment of the life and theology of Martin Luther.[25] But it is phase three (1986–1993) that saw a major development on the doctrine of justification with the publication of *Church and Justification* (1993). This document, as well as numerous others produced by dialogues between Roman Catholics and Lutherans in the United States and Europe, prepared the way for the *Joint Declaration on the Doctrine of Justification* (1999).[26]

The release of the *Joint Declaration* surprised the ecumenical world, but it did not emerge out of the blue. While numerous ecumenical documents had been produced throughout the decades since Vatican II and were gathering dust on the shelves of theological libraries, or were intentionally concealed from the public,[27] this one was a *joint* declaration—a document officially endorsed by both traditions. Edward Cardinal Cassidy described the signing of the *Joint Declaration* as "without doubt an outstanding achievement of the ecumenical movement and a milestone on the way to the restoration of full, visible unity among the disciples of our Lord and Saviour."[28] "Pope John Paul II described the event as marking 'a milestone on the not always easy road towards the restoration of full unity among Christians.' "[29]

This document, more than any other, has led people to respond with some degree of overconfidence that the Reformation is over—forgetting that the Reformation dealt with more than one issue. The *Joint Declaration*'s intention is clearly stated in the preamble:

> [Its intention is] to show that on the basis of their dialogue the subscribing Lutheran churches[30] and the Roman Catholic Church are now able to articulate a common understanding of our justification by God's grace through faith in Christ. It does not cover all that either church teaches about justification; it does encompass a consensus on basic truths of the doctrine of justification and shows that the remaining differences in its explication are no longer the occasion for doctrinal condemnations.[31]

The *Joint Declaration* was made possible with the use of a more meaningful methodological development: a "differentiated consensus" with the recognition of two levels of agreement. The first level is a real and essential consensus on a particular point "that is neither a general, loose agreement nor a compromise." The second level states the remaining differences and varying nuances of emphases. "These differences are also real and essential. But the critical point is that all these differences do not challenge the agreement or consensus on the first level." This schema provides for unity and diversity and does not require a synthesis of the differing positions.[32] This methodological approach has been seen as a breakthrough in bilateral dialogues, with unmistakable implications for the future of the ecumenical movement.

The first section of the document, "Biblical Message of Justification," is saturated with biblical references, mainly from Paul's writings, and touches on all the key Protestant texts speaking of justification by faith. It explains clearly that justification is the forgiveness of sins (cf. Rom 3:23-25; Acts 13:39; Lk 18:14), liberation from the dominating power of sin and death (Rom 5:12-21) and from the curse of the law (Gal 3:10-14). It is acceptance into communion with God: already now, but then fully in God's coming kingdom (Rom 5:1f). It unites with Christ and with his death and resurrection (Rom 6:5). It occurs in the reception of the Holy Spirit in baptism and incorporation into the one body (Rom 8:1f, 9f; 1 Cor 12:12f). All this is from God alone, for Christ's sake, by grace, through faith in "the gospel of God's Son" (Rom 1:1-3).[33]

While theologians of different confessions would likely have used different words to express this "Common Understanding of Justification," the end result is an affirmation of the traditional Protestant forensic view of justification and the beginning point of a new life. "Together we confess: By grace alone, in faith in Christ's saving work and not because of any merit on our part, we are accepted by God and receive the Holy Spirit, who renews our hearts while equipping and calling us to good works."[34]

For Walter Cardinal Kasper, an important conclusion was reached with this document: this is a consensus on the basic truths of the doctrine of justification and other points and questions remain for further discussion, but these should not take away the common ground that has been reached.[35] He added that one must keep in mind that this declaration is a differentiated consensus rather than a complete agreement. "There exists full consensus about the key fundamental issues, in the exposition of the various starting points, yet different thought-forms and expressions, and different emphases and statements are possible. . . . The differences that remain are not contradictory statements but ones that complement and complete each other." And in a most generous statement, he adds, "In this world only a differentiated consensus is possible, and this means that the one, holy, catholic, and apostolic Church is an organic whole composed of complementary opposites." This is an expression of "oneness in diversity." The image of church unity that is sought after is "a unity which does not mean uniformity but a unity in diversity, or . . . a unity in reconciled diversity."[36]

If Catholics were cautiously optimistic about the *Joint Declaration*, so were Lutherans. Centuries of internal debates over details of the doctrine have caused splits between Lutherans and continue to do so. The preparation of this document caused these intra-Lutheran disputes to resurface. Cognizant of this tension among Lutherans, Michael Root stated that the document is nonetheless "an agreement among Lutherans on how rightly to state the doctrine of justification" and "implies that it represents at least one adequate way to state the doctrine of justification."[37] Lutherans remain divided over an ecumenical reading of the document (one that accepts it as an adequate and mediated interpretation of the Reformation view of justification) in contrast to a dichotomist reading (one that intrinsically cannot reconcile differences of emphases or interpretations because the idea of consensus or mediation is itself suspect). In spite of this hesitation on the part of some Lutherans, William Rusch affirms that Lutherans and Catholics can say to each other with "greater assurance that they proclaim the same Gospel of Jesus Christ and are indeed sisters and brothers in Christ."[38] Hans Küng came to the same conclusion in his study. "After four hundred and fifty years of argument about an article of faith with which the Church stands or falls (*articulus stantis et cadentis ecclesiae*), it is established that there had been no need to quarrel and divide the Church on this issue."[39]

While the *Joint Declaration* affirms a common Lutheran and Roman Catholic understanding of the basic truths of the doctrine of justification and therefore the gospel of salvation, other areas remain and will require intense dialogue before common understanding may be reached. For the Reformers, a biblical understanding of justification by faith had a major impact on other doctrines or practices they wished to also see reformed in the Catholic Church. While it may be claimed that the protest of the Reformation is over a common understanding of justification by faith, other difficult areas remain. Luther's protest against the sale of indulgences is, to some extent, valid since Roman Catholic practices still offer indulgences for various good works—although Catholics today understand Penance differently than they did in Luther's time.[40] The *Declaration*'s affirmation of Jesus' sole mediatorship as the basis for justification[41] challenges the Catholic teachings of the ordained priesthood, the sacrifice of the Mass and Eucharistic adoration, and the veneration of the saints and Mary. In these areas, the Reformation is not over, although it seems to be stalling. The doctrine of justification by faith that was agreed to has some real implications for other doctrines and practices still held by Roman Catholics.

Two other documents

Regardless of the number of interpretations given on the *Joint Declaration on the Doctrine of Justification*, the document made a remarkable impact upon the Lutheran–Roman Catholic dialogue. The fourth phase of the international dialogue (1995–2006) ended with the publication of *The Apostolicity of the Church*, a document that explores how both Lutheran and Catholic Churches can be understood as apostolic churches—in itself a controversial area of discussion because each tradition has considered the other heretical. *From Conflict to Communion* (2013), another document published recently to commemorate the five hundredth anniversary of the Reformation, also explores areas of dialogue where significant common ground has been found. These two documents follow the same methodology as in the *Joint Declaration*: discussing areas of broad consensus, followed by Lutheran and Catholic areas of specific emphases or differences. In both documents, the influence of the *Joint Declaration* is significant and raises some important implications regarding the concept of apostolicity.

Because both traditions adhere to the creedal confession of "one, holy, catholic and apostolic Church," parts 1 and 2 of *The Apostolicity of the Church* study the biblical concept of apostolicity in the New Testament and the history of the church. The document affirms that true apostolicity is rooted in the gospel of the New Testament and its faithful proclamation by the church and its ordained ministry. "In general, the study document affirms the oneness of the gospel expressed in a plurality of ways, due to changing times and cultural settings." In the New Testament, the apostles were entrusted with the gospel and "in the traditions that led to Lutheranism and Catholicism, there came recognition that apostolicity is a characteristic not only of individual apostles but of the church as well."[42] With the signing of the *Joint Declaration on the Doctrine of Justification*, both traditions recognize in each other the "faithful proclamation of the good news of Jesus Christ in accord with the apostolic witness"—a recognition that "is not negated by the important differences still to be investigated."[43] Consequently, in a most remarkable change of reality and attitude since the Reformation, Lutherans and Catholics now acknowledge that they both teach the same true gospel of the New Testament and that makes both traditions apostolic.

Yet two contentious areas between Lutheran and Catholic traditions remain. The first one is apostolic succession and ordained ministry in the church (part 3). Lutherans value apostolicity and their bishops provide oversight, but their ordained ministry arises from the leadership of Christ in the community and the priesthood of all believers to serve the church community. For Lutherans, the ordination of a pastor or bishop does not ontologically change the human being. For their part, Catholics hold to the historic apostolic succession in which the office of bishop is constitutive of the church (the church cannot exist without a bishop). That is because the ordination of a priest or bishop ontologically changes the human being into a representative of Christ in the community (henceforth, Christ Himself performs the rites of the church through the priest). A second contentious area is the role of the teaching office of the church in maintaining faithfulness to the gospel (part 4). Lutherans maintain faithfulness to the gospel with a biblically focused teaching ministry in the local community arising from the priesthood of all believers. Catholics, however, refer to the *magisterium* of the church to preserve this faithfulness, where bishops in communion with the pope preserve the truth.

In preparation for the five hundredth anniversary commemoration of the Lutheran Reformation, the Lutheran–Roman Catholic Commission on Unity prepared an ecumenical study document: *From Conflict to Communion*. It offers a common description of the history of Luther's quest for reform and the Lutheran Reformation.[44] And in this small book also, as in *The Apostolicity of the Church*, we find reference to the significance of the 1999 *Joint Declaration on the Doctrine of Justification*. Lutherans and Roman Catholics do not understand the nature of the church and its apostolicity in the same way; this is one of the main variances between them. When it comes to teaching the truth and preserving faithfulness to the gospel, both traditions understand this differently. For Lutherans, the local congregation is church in the full sense and is responsible for faithfulness to the gospel. For Catholics, the local church must be led by a bishop in order to be a church, and it is the *magisterium* of the church (all the bishops and pope together in apostolic succession) that assures faithfulness to the gospel.[45] These points, however, raise some crucial questions and implications for the future of the dialogue between Lutherans and Roman Catholics.

Questions and implications

The signing of the *Joint Declaration* has challenged this ecclesiological distinction between Lutherans and Catholics as highlighted in the documents *The Apostolicity of the Church* and *From Conflict to Communion*. Because both traditions agree that apostolicity is a mark of the true church to preserve the gospel, how is it that the two traditions now understand that they each believe and teach the true gospel and yet they have had different ecclesiastical structures to assure faithfulness to the gospel? Because the basic truths of the gospel are agreed to in the *Joint Declaration*, it must therefore be acknowledged that the Holy Spirit has worked in both traditions to maintain the true gospel during the five hundred years of separation, in spite of the fact that both have different church structures to assure this faithfulness. Even though the Lutheran ministerial office is not within the apostolic succession in the same sense as Roman Catholics understand it, it seems to imply that the Holy Spirit has worked within Lutheran churches to the same extent as He did in the Roman Catholic Church.[46]

These documents raise the same implication: is this not divine evidence that both forms of apostolicity, teaching ministry, and ecclesiology are used by the Holy Spirit and invite some form of mutual recognition?[47] The *Joint Declaration* has led Lutherans and Roman Catholics to ask themselves crucial questions about the exclusive role of the Catholic apostolic succession and the papacy in the preservation of the truth of the gospel. The further impact of this question leads to the very heart of Roman Catholic identity and ecclesiology. If Lutherans preserved the true gospel without the papacy to guide and protect the faith of the church, is the papacy then so crucial, fundamental, and necessary for a future visible unity? This question was at the very heart of the Protestant Reformation and led to Luther's excommunication when he claimed the papacy was not necessary. Has the Roman Catholic Church reached a point in its ecumenical outreach where it inadvertently has corroborated one of Luther's major arguments?

The Lutheran–Roman Catholic ecumenical dialogues over the past fifty years have produced remarkable outcomes that have changed worldwide Christianity, and more changes may still surprise us. The recent document *Declaration on the Way*, produced by the dialogue between Evangelical Lutherans and Roman Catholics in the United States, has also highlighted similar and other agreements that raise further questions and implications between the two confessions. The document boldly brings together a summary of the majority of theological agreements and remaining differences after fifty years of dialogue.[48]

The dialogues the Roman Catholic Church has held with Lutheran churches share basic similarities with the dialogues held with other Protestant churches. Almost all of them dealt with the nature and mission of the church, the nature of unity, the role of Scripture and tradition in the teaching authority of the church, the sacraments (baptism and Lord's Supper), and the apostolic succession and ministry of oversight. While areas of common faith and witness are evident between the Roman Catholic Church and Lutheran churches, numerous areas of doctrinal differences remain. Among them are the ordained ministry and priesthood; the sacrifice of the Mass and Eucharistic adoration; the function, role, and number of other sacraments; papal infallibility and teaching authority; the veneration of the saints and Mary; the role of Mary in the plan of salvation; the role of indulgences in piety and salvation; and issues of gender and sexuality.[49] So far a patient approach to such dialogues is bearing fruit, and many barriers of prejudice are being replaced with avenues of cooperation on social and moral issues. But when it comes to these remaining difficult doctrinal differences, the two traditions have no intention to compromise their traditional positions on any subject and, consequently, may have to admit that they have moved away too far from each other to reach a full consensus or unity of beliefs and practice.[50] A future church unity will likely consist of unity in diversity, not unity in conformity or uniformity. Will that be enough for Roman Catholics and Lutherans to agree to share the Lord's Supper together? The future will tell whether and how these major differences will be dealt with.

In some limited areas, the protest of the Reformation is over—Catholics and Lutherans have reached some surprising agreements on some doctrines that caused the schism of the sixteenth century. A better historical perspective of key events and decisions, along with increased scholarly study of key passages of Scripture, and improved historical perspectives of theological developments since the Reformation have all contributed to these new understandings and agreements. Yet in other areas, the Reformation produced some historically conditioned and biblically based realities and experiences that will remain and, in time, may be embraced by all sides that lead one to arrive at a reconciled unity in diversity. Maybe Cardinal Kasper's vision of the church will become the accepted reality. He states, "The one, holy, catholic, and apostolic Church is an organic whole composed of complementary opposites" and is an expression of "oneness in diversity."[51] Although the Lutheran Reformation began five hundred years ago, many of the issues it raised remain relevant, but the spirit of hostility that marked that era is no longer present. And for all this we are grateful to God.[52]

---

1. In Catholic theology, it is the body of bishops and theologians together in communion with the pope that form the *magisterium* of the church and are responsible for the preservation of the faith. The pope does not act alone or declare something infallible without consultation with the bishops. See Richard P. McBrien, *Catholicism*, rev. ed. (New York: HarperCollins Publishers, 1994), 65, 66.

2. Second Vatican Council, *Unitatis Redintegratio* (Decree on Ecumenism), Vatican, accessed August 10, 2017, http://www.vatican.va/archive/hist_councils/ii_vatican_council/documents /vat-ii_decree_19641121_unitatis-redintegratio_en.html. John T. Ford provides a good assessment of the legacy of Vatican II and its Decree on Ecumenism in "Vatican II's *Decree on Ecumenism* at Age Fifty: An Exhausted Inheritance or a Living Legacy?" *Ecumenical Trends* 45, no. 3 (March 2016): 1–7, 15.

3. This Commission on Faith and Order was one of the building blocks in the formation of the World Council of Churches (WCC) in Amsterdam in 1948 when it merged with the Life and Work Commission. Both commissions were the outcome of the Edinburgh World Missionary Conference. The second WCC assembly was held in Evanston, Illinois, in 1954.

4. John Paul II, *Encyclical Letter Ut unum sint*, sec. 3, http://w2.vatican.va/content/john-paul-ii /en/encyclicals/documents/hf_jp-ii_enc_25051995_ut-unum-sint.html. See Jared Wicks, "The Ecumenical Imperative in Catholic Theology and Life," *Ecumenical Trends* 42, no. 3 (March 2013): 1–4, 11.

5. These elements of truth include a confession of Jesus Christ as God, Lord, and sole Mediator between God and men; a love and reverence of Sacred Scripture; the practice of baptism and the Lord's Supper; and the daily Christian life in their application of the gospel. Second Vatican Council, *Unitatis Redintegratio* (Decree on Ecumenism), secs. 20–23.

6. Second Vatican Council, *Unitatis Redintegratio* (Decree on Ecumenism), sec. 1.

7. In 1988, the Secretariat became the Pontifical Council for Promoting Christian Unity.

8. John A. Radano wrote a summary of the significance of the Lutheran–Roman Catholic dialogue in the United States and shows how the documents it produced influenced the international dialogue between the Lutheran World Federation and the Pontifical Council for Promoting Christian Unity and the documents it produced. John A. Radano, "The Significance

of the Lutheran-Catholic Dialogue in the United States: After Fifty Years," *Ecumenical Trends* 44, no. 9 (October 2015): 1–8, 12–14.

9. The Lutheran World Federation and the Roman Catholic Church, *Joint Declaration on the Doctrine of Justification* (Grand Rapids, MI: Eerdmans, 2000).

10. Lutheran–Roman Catholic Commission on Unity, *The Apostolicity of the Church: Study Document of the Lutheran–Roman Catholic Commission on Unity* (Minneapolis, MN: Lutheran University Press, 2006).

11. Lutheran–Roman Catholic Commission on Unity, *From Conflict to Communion: Lutheran-Catholic Common Commemoration of the Reformation in 2017*, 4th rev. and exp. ed. (Leipzig: Evangelische Verlagsanstalt, 2016).

12. Bishops' Committee for Ecumenical and Interreligious Affairs and Evangelical Lutheran Church in America, *Declaration on the Way: Church, Ministry and Eucharist* (n.p.: United States Conference of Catholic Bishops and Evangelical Lutheran Church in America, 2015).

13. Mark Noll, a professor of Christian thought at Wheaton College and then at the University of Notre Dame, and Carolyn Nystrom addressed this theme in their book *Is the Reformation Over? An Evangelical Assessment of Contemporary Roman Catholicism* (Grand Rapids, MI: Baker Academic, 2005).

14. Bruce McCormack, "What's at Stake in Current Debates Over Justification? The Crisis of Protestantism in the West," in *Justification: What's at Stake in the Current Debates*, ed. Mark Husbands and Daniel J. Treier (Downers Grove, IL: InterVarsity Press, 2004), 81 (italics in the original).

15. This is too brief of an assessment of the historical development of the doctrine of justification in the late Middle Ages. Alister E. McGrath's monumental work provides a rich study of this development: *Iustitia Dei: A History of the Christian Doctrine of Justification*, 2nd ed. (Cambridge, UK: Cambridge University Press, 1998).

16. "When our Lord and Master, Jesus Christ, said 'Repent,' He called for the entire life of believers to be one of penitence." The text from Matthew 4:17 referred to here is *poenitentiam agite* in the Latin, which can be translated "to repent" or "to do penance." Martin Luther argued for the first meaning rather than actions done to be forgiven, which was the basis of the doctrine of indulgences he challenged in the document. True heartfelt repentance should inevitably lead to a changed life; something that he felt was lacking in the piety of most people who bought indulgences. John Dillenberger, ed., *Martin Luther: Selections From His Writings* (New York: Anchor Books Doubleday, 1962), 490. See also James M. Kittelson and Hans H. Wiersma, *Luther the Reformer: The Story of the Man and His Career*, 2nd ed. (Minneapolis, MN: Fortress Press, 2016), 74, 75.

17. According to McGrath, "The Greek verb has the primary sense of being *considered* or *estimated* as righteous, whereas the Latin verb denotes *being* righteous." McGrath, *Iustitia Dei*, 15 (italics in the original).

18. McCormack, "What's at Stake in Current Debates Over Justification?" 82 (italics in the original).

19. Hans Küng, *Justification: The Doctrine of Karl Barth and a Catholic Reflection* (Philadelphia, PA: Westminster Press, 1981). This book was based on his doctoral dissertation at the Pontifical

Gregorian University in Rome. The first English edition appeared in 1964, and the second edition in 1981.

20. Küng, *Justification*, xxxix, xl.

21. Ibid., ix.

22. Kenneth Green, "Kung's Own Justification," *Catholic Herald*, April 2, 1982, 6.

23. McGrath, *Iustitia Dei*, 389. McGrath further explains Küng's methodology and influence in this dialogue. "In his major study *Justification* . . . Küng compared the views of Karl Barth with those of the Council of Trent, and argued that there was fundamental agreement between the position of Barth and that of the Roman Catholic church, seen in its totality. This conclusion was the cause of some surprise at the time (1957), as well as a certain degree of uncritical optimism concerning its significance. A more reliable judgement of the significance of Küng's work would be that he demonstrates that, if the Council of Trent is interpreted in a Thomist sense (rather than a Franciscan sense), and if certain aspects of Barth's doctrine of justification are overlooked, a significant degree of convergence between Trent and Barth emerges." McGrath, *Iustitia Dei*, 388. McGrath explains these various strands of interpretation of the Council of Trent in his book. *Iustitia Dei*, 241–284.

24. Green, "Kung's Own Justification," 6.

25. The other documents from this second phase were *The Eucharist* (1978), *All Under One Christ* (1980), *Ways to Community* (1980), *The Ministry in the Church* (1981), *Martin Luther—Witness to Christ* (1983), and *Facing Unity—Models, Forms and Phases of Catholic–Lutheran Church Fellowship* (1984).

26. The history and development of the ideas presented in the *Joint Declaration on the Doctrine of Justification* owe much to the US Lutheran-Catholic dialogue and are much more complex than I describe here. See Radano, "The Significance of the Lutheran-Catholic Dialogue," 6, 7.

27. Hans Küng claimed the " 'Malta Report' was kept secret by the Vatican, [and] became public only as the result of an indiscretion. . . . Has this perhaps again something to do with the tedious question of infallibility and the fact that it cannot under any circumstances be admitted that the thirty or so anathemas (threats of excommunication) pronounced by the Council of Trent against the Reformation doctrine of justification were based on misunderstanding and lack of understanding; that is, they were mistaken decisions like so many others in the course of history." Küng, *Justification*, xvii, xviii.

28. Edward Cardinal Cassidy, press conference in Rome, June 25, 1998, quoted in Raoul Dederen, "The Joint Declaration on the Doctrine of Justification: One Year Later," *Ministry*, November 2000, 10.

29. Pope John Paul II, Ecumenical News International Bulletin, no. 20 (November 10, 1999): 32, quoted in Raoul Dederen, "The Joint Declaration on the Doctrine of Justification," 10.

30. Not all Lutheran churches are part of the Lutheran World Federation. The Evangelical Lutheran Church in America (ELCA) is the only member from the United States.

31. Lutheran World Federation and Roman Catholic Church, *Joint Declaration on the Doctrine of Justification*, sec. 5.

32. William G. Rusch, "The History, Methodology, and Implications for Ecumenical Reception of the Apostolicity Study of the Lutheran–Roman Catholic International Dialogue,"

in *Celebrating a Century of Ecumenism: Exploring the Achievements of International Dialogue*, ed. John A. Radano (Grand Rapids, MI: Eerdmans, 2012), 90.

33. Lutheran World Federation and Catholic Church, *Joint Declaration on the Doctrine of Justification*, sec. 11.

34. Ibid., sec. 15.

35. See ibid., secs. 40, 41.

36. Walter Kasper, "The *Joint Declaration on the Doctrine of Justification*: A Roman Catholic Perspective," in *Justification and the Future of the Ecumenical Movement: The Joint Declaration on the Doctrine of Justification*, ed. William G. Rusch (Collegeville, MN: Liturgical Press, 2003), 18.

37. Michael Root, "The Implications of the *Joint Declaration on Justification* and Its Wider Impact for Lutheran Participation in the Ecumenical Movement," in *Justification and the Future of the Ecumenical Movement: The Joint Declaration on the Doctrine of Justification*, ed. William G. Rusch (Collegeville, MN: Liturgical Press, 2003), 47.

38. William G. Rusch, introduction to *Justification and the Future of the Ecumenical Movement: The Joint Declaration on the Doctrine of Justification*, ed. William G. Rusch (Collegeville, MN: Liturgical Press, 2003), x.

39. Küng, *Justification*, xviii.

40. It is ironic that the year following the signing of the *Joint Declaration on the Doctrine of Justification* was a great jubilee year and Pope John Paul II offered a full plenary indulgence to pilgrims who visited Rome and other special sites in 2000. Pope John Paul II, *Incarnationis Mysterium* (Bull of Indiction of the Great Jubilee of the Year 2000), Vatican, accessed August 10, 2017, http://www.vatican.va/jubilee_2000/docs/documents/hf_jp-ii_doc_30111998_bolla-jubilee_en.html.

41. Lutheran World Federation and Catholic Church, *Joint Declaration on the Doctrine of Justification*, sec. 18.

42. Warren Harrington, review of *The Apostolicity of the Church: Study Document of the Lutheran–Roman Catholic Commission on Unity*, by the Lutheran–Roman Catholic Commission on Unity, *Journal of Ecumenical Studies* 44, no. 3 (Summer 2009): 498.

43. Lutheran–Roman Catholic Commission on Unity, *The Apostolicity of the Church*, secs. 142, 160.

44. A review of the document was done by David Carter in "Lutheran Catholic Dialogue: The 2017 Anniversary," *Ecumenical Trends* 43, no. 5 (May 2014): 1–6. The book contains three main sections and presents a common perspective on Martin Luther and the Reformation, a historical sketch of the Lutheran Reformation and the Catholic response, and the basic themes of Martin Luther's theology in light of the Lutheran–Roman Catholic dialogues. To be noted, however, is the purpose of this book: "The point is not to tell a different history, but to tell that history differently" and together. Lutheran–Roman Catholic Commission on Unity, *From Conflict to Communion*, sec. 16.

45. Lutheran–Roman Catholic Commission on Unity, *The Apostolicity of the Church*, sec. 284.

46. This thought was openly recognized in *Declaration on the Way*, 43.

47. Lutheran–Roman Catholic Commission on Unity, *From Conflict to Communion*, sec. 194; Lutheran–Roman Catholic Commission on Unity, *The Apostolicity of the Church*, secs. 288–293.

48. A few reviews of this documents are noted: USCCB Secretariat for Ecumenical and

Interreligious Affairs, "Catholics and Lutherans Release *Declaration on the Way* to Full Unity," *Ecumenical Trends* 45, no. 4 (April 2016): 14; William G. Rusch, "*Declaration on the Way: Church, Ministry and Eucharist*: Quo Vadis?" *Ecumenical Trends* 45, no. 5 (May 2016): 1–5, 14, 15; Michael Reid Trice, "*Declaration on the Way: Church, Ministry and Eucharist*: A Commentary," *Ecumenical Trends* 45, no. 6 (June 2016): 1–4, 15; John W. Crossin, "Occasional Reflections on the *Declaration on the Way*," *Ecumenical Trends* 46, no. 6 (June 2017): 1–3.

49. The practice among some Lutheran and other Protestant churches to ordain women to ministry and elect women to positions of leadership is a major roadblock in any future unity with the Roman Catholic Church. William G. Rusch, "A Lutheran View of Where the Ecumenical Movement Stands in the Spring of 2010," *Ecumenical Trends* 39, no. 9 (October 2010): 1–5, 15.

50. *Declaration on the Way* candidly articulates many of these remaining differences regarding the apostolicity of the church, its teaching ministry, the ministry of ordained priests and bishops, and the Eucharist (72–113).

51. Walter Kasper, "A Roman Catholic Perspective," 18.

52. I am grateful to Dr. Michael R. Trice of the Evangelical Lutheran Church in American and professor at the School of Theology and Ministry at Seattle University for his feedback and helpful comments on this chapter.

AUTHOR BIOGRAPHIES

 Sergio Becerra teaches church history, Adventist studies, and prophetic guidance to undergraduate students at the Universidad Adventista del Plata in Argentina. Born in Uruguay to Chilean parents, he is also the director of the E. Irving Mohr Library and director of the Ellen G. White Estate Research Center located on the campus. Prior to teaching, he pastored eleven different churches across both the United States and Chile. Becerra holds a ThD degree in church history from the University of Strasbourg in France. His dissertation was on the Puritan roots of the Seventh-day Adventist doctrine of the Sabbath. He is married to Gabriela, and they have three children.

 Reinder Bruinsma is a retired pastor who lives in the Netherlands. During the past forty years, he has served as a pastor, teacher, and church administrator. He served as the executive secretary of the Trans-European Division of Seventh-day Adventists and as president of the Netherlands Union Conference of Seventh-day Adventists. He has authored numerous articles and more than twenty books. Bruinsma has a PhD from the University of London in the United Kingdom.

 **Heidi Campbell** is the director of the English Center at the Adventist International Institute of Advanced Studies in the Philippines. She has an MA in English from Andrews University in Michigan and a BA in English and history (with honors) from Southern Adventist University in Tennessee. She has taught at both the elementary and college levels.

 **Michael W. Campbell** teaches church history and systematic theology at the Adventist International Institute of Advanced Studies in the Philippines. He has served as a pastor in Colorado and Kansas and was responsible for the Ellen G. White White Estate Branch Office and the Archives & Special Collections at Loma Linda University in California. He earned a BA in history and theology from Southern Adventist

University in Tennessee and an MA and a PhD from Andrews University in Michigan. He teaches classes on the Reformation and enjoys leading tours of sites related to the Reformation.

 Lisa Clark Diller, PhD (University of Chicago), is a historian who teaches on the early modern world at Southern Adventist University in Tennessee. Her dissertation focused on the English Catholic contributions to the Act of Toleration in 1689. Her research and writing looks at the limits of citizenship and toleration in late Stuart England. She is currently researching Gilbert Burnet's vision of church and state in his *History of the Reformation*. Diller travels throughout the world participating in workshops and conferences and teaches on justice, peace, and the history of early modern politics and religion.

 **Abner P. Dizon** served as the founding executive director and later as the research and training director for Philippine Frontier Missions for twenty-two years. He has a doctor of missiology degree from Philippine Christian University. Currently, he serves as an assistant professor of mission and Islamic studies in the theological seminary at the Adventist International Institute of Advanced Studies in the Philippines.

 Denis Fortin is a professor of historical theology at the Seventh-day Adventist Theological Seminary at Andrews University in Michigan. His areas of interest include teaching themes on the doctrines of salvation and the church, as well as Roman Catholic theology and the history and theology of the ecumenical movement. For many years, he was involved in interchurch dialogues for the Seventh-day Adventist Church and on the Faith and Order Commission of the National Council of Churches in the United States. His most recent publication is an annotated 125th anniversary edition of Ellen G. White's *Steps to Christ* (Andrews University Press, 2017).

 Daniel Heinz, PhD, was born in Austria, where he worked as a pastor and taught church history at Bogenhofen Seminary. In 1997, he became the director of the European Archives for Seventh-day Adventist History, located in Friedensau, Germany. Heinz has written widely in the field of Adventist history and the history of the free churches standing in the tradition of Anabaptism. In 2016, he edited the book *So komm noch diese Stunde! Luthers Reformation aus Sicht der Siebenten-Tags-Adventisten*, which investigates the shared heritage and common theological identity of Adventism and the Reformation.

 **Darius Jankiewicz** is a professor of historical theology at the Seventh-day Adventist Theological Seminary at Andrews University in Michigan. Born in Poland, Jankiewicz immigrated to Australia and received his BA in theology from Avondale College in Australia. He worked as a pastor in the Greater Sydney Conference of Seventh-day Adventists. He then moved to the United States, where

he completed an MDiv and a PhD in historical theology. He then served as a pastor in Tasmania and as a senior lecturer of theology at Fulton College in Fiji. In 2008, he returned to the seminary at Andrews University to serve as a professor. Jankiewicz is married to Edyta and has two daughters, Caitlin and Ashley.

Denis Kaiser is an assistant professor of church history at the Seventh-day Adventist Theological Seminary at Andrews University in Michigan and the Annotation Project editor for the Ellen G. White Estate. He earned degrees in tax law and theology in Germany and Austria. He holds an MA in theological studies and church history and a PhD in Adventist studies and historical theology from Andrews University in Michigan. He has published numerous articles and book chapters and specializes in teaching Adventist theology and history, Ellen White studies, and American religious history. He has taught classes in the United States, Europe, and the Middle East.

Joel Klimkewicz grew up Lutheran and studied Luther's *Small Catechism* for his confirmation. He served in the United States Marine Corps, met his wife, Tomomi, on a deployment to Okinawa, Japan, and has three children. He became a Seventh-day Adventist as a result of studying with an Adventist navy chaplain while deployed to the Middle East in 2002. Subsequently, he received a BA in theology from Southern Adventist University in Tennessee, an MDiv from Andrews University in Michigan, and is currently pursuing a PhD in historical theology at Andrews University. He has pastored in Japan, Florida, and Indiana.

George R. Knight has been the foremost leader for the past four decades in the academic study of Adventism. Among his major publications on the topic are *Millennial Fever and the End of the World* (recently revised as *William Miller and the Rise of Adventism*), a major biography on Joseph Bates, a study on Alonzo T. Jones, and a series of historical works that include *A Brief History of Seventh-day Adventists*, *A Search for Identity: The Development of Seventh-day Adventist Beliefs*, and *Organizing for Mission and Growth: The Development of Adventist Church Structure*. Among his editorial projects are the Adventist biographical series (ten volumes published as of 2016, with eight more underway), the Adventist Classic Library (seven volumes at present), and the Library of Adventist Theology (four volumes currently). He was also the originator and consulting editor of the recently published *Ellen G. White Encyclopedia*.

Martin J. Lohrmann is a pastor of the Evangelical Lutheran Church in America (ELCA) and an assistant professor of Lutheran Confessions and heritage at Wartburg Theological Seminary in Iowa. He is the author of *Book of Harmony: Spirit and Service in the Lutheran Confessions* (Fortress, 2016), volume coeditor of *1–2 Samuel, 1–2*

Kings, 1–2 Chronicles in the Reformation Commentary on Scripture series (IVP Academic, 2016), and translator of *The Early Luther: Stages in a Reformation Reorientation* by Berndt Hamm (Eerdmans, 2014).

Douglas Morgan is a professor of history at Washington Adventist University in Maryland. He also serves as the North American regional editor for the forthcoming *Encyclopedia of Seventh-day Adventists*. In 1992, he completed a PhD at the University of Chicago in the history of Christianity, with emphasis in American religious and social movements. His publications include *Adventism and the American Republic: The Public Involvement of a Major Apocalyptic Movement* (University of Tennessee Press, 2001), *Lewis C. Sheafe: Apostle to Black America* (Review and Herald®, 2010), and a chapter in the multiauthored *Ellen Harmon White: American Prophet* (Oxford University Press, 2014).

Jiří Moskala, ThD, PhD, is dean and professor of Old Testament exegesis and theology at the Seventh-day Adventist Theological Seminary at Andrews University in Michigan. Prior to joining the Andrews faculty in 1999, Moskala served in various capacities (pastor, administrator, teacher, and principal) in the Czech Republic. He is a member of different theological societies and has authored or edited a number of articles and books in the Czech and English languages. In addition, he has participated in several archaeological expeditions in Tall Jalul, Jordan.

Richard W. Müller attended the theological seminary in Darmstadt (West Germany) and received a "Prediger Diplom" (BA equivalent) in 1966. He afterward obtained an MA in 1968 and an MDiv in 1970 at Andrews University in Michigan and then a ThD from Lund University in Sweden in 1979 on the topic of the Sabbath and the Reformation. Müller has worked in a variety of capacities, including as a pastor, a professor, and an administrator across Europe and the Middle East.

Trevor O'Reggio is a professor of church history at the Seventh-day Adventist Theological Seminary at Andrews University in Michigan. After spending fifteen years in pastoral ministry, he earned a PhD in history from the University of Chicago in 1997 and a DMin in marriage and family from Gordon-Conwell Theological Seminary in Massachusetts. He has authored several books and articles. He teaches primarily Reformation history, American religious history, and courses in marriage and family. He enjoys cycling, walking, and swimming.

John C. Peckham is an associate professor of theology and Christian philosophy at the Seventh-day Adventist Theological Seminary at Andrews University in Michigan. Previously, he pastored in the Indiana Conference of Seventh-day Adventists and taught at Southwestern Adventist University in Texas. Peckham is the author of such books as *Canonical Theology: The Biblical Canon*, Sola Scriptura, *and Theological Method* (Eerdmans, 2016); *The Love of God: A Canonical Model* (IVP Academic Readers' Choice Award Winner, 2015); and *The Concept of Divine Love in the Context of the God-World Relationship* (Peter Lang, 2014). He has also written numerous articles published in peer-reviewed and professional journals. Peckham is married to Brenda, and they have one son, Joel.

Dennis Pettibone, PhD, is professor emeritus of history at Southern Adventist University in Tennessee. He was a full-time professor at Southern for twenty-four years. Pettibone has taught in Seventh-day Adventist schools for forty years. His doctoral dissertation for the University of California, Riverside, was "Caesar's Sabbath: The Sunday-Law Controversy in the United States, 1879–1892." He wrote *A Century of Challenge: The Story of Southern College*, half of the textbook *His Story: In Our Time*, and one chapter for *The World of Ellen G White*. He has been published in *American Historical Review*, *Journal of the Adventist Theological Society*, *Liberty*, *National Review*, *Review and Herald*, *Ministry*, *Perspective Digest*, and *Guide*. He was married to the late Carol Jean Nelson Pettibone for forty-five years and has two grown daughters and two grandchildren.

Nikolaus Satelmajer started his ministry in New York City and has served the Seventh-day Adventist Church as a pastor, an administrator, and until his retirement, the editor of *Ministry* and an associate ministerial secretary of the General Conference of Seventh-day Adventists. He has attended five postsecondary educational institutions and received BA, MDiv, and DMin degrees from Andrews University in Michigan. He also received a STM degree (with distinction) from the Lutheran Theological Seminary at Philadelphia, Pennsylvania, in Reformation studies. Since retirement, he has continued lecturing, editing, and contributing to books as well as serving as an interim pastor. He is married to Ruth I. Satelmajer (née Nutter), a retired teacher and school administrator.

Dan Shultz taught music for fifty years at all levels in the Seventh-day Adventist school system, including forty years in higher education where he was an award-winning classroom teacher and chaired the music programs at Union College in Nebraska and Walla Walla University (WWU) in Washington. He has written extensively about the historical aspects of music in the Seventh-day Adventist Church, authoring *A Great Tradition*, a book about the history of music at WWU, and more recently *Adventist Musicians Biographical Resource*, an encyclopedia containing the biographies of more than eleven hundred church musicians. Dan was the founder of the International Adventist Musicians Association and served as its president for ten years. For more than thirty years, he has served as the editor of and a contributor to its publications and website. He and his wife, Carolyn (née Stevens), a retired professor of English, live in College Place, Washington.

Mxolisi Michael Sokupa is an associate director of the Ellen G. White Estate in Silver Spring, Maryland. He has a PhD in New Testament from the Adventist International Institute of Advanced Studies in the Philippines and holds a ThD in church history from Stellenbosch University in South Africa. He has served in a variety of capacities within the Seventh-day Adventist Church, including as a pastor, a departmental director, a teacher, and a professor.

Alberto R. Timm is an associate director of the Ellen G. White Estate in Silver Spring, Maryland. He holds a PhD in Adventist studies from Andrews University in Michigan. Born in a German-Pomeranian colony in the south of Brazil, Timm worked as a pastor; the director of the Brazilian Ellen G. White/Seventh-day Adventist Research Center; the dean of the Graduate School of Theology, São Paulo Adventist University in Brazil; and the rector of the multicampus Latin-American Adventist Theological Seminary and the Spirit of Prophecy coordinator for the South American Division (2007–2011). He has published extensively in Portuguese, English, and Spanish. He is married to Marly L. Timm, and they have three children: Suellen, William, and Shelley.

Sigve K. Tonstad completed a BA in theology at Middle East College in Lebanon and Andrews University in Michigan, his MD from Loma Linda University in California, an MA in biblical studies at Loma Linda University, and a PhD in New Testament studies at the University of St. Andrews in Scotland. For a number of years, he worked as a pastor and physician in Oslo, Norway, including eight years as the senior pastor of the Bethel Church, which is one of the oldest Seventh-day Adventist congregations in Europe. He is now a professor of biblical studies at Loma Linda University. Among his books is a commentary on Romans, *The Letter to the Romans: Paul Among the Ecologists* (Sheffield Phoenix, 2016).

Remwil R. Tornalejo is an associate professor of historical theology at the Adventist International Institute of Advanced Studies (AIIAS) in the Philippines. He worked as a district pastor in the North Central Mindanao Conference of Seventh-day Adventists and served as a Literature Ministry Seminary dean and instructor at the South Philippine Union Conference of Seventh-day Adventists. Immediately before coming to AIIAS, he served as the chair of the theology department at South Philippine Adventist College in the Philippines. He is married to Marilou Manatad Tornalejo, and they have four children—two girls and two boys.

Timothy J. Wengert is the emeritus Ministerium of Pennsylvania Professor of church history at the Lutheran Theological Seminary at Philadelphia. A parish pastor for seven years in Minnesota and Wisconsin, he received his doctorate from Duke University in North Carolina in 1984 and was on the Lutheran Theological Seminary at Philadelphia's faculty from 1989 to 2013. He has written many scholarly books and articles on the Reformation, was a coeditor of the English edition of *The Book of Concord*, and translated Luther's *Small Catechism* that is widely used throughout the Evangelical Lutheran Church in America. In addition to several books on Philip Melanchthon, he has written a book on Luther's catechisms (Fortress, 2009). He also wrote *Reading the Bible With Martin Luther* (Baker, 2013) and is the general editor of the *Dictionary of Luther and the Lutheran Traditions* (Baker, 2017). He coauthored (with Susan Wood) a book on Lutheran–Roman Catholic relations (Paulist, 2016). He edited the first volume of *The Annotated Luther*, where his translation of the Ninety-Five Theses has also appeared (Fortress, 2015).

Woodrow W. Whidden II, PhD, emeritus professor of religion (Andrews University), has served as a pastor, a professor of religion at Andrews University in Michigan, and a professor of historical and systematic theology at the Adventist International Institute of Advanced Studies in the Philippines. His published works include *Ellen White on Salvation* (Review and Herald®, 1995); *Ellen White on the Humanity of Christ* (Review and Herald®, 1997); *The Trinity: Understanding God's Love, His Plan of Salvation, and Christian Relationships* (Review and Herald®, 2002; coauthored with Jerry Moon and John Reeve), *E. J. Waggoner* (Review and Herald®, 2008); *The Judgment and Assurance: The Dynamics of Personal Salvation* (Review and Herald®, 2012); and numerous professional and scholarly journal articles and book reviews.

Daniel Wildemann studied theology at Seminar Schloss Bogenhofen in Austria, Theologische Hochschule Friedensau in Germany, and Andrews University in Michigan. He wrote an interdisciplinary thesis on the use of visual media during the time of the Reformation. He comes from Remagen, Germany, and completed an apprenticeship as an advertisement technician and studied at the College of Further Education in Design. He has pastored in the Baden-Württemberg Conference of Seventh-day Adventists for nine years and currently serves as the editor at the German Adventist Publishing House (Advent-Verlag) in Lüneburg. He draws cartoons, and he and his wife have one daughter.